"Art, after all, is nothing but the cause and effect of attuning the senses,
whether sight, hearing, or touch. Why, then, refuse taste its place
in the genesis and triumph of art?"

—Docteur Edouard de Pomiane

Contents

Recipes

Restaurant Menus

Our thanks, from the bottom of our hearts, to:

All of the chefs who made time in their overcommitted schedules to be a part of this book. Through their artistry and generosity of spirit, their lives continue to enrich us all.

Photographers James Bergin and Jessica Zane, who managed to capture such stunningly beautiful images of food and cooking on film; and we join Jamie and Jessica in thanking the following establishments for allowing them to take photographs on their premises: Al Forno, Biba, Blue Room, Daniel, Dean & DeLuca, Florence Meat Market, Jean-Louis, Lespinasse, March, Palladin, Patisserie Café Didier, Picholine, Pignoli, Union Square Cafe, the Union Square Greenmarket, and Vong.

Everyone at Van Nostrand Reinhold/ITP who helped make this book a reality (including Karren Abrams, Michelle Agosta, Paul Aljian, cover designer Paul Costello, marketer Mary Fitzgerald, manufacturing director Louise Kurtz, publisher Melissa Rosati, assistant editor Amy Shipper, designer *extraordinaire* Mike Suh, Stephen McNabb, and Marie Terry) and find a place on bookstore shelves (Audrey Barr, Nancy Brew, Alan Diehlmann, Ellen Goodlin, Lane Jantzen, Joanne Johnston, Diane Kennedy, Sal McLemore, Christopher Nitsch, Don O'Connor, Jonathan Perry, Kevin Posey, Irene Potter, Martina Regan, Roy Sabul, Doug Storm, Elida Tamez, Paul Williams, and Lynda Wright), with a special thank you to VNR President Marianne Russell for her extraordinary enthusiasm and support.

The terrific people at Kitchen Arts & Letters in Manhattan, which is the first place we always turn with baffling questions about obscure culinary resources—and from which we've never left empty-handed.

Everyone who read and told us they enjoyed *Becoming a Chef* and make it so gratifying for us to be authors, and all the booksellers who found a place in their heart for *Becoming a Chef* and hand-sold it into a third printing within four weeks of its initial publication (and a fourth within a few months after that).

All our family members, friends, and colleagues who are so generous with their support and/or advice (especially during our research travels), including Madeleine Kamman, an invaluable sounding board; our thoughtful and hugely talented friend painter Matt Baumgardner, to whom we only turn with simple questions like "What is art?"; and especially Susan Butler, Gail Coleman, Susan Davis, Carla Dearing and Tom Curtin, Bunny Ellerin, Heather Evans, Julie Farrell, Mike Feeley, Margery Fischbein, Albert French, Ashley Garrett and Alan Jones, Stewart Gordon, Misty Gruber, Cynthia Gushue and Leo Russell (and the rest of the Gang of 9, past and present!), Scott Hancock, Russ Hudson, Kate Jackman, Julie Johnson, Tammy Kien,

Acknowledgments

Rikki Klieman, Bruce and Karen Mace, Millington McCoy, Jody Oberfelder and Juergen Riehm, Heidi Olson, Scott and Kelley Olson, Cynthia and Jeff Penney, Marci, Peter, and Sam Pepper, Kathy Reilly, Don Riso, Barry Salzman, Tony Schwartz, Kimberly and Jeff Seely, Karen Springen and Mark Kerber, Brian Taylor, Melissa Weiner and Bill FitzPatrick, Irene Weisband, Trish Wend and Jay Rosenberg, Stephanie Winston, and Donna Zaccaro and Paul Ullman.

Finally, we acknowledge and thank each other—as co-authors, collaborators, and favorite dining partners!

Andrew Dornenburg and Karen Page

*The creation of something new is not accomplished by the intellect
but by the play instinct acting from inner necessity.
The creative mind plays with the objects it loves.*
—CARL JUNG

Don't play with your food.
—PARENTS AROUND THE WORLD

In a childhood diary entry written when I was about eight, I confidently listed my five favorite foods on which I felt I could happily survive for the rest of my life: 1) bacon, 2) bananas, 3) chocolate, 4) peanut butter, and 5) Rice Krispies.

I enjoyed each of these on their own—whether a single ripe banana, or a spoonful of peanut butter—but learned first-hand the meaning of the word "synergy" when I found that I could more than double my pleasure by combining certain pairs of ingredients. In terms of candy, I gravitated toward Nestlé's Crunch bars and Reese's peanut butter cups. At mealtime, I experimented with peanut butter and banana sandwiches, but found I preferred an open-faced version of peanut butter on toast topped with banana slices or, better yet, crumbled bacon. In my food memory, one of the most wonderful discoveries I ever made was of a concoction of melted semi-sweet chocolate chips sandwiched between layers of a mixture that incorporated Rice Krispies and peanut butter—which became the treat I'd choose to bring to school to share with classmates on my birthday. To be able to enjoy not just two but *three* of my favorite ingredients at once was sheer ecstasy.

Thank God I was able to withstand societal admonitions not to play with my food! I ended up sampling a lot of combinations—ones that worked, and many more that didn't—and in the process began to evolve a palate for what I found pleasing (which, in time, admittedly evolved beyond the list above).

Developing a love of cooking was *not* an outgrowth of my passion for food-combining, however. Boston chef Todd English once told us that to have to follow a recipe was, to him, like being put on a leash—and I recall nodding vigorously in immediate understanding of how a recipe exercises control over the cook instead of vice versa. Perhaps because I so loathed recipes, I never found cooking to be a pleasure, and thus never had that means to develop an innate sensibility for a broad range of flavors that "went together"—which might have allowed me to circumvent the need for a recipe and just walk into a kitchen and throw something together that was a little more interesting than pasta with bottled red sauce.

But an amazing thing happened while researching this book. While hungrily working on the list of flavor marriages for lobster, I realized that Andrew had some leftover lobster in the refrigerator. Based on these lists, I had the confidence to buy some tarragon and cream, and to combine them in a pasta dish that turned out to be so delicious I would have felt comfortable serving it to guests. Having access to these lists of foods and flavors that marry well has opened up a whole new interest—not to mention comfort and freedom—in cooking that I've never experienced before.

We hope that the lists within this book will similarly inspire readers to "play with their food," experimenting with listed (or even unlisted) combinations to see whether the results please their palate—the ultimate judge of a particular combination's success. As the reader will soon discover, *Culinary Artistry* is in some ways two books in one. One is a book about culinary composition, which addresses the harmonious combination of foods and flavors. The other is a book about how culinary artists are able to play with component elements so harmoniously that it elevates their dishes and menus and dining experiences to works of art.

Music: *The art of arranging sounds in time to produce a composition that elicits an aesthetic response in a listener.*

Great opera and great art have inspired rhapsodies and moved patrons to tears. Why not great food? Why should we elevate the pleasing of our visual and auditory senses, through museum visits and concert performances, over pleasing our gustatory senses, through the experience of culinary artistry?

The artistry to which we're referring is not simply visual. In fact, we've come to believe that a great dining experience is more on a par with great music than with any other art. Great meals, like great music, have a rhythm and harmony all their own. The most beautiful symphony of food I've ever experienced was in the dining room at The Inn at Little Washington in Virginia, with chef Patrick O'Connell directing the kitchen's preparation of a tasting menu that was a magical concert of flavors, aromas, textures, and visual surprises. It was a meal that touched my palate, my mind, and my heart, and left me speechless. When O'Connell stopped by our table afterward to see how we had enjoyed our dinner, words escaped me. I spontaneously (and uncharacteristically) arose from the table to embrace him. Upon our departure, when we signed the Inn's guest book, one word finally sprang to mind: "Transcendental."

Through researching and writing *Becoming a Chef,* Andrew and I became convinced of the genius of some of the chefs we'd interviewed—which we didn't find properly emphasized in much of what we'd read about them. Too many books and articles seemed to simplify their artistry for the sake of the amateur cook in search of a recipe, instead of acknowledging the complexity and subtlety of their art.

In writing *Culinary Artistry*, we wanted to celebrate the artistry of chefs, and particularly chefs in America who have come to be respected as world class. We wanted to understand their medium of expression in all its components, down to the very flavors they choose to highlight, which in many cases places their "signatures" on their cuisines. What is being expressed in their food? What is being expressed through the restaurant experience? How do they express it? And do customers and critics always "get" their messages?

Culinary Artistry is the result of our desire to explore culinary artists *as artists*, and to discuss with them the basics of their art—treasured ingredients and techniques, and the principles of composition—as well as the potential it contains. You'll find these gifted chefs to be invariably passionate about the subject, doubtless from already having learned the truth of the observation of Aldous Huxley that "The secret of genius is to carry the spirit of the child into old age, which means never losing your enthusiasm."

Karen Page
Summer 1996

The Chef as Artist

Are chefs culinary artists? Certainly not all of them, no more than all sidewalk trumpet players are fine musicians. But are some chefs culinary artists? We believe so. Having experienced extraordinary meals that have moved us—on a level one might expect of great art—we have no doubt of this.

But the potential for achieving a level of artistry within the culinary experience is one that we believe has not received proper emphasis. Understanding this potential has the power to elevate a cook's aspirations— and, we hope, a cook's accomplishments.

Art is the medium in which man and landscape, form and world, meet and find one another.

—Rainer Maria Rilke

What Is Art?

We'll try to be clear what we mean when we say "art"—not that it's an easy task. In fact, your definition of art is certain to sway your belief as to whether a dining experience has the potential to fall into that category.

Generally when people speak of art, they're referring to fine art such as literature, music, painting, and sculpture. But there are also the performing arts, such as theatre, not to mention the applied arts, such as architecture. The potentials within the dining experience can be related to each of these.

This art has its own place among the other arts—painting, literature, or music—to the extent that its affinity with nature is most intense and direct, and also insofar as it responds—even in forms that are sometimes very sophisticated—to what is a vital function; and it also has the advantage of being a popular art, shared by the greatest number of participants.

—Curnonsky

As in literature, there can be a poetry to the way dishes are described on a menu. As in music, there is a rhythm to a great meal, when it flows from one course to another like a symphony. As in painting and sculpture, the visual aspects of a dish can enhance the appreciation of it. As in theatre, the way something is presented—by people in costumes, with music playing, with precise timing—is as much a part of the experience as the thing itself. And as in architecture, while the subjects in question are at their most basic level functional—providing us with food or shelter—great food, like a great building, has the potential to inspire.

As art has become more democratic in recent times, so have common definitions of art expanded to include nearly any branch of creative work. But we would argue that the culinary arts could fit the somewhat narrow definition of "making or doing things, using unusual *perception,* that display *form* and *beauty.*"

It is chefs' extraordinary perceptive abilities that probably go most often overlooked. Because most everyone cooks and has at one time or another fried an egg or grilled a hamburger, knowledge of cooking techniques and ingredients tends to be easily taken for granted. We have been awed by the unusual levels of perceptiveness we've experienced America's leading

chefs as possessing; we believe some to have certain skills of extrasensory perception. In addition, many leading chefs bring nearly encyclopedic knowledge of ingredients to their cooking— from seasonality to recognizing ingredients at their peak to successful flavor marriages. This knowledge allows them to cook with extraordinary depth.

Culinary Artistry

By form and beauty, we're not referring strictly to the increasingly popular, and in some cases misguided, emphasis that some chefs have placed on the visual presentation of food. In determining what form a dish will take, chefs have the opportunity to convey their own sense of beauty with every decision they make about a dish, from the selection of ingredients and their pairing with other ingredients, to its cooking techniques, to its presentation on a plate, to its order of presentation on a menu.

Food is very much theater.
—James Beard

Just as philosophers have suggested that art is "about" something, and conveys feelings toward that subject matter, so does Alice Waters tell us that "Being a really good cook has to do with having a point of view."

Throughout history, great culinarians have likened the culinary arts to arts ranging from architecture to painting to theatre. The press has even used artistic analogies when describing particular chefs. For example, *Los Angeles Times* food writer Charles Perry once likened chef Joachim Splichal to the late rock musician Jimi Hendrix, who was known for his artistic daring.

What Leading Chefs Think

"Cooking is indeed an artistry," says Bradley Ogden. "It's a form of creativity and expression, especially the more defined you become with your cuisine. The direction you decide to take it in—your personal style— usually depends on your background and your education. I grew up in Michigan, and my cuisine is more straightforward American. Unbeknownst to me, I was developing a palate back when I was five or six years old, being reared on organic blackberries and wall-eyed pike."

"We are certainly associated with the arts," Gray Kunz agrees. "There's no question about that. But the affiliation hides an enormous amount of hard work. This work is very stressful—both physically and on the mind. What helps the chef is the simple desire to create dishes that are constantly on a very high level. It's a shame you can't put some of them on canvas!"

Curnonsky's belief that "La cuisine! That's when things taste like themselves," is none other than the artist's precept, "Respect your medium," transposed into the world of food.
—Richard Olney

Wayne Nish, who once studied architecture, points out that "Architecture in the Middle Ages was the mother of the arts. In order to be a practitioner, you had to be a sculptor, a painter, and a musician. It was a requirement that you needed to master these three endeavors before you could build. And I've always thought that the culinary arts were an extention of two of those. Carême was a frustrated architect who constructed edible pièces montée. I see that the relationship exists—cooking for the public is a very visual discipline."

It's more appropriate to compare culinary artists to musicians than to painters or sculptors. In particular, musicians use their musical heritage as a repertoire on which to base their interpretations. I think that chefs use the culinary repertoire of dishes, whether it be Escoffier's or Mexican or Moroccan or Indian or other great repertoires of cuisines that have to be mastered, before they can go on and interpret. Even within them, there are interpretations, much as a soloist would interpret a concerto or a symphony.

There are people who extend the interpretation of food beyond what has gone before them, but very few people do that. Only a few people in a generation might do that. I don't do that. I don't think Alice [Waters] does that. I think we interpret the past.

I think Jean-Louis [Palladin] does extend the normal boundaries of the cuisine and pushes things. And I think there are Japanese chefs that do that. I've had food in Japan that has definitely extended my own consciousness into flavors and textures which I didn't ever think were possible, and which I didn't think actually existed before. I think it's people who bridge two great culinary traditions—like artistic traditions, where there's the Renaissance or Impressionism that was influenced by Eastern arts, or a sense of negative-positive form, or Cubism influencing Picasso—that it's people who are on that edge between two great traditions who, when they synthesize them, create something new. They're not following either-or. Certainly Picasso was not a Classicist painter, and he's certainly not a primitivist. He's basically created a tradition of primitivism in modern Western art.

I don't know that we have that caliber of culinary genius. Food moves slower than art, because obviously it's more personal, it's something that affects the body, it's in the body's experience. It's

Norman Van Aken concurs. "This can be an art, and there are times when it is in the hands of certain individuals," he says. "But it's an incredibly capricious art in that it doesn't last. Ten minutes after it's served, it's gone. I was sort of miserable about that in some respects, and then I think it was Maida Heara who argued with me that I was wrong—because cuisine lives on in memory."

"Chefs can be extremely creative," admits Daniel Boulud, "but our form of art doesn't last—except in cookbooks. In painting, imagination is key. But in food, you must use your senses to create, in a way, a 'virtual reality.'"

The Realm of Culinary Artistry

Why are the culinary arts just now taking their rightful place among the arts?

Perhaps part of the answer lies in history. That the culinary arts are just now coming into their own as an art form is doubtless due at least in part to the fact that only recently have certain factors come together to allow this development.

more like changing sexual mores, which move very slowly. It's part of every day life. It's part of socialization. It's much more complex than doing a painting and hanging it on the wall. Things outside of our normal, every day lives can move very quickly, and—especially in the twenty-first century—are expected to move quickly, whereas food is still tied to its essential, existential roots. That's one of the things that gives it value, and one of the things that makes it very difficult for it to change.

Food is a shared cultural perception. It's a language which we share in terms of experiences. What chefs do is maintain ties to the past and actually sort of unify people in creating a perceptual system that people can share. I think that's one of the great values that they have. It's not that they revolutionize people's thinking about the universe. I think that it's basically that they bring people together on a human scale. The humanity of food is still one of its greatest assets. It's more humane than looking at a painting on a wall or listening to a record.

Some of the greatest chefs are not necessarily some of the greatest technicians or the greatest innovators. They have been some of the people who have created—like Alice [Waters]—a philosophy or a milieu or a community of thinking and philosophy about food, that's been shared not only by the people who have worked there, and the people who have gone to the restaurant, but also by a generation of younger chefs.

Some people would say, "Well, Jean-Louis [Palladin] is a better chef than Alice Waters." Well, that is true technically and creatively, but in terms of who has had more importance, I think there is no doubt that Alice has had more importance.

For example, the emergence of a critical community is a relatively recent phenomenon. While the *Guide Michelin* was first published around the turn of the century in Europe, the first serious restaurant reviewing did not begin to take place in the United States until the mid-to-late-1950s. The *Zagat Surveys* did not begin publication until the 1980s. Without the presence of educated customers and critics, who was to say that some professional cooking could indeed be called culinary art?

In his pathbreaking book *Creating Minds*, Howard Gardner refers to Mihaly Csikszentmihaly's identification of three considerations that are central in any examination of realms of creativity: (1) the *individual person* or talent; (2) the *domain or discipline* in which that individual is working, and (3) the surrounding *field* that renders judgments about the quality of the individuals and products. Realms of creativity are best viewed as based on an interactive process, in which all three of these areas correlate.

Using the above to examine the culinary field, (1) *chefs* (2) *cook* for the public, primarily in restaurants and hotels, and (3) are evaluated constantly

Chefs need recognition in order for food to truly be an art form. It took architects 150 years to get recognition...A fine meal by a creative chef enhances the soul in the same way that a beautiful building inspires; it becomes art.
—Peter Kump

by *customers, food critics, and the culinary community.* How has each of the three considerations played a role in the perception of the culinary arts?

Chefs and Professional Cooking

While the majority of leading chefs we interviewed agree on the potential for artistry within the culinary experience, a few express hesitations about the use of the term. This is perhaps not surprising, given that chefs have evolved from a profession historically viewed as domestic labor into one that now boasts celebrity chef-restaurateurs. Throughout this transformation, they have largely maintained a professional spirit of modesty and service to the customer, and some chefs still feel uncomfortable with the elitist connotations of calling their profession an art.

Michael Romano is one leading chef who has expressed some discomfort with the comparison of food to art. "I think there's a danger of getting too much into the idea that 'I am an artist.' For myself, I like to be in touch with

Cooking is an art that needs to evolve and change on the basis of its methods and materials, its organization—and even of the whole concept of the role of the chef.
—Pierre Troisgros

what I enjoy cooking, and what my customers enjoy eating," he says. "It's not just 'This is my artistic creation—take it or leave it.' A restaurant is about nurturing, about saying, 'Welcome to my home.' It's an interactive process in which you provide your guests with something they're going to ingest, going to put in their bodies. It's a very intimate thing, and they should have a say in it. Chefs should be flexible."

Artistry also carries with it the connotation of originality. However, it took years before chefs dared defy classical tradition to begin experimenting with their own dishes. The French chefs who pioneered *nouvelle cuisine* in the 1960s represented a giant step toward bringing the culinary world into its own. Once creativity was unleashed in French and, subsequently and especially, American kitchens in the last few decades, there was no turning back.

"Before *nouvelle cuisine* hit America, there was not this 'interpretive' spirit. What we learned in school, and what all great restaurants did, was dishes like duck *à l'orange* and veal Oscar. You made the classic sauces—you wouldn't ever have made an orange hollandaise sauce," says Chris Schlesinger. "But *nouvelle cuisine* opened cooking up to interpretation. As long as you stuck to the fundamental principles of good food, then you were allowed to experiment. And that's what I think opened cooking up in this country, because it allowed young people to come to it and we didn't have to do the same junk that went on before us.

"*Nouvelle cuisine* was a movement in France that was a rededication to the basic fundamentals of good food. The chefs said, 'No more sloppiness—we're not going to thicken sauces so much because what the thickening does is cover up lack of flavor with texture. We're going to really be careful with our vegetables.' There was a little bit of Japanese aesthetic in there, too—smaller portions, clearer flavors. They said, 'We're not going to be so concerned about following the classics. We're going to take all the best cooking fundamentals out of the classics, and as long as we stick to those, that's what's important.'"

Chefs have since embraced the opportunity to be creative with, and expressive through, food, and American chefs—widely considered to be the most innovative in the world—are now viewed as world class. Just as the artistic community has over time shifted its center from Paris to New York City, so has the culinary community.

Lydia Shire cites the intense "seriousness among American chefs" as evidence that the profession is moving to new levels of respectability and accomplishment. "American chefs have really jumped ahead in the food world," notes

ARE THERE THREE CATEGORIES OF CHEFS?

	Trade	*Craft*	*Art*
Category	"Burger-Flippers"	"Accomplished Chefs"	"Culinary Artists"
Customer Goal	Survival	Enjoyment	Entertainment
Chef's Intention	Fill/Feed	Satisfy/Please	Transcend/Transport
Price of Lunch	Movie Ticket	Off-Broadway Theatre Ticket	Broadway Orchestra Ticket
Who Determines Meal	Customer ("Have It Your Way")	Customer/Chef	Chef (Tasting Menu)
Chef's Primary Repertoire	Hamburgers	Classic dishes	Chef's own dishes
Number of Senses Affected	5	5	6
Customers Leave Saying	"I'm full."	"That was delicious."	"Life is wonderful."

Shire, "and are cooking some of the most exciting food in the world today."

Yet not all American chefs are culinary artists. We envision chefs as falling into one of three categories along a continuum (see chart on page 7). For the vast majority of America's three million-plus chefs and cooks, this is a *trade*, typically defined as "skilled work." We'd place the majority of (but perhaps not all) "burger-flippers" into this category. While all professional chefs by definition consider cooking to be their trade, there are some who also consider it a craft. As skill is developed with care and experience, and the talent for preparing delicious food on a consistent basis is honed, some chefs elevate cooking to a *craft*, typically defined as "an occupation requiring special skill or art." And still other chefs may embrace both definitions while also seeing the potential for artistry at the highest practice of their profession. At this level, in rare but unforgettable instances, you can find chefs whose culinary skill, combined with unusual imagination and creativity, truly elevates their profession to an art. One's level of competence and intention as a chef largely determines where one falls on the continuum.

Cooking as a Trade

Whether or not they themselves are viewed that way by others, certain leading chefs prefer to view cooking as a trade.

"In trying to understand what art is, and what a craft is, and what a trade is, I've always argued that I don't think cooking should be considered an art, for argument's sake," says Chris Schlesinger. "The reason I say that is because I think it's a skill that grows out of actual human need—everybody needs to cook. People don't need to create art; it's a choice that people make.

"What's at the heart of cooking for me is that it's a profession. It was never something that I chose in order to express myself creatively. I can see other people arguing that it is, but to me it's more visceral and immediate, and its importance and meaning lie in areas other than artistic expression. The art or the magic that's involved in food is not so much in its preparation, but in eating with the people you eat it with. The magic is the mealtime.

"In the beginning of Escoffier's *Ma Cuisine*, he writes that of the many principles in cooking, the main one is to make the person whom you're serving happy. I always read that to mean that, whatever we are, we're professionals—and if we serve food and someone doesn't like it, whether we or the critics think it's the grandest creation, if we don't please the customer, then we've failed. I don't think artists can fail like that."

Cooking as a Craft

Some leading chefs admit that cooking could arguably be called either an art or a craft.

Jimmy Schmidt says, "I think it's safer to call it a craft. To capture the impression or the dynamics of a certain mood or feeling is a lot tougher in food than it is in other media. But that doesn't mean that it's not creative."

Other chefs believe that it starts out as a craft. "Cooking is a craft first," says Terrance Brennan. "Like a carpenter, we learn our trade through hands-on apprenticing."

From its start as a craft, it can evolve into artistry. "The first few years [cooking] aren't a matter of style," says Jasper White. "I tell all my cooks when they come to work for me that it's really a matter of learning how to cook. The techniques and skills are universal, I think, to a certain extent. If I tell my cooks to make lobster bisque and how I want it to taste, the skill that it takes for them to recreate my dish is the same skill that they would need to create their own food. So I really feel that before you reach the point of art, it's a craft. And without being really highly skilled in the craft, I don't believe you can ever attain artistry—even if you get a few write-ups in the magazines."

Joyce Goldstein is also careful to distinguish between those who practice this profession as a craft versus an art. She agrees that "some chefs are artists. And then there are lots of craftspeople. A craftsperson is someone who masters technique and can do a lot of dazzling stuff with technique. And that comes from practice, which is where school really helps a lot.

"Artistry can come from people with virtually no skills with a knife at all. That's cooking in the soul—and some people have that and some people don't. That you don't learn—that either you have, or don't have. It's like being a painter—you can be a very competent painter. You can learn how to grind your pigments and prepare your canvas. You can learn all this stuff—but it's not going to give you soul. There are some people who have shitty technique, but they paint fabulously. The artistic is intuitive—and that comes from God knows where. I couldn't begin to tell you."

How should chefs evaluate their impact? "When you cook, do you reach others with your message?" asks Goldstein. "With lots of technical stuff, diners go, 'Ooooh!' But only the culinary artist wants to make food that people will remember with their mouths, not only with their eyes. So that when others taste it, they want to taste it again and again.

"I don't think you have to be reinventing the wheel to be creative or artistic. Sometimes the most artistic people play with a very limited palate. You pick your palate, you pick your range, you pick what interests you—and then you cook your heart out.

"How do you measure success as a chef? Well, did you get them in the gut? Did you get them in the heart? And, most importantly, did you get them in the mouth? These should be your goals."

Cooking as an Art

What does it take to make the leap into the realm of artistry? "How do you learn to become a great pianist? Where does that come from? It's not just learning how to punch the keyboard," says Bradley Ogden. "It's something more than that. A lot of it is natural ability—it's probably 75 percent natural ability. Either you have it or you don't have it. Some of it can be trained, but a lot of it can't."

Gary Danko says, "Cooking is, for me, the perfect balance of art and science. There's that creative endeavor within you that can think out the seasons and the flavor profiles. Then there's the scientific part—what is actually going on with the whisk? If I'm blanching broccoli, why is it turning brown in the pan? As you study that, you learn that sometimes if you cook a lot of vegetables in the same water, an acid will develop. And if you cook a green vegetable in that acidic water, it's going to turn army brown. So these are things you start to learn through science."

Hubert Keller believes that creativity is rooted in mastering the classics, an argument for mastering the craft of cooking before attempting artistry. "If you have a foundation, you are able to play a little bit," he says. "When you're learning music at the beginning, you practice scales. Once you learn, you start to play other people's songs. And once you've learned those, if you get really good, you might start composing a little bit. It's the same in cooking. Once you have a lot of experience, you might start to include a couple of ingredients that might not have been included by [Paul] Bocuse, by [Paul] Haeberlin, by [Roger] Vergé—otherwise, maybe their hair would stand on end! But if you're in a different country, with a different audience, and if you feel it's not just being done to shock, sometimes it can work. You have to have a guideline, though—and then you can go a little bit right or a little bit left."

In the process of becoming a culinary artist, Gray Kunz says that "there is a point that you are not, and a point that you are. When you're able to bring your feeling and intuition to a dish—the artist is coming out at that point."

George Germon and Johanne Killeen are quick to point out, "There are not that many culinary artists. Only a small proportion of chefs fall into that category."

Part of what characterizes culinary artists is their expressiveness and their ability to cook from their gut. "They have their own way of expressing themselves," says Daniel Boulud. "In food, the expression is more physical and emotional. When creating great food, the taste is always memorable. Buts sometimes the best food is not always the result of deep thought. Sometimes it simply falls together."

Killeen and Germon agree. "We're most influenced—I don't want to say intellectually or theoretically, because that's getting a little bit beyond what it really is—by our gut," says Killeen. "It's also very dangerous, when you start talking in theoretical and philosophical terms," adds Germon. "It really is almost like the death of a dish." Killeen continues, "In terms of art and artistry and food, it has a lot more to do with your gut than your intellect. There are certainly great intellectual artists, but there are also artists who simply create from their gut. And I think that's more what we do than anything else."

Customers

Customers vary greatly in terms of their knowledgeability about food and wine, not to mention personal history, life experience, and likes and dislikes, which affect not only their potential for enjoying a dining experience but also for interpreting what a chef may be trying to express in his or her food. Food's meaning lies as much in the customer's reception as it does in the chef's intention. For example, presenting four different customers with identical, "perfect" strawberry tarts might evoke four very different reactions: fond memories in someone who recalls picking and eating strawberries as a child, alarm in another who is allergic to strawberries, guilt in a third who may be on a diet and concerned about the dish's calorie or cholesterol count, and ecstasy in a fourth who spent the prior evening being fed strawberries by a lover!

Customers' level of knowledge will also color their perception of the chef's profession itself. The same popular cookbooks and television shows that have served to catapult leading chefs into household names have perhaps, in turn, done chefs a disservice. In leading chefs' well-meaning encouragement to home cooks that they, too, can cook the chefs' three- or four-star food at home, they have perhaps omitted any mention of the years of training and experience that are behind the recipes and indeed the practice of professional cooking, leading to the general public's misguided view that "anybody can cook great food."

"Perhaps because everybody eats, and many people cook to some extent, they don't think beyond the daily task-making of it," notes Wayne Nish. "There's simply no reference in their lives to what a really great culinary practitioner can do. It requires a frequent restaurant-goer to even begin to think about that to any extent.

"When you have cooking shows on television that are reaching out to domestic cooks, they by necessity eliminate a great deal of skills in order to make it available to the nonskilled home cook," he points out.

No book of which we're aware (other than the one you're holding) has ever closely examined how a culinary artist composes his or her creations, while scores of books have examined the creative process of painters, musicians, and writers, for example—thereby helping the general public to appreciate the level of sophisticated thought and conscious design that underlies their compositions. This surely enhances the level of appreciation and respect the public has for such artists.

In the economic boom of the 1980s, diners grew increasingly familiar with gourmet ingredients and fine dining, resulting in more educated and discriminating palates. The growth in membership organizations such as the American Institute of Wine and Food and The James Beard Foundation, which sponsor educational events ranging from ingredient tastings to special dinners, reflects an increasingly sophisticated clientele.

As chefs have begun to come into their own, their equally adventurous customers have encouraged their innovation. Diners' voices have become louder with the advent of consumer-poll publications such as the *Zagat Survey* and *Marcellino's*, which summarize their opinions.

There is a triangular relationship among chefs, the ingredients with which they choose to cook, and their customers. Not only does cooking's ambiguity as an art stem from food's utilitarian roots, but doubtless also from customers used to a "have it your way" mentality when it comes to food. There is little room left for a chef's creative expression when they're responding to requests for substitutions and sauces "on the side."

Given the professionalism demanded by hotel cooking especially, Gary Danko admits, "I don't particularly cook for myself anymore. I have my flavor principles, and I have dishes seasoned the way I would season them, and the garnishes on the dishes are for me. But in a hotel restaurant, it is not unusual for people to come in and start ripping your food apart. I don't mind when people request things like serving the sauce on the side, but people will order a meat dish I offer with a tarragon essence and say, 'I don't want tarragon in there.' Chefs really have to learn to remove themselves personally from their food. When we opened, we'd get customers who ordered soufflés even though we didn't have them on the menu. People would get very demanding and say, 'I had a soufflé [at The Ritz-Carlton] in Boston, and I want a soufflé!' So I added soufflés to the menu—including a noncholesterol soufflé, which has become a signature dish—and now 60 percent of our customers order soufflés. Chefs have to be able to allow some flexibility for what the public wants."

"New Yorkers especially need to be pampered," adds Daniel Boulud. "They want to find security, a 'home.' If you understand what they're looking for, you can make them happy."

Countless artists who have had to alter their works according to a patron's wishes in order to receive a commission doubtless know the same feeling! Conversely, educated diners know that they are more likely to experience a chef's best work if they order the tasting menu of dishes composed by the chef.

For some chefs, inspiration can result from this pressure. "Customers come in and tell us what they want, and we're inspired to create it. This happens whether it's a table of ladies who want to have something wonderful yet light, or a table of foodies who are completely open to whatever you want to serve them," says Boulud. "Knowing who I am cooking for determines the direction of my spontaneity."

Boulud cites as an example the time eight years ago that a party of six or seven—including chefs Charlie Trotter and Emeril Lagasse—came in for lunch at Le Cirque, where he was cooking at the time. "We were serving suckling pig as a special, and usually just threw the pig heads away. But for them, I lined a copper pot with smoked bacon and layers of *mirepoix,* and baked the head covered with bacon and *mirepoix,* and served it to them," Boulud remembers. "Spontaneity offers me a chance to have fun with customers who I'm sure will enjoy it. The most beautiful thing in this business is developing a relationship with your guests."

Interacting with art takes place almost solely on a mental plane. In food, the interaction is obviously a lot more personal—you eat it.
—Jimmy Schmidt

Boulud recalls that the photographer Norman Parkinson would come in once or twice a week for lunch, and never opened a menu. Boulud would cook three or four simple courses for him, depending on what was in season. "Then, after every meal, he would wipe his plate clean and would take a marker and write his appreciation on the rim of the plate before sending it back into the kitchen. We had stacks of plates with his scrawlings! He was a character, with great humor—but you could always see how appreciative he was!"

Many chefs were enthusiastic about the fact that their customers had expanded their adventurousness in food. "Moving from Chicago to Los Angeles, I found that customers were so excited about our food. The audience has become so adventuresome and so supportive of chefs that I think it's really been very exciting," says Mary Sue Milliken. "You no longer have to beg people to try things, or sneak things onto their plates somehow so they don't really know they're there."

Critics and the Culinary Community

The critical community extends far and wide, with reviews in newspapers; city, food, travel, and even business magazines; restaurant guides such as those published by Michelin; and organizations such as AAA and Mobil, which recognize outstanding restaurants. To chefs, for the most part, they represent either their biggest champions—or their worst nightmares.

Do critics see the potential for art in cooking? Many leading chefs have expressed their disappointment in food critics' general approach to the practice of restaurant reviewing. Daniel Boulud contrasts the thoughtful critic, who attempts to understand the chef and his or her intention when evaluating a restaurant, with the dreaded "critic with a checklist." Similarly, Mark Miller criticizes what he views as many critics' quantitative as opposed to qualitative approach to criticism. "Dance critics don't say that [a performance] was worth going to or how much it was worth. They educate you that if you should go to this dance, these are some of the things that should help

---

Patrick O'Connell on Creativity

It seems our culture always had it backwards. Creativity isn't something you acquire. In reality, it's the removing of the sandbags that have been laid upon you by the culture, and freeing yourself of the constraints that you've been programmed to deal with so that you can let creativity move through you. And everybody has it. Creativity isn't something you own so much as something that is destined to move through you, and you are a vehicle for it if you can allow yourself to be. I think the control issue is one of the prime reasons that people in our culture have a problem with it, because it is a kind of giving up of control to allow a process to take place through yourself as a vehicle.

A book called *The Gift* figured largely in my reaffirmation of my own thoughts and feelings about creativity. The idea is that our culture, unlike earlier or more primitive cultures, is based on economy, that everything is looked upon as a commodity that can be bought and sold. This is contrasted with the American Indian who, when giving a gift, understood that it was to be kept in continuous circulation. When the Indians gave the white man gifts, they felt that he was supposed to con-

you to understand what you're seeing," says Miller. One chef mentioned how a particular critic wished to abolish the star system for rating restaurants but was not able to do so because it sold newspapers!

The culinary community includes organizations such as The James Beard Foundation, host of The James Beard Awards, the debut of which in 1991 made the culinary arts the only non-performing art with its own televised awards program, and which have played an invaluable role in bringing recognition to America's leading chefs.

The Art of Composition

As previously mentioned, the general public is probably ill-aware of the level of thought and care that goes into culinary artists' compositions. In the evolution or elevation of food from a strictly utilitarian realm to an epicurean one, such compositions become increasingly intricate. The moment of composition is the point at which a chef has the opportunity for expression and to largely determine what a customer will receive. It is important for chefs to understand how their decisions will influence the end result.

Composition: *the act of composing, or putting together a whole by combining parts; an arrangement of the parts of a work of art so as to form a unified, harmonious whole.*

"There are some cooks who create just for the sake of creating. But when it comes down to eating a dish, it has to make sense," insists Bradley Ogden. "If one flavor is fighting with another, and too many different things are going on, it doesn't work."

Similarly, George Germon and Johanne Killeen mention that they heard Fauchon's pastry chef Pierre Hermé discuss "the architecture of taste."

tinue that cycle, whereas white men possessed them and broke the cycle. Then, at one point, the Indians went and stole back the gifts they'd given the white men, and that's where the term "Indian giving" came from.

All of this helped put some perspective on how our present culture is so damaging to the creative process. In terms of what chefs are doing, so often they're trying to figure out what the current trend is and what direction they should go in to please a market. They're so busy orienting themselves commercially that they lose touch with what it is they want to eat. For example, one of my cooks presented for my critique a dish of one fish rolled in another fish with forcemeat stuffed inside, then rolled in something else, served with nuts and mushrooms and herbs and lettuce leaves around it, and two butter sauces. I simply asked him, "Would *you* want to eat that?"

I think it was Gael Greene [of *New York* magazine] who once wrote of Aurora [a now-defunct Manhattan restaurant that was opened in the mid-1980s by Joe Baum and Gerard Pengo], "Right now they're busy trying to figure out what New Yorkers want to eat. We look forward to their getting over that hurdle and cooking what *they* feel like cooking and what *they* would want to eat."

"He pointed out the idea that there is—or should be—structure as well as taste and balance going on in a dish," they say. "Even if there are twelve ingredients in a dessert, each should have a specific purpose—whether it adds sweetness or tartness or texture. And all of them should come together to work as a whole."

The starting point is a classical foundation: some, and preferably much, familiarity with ingredients and techniques. Given the international larder of ingredients and repertoire of techniques available to chefs, the number of different compositions that can result is virtually limitless. History has tamed this potential chaos through the relentless testing of various ingredient combinations and the resulting development of classical flavor combinations and dishes that represent the most successful marriages of flavors and ingredients. These can provide an invaluable starting point for chefs, and are explored in great detail later in this book.

Cooking is for capturing the taste of the food and then enhancing it, as a composer may take a theme and then delight us with his variations.
—Fernand Point

In addition, a chef's individual preferences will, over time and in the right circumstances (of creative freedom), give rise to the chef's own personal style of cooking. While this is a complex and probably largely unconscious process, it is comprised of a chef's reactions to every cooking technique he or she has ever seen used or every combination of flavors he or she has ever tasted—and instantly accepted for or rejected from subsequent use in his or her repertoire.

The Realm of the Senses

The work of a chef and the appreciation of a dining experience is unique—and uniquely demanding—in that it draws upon each of the five senses. While the sense of taste is the one most heavily emphasized, the sense of smell is just as, if not more, important. While the tongue can taste only four basic flavors, the sense of smell provides us with many more sensory impressions. Similarly, the sense of touch—and one's appreciation of textures—comes into play not only with the fingertips but also from the mouth's own sensors, not to mention the ear's appreciation of a good crunch! And while it may be overemphasized in modern cooking, a pleasing visual presentation of a dish can add greatly to one's total appreciation of it.

Bringing Creativity and Point of View to…Asparagus

If cooking were never an art, but simply a skill, you would hand five different chefs a bunch of asparagus each, request that they cook it, and wind up with five more or less identically cooked plates of asparagus.

But leading chefs bring very different points of view to the same asparagus spear. If they're skilled at their craft, they'll know how long to cook it so that its consistency is at its best. But how they choose to cook it, and what they choose to cook it with—these are areas where their creativity and personal preferences come into play.

Need more convincing? Then let's have some fun. Let's see if you can match the dishes with the chefs who have featured them on their restaurant menus:

1. *Dungeness Crab and Green Asparagus Salad with Meyer Lemon*

2. *Grilled Asparagus with Olive Bread Crumbs and Olive Oil*

3. *Asparagus with Dried Shrimp Vinaigrette*

4. *Watercress Salad with Grilled Asparagus and Red Onion*

5. *Asparagus Soup with a Sweet Pepper Coulis*

• • •

a. *Daniel Boulud—Restaurant Daniel, New York City*

b. *Susanna Foo—Susanna Foo, Philadelphia*

c. *Mark Peel and Nancy Silverton—Campanile and La Brea Bakery, Los Angeles*

d. *Chris Schlesinger—East Coast Grill, Boston*

e. *Alice Waters—Chez Panisse, Berkeley, California*

Readers familiar with the chefs' unique styles of cuisine should have a little easier time with this than those who don't. But there are certainly enough clues in the above information to get you started. For example, are there regional or ethnic associations with any of the ingredients or techniques mentioned? Which chef would have the most ready access to them?

Point of view is not limited to the restaurant experience, nor to the plate. It is even expressed through the description of a single dish on a menu.

(Answer key: 1-e; 2-c; 3-b; 4-d; 5-a)

Patrick O'Connell reminds us, "This business affords the opportunity to draw on every single talent that you have, but it's not viewed that way yet. It's viewed as more of a technical expertise or a trade, instead of the art form that it is. Nobody's pushing the outer limits, in terms of what it's really all about."

Our aim is to examine the opportunities for compositional choice open to the chef—specifically, the composition of *flavors*, the composition of *dishes*, and the composition of dishes into *menus*—and how these choices cumulatively evolve into a chef's unique style of cuisine.

Whether the reader is a chef, or a home cook wishing to better understand decision making in the compositional process, or a restaurant diner wishing to better understand some of what goes into the creation of a dining experience, we hope the end result will be the same: a stronger appreciation for the talents, efforts, and accomplishments of America's treasure of culinary artists.

A Final Word

Beauty is often in the eye of the beholder. Some audience members might be moved to tears while attending the opera, while others sitting in the same row are bored to tears. Likely, some of them bring a more educated and knowledgeable appreciation to what they are experiencing, and so the experience is not the same! One's consciousness brings an important element to any aesthetic experience—including that of a diner or chef.

To take a popular example, think of the "Magic Eye" pictures that appear everywhere from the Sunday comics to best-selling books. If you look at them one way, they're merely colorful images on paper—not offensive, but arguably not great art, either. But if you know how to look into the picture, it is possible to see an almost magical three-dimensional image. Not everyone can see the 3-D image; it takes knowledge and practice. But the potential to see it is always there. And just because some people can see it and others can't doesn't mean that it doesn't exist. Similarly, in food, some diners have never had a dining experience that has moved them on the level of art. But those of us who have been so moved know that this potential exists.

For diners, the secret is to know that the potential is there and to open themselves to it. For chefs, the secret lies in aspiring to reach their customers in this manner. "In order to create with food, or to create dishes, you really have to have the end in mind," says Jimmy Schmidt. "You have to perceive a picture or a vision of what you're trying to create, and then your palette to paint with [in order] to create that picture is your ingredients and your techniques. The ingredients are the things that are most visible, that you can see, and how you put them in and whether they're in the

Jimmy Schmidt on Activating the Senses

Robert Del Grande [of Houston] and I were talking about this last week. Food memories are generated by the activation of as many senses as possible. Lots of memories are created the same way, and that's why certain memories in your life are very vivid—because they've got all of your attention. If you look at your food memories, and you can probably remember some of the best meals you've ever had, you can probably remember some really, really bad meals. But tell me what you ate three weeks ago on Thursday night. If it wasn't something brilliant, you probably don't remember. Does it mean it was bad? No. It just didn't create a memory. Because it probably didn't activate or catch the attention of all your senses.

Sight is one of the first things that hits. If something is not pleasant to the eye, it's not going to mean a lot. It doesn't mean a dish is good or bad, but it doesn't activate the sense of sight. *Smell* is extremely crucial. You can smell a lot more things than you can taste—you can only taste four things. Obviously, the *taste* factor is there as well, but beyond that you've got the temperature factor, the sense of *feel*. Even if you've got a cold, you can still tell if something is hot or cold to the palate. The crunchiness aspect is the vibration to your inner ear; you can actually *hear* it.

So, as many of those senses as you get functioning that can work together, the more opportunity you have to make a favorable, lasting, pleasing impression or experience. You want to try to activate *everything*.

foreground or in the background or the center of the identity are really the techniques that you use to cause that all to come together. In order to accomplish that, you have to have experience, continue to try things and experiment. But there are many canvases that are discarded before the final painting is ready and released.

"The medium we work in is so short-spanned that it requires a lot of chemical and technical balance to accomplish it. Likewise, it may need a lot more work on the front side to ensure that the collision of ingredients is at exactly the precise moment

Rick Bayless on Cooking in Context

I'm not sure food can move you in the same way other art can, the way a good piece of literature or music or a painting can. It seems to me that the ability to really move people is a basic criterion of fine art. So should there be a fine-art component to cooking? Is the existence of *haute cuisine*, our equivalent of fine art, really justified? It's easy to relate to food as folk art—it's an easily identifiable cultural expression. But fine art?

In the world of fine art, most artists don't want to be thought of as simply a representation of their culture, something many think of as closer to folk art. They want to be addressing broader questions. If you look at a great painting, for instance, it can mean something profound to people all over the world, Does food exist on a comparable level? Is that what fine dining—*haute cuisine*—is? Or is food less expressive and, by necessity, does it have to stay rooted in the culture that it comes from? I'm not sure we've come far enough to answer that question.

Perhaps *haute cuisine* is like opera, which everyone seems to recognize as an art form, albeit not universal or easily accessible. In fact it's pretty arcane. Though opera can be moving, it's an art form you have to be pretty versed in to appreciate. Rarely can someone who has never heard opera before understand it right off the bat. You have to know what you're listening to, why they're achieving that voice quality. Thinking about it, I wouldn't say opera isn't an art form—that it should be eliminated—just because it's not easily accessible. So I could be convinced to say the same about *haute cuisine*, though I'm not totally comfortable with that conclusion.

I think these are things students in culinary schools—any young people interested in the profession—should think about. They need to understand the cultural, historical, political, and artistic context of their profession. I came of age in the sixties, when it was fashionable to bash *haute cuisine* as elit-

that they are all at their peak. You can have a great idea, and you can put a bunch of ingredients together on a plate, but I think the key is getting all of them down on the plate at the exact time that works perfectly.

"Look, for instance, at beef. It should be aged, because if you ate it right away it would be terrible. Even a chicken needs aging; it needs forty-eight hours, as opposed to two or three weeks. You don't want to eat a

ist. In truth, I don't think it has to be—in fact, it won't be—if we continue to talk about these things, to debate, to understand.

Food—because of the fact that you ingest it and not just look at it—has a unique impression on people. Because it goes across your tongue, because taste and smell are the most evocative of our senses, we react in strongly animal ways—these were protective devices for us for so many millenia. Taste and smell are something we have to reckon with carefully. I mean, we're not going to put out a whole big plate of bitter stuff for our customers, just so that they can have a strong, negative reaction to it. On the other hand, if you go to a good piece of theater, you might see something incredibly ugly put in front of you. You are intended to have a visceral, negative reaction to it. We don't do that with food, do we? Do we have the equivalent of sad or angry or hateful flavors? If we don't, does that make food less an art than a folk art or craft?

Could it be that bitter flavors are the equivalent of ugliness in literature or theater? Take Campari, for instance. My daughter tasted it the other day for the first time, and she washed her mouth out over and over—she thought it was the most vile stuff she'd ever tasted. She couldn't imagine that we could sit there and drink it. I've come to enjoy that bitterness. Is that equivalent to enjoying a heavy novel or play?

If food is art, why haven't we developed a sophisticated way of talking about it? Why isn't it studied in art departments rather than schools that have been historically connected to vocational/technical schools? Why is there still ambivalence about whether or not it's a desired profession? I think historically, worldwide—except for *haute cuisine* in France—cooking has been backroom stuff, out of the limelight, essentially all done by women. It's never been celebrated the way other pursuits have, so perhaps it's hard to talk about because we're not participating in a conversation that's gone on for eons. I hope that by the time I'm old and gray, we'll have made some progress.

chicken right after it's been killed. They're terrible. Whether it's chicken or beef, you want to capture it at the moment in its cycle when it's the most palatable—not only for flavor development, but for texture. Likewise, a vegetable that's picked—especially when you're talking about herbs and such—the best point is right then and there, that exact second.

"So, if you can collide the different ingredients you're putting together at that time when they're all at their peak to create your singular concept of flavor, that's the big challenge. Freshness has got a lot to do with it—sometimes. In other cases, things should be aged. Everything has a cycle.

"The secret is getting in sync with that cycle to get the elements to collide when it's most advantageous to all of them."

Food is all too frequently mistaken as being only about taste. Likewise, the sense of taste is so much more than merely the stimulation of taste buds on the tongue. Food is rich with sensory stimuli—not only of taste but of smell, vision, touch, sound—and, in turn, memories and emotions and cultural connotations. A single aroma has the power to take you immediately back to childhood. (This differs for everyone, but walnuts do so for Andrew and raspberries for Karen.) And a single flavor has the power to suggest an entire region of the world! (When you think of soy sauce, try not to think of Asia.)

Meet Your Medium

The message of any medium is the change of scale or pace or pattern that it introduces into human affairs.

—Marshall McLuhan

Culinary artists must understand the nature of their medium. Cooking is different from perfume-making, for example, in that chefs don't mix pure flavor essences in laboratory test tubes, and different from music-making in that the flavors of ingredients aren't as singular as musical notes—they're more like natural chords. Not only is an ingredient very often a combination of flavors but it also has other characteristics that must be taken into consideration when cooking—its aroma, its color, its texture, and even its common associations, such as with a particular holiday or country. It is critical that cooks become conscious of, and learn to respect, the medium of food.

Sensory Perception

In any encounter with food, taste is probably one of the last senses engaged. Because food is something we ingest, we judge it carefully, critically, and instinctively. All of our senses are used to evaluate whether to put the food into our mouths, and then whether to swallow it. First, you look at it, and then you might smell it. Is it safe? Is it appealing? If a food appears hot, for example, you might first try to touch it to gauge its temperature. Will it burn your mouth? If it passes muster and you bite into it, your first experience is one of texture. Is it soft? Crispy? If it's crispy, you'll probably hear the crunch in your inner ear a split second before its flavor begins to register on your taste buds. So, taste is something that is experienced (and, one hopes, enjoyed) only after the other senses have first been satisfied—and it is where our attention has the pleasure of lingering.

As Mark Miller points out, "Taste is an existential, sensual experience. We don't really understand it. Language is what we use for taste, and yet the body goes through this temporal process; there are highs and lows, intensities, durations, complexities. Taste is a very, very complex thing in the body, where it unifies a number of factors."

Understanding the magnitude of the taste experience has important implications for designing food. "When you design [food] for people, you have to be much more aware of the body's experience, and not get caught in either looking at the object or thinking of how they experience it or using language," says Miller. "Language is descriptive and analytical; it is not about the experience itself."

Food is about much more than what it's called or what it tastes like. "The experience of food is an emotional experience, it's a social experience, it's an existential physiological experience, it's a psychological experience. It unifies, to a great deal, across different cultural traditions as an experience," says Miller. "It exists at all these levels that have nothing to do with saying that it's an apple or an apple pie. That is already abstracted from the experience. It is not an apple pie. The only reason you want to eat it is not because it's an apple pie, but because it's something that you learned to love, that it reminds you of home or your grandmother or a diner or school. People need to go back and realize where the meaning of food comes from for them."

In teaching people to think about food, Miller emphasizes, "I teach people to not use language. Take a raisin, for instance. People would say it's sweet. Well, a raisin when you bite down on it is sweet in the beginning. It has a medium tempo and flavor—it becomes tannic on the edge, it gets a little bit juicier, and it gets highly accentuated sugars and a little bit dusty in the mid-palate over time. There's a certain intensity that goes up. And then the sweetness dies off, and then the tannin dies off, and what you're left with is a kind of seedy little bit of sweetness that follows through. What you have is this curve of experience—from a single raisin!

"When I say, 'What is a raisin?'—it's not that it's sweet. It also has a certain texture. It's also in the body, with the jaw coming down, the interaction of the tongue, the neural receptors, the brain recognizing it and saying, 'Oh, I know what it is.' There's a releasing of anxiety because you have something in your mouth and your body that you know is not a foreign object that may kill you. You're not going to have the same emotional experience from chomping down [on something] and finding that it's a live grasshopper in your mouth."

Flavors are among the things most difficult to describe, and Miller finds it helpful to use musical analogies. "We have polychrome paintings, we have polyphonic music; [in food] we have a tempo, we have a rhythm, we have a bass line, we have a note that goes here, we have another one that goes there—and we can start graphing these things. This is what's happening in your mouth," he says. "With a piece of turkey, it's a protein which is very flat; it doesn't have any highs or lows. Then we get to something like a *mole* [a complex Mexican sauce], which has got twenty or thirty different things going on simultaneously.

"What we're talking about is composition. We're talking about the body as a receptor, and what's interesting to the mind and the brain and their neural capacity," Miller says. "The body is always interested in stimulation; it's physiologically trained to go after stimulation."

By fully understanding how food is a stimulus to much more than just the tongue, one can design food much more holistically.

COOKING WITH THE SEASONS*

SPRING

artichokes
asparagus
avocados
beans, fava
beet greens
beets
blueberries
catfish
chard

chervil
citrus fruits, especially
   blood oranges, Meyer
   lemons
clams
crabs, soft-shell
crayfish
cucumbers
dandelion greens
fava beans
fiddlehead ferns
frisée
frogs' legs
garlic, especially green
greens—arugula, chervil,
   mustard
grouper

guavas
halibut
honeydew melons
lamb
lettuce
mint
mizuma
morels
nettles
onions, Vidalia
papayas
peas
potatoes, new
radishes
rhubarb
salmon
sardines

scallions
sea bass
shad and shad roe
shallots
snow peas
sorrel
strawberries
suckling pig
sugar snap peas
vanilla
veal
water chestnuts
watercress
zucchini

SUMMER

apricots
arugula
basil
beans, green
berries
blackberries
blueberries
canteloupe
celery
chanterelles

cherries
chickpeas
clams
corn
crabs, soft-shell
cucumbers
currants
eggplant
figs
frogs' legs
garlic
goat
gooseberries
grapes
guavas
halibut
honeydew melons
ice cream

litchi nuts
lobster
mangoes
melons
muskmelons
nectarines
okra
peaches
peppers
plums
porcini
potatoes, new
raspberries
ratatouille
red currants
salmon
sardines
scallions

shallots
shellfish
sherbets
squashes, summer
tomatoes
tropical fruits
tuna
watermelon
zucchini

---

* The ingredients most characteristic of the seasons are indicated by **boldface** type. While many ingredients are in fact available year-round, they are listed under their seasonal peak(s).

Culinary Artistry

FALL

apples
beans
beans, green and lima
blood oranges
broccoli
broccoli rabe
brussels sprouts
cabbage
capon

cauliflower
celery root
cèpes
chanterelles
chestnuts
coconuts
cranberries
daikon
dates
duck
eels
fennel
figs
foie gras
game
garlic
grapes

grapes, Muscat
herring
leeks
lemons, Meyer
lobster
maple syrup
mushrooms
mussels
onions
papayas
partridges
pears
peppers
persimmons
pheasants
pomegranates
pork

pumpkins
quail
quinces
rabbits
radicchio
radishes
shellfish
squab
squashes
swordfish
tangerines
turkey
truffles, white
venison
walnuts

WINTER

bananas
beans, black and pinto
broccoli
brussels sprouts
buckwheat
cabbage
cabbage, savoy
capon
caviar
celery root

chestnuts
chicories
citrus fruits—blood
    oranges, grapefruit,
    kumquats, Meyer
    lemons
clementines
cod
daikon
dried fruits
endive
escarole
grapefruit
greens, collard and mus-
    tard
kale
kiwi fruit
kohlrabi

leeks
lentils
lobster
mâche
monkfish
mussels
nuts
nut oils
oranges
oranges, blood
parsnips
passion fruit
pâtés
pineapples
potatoes
rabbit
radicchio
rosemary

rutabegas
salsify
sausages
sea bass
sea urchin
squashes, winter
squid
star fruit
sweet potatoes
tangerines
tropical fruits
truffles, black
turnips
veal shanks
yams

Seasonality

Perhaps no food is more stimulating to the senses and in such an appealing way than that which is made from ingredients at their seasonal peak. Seasonality has emerged as the mantra of the leading chefs we interviewed.

Gary Danko points out, "If you are using ingredients grown in season, you're going to have the maximum amount of flavor those products can deliver. Tomatoes grown in the summer have much more flavor than the ones you get in the winter that have been picked orange, gassed, shipped to their destination, and quite frankly taste like cardboard or cellulose. There's no flavor in them whatsoever. A good cook might be able to doctor them with a little bit of sugar to cut the acid, add some salt and some herbs to bring out whatever flavor is there, and might be able to make a decent sauce. But there's no comparison to the flavor you can get out of a seasonal product by doing less to it, which will also satiate the palate better."

The rhythm of the seasons is wonderful. It has inspired painters and musicians for centuries, and it does the same for me.
—Jean-Louis Palladin

While seasonality is most frequently associated with fruits and vegetables, there is a season to other ingredients as well. "We used to get salmon from all over the place, and now we know that the local salmon is the best tasting, and we just use local salmon when it's available—the season can run from the end of April through September," says Alice Waters. "We never serve it any other time of year."

The reasons for cooking seasonally are not only rooted in seizing an ingredient's peak flavor, aroma, and texture, although these reasons are most important. Cooking with the seasons also has the power to satisfy innate or learned food cravings. "In a big city environment, with international commerce, it's easy for a restaurant to ignore the seasons. But our bodies seem to know them and to crave seasonal ingredients the same way we want to wear linens in the summertime and woolens in the winter," says Michael Romano. "And it's good for chefs to be the ones to point the seasons out to people. That's why you won't find me serving pumpkin ravioli in August or berries in the middle of winter, and you won't see asparagus on my menu any time except spring. If you listen to your body, it will tell you what to cook."

As we'll see in the following chapter on composing flavors, cooking seasonally can also provide a shortcut to culinary artists seeking the most harmonious combinations of ingredients and flavors. "Just working with the seasons, you're half way there," points out Terrance Brennan.

Aromas

Some experts credit aromas with imparting as much flavor as the actual taste itself. It's important for chefs to understand the role and effect of various aromas on a dish. Given the power of aroma to

Culinary Artists on
the Inspirations of the Seasons

Jean-Louis Palladin

Spring
Terrine of Smoked Salmon, Spinach, and Anchovy Butter
or Fresh Cream of Pea Soup with Maine Shrimp and Quenelles
Soft-Shell Crab with Pancetta Butter or Rockfish Sautéed with Basquaise
Farm-Raised Rabbit with Herbs and Portobello Mushrooms
or Veal Loin Roasted with Fava and Ham Ragoût
Coconut Milk Tapioca Croustillant with Saffron Coulis and Pineapple Sherbet

Summer
Coconut Soup with Maine Razor Clams, Vegetables, and Quenelles
Fresh Maine Abalones with Pea Fondue and Saffron
Fresh Duck Foie Gras with Rhubarb
Fresh Sturgeon with Artichoke Barigoule
Farm-Raised Guinea Hen Roasted with Herbs and Green Cabbage Ragoût
Peach Tart with Peach Liqueur Coulis and Apricot Sherbet

Fall
Pumpkin Soup with Tasso, Andouille, and Quenelles
Sea Scallops with Squid Ink Noodles and Parmesan Coulis
Red Snapper with Lemon Confit, Black Olives, Capers,
Tomatoes, Basil, and Lemon Olive Oil
Venison with Fruit Confit and Spinach-Stuffed Pear
with Port and Red Wine Essence
Chocolate Tart with Gianduja Sherbet and Chocolate Coulis

Winter
Fresh Chestnut Soup with Stuffed Squab Legs and Quenelles
Seaweed Salad with Maine Lobster and Ginger Emulsion
Fresh Duck Foie Gras with Quince
Fresh Turbot with Enoki Mushrooms and Enoki Coulis
Milk-Fed Virginia Lamb with Celery Root Risotto
Mascarpone Tart with Spice Ice Cream and Wild Blueberry Coulis

Anne Rosenzweig

Spring

Pasta with Mint-Cured Salmon, Cucumbers, Lemon, and Cream
Sautéed Duck Fillets with Rhubarb Sauce and Cracklings
on a Bed of Arugula with Asparagus
Macadamia Nut Tarts with Coconut Whipped Cream

Summer

Corn Cakes with Crème Fraîche and Caviars
Chimney-Smoked Lobster with Tarragon Butter
and Summer Squash and Potato Fritter
Lemon Curd Mousse with Fresh Summer Berries in Almond Tuiles

Fall

Warm Figs with Gorgonzola and Walnuts on Greens
Roast Quail with Savoy Cabbage and Kasha
Chocolate Bread Pudding with Brandy Custard Sauce

Winter

Wild Mushroom Tarts
Roast Lamb with Celery Root Gratin and Tomato/Red Pepper Casserole
Pear Timbales with Sticky Caramel Sauce and Sugar Biscuits

stimulate and arouse, it's perhaps one of the most underutilized tools at the culinary artist's disposal. An aroma is a dish's built-in appetizer.

A bay leaf dropped into a pot of stew produces an earthy, sweet aroma. Cinnamon adds a different, but still earthy and sweet, aroma to baked sweets ranging from pastries to custards. The smell of garlic advertises a robust tomato sauce. And truffles add a heady perfume that can elevate even simple ingredients like pasta and potatoes to the realm of the sublime!

Jean-Georges Vongerichten plans to tap the power of aroma at his next restaurant by bringing more smells into the dining room. "Half the dishes on the menu will be served tableside," he says. Vongerichten believes that much of the experience of carving a freshly roasted bird, for example, is the fragrance that escapes when it is first cut open, and that customers should be allowed to enjoy this sensory experience.

Dieter Schorner

Spring
Harvey's Lemon Tart with Raspberry Coulis
Rhubarb Tart with Cinnamon Sugar

Summer
Oeufs à la Neige (Floating Island) with Lemon Sherbet
Dutch Rice Flan with Berries

Fall
Plum Tart in Brioche Dough
Alsatian Apple Tart with Vanilla Ice Cream
Tart of Quinces with Lingonberries
Poached White Peaches filled with Chestnut Mousse and Zabaione

Winter
Japonaise—Very Crisp and Thin Hazelnut Meringue
filled with Hazelnut Buttercream
Vacherin—Meringue filled with Blood Orange Sherbet
Apple Pie à la Savoy Hotel—Served in a Soup Tureen covered with
Cookie Dough along with Vanilla Ice Cream

The chefs we interviewed are highly attuned to the aromas of various foods and take them into consideration when composing a dish or a menu, or even—in Vongerichten's case—a restaurant itself. Favorite ingredients are even described as having perfumes instead of mere aromas!

Textures   Even texture can communicate. Many foods thought of as comfort foods have a soft texture to them—mashed potatoes, applesauce, pudding. Foods with this texture can be thought of as homey and nurturing. On the other hand, a lot of snack foods are crispy—potato chips, pretzels. Because of the loud crunch they're capable of producing when eaten, there can be a certain informality, even a sense of fun, to crispy foods. A fried lotus root chip adds both the interest of crunch and of the vegetable's natural lacy pattern.

Emotions

Anyone who's ever gotten a whiff of fresh raspberries and been immediately transported back to one's childhood backyard, happily pulling the berries off a bush, knows that food can indeed trigger memories and emotions and other subjective connotations.

Certain holidays are inextricably linked with certain foods, such as Thanksgiving with turkey, Christmas with eggnog, and Valentine's Day with chocolates. Chocolate is one of several foods ranging from champagne to oysters which have a long history as suspected aphrodisiacs, credited with stimulating romantic feelings. The question of whether there is an actual, physical effect on the body that takes place upon consuming such foods, or whether the power of suggestion is enough to stimulate such feelings, is moot.

In addition, ingredients may have associations that are cultural. Jean-Georges Vongerichten recalls the time he was cooking at an upscale hotel restaurant in Bangkok and tried to add a pineapple tart to the menu. "It created a scandal," he recalls. "At the time, pineapple was considered food eaten only by the poor." Vongerichten was asked to substitute apple tart on the menu, despite the fact that apples were neither local nor fresh.

(If the above scenario sounds far-fetched, then it should be remembered that at one point in United States history, lobster was considered likewise, leading to the passage of legislation regulating how often lobster could be forced upon prisoners and servants!)

Some cultures have distinct ways of thinking about familiar ingredients. For example, the Chinese culture has classified certain foods as either yin or yang. Yin refers to the passive, negative universal energy force, encom-

---

TRADITIONAL HOLIDAY DISHES

Holiday	Typical Dishes
Valentine's Day	Aphrodisiacs like caviar, chocolate, lobster, oysters
St. Patrick's Day	Cabbage, corned beef
Easter	Ham, hard-boiled eggs, lamb
Fourth of July	Barbecue, strawberry shortcake
Thanksgiving	Cranberry sauce, mashed potatoes, pumpkin pie, stuffing, sweet potatoes, turkey
Christmas	Christmas pudding, cookies, eggnog, goose, mincemeat, pheasant, roast beef, Yorkshire pudding

EMOTIVE CONNOTATIONS OF VARIOUS FOODS

Animalistic/Primal:	grilled steak
Aphrodisiac:	caviar, champagne, cinnamon, cloves, game, ginger, lobster, morels, nutmeg, offal, oysters, pepper, saffron, truffles, vanilla
Challenging:	anchovies; stinky cheese
Comfort:	creamy mashed potatoes
Earthy:	grilled mushrooms
Feminine:	fruit, tiramisu
Masculine:	thick-cut steak or chops
Playful:	lamb's tongue with lamb's lettuce
Surprise:	ravioli

passing foods such as sugar; yang denotes the active, positive force, encompassing foods such as chiles.

In another example, Asian cultures have analyzed and categorized various flavors and foodstuffs, relating them to the five basic elements. Bitterness, along with ingredients like apricots, mutton, and scallions, is associated with the element of fire and the season of summer, which represents growth. Sweetness, and ingredients like beef and dates, is associated with the element of earth and the season of Indian summer, said to represent transformation. Pungency, and ingredients ranging from onions to peaches, is associated with the element of metal and the season of autumn, said to represent harvest. Saltiness, and such ingredients as beans, greens, and pork, is associated with the element of water, and the season of winter, a time for storage. And sourness, along with ingredients like leeks, plums and poultry, are associated with the element of wood and the season of spring, said to represent birth.

Beyond this, certain foods seem to trigger more subliminal associations. "Raviolis connote a certain playfulness, and my fascination with them probably extends far beyond the fact that I used to eat them as a child," says Wayne Nish. "It's the little packages, the surprise; it's like being a little kid at Christmastime, getting a little package and seeing what's inside."

Food is a medium rich with potential for communicating in many different ways with the person who eats it—*if* a culinary artist chooses to learn and to speak the language!

Patrick O'Connell

THE INN AT LITTLE WASHINGTON
Washington, Virginia

We used to serve an all-red menu, but I couldn't face that anymore—I didn't want to be that much of a purist! These are tiny little tastes, for the most part, that have a very wonderful progression from delicate and light to a little more substantial.

It's kind of a romantic little dinner. We had a whole team of violinists for Valentine's Day. We have a cross-section of clients, as I'm sure every restaurant does, of people going on their first date and people who've been married for forty years who feel they need to do something special on that date. We used to offer just the regular menu and they would all call and say, "What are you doing special for Valentine's Day?" So we found that they kind of wanted to put themselves in our hands.

The pear ice is shaped in the form of a pear, and has black pepper sprinkled on it—it is extremely stimulating at that point in the meal. For wine enthusiasts, instead of a cheese course—which would probably be too heavy—at that point we just wrap a little piece of good brie in layers of phyllo and fry it on a little griddle, so it goes out looking like the tiniest grilled cheese sandwich in the world.

Based on many years' experience serving Valentine's Day dinners, we've discovered what works and pleases the guest most. So we have a traditional heart-shaped dessert for the purists, and then of course for the chocolate lovers the option of a warm chocolate cake.

For years, we had the sense that while customers might have a wonderful experience, they still craved to have some tiny little thing to take with them to be sure it wasn't all a dream. We have a little miniature picnic basket that provides that, which is what our little chocolates are presented in. It's about three inches by two inches, lined with a tiny little picnic cloth, with a porcelain oval logo on the top and a miniature bee hovering above it, and in it would be various little chocolates and truffles, and some tiny little miniature tea cookies with nuts and poppy seeds, and our candied grapefruit rinds.

Valentine's Day Menu
February 14, 1996

Barbecued Rabbit Turnovers
Smoked Oyster Canapés

. . .

A Demitasse of Sweet Red Bell Pepper Soup

. . .

Two Eggs in an Egg
(Caviar and Scrambled Eggs in an Eggshell)

. . .

Native Rockfish Roasted with White Wine, Tomato, and Black Olives
on Toasted Couscous

. . .

Grilled Quail with Homemade Blackberry Vinegar
on a Crispy Potato Galette

. . .

Pear and Pepper Sorbet with Poire William

. . .

Rack of Baby Lamb on Roasted New Potatoes
with Pearl Barley and Wild Mushrooms

. . .

A Miniature Croque Monsieur
on Field Greens with Spiced Walnuts

. . .

A Mascarpone Cheese Coeur à la Crème with Raspberry Sauce
Warm Chocolate Cake with Roasted Banana Ice Cream

. . .

Coffee or Tea
Chocolate Bonbons

The essence of ingredients—which encompasses their appearance, aroma, and texture as well as their flavor—is the starting point of all cuisine. Culinary artists go to great lengths to understand their ingredients as well as possible—everything from their historical origins and uses to exactly how they're grown or raised.

Only when you understand and respect the essence of an ingredient can you properly come to enhance its flavor through cooking. This takes place in two primary ways: through the application of cooking techniques which serve to change

Composing Flavors

Cooking is like matrimony—two things served together must match.

—Yuan Mei

(and, one hopes, enhance) the characteristics of an ingredient, and through combining flavors harmoniously and even synergistically with other ingredients whose properties serve to enhance one another.

But the best cooking of all is when ingredients taste like themselves. A culinary artist must respect the essence of ingredients, and take care to choose those of the highest possible quality.

"There's a lot more to it than just learning how to cook well, and then cooking," says Jasper White. "A lot of what determines the quality of the final product has to do with buying—what you buy, and what your standards are."

Jean-Louis Palladin agrees. "The products we use are all important—and we only use top-level products," he says. "When you've got a perfect fish, it's a crime to kill it and hide it! However, this is not a sushi restaurant, so we have to do *something* to it, but we take care to give it the flavor the fish deserves."

"Great cooking really has a lot to do with how perfect the ingredients are," says Johanne Killeen. Her husband and cooking partner George Germon jumps in with an example. "Take parsley from the market, and then take parsley out of your windowsill off a plant, and use them side by side. You'll discover the difference," he swears. "After a few days at the supermarket, it still looks good and it still certainly has taste, but when you take it off a plant and just use it right away, there's no comparison." Killeen adds, "Once it's lost that life…You can't put life back into things that have none. So if you're dealing with really simple dishes with only a few ingredients, then each ingredient has to stand on its own. Each has to be good by itself."

Aside from sharing a commitment to seasonality and both using and respecting the essence of the best possible ingredients, culinary artists differ as much as other artists do in the way they approach the process of composition. There is no set starting point, no set point of conclusion. There is certainly no conscious, consistent chronology of creativity that leads a chef neatly from point A to point Z, from inspiration to finished plate. As authors, we don't mean to suggest one in presenting leading chefs' ideas on the topics discussed in a chronology of our own devising—that of starting with the smallest elements (the composition of flavors) continuing through their combination into composed dishes and menus—but it's as good a way as we know of to start!

A Matter of Taste

Both the creation and the enjoyment of food centers around the palate. The four basic flavors that can be perceived on the tongue are sweet, salty, sour, and bitter. As Mark

Miller points out, "In China, there are five—there's also 'hot.' In southeast Asia, there's also 'aromatic.' There's also 'pungent'—something like fish paste which is not sour or bitter, but its sour, bitter, sweet, *and* salty."

Gary Danko mentions yet another "fifth flavor": "It's called *umami*. The best way to illustrate it would be the taste of the combination MSG and water. Those are amino acid-like proteins. Or another example would be to put a raw oyster in your mouth. The feel or taste is of the sort of numbness in your mouth. It's hard to describe.

"If you close your nose when you start to eat, those five flavors are the only things you can taste," says Danko. "A pure taste is something that goes from your palate to your brain immediately, without going through your olfactory sensors and then filtering up. It's an immediate sensation from tongue to brain."

How can chefs use this knowledge to improve their cooking? "You hear a lot about balancing the four points of the tongue," says Danko. "There are people who say, 'If you just add more lemon juice, you won't need so much salt.' But I would disagree with that. I look at it more as a balance—you need a little bit of this, and a little bit of that, and these are all essential in satiating you. You can leave a huge meal 'hungry' if your palate was not satiated. On the other hand, you can be satisfied with less food if you've had good, balanced flavors coming into your mouth."

In thinking about food, cooks should aim to become conscious of what's going on in a particular dish. Which ingredients are contributing to the dish's sweetness, or saltiness, or sour tones, or bitter notes? Through understanding a particular ingredient's flavor properties, a chef can more expertly handle that ingredient and combine it with others, being aware of what the ingredient is contributing to a dish.

Affecting Flavors

The nature of the cooking process is change—transforming raw ingredients in ways that maximize not only flavor but enjoyment. There are two primary ways to do this: through the application of optimal cooking techniques, and through a harmonious combination of flavors. While it can be pleasurable to eat a perfect raw carrot, for example, in the middle of winter it can be even more satisfying to eat that same carrot hot, perhaps puréed or as a soup. And those who enjoy the flavor of carrots may find it even more appealing after the addition of a pat of butter, or a squeeze of lemon or orange.

So, a chef must take the essence of an ingredient into consideration when deciding what to do with it. It is vital for chefs to become familiar with the effect of using different techniques in combination with various ingredients. As Gray Kunz declares, "Proper technique is the backbone of cuisine." In addition to making raw ingredients either edible or merely more palatable,

*As cooks, we have the right to enhance or
heighten flavors, but we do not have the right
to destroy them.*

—Joel Robuchon

the process of cooking changes the flavors and textures of the ingredients being cooked.

Take sugar, for example, which is a recognizable flavor in and of itself. Yet if it is heated to a certain point, it will begin to brown and melt—the process of caramelization. Through the application of cooking techniques to sugar alone, new flavors and textures can be created.

The same is true for nuts. Taste a walnut fresh from its shell. Then toast some walnuts in the oven, or in a sauté pan, until they begin to brown slightly, and you'll find that a deeper flavor and crunchiness are released. Toasting may also increase the perceived bitterness of walnuts as well as of aromatics such as caraway or mustard seeds.

Roasting, on the other hand, can increase the sweetness of a dish through the carmelization process. "There's something called the 'Maillard effect' that occurs when the natural sugars in foods are exposed to high temperatures in the presence of acids, which results in a natural carmelization," explains Jimmy Schmidt. "When you roast things like garlic or onions, it creates broader flavors with more depth than the ingredients would have raw or even cooked at a lower temperature. Through roasting, certain gelatinous vegetables, such as shallots and parsnips, break down, giving the dish a naturally rich mouth-feel."

Techniques affect not only the actual flavor but also the perceived flavor of a dish. For example, heating food can increase its perceived sweetness, while chilling it makes its sweetness less perceptible. As a case in point, the mixture about to be poured into an ice cream maker often tastes unbearably sweet. However, once frozen into ice cream, the same ingredients taste merely pleasantly sweet.

A particular ingredient and its characteristics will sometimes suggest use of a particular technique. "If you have a perfect lobster, you probably don't want to do anything more than boil or steam it," says Jasper White. "But if your lobsters aren't fabulous, you might want to turn them into a bisque. To get the most flavor out of the lobster, it's not going to come from the meat, which might be bland that particular time of year; it's going to come from slowly simmering the carcasses and making a really strong broth with them. And if the season is spring, and it's chilly, soup is appropriate. Plus, lobster is an expensive ingredient, and making a soup with it is a great way to stretch it."

Different kinds of fish lend themselves to different methods of preparation. "You can't grill black cod, for example, or Chilean sea bass. They just fall apart," explain Mary Sue Milliken and Susan Feniger. "But they're both great pan-searing fish. It's just that their texture is not right for the grill and you'd lose all that juice, since they're both juicy fish. Tuna and swordfish are

BASIC FLAVORS CONTRIBUTED BY VARIOUS FOODS

While every ingredient has more than one flavor, understanding an ingredient's dominant flavor will allow you to use it when you want, for example, sweetness in a dish without relying too heavily on sugar. When you're next willing to experiment with the seasoning of a dish, consider reaching for this chart instead of the salt or sugar to look for examples of other appropriate ingredients you might incorporate to add saltiness or sweetness. And consider the variety of options for adding sourness or bitterness to a dish. Doing so can lead to deeper, more complex flavors.

sweet
bananas
beets
brown sugar
carrots
coriander
corn
corn syrup
dates
figs
fruits
grapes
honey
maple sugar
maple syrup
molasses
onions
poppy seeds
saccharine
sesame
sugar
vanilla

salty
anchovies
bacon
baking powder
baking soda
caviar
cheeses such as Cheddar,
    Parmesan, Provolone,
    Romano
ham
meat juices
oysters
prosciutto
salami
salt
sardines
seaweed

soy sauce
sun-dried tomatoes
tapenade

sour
apples
buttermilk
crème fraîche
grapefruits
lemons
limes
pickled vegetables
pickles
rhubarb
sorrel
sour cream
sumac
tamarind
tarragon vinegar (and
    other flavored vinegars)
vinegars
yogurt

bitter
almonds
beer
caraway
cardamom
chocolate (unsweetened,
  of course)
coffee (caffeine)
cumin
fenugreek
ginger
grapefruit
greens
mustard
quinine
rosemary
saffron

sage
tea
thyme
walnuts
wines, red

hot
cayenne
chiles
curry
paprika
pepper

pungent
allspice
dill
turmeric

sweet/sour
apples
cherries
oranges
pomegranates

sour/salty
salt-rimmed glasses dipped
    first in lemon juice (as
    for a margarita)

bitter/salty
olives

bitter/sweet
caramel
cassia
bittersweet chocolate
juniper

bitter/hot
cloves

Gary Danko on Techniques

Braising:	"It's a streamlined way of getting a dish and a sauce at the same time."
Caramelizing:	Increases sweetness: "Caramelization equals flavor."
Grilling:	"Any time the flame licks the meat, you get a carbon deposit on the meat. There's a difference between carbonization and caramelization. To me, when that burned flavor is on your food, it's not pleasant. So it's important to grill properly."
Marinating:	"Modern marination is really only a flavor principle. It never really tenderizes. It's said to penetrate only about one-sixteenth of an inch every twenty-four hours."
Roasting:	Increases sweetness via caramelization in the presence of acids and high heat: "Through the process of roasting, you can develop a higher flavor profile than, say, just boiling something—through the process of developing the natural sugars through caramelization."
Toasting:	Increases bitterness (of aromatics such as caraway, cardamom, cumin, mustard)

better for grilling. They're more fine-textured fish, and they tend to taste better undercooked."

Even vegetables may suggest a particular method of preparation. "If we make a red pepper *chermula*, the peppers will be peeled. If you get the pepper skin in there, it sometimes sticks in the throat or attaches itself to the roof of the mouth. I find it very unpalatable. In digestion, it actually causes gaseousness," says Gary Danko. "So I find that if I peel the pepper, it becomes a much more elegant and really different vegetable than if you leave the skin on. It takes a little more work, but that brings you into the discipline of cooking—going that extra step, although you don't necessarily have to. But if you take that extra minute and learn how to do it, and then do it faster, it becomes embroidered in your repertoire."

It's important to use ingredients in the way they are most naturally suited. Joachim Splichal points out that there are more than forty different types of potatoes. "Most customers are only familiar with Idaho and Red Bliss," he says. "I use Yukon Golds exclusively for mashed potatoes, for example, because of their texture and golden color. And I'll use fingerlings [tiny potatoes the size of a fingertip] for salads."

Utilizing Kitchen Tools

Even the particular kitchen equipment used can affect the flavor of the finished product. Gray Kunz uses only the freshest herbs, and wants the same freshness from his spices. "That's why we grind all our spices at the restaurant, using a small coffee grinder," says Kunz.

Mark Peel believes that using simple tools often results in better food than is possible from high-tech gadgets. "If you take exactly the same recipe and you make pesto or an aioli with a Cuisinart, and then you make it with a mortar and pestle, they're completely different," explains Peel. "You can see—and taste—the difference.

"In a Cuisinart, when garlic comes in contact with the air, you get bitterness. The air is reacting with the juice of the garlic, which results in a sharpness. With a mortar and pestle, you're not getting the heat [from the motor of the Cuisinart]. The garlic stays continually coated with olive oil, and you're not incorporating air into it. In a Cuisinart, you're incorporating so much air into it, you're making a mousse!" For that reason, mortars and pestles are staples in Campanile's kitchen. The restaurant makes all its own mayonnaise, for example, using a mortar and pestle.

"A lot of times people will use a burr mixer [a "blender-on-a-stick"] for puréeing things," says Peel. "It's really fast, but you're better off using a food mill. It takes longer, and it's a lot messier, but you end up with a better product. The food mill will take fiber out, while the burr mixer just chops it up. When making, for instance, mashed potatoes, a food mill is essential. With a burr mixer, they can turn into a greasy mess. The granules of starch, which

have been puffed up in the water, are still intact. If you burr-mix it, you break them open, and it ruins the texture.

"We used to make a fish soup that was almost a bouillabaisse, and we would burr-mix it, then pass it through a food mill, but we'd leave some texture behind. The burr-mixing released a lot of the flavor from the lobster shells, and then the food mill meant that we could extract the juice and the larger fibers, yet leave enough behind to give the soup density."

Global Techniques

Travel provides opportunities to learn and be inspired by new techniques, even for seasoned chefs. George Germon experiments with Asian techniques within the realm of the Italian-inspired cuisine served at Al Forno. "If something has a vinegar and oil base, generally the process would be to cook it in oil first, and then add vinegar afterward. But I'll do a flip-flop of that—cooking in vinegar first keeps a real sprightly texture, and then I'll just dress it with oil at the very end. It gives a whole different spirit to the dish.

"I think that what appeals to me most about Asian technique is locking in the flavor, and their methods for doing that," says Germon. "That's what got me to start thinking, If they can do it in their cooking—which I feel is so close to Italian—then why shouldn't we be applying the same principles? Why does something have to be cooked for hours and hours and hours, when it can be cooked for a much shorter time and have more flavor to it? We just try to take different approaches to our food."

Rick Bayless on Combining Mexican Flavors

Basically, Mexican flavors fall into a couple of categories: those that are based on dried chiles, and those that are based on fresh chiles.

Dried Chile Flavors: Because of the nature of the drying process and what it intensifies, a certain kind of fruitiness is drawn out, this dried-fruit fruitiness. Then that's balanced against a lot of other flavors that range from bitter, like unsweetened chocolate or an almost tobacco-like bitterness, to a real fruitiness like the kind you'd get in a dried tomato. When you mix all of that kind of stuff together, you've got really deep, rich flavors. That's the basis of a whole category of Mexican dishes. Almost always, everything in this category is toasted before it's used, which adds another dimension, another level of complexity to the flavors. Clearly, when you're working with dried chiles, there are some pretty untamed flavors in there as well, so you have to work with those and figure out how to balance them or play them down or in some cases eliminate them by, for example, soaking the chiles and then throwing away the soaking water.

Because this is such a major category of Mexican flavor, it's where I put a lot of my attention, because I want to draw out as much of the flavor as I can from the chile and elaborate on that without trying to undo it in any way. I really capture the very spirit of the flavor the chile has to offer without compromising it in any way. A lot of chefs might try to eliminate a lot of its flavor so that it becomes very subtle, but then I think you've really missed the point of the chiles. We try to really let them be

Johanne Killeen points out that "In Asia, when poaching a chicken, sometimes it will be left out to air-dry, so that the skin becomes really crisp. Sometimes they'll deep-fry it, but we'll do something like poaching it, drying it briefly, and then roasting it—and that produces a really crispy, crispy skin and a succulent interior that is really juicy."

Jean-Louis Palladin says he was inspired by the best duck of his life at the Empress Room when traveling through Asia. "I ate there five times in a row," he says. "Unfortunately, I don't have the ovens that they have there, where they can leave the duck for hours to cook, painting it with sauce until it turns golden. Then they served only the *skin* of the duck!"

Living and working in Asia is also what Jean-Georges Vongerichten credits with "waking up" different flavors for him. While flavored oils have been around for hundreds of years, Vongerichten says he enjoyed experimenting with oils and different spices: "It was new to see parsley oil." When his customers started watching their waistlines and cholesterol levels more closely, Vongerichten took the *beurre blanc* with parsley purée off the grilled scallops he served, replacing it with a lighter parsley oil.

Gray Kunz credits his multiracial staff at Lespinasse with influencing his experimentation with flavors and ingredients from around the world. "My

---

what they are but yet, at the same time, put their best foot forward. And that sometimes comes in the way that we prepare them—the initial steps of preparation are in the toasting and the soaking—or it might come in the way that we cook them. There's a very standard method for cooking dried chiles where a purée is made out of them, and then that's cooked in a very hot pan with just a little bit of oil in it so you're searing it and reducing it. When it's reduced to a really thick paste, at that point you can add stock and bring it up to a brothy or sauce-like consistency. That's one of the ways we work with that [category of] flavor. There's a kind of triumvirate that runs through a lot of those dishes: black pepper, cloves, and cinnamon, although sometimes the cinnamon will be replaced with a little bit of cumin. And then always garlic.

Fresh Chile Flavors: On the flip side, the fresh chile flavors are typically associated with things like lime and cilantro, and they're much easier to work with. When they're the really small chiles, frequently they're not cooked, so you get a lot of grassiness out of them. You're thinking more in terms of heat and sharpness; obviously, if you're balancing them with cilantro and lime, you're just underscoring even more the brashness they can offer. When you get into the larger chiles, like poblanos, usually they're roasted, which turns the flavor from grassy to more like a deep, rich herb like rosemary or even a hint of the flavor you get in very green olive oil. It's more a vegetal flavor than it is a fruit flavor. When you're dealing with fresh chiles, garlic is usually replaced by raw onion—and it's always white onion, never yellow, because it has a much cleaner, brighter flavor than the yellow ones do.

sous chef is from India and brings in ideas from traditional Indian cooking," he says.

Terrance Brennan credits his stint at Gualtiero Marchesi, a Michelin three-star restaurant in Italy, with teaching him the importance of preparing pasta from scratch. "It was there that I learned that if you add more egg yolk to the pasta dough, it results in a richer-tasting pasta," says Brennan. "Now we make our own pasta at Picholine, to ensure a fresher taste." Picholine serves no flavored pastas, except an occasional black pasta made from squid ink: "All the other flavors cook out in the pasta-making process, and all you're left with is the color," he explains.

Brennan was also inspired to bring the same perfectionism to his preparation of risotto, which some consider to be among the best in the city. The secret to risotto? "When risotto sits around, whether it's half-cooked or not, it starts to break down. So it's only done to order. And the rice I use is very important—it's a *semi-fino*, as opposed to arborio, which is a *fino*. So it's a larger grain, with a harder core to it. It's what the Venetians use, although they make a more soupy risotto and I keep it tighter. I like it because it's very hard to overcook, since it has a very hard center. It's creamy, and I like the way it stays together in your mouth when you eat it. There's even a larger grain, called *carnaroli,* which when it cooks up has the grains stay very separate, but I just didn't like the feel on the palate. Some chefs may think it's superior to the *semi-fino* I use, but I don't think so. I think it's a matter of taste."

It is important for chefs to hone their knowledge and judgment of techniques so that they can be effective in devising new approaches to solving culinary dilemmas. One clever New York City café, trying to devise a low-fat way to cook eggs, stuck a bowl of raw, beaten eggs under the nozzle of their cappucino machine's milk steamer. The steamed scrambled eggs have since become one of the restaurant's specialty breakfast items.

Dieter Schorner says, "Chefs need to think about what it is necessary to do to get the effect that they want, or to make things better. For example, I make tarte Tatin [carmelized apple tart]. In France, the apples are cooked with the caramel, with a crust on top. But the apples needs to steam, which usually makes the crust soggy. So I learned to cook the crust separately, with aluminum foil on top, which results in a crisp crust. An old French chef once asked me, 'Why do you cook the crust like that? Nobody does it like that in France!' And I said, 'That's right. But if I copy everything I see exactly, then I don't have a brain!'"

Still, in Jean-Georges Vongerichten's opinion, flavor is paramount over "proper" technique. "If my cooks make a mistake on something technical, I close my eyes," he says. "But if they make a mistake with seasoning, I yell all night."

Tarte Tatin

by Dieter Schorner

Melt 1 1/2 cups granulated sugar in any small-size saucepan (add sugar slowly on a medium flame) until sugar is completely melted and looks honey-brown. Pour into a 10" cake mold, let cool, and arrange 10 peeled, cored, and quartered cooking apples (like Rome or Golden Delicious) in concentric circles, facing the same direction, covering the caramel. Add a tablespoon of butter on top of the apples. Cover cake mold with aluminum foil. Place on a sheet tray and bake for about 1 hour at 375° or until the juices of the apple float out of the mold. Remove aluminum foil and let cool. On a floured table, roll out puff pastry or pie dough 1/16" thick into a 12" circle. Place the circle on a sheet tray, prick with a fork, and let rest in the refrigerator for 1 hour. Bake in a 375° oven until golden brown on both sides (about 15 to 20 minutes). Cut out a 10" circle and place on top of the apples. Place a finemesh grill on top of the dough and turn over. The juice from the baked apples should then be boiled for a few minutes; add a few drops of Calvados brandy and use it as a glaze. To give the tarte the original crunchy, caramelized taste, melt a few tablespoons of sugar, cool for a few seconds, and use a fork to make a lace pattern of caramel on buttered parchment paper. Place the lacy caramel on each slice of tarte Tatin or make a lacy pattern in caramel over the whole tarte.

Intensifying Flavors

When discussing the effect of combining flavors, an important factor is the level of each flavor that is present. One flavor can overwhelm another, while in a smaller quantity, as an accent, the same flavor has the power to bring out the other. For example, recipes for sweet desserts, such as cookies, often call for a pinch of salt. If too much salt were used, the cookies would taste unpleasantly salty, but in such a small quantity the salt serves to accent the sweetness of the cookies and to balance the resulting sweet flavor. Likewise, a pinch of sugar can be added to savory foods, such as sauces, to enhance their flavor.

Sometimes a chef's aim will be to intensify the flavors in a dish. This can be accomplished through employing either specific techniques or additional ingredients. For example, a well-flavored stock will taste even more intensely like the meat it was made of when it's reduced. In other cases, some chefs will combine multiple versions of an ingredient in order to intensify the flavor delivered. For example, Jean-Louis Palladin combines fresh, raw toma-

Cooking Techniques and Alternatives

When using culinary techniques, chefs should consider alternatives to the usual methods that might result in more interesting flavors or textures:

Breading   Instead of ordinary bread crumbs, consider using:
  - buckwheat
  - pecans, crushed
  - plantains, crushed

Dredging   Instead of flour, consider using:
  - cornstarch
  - Cream of Wheat
  - rice flakes
  - water chestnut flour

Skewering   Instead of simple wooden skewers, consider using:
  - rosemary branches
  - sugar cane

Thickening   Instead of flour, cornstarch, or arrowroot, consider using:
  - blood
  - bread
  - butter
  - carrots, puréed
  - cream
  - coral, shellfish
  - egg yolks
  - garlic, roasted and puréed
  - instant mashed potato flakes
  - nuts, ground
  - pecans, ground
  - potatoes, puréed
  - *roux*

toes with sun-dried tomatoes in order to give a different spin to the tomato flavor in a dish. The same principle applies when adding corn kernels to corn bread, or featuring chocolate desserts with multiple chocolate sauces.

In the same vein, Gary Danko illustrates how the flavor of apple can be intensified to enhance a duck dish. "You want to get the apples, as a fruit, to be a little more savory. That would be accomplished by lightly cooking them until they start to caramelize. You want to develop that flavor as well as cook the apples during this stage," he says. "When they're done caramelizing, you might wipe all the fat out of the pan—hopefully, it's a nonstick pan—and then deglaze it with a little bit of Calvados and some apple cider in small quantities, bringing it down to a glaze. Again, you're going to get that next step of caramelization. With every step of caramelization, you're going to get more flavor."

Mary Sue Milliken recalls the process of experimenting with the ingredients involved in making "the world's best flan," as Susan Feniger describes it, and achieving exactly the right milky taste. "First we used sweetened condensed milk. Then we used whole milk. Then we eventually used nonfat milk reduced 50 percent to which we added sugar," Milliken says. "When we make the flan with it, it has the most incredible rich, milky flavor. But we've spent nine years working on it."

Enhancing Flavors

Bradley Ogden finds that too many cooks overreach their abilities when it comes to combining ingredients. "If most cooks would just try to enhance the natural flavors that are already there, they'd be a lot better off," he says. "Some of them don't have the education or the palate to pull things off. Instead of keeping things simplified, they create a mishmash of flavors and tastes and textures and countries, and you don't know what you're eating by the time it's all done."

"Seasoning should not kill the taste; it should enhance the flavor of the ingredient," says Dieter Schorner. "If you're eating fish, it should smell and taste like the fish—not, for example, like you're eating just saffron. I found that in some French kitchens there would be so much liqueur used in desserts that it was almost all you could taste."

It is often the role of seasonings and herbs, such as salt and lemon, to enhance the essential flavor of ingredients. "Salt's potency in heightening the taste of food is unmatched," writes Edward Behr in his book *The Artful Eater*. "Salt deepens flavors and to an extent unites them, and it balances acidity and sweetness, helping to restore equilibrium when they are in excess."

It is important to use proper technique when seasoning with salt, which will affect the flavor. "Different foods call for different methods of salting," points out Gary Danko. "For example, with things like meat and fillet that have been trimmed down to the bare muscle, I cook them, let them rest, and while they're resting I salt them. In a *braisée*, you would season your liquid slightly because there is an exchange between the juices of the meat and the sauce, and they eventually become one. If you're cooking, say, a trout, you're going to salt it first, then flour it."

Escoffier subdivides condiments into three classes:

1) the pungents (e.g., chives, garlic, horseradish, onions, shallots)

2) hot condiments (e.g., capers, chili sauce, gherkins, ketchup, mustard, Tabasco sauce, Worcestershire sauce)

3) fatty substances (e.g., animal fats, butter, edible oils, margarine)

Gray Kunz cautions, "Seasoning is an uphill battle every day. That final seasoning of salt or pepper can make or break a dish!"

Bradley Ogden mentions that some seasonings serve as "taste exciters" that are essential to incorporate in good cooking. "You can use them without even having it known that they're there," he says, "and by doing so, you can add less salt, less fat, less oil to particular dishes and still have them taste good." Ogden places into this category such seasonings as fresh herbs and spices, vinegars, chiles, and citrus. Noted English writer Jane Grigson advocates sprinkling liqueurs on fruit to enhance their flavor: "With a bottle of Kirsch and a bottle of Cointreau, you can cover most fruits of the year."

Combining Flavors

When you think about all the ingredients that exist around the world, it soon becomes clear that there is an infinite number of combinations of ingredients. So how on earth is any cook supposed to figure out which ingredients go best together?

Happily, it is not necessary to reinvent the wheel. Probably almost as long as people have had to eat, people have been experimenting with combining various ingredients. While the most ill-conceived of these experiments did not produce lasting results, other charmed combinations have since gone on to become classics.

"While in recent decades cuisine has become much more 'compact' with all the cross-cultural influences, prior to that cuisine was the intersection of where people lived and the food that lived there," explains Chris Schlesinger. "Dishes were developed that stood the test of time, from combinations that were found to work together after trying millions and millions of different combinations and throwing out the stuff like scallops with raspberry sauce that they tried but found didn't work.

"But they kept the combinations that did work—like ginger, soy, and sesame in Asia, and lemongrass and chiles in Thailand—which became classics. That's how each cuisine developed its own identifiable 'flavor footprints'

from its distinctive larder and techniques, and from the non-nutritive seasonings and flavorings that helped develop the characteristic flavors of its country of origin," he says.

Schlesinger argues that it's important to understand food history and classic combinations because there isn't any 'new' food. "I don't think anybody 'invents' anything," he says. "I don't think there are any new combinations. I think it's all been done before."

Alice Waters agrees. "There is probably one person in tens of thousands who can pick up ingredients and put them together in a new way that makes them greater than the sum of the parts," she says. "But most people don't have that kind of taste capacity and understanding of food. So it's terribly important to know the classics of a cuisine.

"I really believe in classic preparations," she continues. "I think they have withstood the test of time, and there are reasons that certain flavors go together, reasons that people put them together. I think it's very important to appreciate that in cooking.

"In France, you have the combination of a leg of lamb and flageolet beans. In Italy, you have pasta pesto as a classic—basil and garlic going together," Waters explains. "In Japan, I think of the preparation of frying vegetables—the tempura and the little dipping sauces, those classic soba soups, really tasty broths."

There are other classic combinations which are widely regarded as mutually enhancing. "When you say tomato, I say basil," says Gray Kunz, providing a classic example of this phenomenon. Similarly, English food writer Elizabeth David has noted that "somebody long ago discovered that basil works some sort of spell with tomatoes, fennel with fish, and rosemary with pork."

When chefs do experiment with combining ingredients, it's still a never-ending learning process. "When you work with an ingredient over a period of time, and you have a lot of different herbs and vegetables to think about, it involves trial and error," says Alice Waters. "Yes, you begin with the classic things. With salmon, it's a lot easier to imagine; it's much more adaptable than other things. Sometimes you do want to have that ethereal butter and Champagne sauce on salmon, especially that so-delicate first-of-the-season salmon. But then, as the fish gets bigger toward the end of the season and becomes more oily, we end up preparing it in a different way, putting stronger herbs on it and grilling it. Or I'll make a vinaigrette with lots and lots of shal-

"Flavor Pals"

Certain flavors are known to marry well with others. We credit our interview with Jean-Georges Vongerichten as where we first heard the term *flavor pals*, which we've adopted for this section of well-matched flavors:

allspice
curry
ginger
juniper berries
nutmeg

anchovy
capers
chiles
garlic
lemon
pimientos
sage

basil
cilantro
garlic
mint
olive oil
oregano
parsley
saffron
thyme

capers
anchovy
horseradish
mustard
raisins

caramel
brandy
chocolate
coffee
salt

A little salt will bring out the flavor of caramel.
—François Payard

caraway
dill
garlic
honey
oregano

cardamom
coriander
curry
grains of paradise

cayenne
cilantro

chervil
chives
lemon thyme
parsley
tarragon
thyme

chiles
cilantro
garlic
ginger
lime

chives
chervil
dill

chocolate
spices

Spices are nice in combination with chocolate.
—François Payard, who has combined chocolate with everything from coriander to pepper to tarragon

cilantro
basil
chiles
coriander seed
cumin
curry
fennel

garlic
marjoram
mint

cinnamon
cloves
ginger
nutmeg
sugar
vanilla

cloves
cinnamon
garam masala
ginger
grains of paradise
nutmeg
saffron

coriander seed
cilantro
cumin
mint
parsley

cumin
chiles
cilantro
cinnamon
coriander seed
garlic
mint
orange
parsley
saffron
scallion

dill
caraway
chives
mint
oregano
parsley

fennel
basil
cilantro

garlic
olives
oregano
parsley
thyme

fenugreek
garlic
red pepper

garlic
basil
chiles
chives
cilantro
cumin
ginger
mustard
olive oil
oregano
parsley
sage
thyme

The combination of garlic and olive oil has been described by Richard Olney as belonging to "the realm of voluptuous experiences."

ginger
allspice
chiles
chives
cinnamon
cloves
coriander
cumin
curry
fennel
garlic
mace
nutmeg
pepper, black
saffron

grains of paradise
cardamom
cloves

horseradish
capers
dill
lemon
mustard

juniper berries
allspice
garlic
marjoram
pepper, black
rosemary

lavender
garlic

lemongrass
chiles
cilantro
coriander
garlic
peppers
shallots

marjoram
basil
cilantro
cinnamon
dill
nutmeg
parsley
thyme

mint
basil
chocolate
cilantro
coriander
garlic
parsley

mustard
capers
fennel
honey
turmeric

nigella
allspice
coriander
savory
thyme

nutmeg
allspice
cinnamon
cloves
cumin
ginger

orange
cumin

oregano
basil
cinnamon
cumin
garlic
parsley
savory
thyme

parsley
basil
bay leaf
chervil
chives
dill
garlic
oregano
thyme

*Parsley is the perfect foil
for garlic.*
—Elizabeth David

rosemary
garlic
oregano
parsley
sage
thyme

saffron
basil
chives
cinnamon
cloves
coriander
cumin
fennel
garlic
ginger
mint
parsley

sage
anchovy
garlic
parsley
rosemary
thyme

sassafras
allspice
anise
chiles
pepper, black

scallions
lime

shallots
wine

sorrel
chives
oregano
parsley
thyme

star anise
cassia
cinnamon

Szechuan pepper
cassia
ginger

tamarind
curry

tarragon
chervil
garlic
oregano
parsley
thyme

thyme
basil
bay leaf
chervil
dill
marjoram
mint
oregano
parsley
sage

turmeric
mustard

vanilla
caramel
chocolate
cinnamon
coconut
coffee
rum

lots in it, so that it's almost a shallot sauce that's macerated in vinegar with some olive oil added and black pepper, and I'll spoon that over it. So you're constantly making those kinds of considerations and evaluations. Every day, these things change."

Chris Schlesinger believes that when experimenting with spices, Americans are at a disadvantage. He says, "We don't have a lot of experience working with spices. If you go to Mexico, Central America, the Middle East, India, they use a tremendous amount of spices, and there are developed ways to use spices, developed combinations of spices, all sorts of precedents. In India, the skill and attention and detail that go into the buying, handling, storing, combining, and cooking of spices is on a par with a

---

"Flavor Cliques"

There are some groups of "flavor pals" that are so fond of one another that they hang out together in cliques, and the cliques have become so popular as to merit their own names:

Bagna cauda: Italian for "hot bath"—a sauce of olive oil, butter, salt, pepper, anchovies, and lemon zest, typically served with vegetables

Bouquet garni: bay leaf, parsley, thyme

Chinese five-spice powder: cassia or cinnamon; cloves, fagara, fennel, star anise

Fines herbes: chervil, chives, parsley, and tarragon

Gremolata: garlic, parsley, lemon zest, anchovies

Herbes à Tortue: basil, chervil, fennel, marjoram, savory

Mirepoix: carrot, celery, onion

Spanish picada: garlic, parsley, and saffron ground with almonds or pinenuts

Quatre-Epices: cloves, ginger, nutmeg, pepper

Tunisian five-spice mix: cinnamon, cloves, grains of paradise, nutmeg, pepper

saucier in the French system. A lot of Americans see spices as things that are shaken out of a can and added to a dish."

If any of his cooks come up with an idea for a dish featuring an unusual combination of ingredients, Schlesinger makes them defend the dish by explaining where they've seen that combination of ingredients used before. "That's my guide. If there's a culture that's used it before, and it's stood the test of time, then in my mind it's a good combination," he says. "I think I've gone outside that maybe two or three times in my life, combining things that I felt intuitively went together without having any corroborative historical evidence. They're combinations that may exist, but I just couldn't find any evidence of them. They were leaps, in my mind, but they worked."

Simply studying and learning about ingredients can trigger a cook's creativity when trying to think of what ingredients might taste good together. "We never knew that cumin was in the parsley family," says Mary Sue Milliken. Susan Feniger adds, "We learned it's the dried seed of a plant related to parsley. So the next time I see parsley root at the farmers' market, I'll bring it home and I'll want to do something with it and cumin, because they're in the same family and I'll want to see how they are together."

What About Sauces?

Throughout history, sauces have evolved as classic flavor (not to mention textural and color) complements to a variety of ingredients. Sometimes the role of a sauce is to intensify the desired flavor; in other cases, it serves to add interest through contrast. The art of sauce making—and matching—is subject for a book in and of itself. In fact, those interested in the topic can do no better than to refer to James Peterson's book *Sauces: Classical and Contemporary Sauce Making* (see Resources).

Michael Romano describes stock as "the backbone on which you can hang other flavors, like herbs, in a sauce. It can provide the structure for a sauce, if it's balanced. For example, if you're making a wine sauce with an intense reduction, if the stock is off, the sauce will be off-balance. It takes tasting and tasting to get a sense of what needs to be done to make a sauce 'right.' And as a chef, you must be able to judge what to do. If you're trying to get the right consistency just through reduction, you can end up de-naturing a sauce. You're better off stopping and thickening the sauce when you've got the flavor right."

While Romano says he'd like to honor the principle of cooking *à la minute* when possible, given Union Square Café's volume, doing so with his sauces is out of the question. "Michel Guérard used to say, 'A good sauce in a *bain-marie* is better than a bad sauce made *à la minute*,'" he remembers, "and I agree with him."

There was a period of time when I was out of the kitchen, and I had taken over a liquor store for my mother. The one satisfaction I got out of the whole deal was studying wine, where I kept coming across descriptions of wine as having "body," and descriptions of wine talking about the "fleshiness" and the "flabbiness" and the "structure"—those were the types of metaphors used.

When I went back into the kitchen a few months after that, I began to try to describe for my younger cooks and sous chefs why I was doing certain things, particularly with sauces. I thought of the human body as an easy and readily available metaphor. I could hold their arm and point to the muscles within their arm, or the bone underneath their muscles, or the flesh that covered all of those things, and describe the characteristics or tendencies each of those things had, and how sauces needed to have a balance between those things or they would be out of proportion.

In essence, if the body had too much fat—or if the sauce had too much fat—that would be evident in that there would need to be a way of working it back into a proper mesomorphic relationship. If it's got too much fat, then it doesn't have enough acidity or protein. Or if a sauce is overreduced—if you reduce a demi-sauce down, it's just all this muscle, like a guy on steroids—it's a grossly disproportionate thing. But when you finally get them all together in a harmonious relationship with each other, you can have a very beautiful, balanced ideal of what a sauce is about.

Different ingredients used in making sauces have different properties. The acidity of the structure,

Terrance Brennan recounts with a laugh that when he was cooking at Le Cirque, then-chef Alain Sailhac would taste his sauces and sometimes exclaim, "You were born like this—you were born a *saucier!*" But Brennan is the first to admit that becoming skilled at sauce-making is a long road.

"To make a fine sauce, you can't just follow the recipe exactly; it's never exactly the same, so you always have to adjust. But that takes experience," he says. "Do you need to add a touch of port to it, add a few more beets to the Bordelaise, reduce it down a bit to achieve a deeper, richer color? There are different things you need to adjust each time to make a sauce consistent. You don't achieve consistency just by doing it the same way every time."

Sometimes enhancing a flavor involves *not* repeating it within a dish by way of the sauce. Brennan says, "I don't use fish *fumé* for my fish sauces; I use chicken broth instead. I've found it has a more neutral flavor, so that it doesn't taste like fish—the fish tastes like fish. Especially if you do a reduction, the *fumé* gets more powerful and fishy, and I don't want fish stock to overpower the fish. That's not to say I don't use it for a good fish soup—you need it then."

whether in the form of vinegar or wine or citrus juices—gives a sauce the ability to "stand up." It's like the skeletal structure. Meat products, stocks, are the "muscles" of the body. The fat, the cream, or the butter that might finish a sauce are the "flesh." The spices and herbs and vegetables are like the "personality."

Now the body needs to stand on something, and so typically that came in the form of rice, pasta, bread, and those types of things. Those are the foundation. In Japanese cooking, it's called *fan,* which means rice. Everything else that circles around it is called *t'sai.* All food revolves around the idea of 'everything around the rice.'

I'd been looking for a way to describe to my cooks the balance I was looking for. I didn't want them to say, "Why did he just add a little bit of mustard to that *beurre blanc?*" I would say, "I didn't just add mustard—I added acidity."

It was a metaphor that I used to try to help people look beyond the ingredient to its function. Instead of thinking about soy, I wanted to think about what soy was in terms of a property. Or what balsamic vinegar was in terms of a property.

Sometimes, if a chef was interested in music, I'd try to describe food in musical terms, like "soy is this kind of smoky, bluesy note," and "balsamic is a brighter, melodic sort of intensely sweet note." And then, "Why do these two notes work together in some kind of chordal harmony?"

I believe that understanding the role each component ingredient plays in a dish can help a chef create more complex flavors that can move across the palate in waves.

Brennan credits the advent of *nouvelle cuisine* with having changed chefs' approach to sauces. "[Roger] Vergé used to finish some of his sauces with cornstarch. But now, even [the classic French Manhattan restaurant] La Côte Basque probably doesn't even use *roux* anymore. I'd be surprised to see a big pot of *roux* hanging around a kitchen these days."

Lydia Shire credits the sauce as one of the keys to her wildly popular steak *au poivre* dish. "My cooks have to learn to get it right," she says. "It calls for a lot of black pepper, a third- to a half-bottle of red wine, demi-glace, and butter—per serving."

This amount of wine in a sauce might sound like a lot, but it's not unusual among leading chefs. "Some of my sauces involve reducing a half-bottle—or more—of wine per serving," says Terrance Brennan. "They're incredibly expensive."

Bradley Ogden's aim is to include more than one dimension of flavor within a sauce in order to heighten interest. "For example, I make a particular sauce for quail from quail stock, which is reduced down with some root vegetables, wine, and balsamic vinegar, and then strained," says Ogden. "It's a complex sauce, yet it still enhances the flavor of the quail without dulling the palate."

Experimenting with Flavors

When leading chefs experiment with flavors to bring out the ones that will tantalize us most, how do they approach the challenge?

Hubert Keller starts with a recipe on paper. "If you think about it, you can combine the flavors in your mind and envision how something will taste," he says, referring to an ability that comes easier to more experienced chefs. Given the direction toward lighter food that Keller sees as having influenced cooking over the last decade, he also likes to demonstrate that food, even old combinations, can be updated. "Lamb has traditionally been served with a rich red wine sauce," he points out. "Now I do it with a Merlot. Today when you say Merlot, everybody jumps! The Merlot has a hint of vanilla flavor in it, and instead of using butter to add richness and flavor to the sauce, I add some fresh vanilla, which emphasizes the vanilla flavor in the Merlot."

The next step for Keller is trying out his ideas on the line of his restaurant kitchen. "I'll prepare the dish and taste it to find out if it works. Then the eye comes in—I'll made a drawing, illustrating how to display the garnishes for the dish on the plate. This might take four or five, even six, tries. Finally, I'll try it out on some good customers and see what they think. I've got customers who are open enough to say to me, 'Well, it's not my favorite...' That's when it's important for a chef to be flexible enough to either change a dish or take it off the menu completely if it's not right."

Joyce Goldstein says, "I only know something's right when I eat it and it's complete in my mouth—and when other people eat it, they get it. I'm coming out with a new book called *Kitchen Conversations* that will ask read-

---

"Flavor Enemies"

While flavor pals can't get enough of each other, flavor enemies are ones that you probably don't want to invite into the same dish, unless you do so with great care!

basil	wine
dill	acidic foods
tarragon	artichokes
	asparagus
Sauternes	chocolate
chocolate	coriander
citrus fruits	hot, spicy foods
	ice cream
tarragon	MSG
most other herbs	tomatoes

ers, once they've cooked a recipe: Are you there yet? Did you get what you were aiming for? What were the elements you were playing with? If you like bitterness, how do you play it up? How do you keep the plate in balance without going over the edge and getting too bitter? If you like sharpness, or acidity, how do you keep that in the forefront without making the dish too tart and killing everything else? It helps to think about why you like certain dishes. Why are you playing in this ballpark? Why are you interested in that? Certain things are texture, certain things are taste—when you play with them, the whole becomes more than the sum of the parts. That's when you've hit it."

According to Jean-Louis Palladin, a chef works exactly like a painter. "You start with the basics, and build the painting you want," he says. "After thiry-seven years in the kitchen, I can make matches pretty well," Palladin adds, too modestly. "I can see in my mind the matching without even tasting it. Of course, I always try it and taste it first, and I may change it a little bit. But 95 percent of the time, it's a winner."

Gary Danko on Cooking with Wine

Because we're a restaurant of the caliber that serves expensive wines, all the food here has to be more delicate. So we'll never do, for example, a Moroccan dish in its authentically hot-hot-hot seasoning, but I'll use the same flavor principles and balance the dish more delicately so that it can actually work here.

Wine and artichokes are very difficult to match. The way you would deal with that is to use the artichokes as a garnish in a dish, but you would have a sauce that would make the bridge between the dish and the wine. Asparagus and wine aren't the best of friends, although you can use the grassy character of a Sauvignon Blanc to match that grassy character of the asparagus. If I had to match a wine with it, I would put another component into the dish, maybe some crumbled goat cheese, and work from that point of match, and then put a vinaigrette on it which would sort of lubricate or insulate that direct asparagus-wine taste. And, quite frankly, vinegars and wine don't match. But there are remedies—Jim Neal has made *verjus*, which has solved a lot of problems with un-wine-friendly salads.

A dish, like any work of art, is composed with a purpose. When examining a work of art, whether a building designed by a great architect or a dish prepared by a culinary artist, its basic components can be reduced to a message (function) and its medium (form). As a chef, you must know your aim. And while it may be achieved through a variety of forms, it is up to you to select the most appropriate or effective.

The purpose or function of a dish is its starting point. "When I taught art in college, I learned that the most difficult assignments for my students were the ones without

Composing a Dish

I consider the invention of a new dish, to whet our appetite and prolong our pleasure, to be far more interesting an event than the discovery of a new star.

—Jean-Anthelme Brillat-Savarin

guidelines. The students wouldn't know where to begin or how to have a reaction," says George Germon. "Similarly, cooks say they want freedom in the kitchen, and it makes me chuckle. I know they'd fall apart without the structure. The truth is, they need reference points to build on."

Johanne Killeen agrees. "In the worlds of art or architecture, you always have a reference point for whatever it is you're creating. If you're building a house, for example, and you want it square, there will be one wall that is your reference point and you'll take all your measurements from that one wall," she says. "Likewise, Italy is our reference point in our cooking."

"And within that structure, we make our own rules," adds Germon. "But it's good to have that reference point. It keeps us in focus. It's extremely important to have a philosophy in cooking; it even helps build trust among your employees, who begin to see that there is a rationale behind your critique of their food, that there's something specific you're going after."

Where does a dish originate? Its starting point, or reference point, can be anything! It might stem from the request of a customer to satisfy a particular craving. Or from the arrival of the season's first bounty—of produce, of wine—which demands a dish that celebrates it. Or from a chef who may wish to experiment with a particular technique, in a dish that employs it. A dish can be created to achieve any of these ends, and at its best may achieve many ends at once. One created primarily for nourishment, for example, will ideally also please the taste buds—even charm the spirit!

Classic Dishes

Even so-called classic dishes first came into being through a starting point. As Chris Schlesinger points out, "Classic dishes, such as bouillabaisse and Caesar salad, were not individual dishes created out of people's minds; they were based on things that were already there, that they had to work with. The creativity was in the interpretation of the ingredients, not necessarily in choosing *and* interpreting them. Often, creating a dish is not a strictly creative process—one beginning with a blank slate—but one where you've got these ingredients that you're moving around, and you're researching what works together."

History represents the roots of my cuisine.
—Daniel Boulud

Classic dishes typically consist of combinations—of flavors, textures, even aromas and colors—that history has been hard-pressed to offer improvements upon. Their having stood the test of time speaks to the elegance of their form, in combining flavors not only harmoniously but, in many cases, synergistically, such that the whole is indeed greater than the sum of the individual parts.

Other classic dishes range from *cassoulet* to *paella*, from *coq au vin* to *steak au poivre*. "In each of them, all the ingredients that are there are there for a reason—because they work," points out Terrance Brennan. This, too, should be the aim when composing new dishes—in Brennan's words, "A real solid, thoughtful marriage of ingredients resulting in high-quality cooking."

Rick Bayless tends to agree. "Too many people always worry about creating something new," he believes. "I'm more interested in perfecting something for myself, and knowing it's perfect. Only then would I consider tweaking it. 'Mastering the classics' doesn't mean doing the same things the same way they've always been done—it means making them exactly right for you today. There's genius in those classic dishes that isn't always appreciated."

Researching classic dishes can inform chefs of those food matches that history tells us are the most successful of all time and prevent them from having to start from scratch. Chris Schlesinger, like other leading chefs, looks to the past when creating food for the present. "I was reading a book on pickling from the 1950s. These people pickled everything—even grapes! That's what's so mind-blowing. You could name a decade and I could make a menu from old cookbooks from that decade, using only those recipes, and customers today would go, 'Wow—that's so creative! How did you think that up?' When we first served plantains at the East Coast Grill, not a lot of people had seen them and customers would say, 'Wow—these are unbelievable!' But plantains are so common that they're eaten like French fries in a lot of other cultures.

"I was researching Brazilian cuisine and found that the northern part of Brazil has a lot of diverse influences with the slaves from Africa. For example, there's a classic combination of ingredients—tomatoes, peanuts, and coconut milk—that's served in a relish, and I served it on some grilled lamb in the restaurant. Customers went wild over it and asked me, 'How did you ever think of combining those ingredients?' I had to tell them that it's a classic dish of this region that's been prepared for hundreds of years."

Wayne Nish recalls experimenting with pasta blankets embedded with herbs when he cooked at The Quilted Giraffe. "Immediately afterward I came across a reference of the same exact technique in one of [Giuliano] Bugialli's books, which was referenced back to fourteenth century Siena—I think that was the first time the technique shows up in any cookbooks or records," says Nish. "So here I was, thinking I was doing this really neat new thing, only to find out that there had been people rolling the same thing out by hand six hundred years ago."

Borrowing from the Classics

Where is the line between copying and finding inspiration in a cuisine? And how far can that line be pushed? Chris Schlesinger points out, "My food, while not exact duplication, is true to the flavors and ingredients of the culture that inspired it. If a dish is inspired by a dish that I had in Thailand, for example, it won't have any ingredients that can't be had in Thailand, and it won't have any flavors that don't exist in Thailand.

"I feel that cooks have an obligation, if they're inspired to borrow from another culture, to have some knowledge of it, some appreciation for it, and some respect for the integrity of the flavors and the ingredients. I don't believe that cooks should ever combine two totally unconnected ingredients, like soy sauce and tortillas, for example. If you want to combine two ingredients like that, you can find tortillas in the Chinese culture—in the form of moo shu pancakes, for example. In a lot of cases, if you look hard enough, you can generally find something within a single cuisine. Why call something an Indian salsa, when they have something like a salsa called a chutney? Or why call something an Asian salsa, when they have something like a salsa called a sambal?"

Likewise, Joyce Goldstein tries to communicate a respect for the culture and authenticity of the food she's serving. "That is, unless I'm screwing around," she notes. "But then, I'll indicate on the menu that I'm just screwing around."

"Screwing around" sometimes leads other chefs to experiments in fusion cooking—trying to meld the ingredients of more than one cuisine—of which too many are misguided, in Goldstein's opinion. "In principle, fusion cooking is fine. But the flavors have got to work together," she insists. "You might have a beautiful blouse and a favorite skirt, but they might not go together as an outfit. About 95 percent of the time, fusion doesn't work. It's only through eating and tasting and travel and understanding where food comes from that you can come to know what flavors work together."

Terrance Brennan describes how he came up with his signature dish of salmon and horseradish crust, which has classic roots. "At Le Cirque, we used to do herb crusts for fish, like Dover sole. There's a classic preparation of a crust of butter and bread crumbs and mustard that was put on rack of lamb. Knowing the classic combination of salmon and horseradish, I decided to make a horseradish crust. I just adapted the recipe, putting mustard in it along with cured salmon, cucumber, salmon caviar, and a little *crème fraîche*.

"When you've been cooking a while," Brennan says, "you just know what things are going to work together." His principles include "Pairing sweetness with acid, or sweetness with hotness. Cutting richness with acid. Not overpowering delicate flavors. Cooking Mediterranean is easy because garlic, tomato, and olive oil all have a natural affinity to each other. From working with the classics, you know what flavors go together, so you can serve them together in different ways. The classics are classics for a reason. These flavor combinations have been tested over years and years—and they're great, great dishes."

Understanding as much as possible about a particular ingredient can help inform what to do with it and which other ingredients to combine it with, in a kind of culinary free-association. "If you're working with duck, and you know that ducks eat grains, like corn, then you can serve a corn cake with *foie gras*, because it's part of their environment. Serving grain with duck goes back to ducks and wheatfields," says Brennan. "It's game, it's fall, there's mushrooms. The gaminess of game goes well with squash, because there's a nice sweetness to it. I love purées in the wintertime; they go really well with game. So just working with the seasons, you're half way there."

After starting with the seasons, "Good taste leads you to combinations that work," says Lydia Shire. She believes chefs can develop taste through eating out in restaurants and experiencing firsthand which combinations are pleasing and which miss their mark.

Michael Romano agrees that "a chef has to have taste in terms of knowing how to put things together. As in every human endeavor, you can improve to a certain extent through training and practice," he says. "But beyond a certain level, you either have it or you don't. You can give two people the same budget and send them into a clothing store, and one will come out looking like a frump and the other will look like a million dollars. The difference is taste."

Classic dishes raise the question of recipes. Do professional chefs ever follow them? "I think they can be likened to training wheels," says Romano. "If you follow a good recipe carefully, you should be able to come up with something good. But as you gain more experience, you can take off the training wheels. Then you look at recipes to get a sense of interesting combinations of ingredients, rather than a teaspoon of this or a cup of that."

> *It is not just a haphazard affair, a new dish. It is a pondering on a new combination of tastes and then a reconciliation with a technical base.*
> —The Troisgros Brothers

Deconstructionism/Reconstructionism

"Most of my experimentation is rooted in the past," admits Charles Palmer. "It's involved taking what I knew—classic French cuisine—and applying it to great ideas in a modern American approach. And a lot of the products you find here, from beef to lamb, are even better than what you'll find in France, so it makes the experimentation that much more enjoyable."

Similarly, Rick Bayless describes the cuisine he serves at his Chicago restaurants as "classic Mexican food with contemporary twists in a contemporary context." But, in his opinion, "the most important thing we do is understand the soul of what's being done in the cuisine and capture that in our food. Flavors should take you to the heart of a cuisine." Bayless believes that the culture and substance of Mexican cuisine lie in its sauces, so he is careful to respect the integrity of all the sauces prepared in his restaurants. "They're all prepared traditionally; we don't take any liberties at all. Deciding which meat or seafood to pair it with is almost an afterthought," he says. "And we also respect another tradition of using lots of sauce on the plate."

Beyond this, Bayless's own interpretation comes into play when deciding which meat to pair with which sauce, whether the meat should be roasted or stewed, and how the dish will be plated and presented to the customer. The success of his interpretations is determined in part by his restaurants' Mexican customers, to whom he says he listens carefully. "When they tell me 'this dish tastes just like home' or 'that transported me back to my childhood,' I know we're on the right track," he says.

Susanna Foo says she always goes back to classical Chinese dishes when she's working on a new dish. "I'll use them as a base," she says. "But I like to adapt to American preferences. For example, American customers tend to prefer fillets as opposed to having fish served whole. And because Americans tend to like a big portion of meat, I might serve eight ounces of meat, but in one-ounce fillets. Besides, when preparing them using Chinese techniques, the flavor penetrates smaller pieces more quickly."

Foo says she's come to believe, "Why should you use tradition if it doesn't work? In Taiwan, unpasteurized rice wine is used in cooking, but the pasteurized wine that is exported to the United States—when you can find it— is far inferior in quality. I've found that vodka has a naturally light sweetness and gives a wonderful flavor to fish and shellfish, so I use that instead, even though no one knows vodka in Taiwan."

If your foundation of understanding is strong enough, it is possible to successfully give a twist to classic preparations. While a bordelaise sauce (of veal stock, shallots, and bone marrow) is typically paired with beef, Terrance Brennan makes a shellfish bordelaise, substituting lobster stock for veal stock. "For Valentine's Day this year, I served lobster with celery root purée, fresh porcini, and shellfish bordelaise," he says.

At Picholine, he's also served a variation on the dish of white gazpacho, which predates the introduction of tomatoes to the new world. "A lot of times I'll take a classical idea and give a little something different. It's made with almonds—used to make an almond milk—white grapes, garlic, olive oil. You purée all this up, and it's a white consistency, and you can put a little *verjus* in it and some white bread crumbs. It's basically a garlic soup, but I tame it down a bit," says Brennan. "Then I take all the things you make a red gazpacho with, juice them, and make a granita out of it, and garnish the soup with granita and shrimp and coriander. Sometimes you taste something and go 'Wow!' That's what this soup is."

Once you understand the classics, you can more easily and confidently substitute ingredients that are similar. Johanne Killeen and George Germon find themselves inspired by ingredients that they haven't used before. "The other day, one of our wholesalers dropped off a case of tomatillos [green Mexican tomatoes] for us, no charge. So we looked at them and wondered, 'What the hell are we going to do with tomatillos?'" admits Killeen. "But we also had some beautiful, fresh cod come in. We were influenced by a Mexican kid who had just recently been at our house, and we decided to toast the tomatillos like he had, and I started making a sauce with a lot of onions and garlic, and we threw in these toasted tomatillos and bay leaf. It made a dark, rich sauce out of just a few ingredients, and it became the sauce for the cod. In thinking of the tomatillos and the kind of citrusy acid that it has, we thought it would be a really good balance for the fish, and it worked out to be a great dish."

You have to leave room for you to put you into the food. Every cook should have this license to insert their will, their talent, their prejudices.
—Joyce Goldstein

Killeen brought the same sense of creativity to composing a new dessert based on the classic flavors of cheesecake. "I don't eat a lot of cheesecake, but I'm kind of intrigued by it," says Killeen. "I've included all the basic ingredients—some of the flavor of a graham cracker crust, a cream cheese *crème anglaise*, and a cream cheese vanilla soufflé. So we have all of the ingredients, but in a completely different way. We make our own kind of graham cracker cookie batter and bake off a big, five-inch diameter cookie. Then we make the vanilla soufflé, which we fold *crème anglaise* and cream cheese into, and that goes on top of the cookie and bakes.

"So it's a free-form soufflé that looks like a big cloud that comes to your table, and we serve it on top of a *crème anglaise* that's been enriched with cream cheese. It's lighter than cream cheese, because you're dealing with mostly egg whites in the soufflé, but it's got all the flavor of it. So it's kind of a traditional American dessert that's been deconstructed and then reconstructed. This is the kind of thing that I have fun with."

But how far is going too far? Jeremiah Tower recalls a classic Taillevant dish from the 1500s calling for turkey or guinea fowl to be marinated in raspberry vinegar and then flattened and grilled before being garnished with a handful of raspberries. But in the 1970s, with the advent of other berry vinegars, balsamic vinegar, and Asian fruits, he eventually saw a bastardization of the dish in the form of squab with kiwi and star fruit made

If you're making tarte Tatin, it would be okay to put raisins in or soak the fruit in liqueur first. But I'd draw the line at mango tarte Tatin.
—Lindsey Shere

with balsamic vinegar. "Star fruit is pretty, but it's inedible," comments Tower. "Anybody who cuts into a star fruit and sticks a piece in their mouth can tell you that. It's rare that they're ever ripe."

Similarly, Daniel Boulud recounts, "Some young chefs believe they are more creative than the genius. Twenty years ago, Michel Guérard came up with the *salade gourmande* of *haricots verts, foie gras,* and truffles. It was simple, but perfect. But then some young chef tries to make it with raspberry vinegar. It's silly. When making a dish, you experiment with it until there is nothing else that can be done to improve the flavor. Then you must stop."

Being Touched by Inspiration

A dish represents the resolution to a dilemma. How can I satisfy this craving? How can I use up this particular ingredient? The creative process leading to a successful resolution can be sparked by anything—flipping through a book, traveling on vacation, eating something at a restaurant, strolling through a market—that sets the imagination in motion.

"Inspiration is difficult to talk about, because it's nonverbal," says Jeremiah Tower. "But it usually comes sometime between the first and the third glass of wine, at that point of relaxation. You might be skimming through a great cookbook and have some kind of reaction, or be looking through a nineteenth-century cookbook thinking 'I can't do it that way—so how would I do it?' Or you could be flipping through a bad cookbook, or a magazine, or some old menus—it's one particular stimulus, usually."

Sometimes the ingredients themselves provide the inspiration. Terrance Brennan recalls that as a young cook at Le Cirque in New York City, "We used to get the first and the best of everything in season. I loved to experiment with things like porcini mushrooms, white truffles, and *espillende* (seaweed)."

For Lydia Shire, composing a dish begins with something you love. "Go to the market to see what catches your eye—what's perfectly ripe and gets you excited," she says. "Then you can take it from there." When one of Shire's restaurant purveyors offered her some fresh grape leaves about the same time one of her cooks suggested putting a brochette on the menu, Shire was inspired to marinate chunks of chicken in yogurt, which were then wrapped in grape leaves before skewering. "We decided we wanted to be in Greece," she remembers, adding that she took the liberty of coloring and seasoning the marinade with turmeric, a spice not native to Greek cuisine.

Mary Sue Milliken recalls visiting Thailand, where she once bought a salad from a man on the street who had no legs. "He was making them on the street with a mortar and pestle, selling the salads in little baggies," she remembers, "and it turned out to be absolutely delicious." The combination of ingredients, which included melon, dried shrimp, serrano chiles, lime, and garlic, she recalls, inspired her to experiment with similar flavors when she returned home.

I travelled to Morocco, China, and India, and found that eating Oriental and other ethnic foods really opened the doors to my mind, in terms of the way I thought about flavors, textures, and combinations.

—Lydia Shire

Norman Van Aken on Inspiration

Inspiration can come when you're stuck at a red light. The creative process is something that is very, very difficult to describe. In some ways, it's kind of like a lovers' quarrel that happens in your mind. I think some of the most creative moments I've ever experienced made me a little sick like a lovers' quarrel—and then suddenly, incredibly happy, once there was a resolution to it.

It's the marriage between thought and the ingredients—and what a child of that marriage would produce. I've trained myself to know my ingredients really well, so that I can shuffle them in my mind. Certain ingredients or combinations might trigger a memory, or trigger a hunger—the past or the future, I guess—that will set me into motion, and then creative things can occur.

I think it was Pasteur who said that "Chance favors the prepared mind." There is a tremendous amount of preparation you have to have in order for this creativity to spawn. It's not just like winning the lottery.

Jean-François Revel said, "To as great a degree as sexuality, food is inseparable from imagination." Imagination for me is just another word for creativity. When you take the freedom to use your imagination, then the portals of creativity have no locks.

It's one of the truest things, in terms of chefs. We have to have an extraordinary self-editing process. We need to be able to walk into this natural garden that exists for us out there in the world—and, of course, politically we have to help protect that natural garden, because as chefs if we don't, then we won't have it—and get past our own personalities at times and get into the aromas and the textures. We have to shut our minds off to all the little things, like the fact that the air-conditioning unit's broken or whatever, and for a moment, the doors of perception can swing open and we can come up with some way of presenting food and making that memory of food be something that people can carry with them forever—or at least for a very long time.

Milliken also remembers when her partner Susan Feniger returned from a vacation in India. "She was so excited and said, 'I've got to make these fritters for you—they're really unbelievable!' So she made these vegetable fritters with chickpea batter, served with mint-cilantro chutney and a yogurt sauce, and later we put them on the menu as an appetizer. It was just kind of an experiment, but they went over really big. And what our experience at Le Perroquet [the Chicago restaurant where the two first met] taught us was that we could take any kind of food, including these country-style fritters from India, and we could kind of elevate the dish by using some of the finest techniques of handling food, which is what the French are brilliant at."

Jean-Georges Vongerichten recalls paging through a cookbook from the 1800s by Urbain Dubois and running across a recipe calling for the unusual combination of raisins and capers. "I knew the combination would need a spice. First I tried clove, which didn't work, but then I tried nutmeg, which is kind of 'pals' with raisins," recalls Vongerichten. "I made a purée of the raisins and capers, which was delicious, even if the color was not very appealing. In trying to decide what to use the sauce with, I knew that capers and skate were 'pals,' so I tried it." The unusually delicious dish that resulted was added to his restaurant menu.

How do chef-couples like Mark Peel and Nancy Silverton collaborate on developing dishes? "I did the original menu," says Peel. "And Nancy is the one who goes to the farmers' market and gets a lot of ingredients, and those end up in dishes. Tina [Wilson, Campanile's chef] also comes up with a lot of dishes, within parameters."

The idea doesn't always start with the main ingredient. "Nancy found some wonderful sprouted legumes at the farmers' market," recalls Peel. "When they sprout, a chemical change occurs inside the beans, causing them to become sweeter." Peel and Silverton decided to use a bed of the sprouted legumes to showcase a perfectly cooked piece of salmon.

For George Germon and Johanne Killeen, whose training as artists predates their entry into professional cooking, the starting point is visual. "I think it's a gift of our training," says Germon. "We use our brains as an empty canvas." They recall hearing the description of a thin lasagna, a layered pasta creation less than one inch thick, as making their mouths water. "American lasagna is filled with so much goop," says Killeen. "We started experimenting with thin lasagna that was still two or three layers high, but only three-quarters of an inch thick. From the initial visual idea, our minds created the dish and brought it to reality on the plate—one with a béchamel sauce glazed with Parmesan cheese, which we now cook to order."

The day's weather often dictates the kind of food people want to eat—or chefs want to cook. Obvious examples include craving hot food in cold weather, and vice versa. "I think the weather is one of the most dominating factors in terms of the mood I'm in and what I feel like cooking," says Norman Van Aken. "But after living here [in Miami] nearly twenty-five years [as a trans-

Cooking and music are alike, in that a finished dish and a performance depend on an element of improvisation which are never part of the recipe or score. When this goes right, the results are magical. It is the magic that matters.
—Paul Bocuse

plant from the Chicago area], our perception of what is 'cold' has definitely changed. Yesterday was 53 degrees and rainy, and we were thinking 'lamb stew'!"

Weather conditions can also directly affect the availability or quality of certain ingredients. "We certainly get rained out in terms of tuna or shrimp being available," says Van Aken. "When the moon is full, the shrimp go down, and the shrimpers just don't go out." And across the country in Los Angeles, Nancy Silverton pays attention to the weather in planning her desserts. "After a recent rainy spell, I took strawberries off the menu because I knew the strawberries weren't going to be good enough after having soaked up all that water," she says.

The Mother of Invention

As Chris Schlesinger previously pointed out, it's rare that chefs have the luxury—or challenge!—of creating out of thin air. "Getting back to the idea of a chef as a professional, my job as a chef-restaurateur is to run a profitable kitchen," says Schlesinger. "One of the major realities facing cooks throughout time is that it's a rare thing that a cook gets to create in a vacuum. I go into the walk-in [refrigerator] in the morning and I look at what I have and what I need to use. Then I'll call up my purveyors, who'll tell me that leeks are looking great, for example, or that striped bass season just started. So I'm never starting from a blank sheet of paper—I'm always starting from something. I have all these things to which I need to apply my experience and knowledge in order to tie them together."

Mary Sue Milliken and Susan Feniger once found themselves with an abundance of chicken in their walk-in, and used that situation as an impetus to create a way to use it. The result was one of the most popular dishes ever on their menu: Stuffed Rigatoni with Chicken and Fennel. "We had ordered some pasta, and the rigatoni had come in really long. And I thought, Well, maybe I can do something with the pasta and that chicken. I was thinking about Italian sausage and pasta, which we both love. But people don't like pork, and they don't like all that fat in sausage. Then we were talking about it, and we decided to grind the chicken up and make a mousse, like we used to make at Le Perroquet. We decided to take a pastry bag and stuff the mousse inside the blanched rigatoni. We realized we had to flavor it with something, and we

A Chef's Palette of Flavors

Jean-Louis Palladin

"This list reflects exactly what I've got in the refrigerator, or exactly what I'm going to receive," says Jean-Louis Palladin, of those ingredients indicated in boldface.* Palladin would go into his office at 1 P.M. every afternoon to compose the restaurant's daily specials based on such a list.

INVENTORY—JANUARY 10, 1996

FISH

Abalones	Crawfish	Lamprey	Rockfish	Skate
Anchovies	**Eel**	**Lobster**	Rouget	Soft Shell
Bass, Sea	Flounder	**Monk**	Salmon	**Spotted Tile**
Clams—Razor,	**Frogs' Legs**	Monk Liver	Sardines	Squid
Countneck	Goeduck	**Mussels**	**Scallops**	Sturgeon
Cod	**Grouper**	**Onaga**	**Sea Urchins**	Swordfish
Cod Cheeks	Hake	**Oysters**	**Seaweed**	**Tuna**
Crab	Halibut	Periwinkles	Shad Roe	**Turbot**
Spider Crab	Herring	Piballes	**Shrimps**	

MEATS

Caul Fat	Legs Confit	**Lamb**	**Squab**	**Rabbit Sausage**
Capon	Gizzard	Marrow	**Legs**	Buffalo
Chicken	Heart	Pig Feet	**Sweetbreads**	Buffalo Testicles
Chicken Wings	Kidney—Black, White	Pig Ear	**Veal**	
Duck:	**Foie Gras**	**Rabbit**	Venison	
Moscovite	**Guinea Hen**	**Leg**	Faisan	
Magrets	**Ham**	**Loin**	**Confit Gizzard**	

FRUITS

Strawberries	Blood Oranges	Prunes	Persimmons	Tangerines
Raspberries	Mandarines	Raisins	**Pineapples**	Ugly Fruit (Thierry)
Dates	**Melons**	**Oranges**	Lemons	Sapotes
Blueberries	Grapes	Passion Fruits	**Limes**	Star Fruits
Bananas	Kumquats	Peaches	Pomegranates	
Huckleberries	Figs	Apricots	Plums	
Gooseberries	**Mangoes**	**Pears**	**Quinces**	
Cranberries	**Papayas**	**Apples**	Rhubarb	

VEGGIES

Artichokes	**Corn**	Parsley Root	Radishes	Yucca Roots
Asparagus	Cucumber	Parsnips	Rutabagas	Ramps
Green	**Eggplant**	Peas	**Salsify**	Bok Choi
White	**Fennel**	Snow Peas	Squash	Avocados
Beans	**Garlic**	**Peppers**	**Zucchini**	**Beets**
Fava Beans	**Ginger**	**Red**	Jerusalem Artichokes	Chestnuts
Broccoli	Horseradish	Green	**Taro Root**	Pumpkins
Carrots	**Lemongrass**	**Yellow**	**Tomatoes**	Spinach
Cauliflower	**Leeks**	**Potatoes**	Red	
Celery	Onions	Finn	Yellow	
Celery Root	**Pearl Onions**	Red	**Turnips**	
Cabbage	Scallions	**Idaho**	Water Chestnuts	

*Bold indicates the items in stock.

HERBS

Bay Leaf	**Dill**	Oregano	Sorrel	Ti Leaf
Basil	Epazote	**Parsley**	Tarragon	Juniper Berries
Chervil	Lavender	Rosemary	**Thyme**	
Chives	Marjoram	**Sage**	**Lemon Leaf**	
Cilantro	**Mint**	Savory	Shiso (Oba) Leaf	

BUTTERS

Anchovy	**Coral**	**Enokis**	**Sea Urchin**	Tarragon
Black Olive	Coriander	**Ginger**	**Smelt Roe**	Chive
Caper	Curry	Lemongrass	Watercress	Chervil
Caviar	**Dill**	Parmesan	Basil	

SAUCES

Garlic	Huckleberries	Lemon	**Meat Juice**	**Quince**
Shallot	Lime	**Red Wine**	Rhubarb	

SALADS

Arugula	**Green Romaine**	Bibb	Mâche	Mustard
Collorosa	**Red Romaine**	Chard	**Mesclun**	Watercress
Green Oak	**Mixed Lettuces**	Dandelion	Misuna	**Heart of Palm**
Red Oak	Endives	Frisée	Trevise	

PREPARATIONS

Barigouce	Basquaise	**Niçoise**

SMOKED FISH

Eel	Salmon	Sturgeon	Trout	**Seaweed Salad**
Mussels	Scallops	Halibut	Tuna	Octopus Salad
Rockfish	Skate			

SOUPS

Corn	Eggplant	Tomato	Cauliflower	Onions
Mushroom	Petits Pois	Artichoke	Broccoli	Shallot
Chestnut	Fava	Asparagus	Carrot	**Salsify**
Coconut	Pepper	Bean	Celery Root	**Crab**

TERRINES

Mushroom	Cèpe	Fresh Salmon	Venison	**Foie Gras**
Vegetable	Duck	Scallops		

FISH EGGS/CAVIAR

American	Beluga	Smelt Roe	Cod Roe	**Quail Eggs**
Osetra	Sevruga	Flying Fish		

MUSHROOMS

Chanterelles	Hedgehogs	**Shiitake**	Wood Ear	Lobsters
Crimini	**Cèpes**	Trumpets	Yellow Foot	Matsutake
Enokis	Portobellos	Truffles	Morels	Bottom Mushrooms

came up with fennel, which is a traditional seasoning for sausage. So we assembled the dish and put it on the menu—and that dish was on the menu for thirteen years!"

Sometimes it's a lack that creates the need to find a suitable substitute. "When we opened Al Forno, we started out without a wood-burning oven," recalls George Germon. "It was a constant source of frustration that we didn't have the space for one in the original Al Forno. But it was something that forced us to experiment with different cooking techniques that would allow us to give a similar flavor to certain foods, and that experimentation led us to develop grilled pizza. It's our own technique in that it didn't exist in Italy when we experimented with it, but it was certainly Italian in spirit." The technique, whereby pizza dough is cooked on a grill to impart a unique flavor and crispy texture to the pizza, has since been widely copied.

Composing Dishes

How does the creative process of developing a new dish unfold?

In coming up with a dish, the starting point for Anne Rosenzweig is the ingredient's essence. "Then I go into taste memory to see what the ingredient evokes," she says. "And I'll either bring it back—or bring it back in an even better incarnation." She cites as an example the meatloaf offered on her menu at her second restaurant, The Lobster Club. "We interviewed customers, and talked among ourselves, and found that the thing everyone remembers about eating meatloaf growing up was the tomato sauce. So we'll use different meats, and different seasonings, but we always incorporate a tomato sauce with it. And sometimes we get very playful!" "Playful" certainly describes "Julio Iglesias's Mother's Meatloaf," a fictional creation incorporating roasted peppers and ancho chiles!

Jasper White never hesitates in saying, "The starting point is the ingredients. What is the focus of the dish? I guess I'm traditional to the extent that it's usually the protein—what is the fish or meat or caviar? Whatever it is, there's something that's the reason why I'm cooking the dish. And I try not to let the dish go too far away from that reason.

"So the first thing I do is identify the product, and that's the theme of the dish. And I identify the characteristics of that particular product—was the fish freshly caught and bled, for example? Then it will have slightly different properties than a fish that's not. So then I go into the memory bank. I already know what this fish tastes like. And I already know which ten ingredients go best with it. And then I would see what those ten ingredients are, and what the season is for them, and then start developing a dish out of them.

"I'm into kind of the TV dinner approach—the three compartments: protein, vegetable, starch. A lot of times they can all be mixed together or they could be handled in different ways. But I still kind of stay with that because, for me, a plate needs to have those three elements," says White.

"So it starts with the season. And you also have to take into account the occasion. Is it for a restaurant menu, or is it for a special dinner? Is it for friends at home? Is it casual, or am I trying to be fancy? Or it might have to do with the rest of the menu, too," he says.

Jimmy Schmidt is one of a number of chefs who point out the importance of designing food to complement the wine with which it is to be served. "But in the cases when you're not accounting for any kind of beverage mar-

Contrasts Between Ingredients

Providing contrasts within a dish offers powerful opportunities for heightening interest as well as expressing one's point of view. Most importantly, it is a way to achieve an all-important sense of balance in a dish:

Characteristic	Spectrum	Example
Aromas:	Faint/Strong	Vanilla custard with cinnamon
Colors:	Varied	Tropical fruit salad
Consistency:	Fatty/Astringent	Salmon with horseradish
Cooked States:	Cooked/Raw	Zabaione with strawberries
Cost:	Inexpensive/Expensive	Potatoes with caviar
Density:	Heavy/Light	Lemon meringue pie
Familiarity:	Common/Exotic	Mashed potatoes with *huitlacoche*
Flavors:	Sweet/Sour/Salty/Bitter	Pad Thai
Flavor Strength:	Sharp/Bland	Lemon sole
Moistness:	Wet/Dry	Soup with a crouton
Size:	Big/Little	Steak with fingerling potatoes
Spiciness/hotness:	Spicy-Hot/Bland-Cool	Wasabi on tuna sushi
Temperatures:	Hot/Cold	Hot apple pie with vanilla ice cream
Textures:	Crispy/Soft	Grilled cheese sandwich

riage per se, you start with the ingredients themselves. The direction of the thought process then proceeds to 'How do you take these natural ingredients and enhance their natural beauty?'"

"If you take a fish, for instance, and apply heat to it, you'll end up with a piece of fish. It's going to taste like fish, and it may be fresh, but not much other excitement is added to it, from a gustatory point of view. There's not much visual. There's not much from a textural, contrasting point of view. And the flavor is kind of one-dimensional.

"If you were to add a sauce to the dish, and either vegetables or starches that would offer color, flavor, contrasting texture—all of those elements would preferably not cover up the flavor of the fish, but would enhance it. For example, combining the crunchiness of snow peas with salmon would make the flesh of the fish seem silkier in contrast. Likewise, a more acidic sauce with the salmon would balance out some of the natural sweetness and fatty characteristics of the salmon.

"Then, you might grill the salmon, or pan-roast it, or dust it with spices and sear it. With each one of those different techniques, you're quite able to bring out more flavors, or potentially even caramelize some of the natural sugars in the presence of acids and build an additional flavor profile."

Lindsey Shere believes the same kinds of contrasts make for a good dessert. "Our focus is always on the flavors, textures, and temperatures in a dessert," she says. "We want to let people know what really good stuff tastes like, since Safeway [the grocery store chain] seems to be the flavor standard in the United States."

What comes first in creating a dessert, according to Shere, is tasting the fruit. "You have to know how it behaves," she says. "What happens when it's cooked or puréed? Does it turn brown? The fruit tastes different from year to year and from farmer to farmer. Every year when apple season starts, we bring back one of every type of apple, and then cook and taste them. Good eating apples are not always good cooking apples. Red Delicious apples, for example, don't have a lot of flavor when cooked. We see which ones we like the texture of, and which combine well with others."

Next comes "thinking about all the possibilities for what that fruit could be," says Shere. "Sometimes something will come out of the blue, and other times you'll work at it. Do you want to make a tart? What about cream puffs? We can't fry here [at Chez Panisse] because we don't have a hood over the pastry section, and we don't have a broiler so we can't do things like gratins. It's limiting not having those possibilities."

Even though Chez Panisse doesn't have a liquor license, the restaurant is allowed to use hard liquor in the kitchen, and Shere will take advantage of that freedom by serving pear sherbet with grappa, or berry, peach, or nectarine sherbet with framboise. "And I like Kirsch on peach, pear, strawberry, or raspberry sherbet," Shere says.

What about chocolate? "Chocolate is a real standby in the winter here, when the supplies of fruit are low," says Shere. "In coming up with new desserts, we run experiments in the kitchen a lot, testing recipes. There's a lot of pressure to come up with new desserts, both pressure from our customers and self-imposed."

When composing a dish, Gary Danko starts by asking himself, "What is the main ingredient here? What is the center of the plate? Is it a roast eggplant with lamb loin, or is it roast lamb loin with eggplant? Ideally, I will choose by the season.

"When I cook with lamb, because I take all the fat and connective tissue off the meat, I have to somehow insulate that meat. In the spring, I'll take dried morel mushrooms and powder them, and use that with bread crumbs and aromatics, onions, garlic, parsley, thyme, and make a very delicate crust. I'll sear the lamb in a little bit of hot oil, cool it down quickly, brush it with egg white, and then roll it in this crust. From that, I'll decide, 'What am I going to put this on?' I'll think, 'Well, lamb like to graze on fennel, and fennel's just coming into season, so I'll make a really simple fennel compote,'" Danko says. "Then I'll think, 'Do I want this to go more Mediterranean, or what style do I want to take this in?' In my mind, I'll think Easter, Easter bunnies, ham, asparagus, eggs—these are certain things from my childhood that I remember. This is the individual style of the chef coming out here—basically, where you were born, what your life experiences are, et cetera. If I travel and I see a dish that's quite interesting, and I like the philosophy and it blends with mine, then I might incorporate those flavors. Or I'll take a specific cuisine—I love Moroccan and Indian food—and I will use the love of those spices in a much more delicate manner in the food that I prepare at The Ritz-Carlton Dining Room."

What's the goal when building a new dish? "Simplicity," says Rick Bayless, "and wholeness of flavor and texture. Recently, I kept encouraging a sous chef to pull back on an appetizer of grilled scallops, and to take everything away except what would naturally meld really well with the salsa it was paired with. This way, when the diner started at it, there would really be a sense of completeness about scallops, and a counterpoint of this absolutely delicious salsa, and then some other element that would stay in the background as the element you needed to tie it all together.

Some of the best dishes in the world have no more than three major components.
—Lydia Shire

"What we ended up with was taking some napa cabbage and cutting it really very thin, heating a skillet until it was quite hot, putting just a tiny bit of dressing in that hot skillet, and then putting the napa cabbage in and just tossing it off the heat so it just barely wilted the napa. It went on the plate, and then the rest of the components were built on top of that," says Bayless. "When it was done, you could eat it and it felt as if everything was in perfect balance, but you didn't really even know what that was; it was the kind of background against which all these other flavors and textures worked themselves out. That's a good example of how we are able to build dishes here, and what our goal is, basically."

Understanding and always respecting the essence of the ingredients is key. Mark Peel says, "Let's say you start with a quail. A quail is a little thing. So I would always put something substantial with quail, to kind of build it up. It needs more support than, say, a prime rib. I might put some parsnip potatoes or mashed potatoes with it, as kind of a base.

"A lot of dishes have a base—literally, a physical base, something that's going to kind of hold the dish up. It's something that's going to accept the flavors and pull everything together. For example, we serve sweet potatoes with baby chicken, which comes with a garlic confit and escarole. The sweet potato purée accepts the sharp, bitter flavors of the escarole and the garlic confit and the juices that are coming out of the chicken. And the sweetness contrasts with the bitterness, and the garlic really rounds out the flavor of the sweet potato." "And all those soft textures are textures that people really love," adds Nancy Silverton. "The creaminess of the garlic and the softness of the potato all kind of melt together."

Juggling Flavors

The greater the complexity of dishes, the more flavors and other properties that must be juggled and juxtaposed against one another, providing plenty of challenge for a chef. "You often think up dishes in your head," says Jimmy Schmidt. "And with ingredients, some people think, 'Well, if one's good, two's better, three's great, four's terrific, and five is fantastic!' And I don't necessarily agree. I think that the flavors between the ingredients have to tie together. I don't think your palate tastes them all individually. When you drink a glass of wine, you're tasting all the wine. You're tasting one flavor, even though it's made up of multiple components. Likewise, with a dish, the flavors should come together to create one image, that hybrid image. So you need to use supporting flavors to make that work."

How to make sure you are able to accomplish that? "I remember hearing about a kind of triangle theory, whereby if you were combining two ingredients that didn't really go together, you had to have a third ingredient that related to both in order to tie the dish together," says Chris Schlesinger.

Put another way, "If you look at ingredients like characters in a play, there are times that there are twenty characters on stage and times when

George Germon on the Power of Simplicity

George Germon recounts an experience that he says he'll never forget, which had a powerful influence on him as a cook. "I was visiting some people in England who had a four- or five-year-old daughter. They weren't around, but I was in the kitchen and the little girl pulled a chair over to the stove and started heating up a pan, saying she was going to make tomato soup," he remembers. After getting the girl's assurance that her parents allowed her to do so, Germon says he watched her heat some butter in the pan, then take out a knife and cutting board and chop some tomatoes. She cooked the tomatoes in the butter about three minutes, and then added a little salt and a little cream. "Would you like some?" she asked Germon, who politely replied, "Sure!" Once he tasted it, Germon says he was absolutely floored. "It was unbelievable," he says. "I couldn't believe that something tasted as good as it did with so few ingredients."

Al Forno's menu features a potato soup that's equally simple. "It has just four ingredients: potatoes, onions, butter, and water. That's it," says Germon. "And when our cooks first made it, they kept asking, 'What's the next step?'" Johanne Killeen remembers, "They found it impossible to believe that anything wonderful could result from four ingredients!"

there are just two. So what you pair an ingredient—say, ginger—with depends on how many characters are on the stage," explains Norman Van Aken. "In the latter case, you might add ginger to a simple vinaigrette of oil and an acidic component. And the three are quite different from one another. If there were many characters on the stage, it might be a ginger-soy vinaigrette with grilled chicken and some caramelized plantains. The resonance between the caramelized, smoky plantains and the soy and the pungency of the ginger working against the meaty simpleness of the chicken—I'm thinking of them all talking together, and what they're able to say to each other.

"I find the number of ingredients on a plate to be a common discussion in this day and age. The California food movement really seems to say to itself, 'Well, simplicity is really where the purity lies.' They might look at some of my recipes and say, 'Oh, this is too complicated.' But then I'll look at a cuisine that is much older than most of the cuisines of the world, like China's or some Thai cuisines, and say, Look what they've done after many more centuries of civilization, in terms of having these disparate ingredients. You'll look at their recipes and you'll see twelve ingredients in a recipe. And over a period of time, you might think that you'd get it down to only two or three ingredients and become quite minimalistic. But the reverse is true in these more ancient cuisines. And it's not because it's hodgepodge."

Bradley Ogden agrees. "Sometimes you'll have a dish that's too heavy—a risotto that's too rich, or a sauce that's overreduced—and you feel really terrible after you've eaten it. It's usually because it's one-dimensional," he says. "If there were two or three dimensions, it would be sparking up your taste buds instead. That's why you need the blending of flavors that will take away some of that richness and stir up the taste buds and cleanse the palate a little bit. That's where a cook can put his or her creativity into play. You know when you have a bad bottle of wine, where the first sip might make you say, 'Wow!' but then it's sort of flat after that? It's one-dimensional. And it's no difference from a meal that's one-dimensional. I like to go for two or three dimensions, but yet without getting too complex.

"For example, I did a *foie gras* dish the other night with Fuji apples, which I'd roasted and marinated with a little balsamic vinegar. They were still crisp, with a bite to them, and lightly caramelized," says Ogden. "The richness of the *foie gras* was balanced by the tartness of the apple, so you walked away from the dish thinking, 'That was really great' instead of 'That was really heavy.' Balancing tastes and textures sparks your palate instead of leaving it coated and blah."

Achieving a balance, whatever the particular characteristics of a dish, is the goal for Rick Bayless. "If I serve a fried dish, I always like to pair it with an acidic component," he explains. "And when I serve something exotic, I like to pair it with something well known."

"I'm able to throw in an accent," says Nancy Silverton, "but I can't always come up with the whole dish. Mark [Peel] and Tina [Wilson, Campanile's chef] will take it to a certain point, and sometimes I'll say, 'Why don't you also add this?' and that's my contribution." Peel characterizes his wife's contributions as "typically trying to add a little crunch to things." How? "Fava beans," says Peel. "Or bread crumbs," they say, almost simultaneously.

"Sometimes for me, creating a dish is a way to use something that I really love," says Silverton. "When I fell in love with the combination of warm apple sauce and cold cream, I said I wished that I could serve that at the restaurant, but nobody would buy it if they saw it next to a piece of twenty-five-layer chocolate cake. But it's probably one of the most exquisite combinations in the world. So I came up with a dessert that went with it, to embellish this perfect combination, and that was a vinegar pie. Somebody had made me what they call a chess pie, which has vinegar in it, and I liked it, but it wasn't vinegary enough for me—but that was the starting point.

"I never like desserts, certainly not fruit desserts, to be on the sweet side; I always like them to be somewhere between savory and sweet. And I love acidic things with apples. Cold cream provides a contrast in temperatures—you don't want ice cream with everything—and is also neutral, in a sense. So it sort of gives your palate a place to rest."

Visual Presentation

"The first way you encounter a dish is through seeing it with your eyes," points out Dieter Schorner. "And over the last thirty years, we've seen chefs making mountains and monuments on a plate—and they're so impractical. I always hate it when people cover the whole plate with cocoa. Even a little bit of a breeze when you have a white shirt on, and...forget it!

"With *nouvelle cuisine*, it would take half an hour to decorate the plate, and by the time you got the food, it was cold," says Schorner. "A lot of presentation was done just to show off, and I have always been against just showing off."

Nancy Silverton believes that most diners are very heavily influenced by the elaborate presentation of a dish. "Ninety-eight percent of the population probably sits down and says, 'Whoa! That's incredible! That chef is so talented!' Those are a lot of the chefs who get the attention from the press and are making the waves these days across the country. But because of that, we're getting a lot of muddled food. People who don't know how to do a lot of those very technical things correctly are trying, and they're just falling on their faces. It makes it difficult for me to find places to eat these days.

"The more whimsical or the more complicated you get with your food, the more you have to do ahead of time, and the more you sacrifice the flavor. No matter what anybody says, you can't do it all. All you can do *à la minute*..." ("...you have to be able to do in a minute," quips Mark Peel.) Silverton continues, "The more complicated a dish, the more spectacular a dish, the more stale it's going to taste. There's no way anyone can prepare all the elements the same day."

"I think we've really achieved a great presentation when a dish looks as though that's they way it ought to be—and should always be," says Mark Peel. Silverton agrees. "When we do it right, and we've done what we set out to do, you see the dish and you think, 'Yes, that's how that dish should always be and why would anyone ever do it any different?' That's when we've hit the mark."

George Germon agrees. "I think that food should look as natural as possible. And I like food to look fresh, like it was born on the plate," he says. "I don't like tall food, squeeze bottles, drizzles, or sprinkles." In terms of the presentation of food, he says, "Our art backgrounds are the best things that ever happened to us. Presentation comes naturally to us. It's part of our vocabulary."

Even if you know what look you're going after, it's not always easy to communicate it to those who will have to execute it. "I find that the most difficult thing to do is to impart the concept of 'free form.'" says Patrick O'Connell. "If you draw something on graph paper, cooks are very comfortable and say, 'I can follow this—this goes here and this goes there.' But to me, that's what we call 'tense' food. So I said to this young man the other day, 'What we're trying to do here with this plate is to make it look like you picked the asparagus and you waltzed through the garden, and a little breeze blew the stuff across the plate.'

"We have dishes where sauces are thrown, and some cooks think that means splat! No, no, no, no, no. It's a very delicate balance. If you're going to make it look wild and crazy, you're going to have to have the element of total and complete control and precision there with it to balance it out. Some cooks don't understand it yet, what a dish is saying—[that it's] saying a whole bunch of things," O'Connell says.

"Michel Guérard has a very light touch, and since working with him in France, I've always carried that with me," says Michael Romano. "He taught me that if a plate looks too full, it's unappealing. The presentation of his food has a certain airiness and lightness to it, and I try to remain inspired by the same delicateness."

Even among leading chefs, there is a wide array of opinions as to what constitutes great presentation. "There always has to be height in a dish," argues Joachim Splichal. "There has to be a focus in the way it's placed on the plate. A dish should be a visual experience for the customer. It was with [French chef Jacques] Maximin that I learned presentation, how to get something to look perfect."

On the other hand, Joyce Goldstein says, "I don't believe in tall food. There are some dishes that you have to crash in order to eat. I don't believe in squeeze bottles, and I don't believe in little dots of sauce around the rim of a plate. And I don't want my customers to leave with parsley or cocoa on their sleeves because someone in the kitchen's gone crazy sprinkling it all over the rim of a plate.

"I don't think you should put anything on a plate that doesn't relate to the dish," she says. "Why would anyone want a rosemary branch standing up in the middle of their plate? Are you supposed to eat it? Pick your teeth with it? If not, then what on earth is it doing there?"

Some chefs feel that the natural beauty of their ingredients provide them with a leg up, in terms of attractive presentation. "I don't build architectural food, but I do look very much at dramatic presentation," says Norman Van Aken. "It's kind of easy, in certain respects, because we work with such beautiful colors with the tropicality of where I'm at [Miami], to invest my plates with technicolor-like opportunities. It's not autumnal—it's riotous, in many respects, and it can be made to be more so. And I can work with three or four colors, but they're such strong primary colors that the plates will seem nearly electric in terms of their presentation.

I love edible garnishes. I want every little piece of greenery on a plate to be there for a purpose.
—Alice Waters

"One of my key dishes is my rum and pepper painted fish, with a mango moho, which is nearly black from this rum paint that I make, on the fish, in stark relief to the brilliant mango purée—pure, simple color. Then I have this bright green poblano that's stuffed, with the stem still coming off of it. So there are really only three colors with a little bit of lime and a little bit of ripped flowers, but they're all so different that it allows for an extraordinarily dramatic presentation.

"I can do that because of my raw materials here, which are not affected by me as the chef, but are affected by Mother Nature and her extraordinary palette of colors. I can select these things and put them together in very natural ways that will look very bright to people who are coming from areas that perhaps don't have these things so much within their larder.

"One of the most important things in food is texture," says Van Aken. "I think that one of the reasons we began stacking things in a napoleon-like way wasn't really to press the phallic opportunity but to offer a chance for the fork, as it delivers an intrusion to a presentation, to get a stratum of textures that you'll push through, so that when you get your bite, you'll have your little bit of mashed potatoes and your little bit of crunchy potato or plantain chip and your dense meaty protein from your fish or pork or whatever in one nice bite, so that when it's in your mouth, it's like, 'Wow!' It's all kind of bouncing around in there and offering this chordal opportunity, as opposed to just a note."

"Presentation is a consideration," admits Alice Waters. "I don't like for everything to be flat on a plate—and I don't like, obviously, for everything to be tall. But, again, I like to rely on the classics. I like the look of lime-green fava beans with a little pink prosciutto or salami. I love those colors. And I love all the maroon colors of food, like the radicchios that look like parrot tulips, all striped. It's just fantastic. I love all the colors of tomatoes together, including the unlikely ones—the sort of brown ones and yellow ones. There's a whole palette to be considered, and I'm very influenced by that, by color. But, obviously, taste is number one; I would never use the color if it didn't taste good."

Mary Sue Milliken agrees that her first priority in a dish is taste. "Nothing is more important to me than how that food's going to taste," she says. "For me, I like my salads to have every single leaf covered with exactly the right amount of dressing. Those leaves aren't going to stand up."

"We do lots of great sauces that are very thin," adds Susan Feniger. "And they don't look that great on a plate; they don't look nearly as good as something that's reduced and sort of demi-glace-like, because they don't coat the plate as well."

The problem, it seems, comes when taste is sacrificed to appearance. "Now there are some people, like [Charles] Palmer, who do vertical food beautifully. But people will always go to see the latest madness," says Jeremiah Tower. "When I see an army of peas around a plate, I know that they've been handled and are probably cold. In terms of the appearance of a dish, I find few things more beautiful than a bowl of sliced white peaches, maybe with some raspberry cream on top."

Lindsey Shere admits that when it comes to desserts, "I'm a minimalist at heart. I'd rather see a really beautiful combination of colors, flowers, and leaves on a plate, rather than fireworks. I find it often detracts from the taste of desserts. When you put too many things together, not everything can be perfect. The caramel can get tacky sitting on the plate while the dessert is constructed, or the cookies can get soft. Another thing I don't like is seeing an even number of things on the plate; I prefer seeing, for example, three sorbets, which I think appears more balanced."

"One of the most important things in any dessert is texture," adds François Payard. "There is nothing more boring than a dish with no texture. Even in a dish like *oeufs à la neige* [floating islands], which emphasizes the softness of the fluffy egg white, there is caramelized sugar to add crispiness."

Payard recalls proudly that *New York Times* food writer Florence Fabricant had paid him a compliment at a recent food event. "She pointed out that in my desserts I work more on flavor than on structure," says Payard. "When you think about it, you realize that when your grandmother made a good dish, what made it good wasn't how it looked but what it tasted like. For example, a floating island dessert has no structure. But when your grandmother made it, how was it? Perfect!"

A Final Word

No matter how many guidelines are offered on how to compose a dish, in the end its beauty lies only in the eye of its beholder—or taster! Knowing this, Rick Bayless says, "I get really frustrated with a number of my cooks these days who want me to explain to them, why? 'Why?' 'Why do you do this?' 'Why do you do that?' What I usually answer is, 'Well, just taste it.' And I let them see if they can internalize it. Sometimes chefs need to sort of commune with the ingredients and then taste the final dish to know whether they've gotten it right or not. I feel very strongly that you just have to taste it and

Personally, I have ceased counting the nights spent in the attempt to discover new combinations when, completely broken with the fatigue of a heavy day, my body ought to have been at rest.
—Auguste Escoffier

Culinary Artistry

that's what cooking's all about—it's got to be something that you appreciate and understand at an intuitive level, much more than just on paper."

The most difficult dishes to make generally
appear to be the simplest.
—Fernand Point

And "getting it right" is its own reward for a chef. "One of the reasons
that I became a chef is that I felt very much in love with and hurt by the
world during my childhood, so that I wanted to remake it in a way that would
make me and my friends happy," says Norman Van Aken. "Annie Dillard [the
author of *Pilgrim at Tinker Creek*] was talking with people about writing once,
and someone asked her, 'How can I become a great writer?' She said, 'The
first thing that you have to do is love sentences.' People ask me why I like to
cook, and my answer sometimes is 'Because I like to make plates.' If you don't
like to make plates, you're not going to like making menus. You're not going
to like presenting *dégustations*. You've got to start off with the simplest form
of it. And then everything else is just a continuation that builds, like drops
of rain will build finally into a lake."

A dancer's graceful and seemingly effortless performance on stage can
belie years of training and practice and long hours of rehearsal. So, too, can
chefs' creations belie their own history. "Sometimes a customer will say to
one of us, 'What's so spectacular about this dish? It seems so simple,'" says
George Germon. "And I chuckle because that's when I know we've hit it.
The customer has no idea of all the stumbling blocks we've overcome in order
to make that particular dish, and all they know is that it seems simple—and
that it's delicious."

Because he loves the very, very delicate taste of turbot, Jeremiah Tower can't imagine pairing it with anything more complicated than a hollandaise sauce and some little boiled potatoes. "With the hollandaise, there's an enrichment of the flavor without adding lots of distracting flavors," he says. And Tower thinks that pork doesn't need more than a sprinkling of black pepper: "I believe strongly in the marriages of flavors!"

When we asked leading chefs how they knew that certain flavors or foods would complement each other, the usual response was something along the lines of, "You just know. After tasting so many different foods and food combinations, you store the ones that work in your head. When you've accumulated enough, you can even get pretty good at predicting which combinations you haven't yet tasted will work, based on the ones you know that work."

Wondering how we might shortcut the process of gaining decades of firsthand experience led to our research and development of the following charts. Based on our conversations with chefs as well as our researching some of the best respected culinary books (including those written by leading American chefs and recommended by them as critical to an aspiring chef's education), we compiled a treasure of food combinations that are known to work.

How to use them? When your starting point for composing a dish is a particular ingredient, you may wish to scan the list for inspiration for a possible complement or complements. While many ingredients are available year-round, seasonal peaks are noted for certain items. In addition, in some instances, preferred cooking techniques are indicated. You might also be inspired by the examples of how our chefs have combined the ingredients and complements on their own menus.

How *not* to use them? You should remember that your own palate is paramount. There may be some combinations listed that are not to your personal liking, and there are certainly combinations not listed that work as well—or even better—than those included. Your goal should be to cook to please yourself and those for whom you cook—and not in conformance with any chart in any book!

Jean-Louis Palladin claims that food pairing isn't difficult, given the years he's spent cooking. "Many combinations eventually become second nature," he claims. So how does a less-experienced chef develop the same sense of what works? By referring to the extensive flavor combining charts on the following pages, which bring into one convenient place, for the first time, the intuitive knowledge gained over centuries by some of the world's greatest culinary minds, as culled from interviews and menus of contemporary chefs and our historical research.

Why Food Matches?

FOOD MATCHES MADE IN HEAVEN*

ALMONDS

apples
apricots
caramel
chocolate

coconut
cream
plums
prunes

raisins
rice
strawberries

ANCHOVIES

eggs, hard-boiled
garlic

lemon
olives

onions
parsley

APPLES   (Fall)

almonds
applejack
bacon
blackberries
blue cheese
brandy
brown sugar
butter
butterscotch
Calvados
caramel
cassia
celery
cheese
chestnuts

cider
cinnamon
cloves
Cognac
Cointreau
coriander
cranberries
cream
currants, black
custard
dates
ginger
Grand Marnier
hazelnuts
honey
horseradish
Kirsch
lemon
Madeira
maple syrup
molasses
nutmeg
nuts, especially almonds
    or pecans

oatmeal
oranges
pears
pepper, black
pignoli
pistachios
praline
prunes
quinces
raisins
rosemary
rum
sauerkraut
sausages
sherry
sour cream
sugar
vanilla
vermouth
vinegar
walnuts
wine, red
yogurt

(continued on facing page)

---

* Many of these combinations are considered classic and are especially widely practiced. These are indicated by **boldface** type.

Apple Empanada with Cinnamon Ice Cream—Terrance Brennan

Jerry's Sour Cream Apple Pie served with Brown Sugar Ice Cream
—Joyce Goldstein

Apple Custard Pie with Calvados Cream—Joyce Goldstein

Chilled Soup of Apples and Cider with Warm Vanilla Maple Syrup—Gray Kunz

Fresh Macintosh in a Light Apple Syrup with Apple Sherbet and Apple Chips
—Francois Payard

Spiced Napoleon of Baked Apple with a Caramel Mousse—Francois Payard

Apple Tart with Cinnamon Ice Cream—Lindsey Shere

Warm Vinegar Pie with Applesauce and Cold Cream—Nancy Silverton

Caramelized Apple-Pear Bread Pudding with a Burnt Almond Sauce
—Joachim Splichal

Calvados Apple Turnovers with Black Pepper Feuilletés—Norman Van Aken

Apple Compote with Rosemary—Jean-Georges Vongerichten .

APRICOTS (Summer)

almonds	lamb	Sauternes
brandy	**lemon**	sesame
caramel	lime	sour cream
cherries	lingonberries	strawberries
coconut	maple syrup	tarragon
Cognac	nectarines	**vanilla**
Cointreau	oranges	yogurt
cream	peaches	wine
custard	pineapple	
ginger	pistachios	*bake*
Grand Marnier	plums	*poach*
hazelnuts	**raspberries**	*raw*
honey	rice	*stew*
Kirsch		

Apricot Tarte Tatin with Apricot Custard Sauce—Jean-Louis Palladin

Apricot Sherbet Bombe with Almond Mousse—Lindsey Shere

Apricot and Almond "Ravioli" with Toasted Almond Anglaise—Norman Van
Aken

Apricot Gratin with Almond Milk Ice Cream—Jean-Georges Vongerichten

ARTICHOKES (Spring)

aïoli
anchovies
bacon
basil
bay leaves
bread crumbs
butter
cheese, goat
chervil
cream
cumin
fennel
garlic
hazelnuts
hollandaise sauce
lemon
mayonnaise
Mornay sauce
mousseline sauce
mushrooms
olive oil
onions
Parmesan cheese
parsley
pepper, especially black
  and red
rémoulade sauce
salt
sausage
thyme
tomatoes
truffles, white
vinaigrette
wine, white

bake
braise
marinate
roast
steam

Artichokes, Carrots, and Zucchini with Lemon and Dill—Joyce Goldstein

Baby Artichokes Fried with Lemon, Roast Garlic and Shaved Parmesan
—Jimmy Schmidt

Artichokes Stuffed with Bread Crumbs, Anchovies, Garlic and Parsley
—Alice Waters

ARUGULA (Summer)

avocado
butter
carpaccio
cheese, blue
garlic
lemon
olive oil
Parmesan cheese
pasta
pears
pecans
pignoli
potatoes
ravioli
walnuts

Arugula and Radicchio with Gorgonzola, Pear, and Walnut
—Susan Feniger & Mary Sue Milliken

Apple and Arugula Salad with Lemon and Capezzana Olive Oil
—George Germon & Johanne Killeen

Arugula Salad with Smoked Pears, Spiced Pecans, and Stilton Cheese
—Chris Schlesinger

Avocado, Papaya and Arugula Salad—Jeremiah Tower

Meyer Lemon and Arugula Soup—Alice Waters

ASPARAGUS   (Spring)

anchovies
bread crumbs
butter
cheese sauce
chervil
chives
crabmeat
cream

eggs
garlic
ginger
hollandaise sauce
horseradish
lemon
Maltaise sauce
mayonnaise
morels
Mornay sauce
mousseline sauce
mushrooms
mustard
new potatoes
nutmeg
offal
olive oil

onion
orange
pancetta
Parmesan cheese
parsley
pepper
rosemary
shallots
soy
velouté sauce
vinaigrette

boil
grill
steam

Asparagus-Pistachio Soup Avgolemono—Joyce Goldstein

Grilled Asparagus with Olive Bread Crumbs and Olive Oil—Mark Peel

Green Asparagus Soup with Morels—Alice Waters

AVOCADOS

basil
beef, spiced or salt
bread, whole wheat
chiles
chives
cilantro
crab
cucumber
garlic
grapefruit
leeks

lemon
lemongrass
lime
mangoes
mint
onions, especially red
oranges
parsley
pineapples
pistachios

salt
shrimp
smoked fish, especially
  salmon and trout
sugar
tomatillos
tomatoes
vinaigrette
vinegar, especially bal-
  samic

Avocado and Orange Salad with Black Olive Dressing—Chris Schlesinger

Avocado Salad with Pancetta, Spring Garlic, and Hot Pepper Vinaigrette
—Jeremiah Tower

Avocado and Tomato Salad with Smoked Trout—Norman Van Aken

BANANAS (Winter)

alcohol
almonds
apricots
Armagnac
bacon
blueberries
brandy
brown sugar
butter
Calvados
caramel
cardamom
chicken
chocolate
cinnamon
coconut
Cognac
coriander

cream
cream cheese
custard
eggs
fruits, especially tropical
    (e.g., mango, papaya,
      pineapple)
gin
ginger
honey
ice cream
Kirsch
lemon
lime
malt
maple syrup
nuts
oranges

passion fruit
pecans
pineapples
pralines
raspberries
rum
sour cream
strawberries
sugar, brown or white
vanilla
yogurt

bake
broil
poach
raw

"Rum can bring up the flavor of bananas."—François Payard

Banana-Toffee French Toast—Susan Feniger & Mary Sue Milliken

Honey-Fried Bananas with Caramelized Ginger Sauce—Susanna Foo

Banana-Rum Ice—Chris Schlesinger

Grilled Sausage Skewers with Fresh Apricots, Jalapeños, and Chipotle Vinaigrette and Whole Grill-Roasted Banana—Chris Schlesinger

Roasted Banana Kugelhopf...Double Dark Chocolate Semi-Freddo—Lydia Shire

Cuban Banana-Rum Custard Tart—Norman Van Aken

BARLEY

almonds
cabbage
ham

mushrooms
onions

parsley
peas

BASS

almonds
anchovies
artichokes
butter
capers

carrots
chives
citrus
coriander
fennel

garlic
ginger
leeks
lemon

(continued on facing page)

mint	potatoes	*bake*
mushrooms	shallots	*braise*
olive oil	thyme	*fry*
oranges	tomatoes	*grill*
peppers	wine, red	*roast*

BASS, STRIPED (See also BASS)

basil	eggplant	*roast*
cream	mustard	
dill	olives	

BEANS, BLACK   (Winter)

avocados	*crème fraîche*	oranges
bacon	*epazote*	peppers
cheese, especially goat	**garlic**	rice
chiles, especially serrano	ham hocks	salt pork
chives	jalapeños	sour cream
cilantro	Madeira	tequila
coriander	mint	tomatoes
cumin	onions	

Frijoles Refritos: *Black Beans Fried with Garlic, Onion and* Epazote, *Topped with* Queso Fresco—Rick Bayless

Habañero Black Bean Soup with Avocado-Shrimp Salsa—Mark Miller

BEANS, FAVA   (Spring–Summer)

bacon	mushrooms	**savory**
butter	olive oil	spinach
cilantro	pancetta	thyme
cream	parsley	vinaigrette
garlic	Pecorino cheese	
ham	rosemary	*boil*
leeks	sage	*purée*
lemon	salt	*steam*

BEANS, GREEN   (Summer–Fall)

almonds
anchovies
bacon
basil
béchamel sauce
butter
chives
cream
dill
garlic
lemon
mint

mushrooms
mustard
nutmeg
nuts, especially hazel-
  nuts
olive oil
onions
oregano
Parmesan cheese
parsley
pimentos
rosemary

savory
sour cream
tomatoes
vinegar, especially
  white wine
walnuts
Worcestershire sauce

boil
purée
steam

BEANS, LIMA   (Fall)

bacon
brown sugar
butter
cheese, especially
  Cheddar
chives
cream
dill

garlic
lemon
molasses
mushrooms
nutmeg
olive oil
onions

parsley
pepper, black
salt pork
sour cream
tomatoes

simmer

BEANS, PINTO   (Winter)

bacon
beer
cheese, especially
  Cheddar and
  Monterey Jack
chiles

cilantro
garlic
onions
oregano
rice

salt pork
tomatoes

refry
simmer

Frijoles Charros: *Pinto Beans Simmered with Bacon, Poblanos, Tomato, and Cilantro*—Rick Bayless

BEANS, WHITE   (Winter)

bacon
bay leaf
chervil
chives
cream
garlic

maple syrup
molasses
olive oil
onions
parsley
pork and salt pork

rosemary
rum
sage
shallots
wine, red

BEAN SPROUTS

ginger	soy sauce	vinegar, especially wine
sesame oil		

BEEF

basil	marrow	soy
beer	**mushrooms**	vinegar, balsamic
béarnaise sauce	mustard	wine, especially red
bordelaise sauce	onions	
Burgundy	orange	*boil*
carrots	parsley	*braise*
chiles	**pepper, black**	*grill*
chives	peppers	*marinate*
corn	potatoes	*pot-roast*
hazelnuts	prunes	*roast*
horseradish	scallions	*spit-roast*
Madeira	shallots	*stew*

Fillet of Beef with Oysters, Black Pepper, and Port Wine—Gary Danko

Grilled Beef Tenderloin with Onion Beer Sauce, Horseradish Mayonnaise, and Marble Potatoes—Bradley Ogden

Patina Smoked Beef Tenderloin with Horseradish Glazed Potatoes and Spinach—Joachim Splichal

BEEF HEART

bacon	paprika	*bake*
horseradish	parsley	*braise*
marjoram	rosemary	*grill*

BEEF RIBS (Winter)

ginger	mustard	tomatoes
horseradish	potatoes	

BEET GREENS

anchovies	mustard	*sauté*
butter	sour cream	
horseradish		

BEETS

allspice	fennel	smoked fish, especially
anchovies	ginger	trout or whitefish
apples	horseradish	**sour cream**
bacon	**lemon**	tarragon
béchamel sauce	*mâche*	vinaigrette
brown sugar	mustard	**vinegar**, especially bal-
butter	nutmeg	samic, sherry and
cheese	onions	white wine
chives	oranges	walnuts
cloves	paprika	walnut oil
cream	**parsley**	watercress
crème fraîche	potatoes	
cucumber	prosciutto	*bake*
curry	salt	*boil*
dill	salt pork	*steam*
eggs, hard-cooked	shallots	

We were not the first to do a beet risotto, but I think the risotto we serve is exciting. We use organic beets from a farm, which were picked that morning. The color is the most intense fuschia, a vibrant purple-red. I used to hate beets, but I'm mad about beets right now. I love the richness and deepness of their flavor—it's like an explosion.—Lydia Shire

Salad of Pickled Beets, Oregon Blue Cheese, and Walnuts—Gary Danko

Beet Salad with Watercress and Horseradish Vinaigrette—Mark Peel

BERRIES (See also specific berries)   (Spring–Summer)

brown sugar	Framboise	sour cream
cream	maple syrup	yogurt

BLACKBERRIES (See also RASPBERRIES)   (Summer)

apples	lemon	peaches
cinnamon	maple syrup	raspberries
cream	milk	rose geranium
custard	muesli	strawberries
honey	oranges	sugar

BLUEBERRIES   (Spring–Summer)

apples
apricots
blue cheese
bourbon
brown sugar
cinnamon
Cognac
Cointreau
cream

currants
custard
ginger
Grand Marnier
honey
lavender
lemon
lime
maple syrup

peaches
pineapple
raspberries
sour cream
strawberries
sugar
thyme
yogurt

Blueberry Sorbet served with Lemon Snaps—Joyce Goldstein

Crispy Blueberry Fritters in Lemon Crust with Vanilla Bean Ice Cream
—Mark Miller

Blueberry Bourbon Pancakes—Jimmy Schmidt

Peach and Blueberry Cobbler—Lindsey Shere

BLUEFISH   (Spring)

bacon
basil
cabbage
garlic
lemon
lime

mustard
juniper berries
tomato
vinegar
wine

bake
broil
grill
sauté
smoke

BRAINS

bacon
bread crumbs
**butter, especially
    brown**
capers
cèpes
cheese, especially
    Gruyère
cherries
cream
eggs

garlic
hollandaise sauce
lemon
mushrooms
mustard
onions
paprika
parsley
spinach
sweetbreads
tomato sauce

vinegar
watercress
wine
Worcestershire sauce

bake
broil
sauté

BROCCOLI (Fall–Winter)

anchovies
bacon
bread crumbs
butter
cheese, especially
  Parmesan, Romano,
  or Swiss
cream
cumin

garlic
hollandaise sauce
lemon
Maltaise sauce
nuts, especially almonds
  and walnuts
olive oil
onions
orange

peppers, especially hot
pimiento
potatoes
vinaigrette
watercress

deep-fry
sauté
steam

BROCCOLI RABE

garlic
lemon

olive oil
red pepper flakes

Romano cheese

BRUSSELS SPROUTS (Fall–Winter)

almonds
anchovies
apples
bacon
bread crumbs
butter
carrots
cheese (e.g., Parmesan,
  Swiss, Taleggio)
chestnuts
cream
duck fat
eggs, hard-boiled
garlic

grapefruit
ham
hollandaise sauce
lemon
mushrooms
mustard
nutmeg
onions
pancetta
parsley
pepper, black
peppers, sweet
pignoli
rosemary

salt
thyme
veal gravy
vinegar
walnuts

bake
boil
braise
parboil
sauté
steam

BUCKWHEAT (KASHA)

asparagus
eggs

mushrooms
Parmesan cheese

pignoli
sour cream

BULGUR

lemon
mint

olive oil
onions

parsley

CABBAGE, COOKED
(Fall–Winter)

apples
bacon
béchamel sauce
beets
butter
caraway seeds
caviar
chestnuts
coconut
cream
garlic
ham
horseradish

leeks
lemon
juniper berries
Madeira
mustard
nutmeg
onions
paprika
parsley
pepper
poppy seeds
potatoes
salt

salt pork
sausages
sorrel
spinach
vinegar

bake
boil
braise
sauté
steam
stir-fry

CABBAGE, RAW
(Fall–Winter)

apples
carrots
celery root
chervil

chives
lime
nut oil
olive oil

peppers, green
vinegar, especially sherry and white wine

CABBAGE, RED
(Fall–Winter)

apples
bacon
bay leaves
brown sugar
cheese, especially goat
chestnuts
cinnamon
cloves

garlic
olive oil
onions
pepper
prosciutto
salt
thyme

vinegar, especially wine
walnuts
wine, especially red

blanch
braise

CALVES' BRAINS (See also BRAINS)

butter, especially brown
capers
chervil
chives
hollandaise sauce
lemon
onions

parsley
pepper
tarragon
thyme
tomato sauce
truffles, especially black
vinegar, especially white

watercress

fry
sauté
simmer

Calves' Brains with Crisp Fried Capers and Sherry Vinegar—Lydia Shire

Calves' Brains with Sautéed Baby Artichokes and Balsamic Vinegar
—Joachim Splichal

CALVES' HEAD

bay leaves	Madeira	vinaigrette
cloves	sherry	wine, white
lemon	tomato sauce	

CALVES' LIVER

apples	Madeira	**shallots**
bacon	Marsala	sherry
basil	**mushrooms**	sour cream
béarnaise sauce	**mustard**	tarragon
bread crumbs	**onions**	tomato
chervil	pancetta	**vinegar**, especially sherry
chives	**parsley**	**wine, white**
Cognac	pepper, black	
garlic	peppers, green	*braise*
grapes	port	*broil*
leeks	potatoes	*grill*
lemon	raisins	*sauté*
lime	sage	*stew*

Grilled Veal Liver with Onion Soubise and Crispy Shallots—Mark Peel

Walnut-Crusted Calf's Liver with Shallot and Red Onion—Lydia Shire

Sautéed Calf's Liver with Slab Bacon, Applejack Brandy and Green Onions
—Norman Van Aken

CAPON   (Fall–Winter)

apples	oranges	thyme
garlic	rosemary	truffles
mushrooms	tarragon	

Open Ravioli of Smoked Capon and Wild Mushrooms with Sweet Garlic-Infused Pan Broth—Charlie Palmer

Capon with Wild Mushrooms and Mint Béarnaise—Jeremiah Tower

(See Michael Romano's menu featuring capon on the next page.)

Michael Romano

UNION SQUARE CAFE
New York, New York

To my mind, this menu is kind of a snapshot of what we do best at Union Square Cafe — that is to say, it is a blending of classical Italian and French dishes, with a dash here and there of the new and the different thrown in. The risotto with *foie gras* is an example of this. The dishes are teamed up with excellent wines which work in great combination with the food. Beyond the descriptions, which sound good, is just good solid cooking, which makes the dishes work.

New Year's Eve
Saturday, December 31, 1994

Assorted New Year's Hors d'Oeuvres
House-Salmon with Chives, Osetra Caviar Canapé, Brandade Phyllo Purse
Billecart-Salmon Blanc de Blancs "Cuvée N.F." Vintage Champagne (Reims)
1983

• • •

Frisée Salad with Prawns, Fennel, and Clementines
Tokay d'Alsace, Grand Cru, "Brand," Albert Boxler (Alsace) 1988

• • •

Risotto with Foie Gras, Sauternes, and Cabbage
Château Clos J. Kanon (St. Emilion) 1990

• • •

Oxtail Tortellini and Winter Vegetables in Brodo
Château de Fonsalette, "Cuvée Syrah," Jacques Reynaud (Southern Rhône)
1986

• • •

Roast Capon en Demi-Deuil with Fresh Black Truffles,
Cardoon Gratin, and Leeks
Hermitage, "Le Meal," Bernard Faurie (Northern Rhône) 1989

• • •

Mocha Semifreddo with Toasted Hazelnut Dacquoise
Billecart-Salmon Brut Champagne "Cuvée Union Square Cafe" (Reims) NY

• • •

Chocolate Truffles and Coffee

CARDOONS (Summer–Winter)

anchovies
butter
chervil
cream
hollandaise sauce

lemon
olive oil
Parmesan cheese
parsley
truffles, white

vinaigrette
vinegar
fry
simmer
stew

CARROTS (Spring)

almonds
bacon
basil
beef
brandy
butter
cayenne
celery
cheeses (especially
   Cheddar, Parmesan,
   Provolone, Romano)
chervil
chives
cilantro
cinnamon
cloves
cream
cumin
dill
fennel
garlic
ginger

honey
lemon
Madeira
maple syrup
marjoram
Marsala
mayonnaise
mint
mushrooms
mustard
nutmeg
nuts, especially hazel-
   nuts and walnuts
olive oil
olives
onions
oranges
paprika
parsley
peas
pignoli

potatoes
raisins
rosemary
sage
shallots
stock
sugar
tarragon
thyme
tomatoes
turnips
vinegar, red wine
walnuts

bake
boil
fry
purée
raw
sauté
steam

Organic Carrot and Ginger Soup—Bradley Ogden

Orange-Glazed Carrots and Mangoes—Chris Schlesinger

Carrot and Cilantro Soup—Alice Waters

CATFISH

bacon
capers
ginger
ketchup
mustard

olive oil
olives
pecans
peppers, especially
   sweet

bake
broil
fry
sauté

CAULIFLOWER   (Fall)

aïoli
almonds
anchovies
bacon
béchamel sauce
bread crumbs
butter, especially
   brown
cheese, especially
   Cheddar, **Gruyère** or
   Parmesan
chervil
chives
cracker crumbs

cream
crème fraîche
curry
garlic
ham
hollandaise sauce
lemon
Mornay sauce
mousseline sauce
mushrooms
mussels
nutmeg
nuts
olive oil

parsley
pepper, especially hot
tomato sauce
walnuts

bake
boil
deep-fry
purée
raw
sauté
steam

CAVIAR   (Winter)

blini
bread, black
cream
lemon

parsley
potatoes
shallots
smoked salmon

sour cream
toast
vodka

Freshly Made Hot Potato Waffles with Ounce of Osetra Caviar—Lydia Shire

Osetra Caviar, Lemon-Marinated Potatoes, and Some Traditional Garnish
—Joachim Splichal

CELERY   (Summer)

almonds
béchamel sauce
blue cheese
bread crumbs
butter
celery seeds
cream

curry
dill
fennel
hollandaise sauce
lemon
nutmeg
parsley

walnuts

boil
braise
raw
steam

CELERY ROOT   (Fall–Winter)

bacon
bread crumbs
butter
caraway seeds
cheese, especially
  Parmesan and Swiss
cream
fennel
garlic
hollandaise sauce
lemon

mayonnaise
mustard
nutmeg
olive oil
onions
parsley
potatoes
squash, butternut
thyme
vinegar, especially
  white wine

walnuts

boil
braise
deep-fry
fry
purée
raw
sauté
steam

Savory Celery Root Flan and Vegetables à la Grecque, *Essence of Sweet Garlic and Kalamata Olives*—Charlie Palmer

Celery Root Gratin—Anne Rosenzweig

Celery Root with Mustard Mayonnaise—Alice Waters

CÈPES   (Fall)

bacon
bay leaves
béarnaise sauce
bread crumbs
butter
cheese, especially
  Gruyère or Parmesan
cream
eggs
fennel
fish
foie gras
garlic
lemon
lemon thyme

mustard
nutmeg
olive oil
olives
paprika
Parmesan cheese
parsley
pasta
pepper
potatoes
poultry fat
risotto
rosemary
saffron
shallots

sour cream
truffles, white
vermouth
vinegar, especially wine
walnuts
walnut oil
wine

bake
broil
fry
grill
raw
sauté

CHANTERELLES   (Summer–Fall)

béchamel sauce
butter
chervil
chicken
cream
crème fraîche
eggs

fish
game
garlic
herbs
leeks
lemon
offal

olive oil
onions
parsley
pepper, black
rabbit
shallots

(continued on facing page)

shellfish	veal	*sauté*
steak	vinaigrette	*stew*
tarragon		

CHARD   (Summer–Winter)

lemon	*braise*	*sauté*
peppers, especially hot	*parboil*	*steam*
saffron		

CHERRIES   (Summer)

almonds	goat cheese	plums
apricots	Grand Marnier	port
Armagnac	ice cream	sour cream
brandy	**Kirsch**	verbena
caramel	**lemon**	vanilla
chocolate	mint	vinegar, balsamic
Cognac	nectarines	zabaione
cream	nuts	
currants, red	peaches	*flambé*
custards	pepper, black	*raw*

Fresh Cherry-Vanilla Ice Cream—George Germon & Johanne Killeen

Cherry Compote with Lemon-Macaroon Cream—Lindsey Shere

Warm Preserved Cherry Clafoutis with Speckled Vanilla Anglaise—Lydia Shire

Brandied Cherries on Ice Cream—Nancy Silverton

French Sweet Cream served with Port-Soaked Sour Cherries—Jeremiah Tower

Hot Cherries with Honey Kirsch—Jean-Georges Vongerichten

CHESTNUTS   (Fall–Winter)

apples	cloves	prunes
brandy	cognac	raspberries
brown sugar	cream	rum
brussels sprouts	crème fraîche	stuffings
butter	fennel	sugar
cabbage	ginger	vinegar
carrots	lemon	
cayenne	Marsala	*bake*
celery	**mushrooms**	*boil*
Chartreuse	**onions**	*roast*
chocolate	orange	*steam*
cinnamon	parsley	*stew*

Hubert Keller

FLEUR DE LYS
San Francisco, California

For this menu for the Queen of Thailand's entourage, Hubert Keller received two requests: to serve chicken as the main course, and to serve something from Thailand. He wished to keep the menu simple and uncomplicated.

The response to the soup dish was so great that it was subsequently added to his restaurant menu at Fleurs de Lys. The chocolate *crème brûlée*, despite its popularity now, was then unusual. Keller decided upon that combination "because everybody likes chocolate—and bananas and chocolate are a great combination that really work well together!" This dessert is still on his restaurant menu.

In the Presence of
Her Royal Majesty the Queen of Thailand
Monday, May 24, 1993

Crab Strudel with Citrus and Basil Oil

• • •

Lobster and Coconut Milk Soup
Flavored with Lemongrass and Ginger

• • •

Roasted Striped Bass on Mashed Potato
Topped with Marinated Peppers and Olive Oil Essence

• • •

Free-Range Chicken Breast Rolled over Wild Mushrooms
Tomato Consommé and Truffle Oil

• • •

Bittersweet Chocolate Crème Brûlée
with Caramelized Bananas and
Homemade Vanilla Ice Cream

• • •

Assortment of Miniature Pastries

• • •

Coffee and Tea

CHICK PEAS   (Summer)

carrots
cilantro
coriander
couscous
cumin
garlic

lemon
lemon, preserved
mint
olive oil
onions
parsley

peppers, especially red
rosemary
spinach
tahini
tomatoes
yogurt

CHICKEN

achiote
almonds
apples
Armagnac
asparagus
bacon
barbecue sauce
basil
beer
béarnaise sauce
blood
brandy
bread crumbs
cabbage
Calvados
Champagne
cheese, especially Swiss
cherries
chervil
chestnuts
chives
cider
coconut
Cognac

coriander
corn
cranberries
cream
curry
dill
endive
escarole
fennel
five-spice powder
foie gras
Fontina cheese
garlic
ginger
go chi berries
grapes
herbs
honey
horseradish
lemon
lime
Madeira
mangoes
marjoram
mint
morels
mushrooms
mustard
mussels
nutmeg
olive oil
olives
onions
oranges
oregano
oysters
paprika
Parmesan cheese

parsley
peas
pecans
pepper
pineapples
plums
prunes
Riesling
rosemary
savory
sour cream
soy sauce
star anise
stuffings
sweetbreads
sweet potatoes
tarragon
teriyaki sauce
thyme
tomatoes
truffles
vinegar, especially red
    wine
walnuts
wine, especially white
yogurt

bake
braise
broil
fry
grill
marinate
roast
sauté

(continued on next page)

CHICKEN *(continued)*

With an ingredient as versatile as chicken, how do you decide which direction to take it in? "Start by thinking about what else is in season and available. That will, in part, determine whether you're going to put truffled mashed potatoes with it, or little baby marbled potatoes roasted with a little spring asparagus and poached spring garlic, or a morel mushroom sauce," says Bradley Ogden. "And what is the occasion—are you doing just a simple summer barbecue, or is it part of an elaborate five-course meal? If it's a summery buffet, you might serve it with a great shortcake for dessert. If it's more formal, you might serve it with the truffled potatoes and a salad, and finish with a light dessert. It really depends on what's around, and what you're trying to do."

Pollito a las Brasas: *Free-Range Baby Chicken, Border-Style (Half-Boned, Marinated in Garlic and Sweet Spices, and Grilled) served with* Frijoles Charros, *Charcoaled Green Onions, and Jicama Salad*—Rick Bayless

Stuffed Rigatoni with a Chicken-Fennel Mousse
—Susan Feniger & Mary Sue Milliken

Grilled Chicken Breast Braised with Fresh Tomatoes, Lemon, Onions and Herbs, served with Mashed Potatoes—George Germon & Johanne Killeen

Pollo al Ajillo—*Sautéed Chicken with Garlic, Prosciutto, Sherry, Olives, and Almonds, Served with Saffron Rice and Asparagus*—Joyce Goldstein

Oak-Roasted Chicken Breast with Pan Drippings, Basil Mashed Potatoes, and Fresh Bean Casserole—Mark Miller

Spit-Roasted Free-Range Chicken with Lemon, Herbs, Buttered Spinach, and Mashed Red Potatoes with Chives—Bradley Ogden

Garlic-Crusted Chicken with Slow-Roasted Artichoke, a Purée of Barlitto Beans, Tomato Oil, and Fresh Rosemary—Charlie Palmer

Roasted Baby Chicken with Sweet-Potato Purée, Escarole, and Garlic Confit
—Mark Peel

Spit-Roasted Herb and Lemon-Rubbed Chicken with Mashed Sweet Potatoes and Seared Kale—Chris Schlesinger

Chicken Roasted with Ginger, Green Olives, and Coriander Juice with Chickpea Fries—Jean-Georges Vongerichten

Lydia Shire says that there are certain things she knows her customers won't eat. "One of the best chicken dishes I've ever had was at the China Pearl in Chinatown in Boston—a boiled chicken, cooked medium, made with star anise and served with plum dipping sauces. To serve it, they cut right through the bone, and all the meat around the bone is pink. It's so moist, and so delicious. But it's sad that we couldn't do that dish here, because customers wouldn't eat slightly undercooked chicken."

(See also Hubert Keller's menu featuring chicken on page 106.)

CHICKEN LIVERS

bacon	Madeira	salt
brandy	mushrooms	sour cream
Cognac	onions	
cream	parsley	*sauté*
garlic	pepper	

Grilled Chicken Liver Crostini—George Germon & Johanne Killeen

Buttermilk-Fried Chicken Livers with Apple Raisin Chutney, Spinach, and Warm Bacon Dressing—Chris Schlesinger

Roasted Chicken Wings with Unorthodox Chopped Liver—Joachim Splichal

CHICORY   (Winter)

apples	figs	vinegar
bacon	ham	walnuts
cheese, especially	nuts	
Gruyère	pears	*grill*
crème fraîche	vinaigrette	

CHOCOLATE

almonds	lemon	pecans
bananas	liqueurs	pistachios
caramel	malt	raspberries
cherries	maple	rum
cinnamon	mint	tea, especially Earl Grey
citrus peel	mocha	vanilla
coffee	**nuts, especially hazel-**	verbena
coconut	**nuts**	violets
cream or milk	orange	walnuts
ginger	passion fruit	

Chocolate with a little tea flavor at the end of the taste is nice, as an accent. You just don't want to bite into something chocolate and get a whole mouthful of tea flavor—it's too strong.—François Payard

Mexican Chocolate Cream Pie with Bittersweet Chocolate, Almonds, and Cinnamon—Susan Feniger & Mary Sue Milliken

Fresh Mint Chocolate-Chip Ice Cream—George Germon & Johanne Killeen

Warm Chocolate Cake with Hazelnut Caramel and Honey-Spiced Bananas—Mark Miller

Chocolate Bread Pudding with Brandy Custard Sauce—Anne Rosenzweig

(continued on next page)

CHOCOLATE *(continued)*

A Little Hot Chocolate Cheesecake and Cool Espresso Cream—Lydia Shire

Sourdough Chocolate Cake with "Iced" Cream and Coffee Sauce
—Nancy Silverton

Caffeine Three Ways: Chocolate, Espresso Cake, and Toffee Coffee with Sambuca Sauce—Joachim Splichal

CHOCOLATE, WHITE

bananas	hazelnuts
berries	loganberries
blackberries	**oranges**
boysenberries	**raspberries**
cherries	rum
coconut	violets

Lime and Raspberry Tartlette served with White Chocolate Raspberry Swirl Ice Cream and Raspberry Sauce—Joyce Goldstein

Gratinade of Fresh Berries with White Chocolate Mousseline—Gray Kunz

WAM! White Chocolate Ice Cream, Passion Fruit, Raspberry Sauce, and Macadamia Nuts—Jimmy Schmidt

White Chocolate Ice Cream with Warm Berry Compote—Lindsey Shere

CLAMS (Spring–Summer)

bacon	onion	thyme
bread crumbs	paprika	**tomatoes**
butter	**parsley**	vinegar
chiles, especially red	pepper	**wine, white**
chives	Pernod	Worcestershire sauce
cream	potatoes	
curry	sake	*bake*
garlic	shallots	*broil*
ginger	sour cream	*fry*
horseradish	Tabasco sauce	*raw*
lemon	tarragon	*roast*
olive oil	tartar sauce	*steam*

Clam Roast with Mashed Potatoes and Very Spicy Sausage
—George Germon and Johanne Killeen

Spritz of Rice Wine Vinegar on Clams Hearth-Roasted over Pine Needles with Foaming Sauce of Pine Nut—Lydia Shire

COCONUTS  (Fall)

apricots
bananas
chocolate
custard
fruits, especially tropical (e.g., banana, lime, mango, passion fruit, pineapple)
nuts, especially tropical (e.g., Brazil, cashew, macadamia)
pineapples

Coconut Milk Tapioca Croustillant with Saffron Coulis and Pineapple Sherbet —Jean-Louis Palladin

Macadamia Nut and Coconut Tart—Lindsey Shere

Coconut Flan with Mango in Sauternes and Coconut Chips—Norman Van Aken

COD

aïoli
bay leaves
beans, black, fermented
black olives
butter
capers
caraway seeds
Champagne
chervil
coriander leaves
eggplant
garlic
ginger
hollandaise sauce
horseradish
juniper berries
leeks
lemon
milk
mushrooms
mustard
olive oil
olives
onions
parsley
pepper
potatoes
rosemary
sake
shallots
soy sauce
thyme
tomatoes
truffles
vinaigrette
vinegar, especially sherry
wine, white

boil
braise
broil
fry
pan-fry
poach
roast
sauté
steam

Sautéed Fresh Codfish with Vegetable Basquaise—Jean-Louis Palladin

Eggplant-Crusted Maine Cod with Bay Shrimp, Thyme-Roasted Vegetables, and Port-Wine Essence—Charlie Palmer

Pan-Fried Cod with Tomato-Mint Yogurt Sauce—Chris Schlesinger

Cured Atlantic Cod in Provençal Tomato, Garlic, and Basil Broth—Alice Waters

COFFEE

cinnamon	cream	lemon
Cognac	hazelnut	vanilla

Mocha Semi-Freddo Layered with Toasted Hazelnut Dacquoise
—Michael Romano

Espresso-Cognac Mousse—Lindsey Shere

Java Granita with Cinnamon Crème Fraîche—Lydia Shire

If you rub a little lemon around the lip of the cup, an espresso tastes better. The dash of lemon on your lip combined with the bitter flavor of the coffee bean gives a real excitement.—Dieter Schorner

CORN   (Summer)

bacon	**cream**	salt
basil	garlic	scallions
butter	lemon	sweet pepper
cayenne	lime	Worcestershire sauce
chanterelles	lovage	
cheese, especially Feta	marjoram	*boil*
or Parmesan	onions	*grill*
chiles	parsley	*roast*
chives	pepper, black	*sauté*
cilantro	peppers, green	*simmer*

CORNED BEEF   (Spring)

beets	**mustard**	*braise*
cabbage	nutmeg	*simmer*
carrots	onions	
garlic	parsley	
horseradish	**potatoes**	

CRABS

almonds	coconut	garlic
avocado	Cognac	ginger
bacon	coriander	grapefruit
butter	**corn**	hollandaise sauce
cabbage	cream	leeks
celery	*crème fraîche*	**lemon**
chiles	curry	lemongrass
chives	fennel seeds	*(continued on facing page)*

lettuce, Bibb
Louis dressing
Madeira
mangoes
mayonnaise
mornay sauce
mushrooms
mustard
nutmeg
onions
oranges

parsley
pepper, black
potatoes
rémoulade
rice
scallions
sherry
sour cream
tarragon
Thousand Island dress-
   ing

Tabasco sauce
tomatoes
truffles, black
vinaigrette
vinegar
wine, white
Worcestershire sauce

boil
poach

Peeky Toe Crabmeat Salad with Avocado and Citrus Vinaigrettes
—Terrance Brennan

Portuguese Crab Cake, Avocado, Papaya, Watercress, and Mint with Citrus-Hot-Pepper Vinaigrette—Joyce Goldstein

Timbale of Virginia Lump Crabmeat and Spinach Mousse—Patrick O'Connell

Mustard-Crisped Crab Cakes on an Acorn Squash Ratatouille
—Anne Rosenzweig

Crab Ravioli with Black Truffles—Jeremiah Tower

Crab Salad with Mango, Cumin Crisps, and Grainy Mustard
—Jean-Georges Vongerichten

Dungeness Crab Cake with Meyer Lemon and Pepper Sauce—Alice Waters

CRABS, SOFT-SHELL   (Spring–Summer)

almonds
basil
beans, black
butter
capers
carrots
cayenne
chives
dill
garlic
ginger

honey
lemon
lemongrass
lime
mayonnaise
pancetta
parsley
pepper
Pernod
pignoli
soy sauce

spinach
tartar sauce
tomatoes
vinaigrette
vinegar

broil
deep-fry
grill
sauté

Soft-Shell Crab with Pancetta Butter—Jean-Louis Palladin

Sizzled Soft-Shell Crabs with Spicy Carrot Sauce—Michael Romano

Pan-Cooked Soft-Shell Crabs with Papaya and Lime—Norman Van Aken

CRANBERRIES (Fall)

apples
cinnamon
cloves

oranges
pears

sugar
walnuts

CRAYFISH (Spring)

avocados
basil
bay leaves
brandy
bread crumbs
butter
carrots
cayenne
cheese, especially
   Gruyère and
   Parmesan
Cognac
coriander

cream or milk
dill
garlic
hollandaise sauce
leeks
lemon
mayonnaise
nutmeg
onions
parsley
saffron
shallots
sherry

sorrel
tarragon
thyme
tomatoes
truffles
vinegar
wine, white

boil
grill
sauté
stew

Chilled Crayfish and Cranberry Bean Soup with Ratatouille and Opal Basil
—Daniel Boulud

Warm Salad of Crayfish with Cucumbers and Dill—Jeremiah Tower

CUCUMBERS (Spring–Summer)

anchovies
basil
butter
celery seeds
chervil
chiles
chives
cilantro
cream
cream cheese
dill
fennel
Feta cheese

garlic
ginger
horseradish
lemon
lime
mangoes
mayonnaise
mint
mushrooms
nutmeg
olive oil
onions, especially red
parsley

pepper
salt
sour cream
strawberries
tomato sauce
tomatoes
vinegar, especially
   white wine
yogurt

raw
simmer

CURRANTS (Summer)

almonds	cream	prunes
cherries	pears	raspberries

Red currants are quite often used to reinforce the flavor of other fruit, as if they were a kind of lemon.—Jane Grigson

CUSTARDS

almonds	**coffee**	passion fruit
bananas	Cognac	pineapple
berries	Cointreau	rice
caramel	ginger	rum
cherry	lemon	strawberries
chocolate	maple	vanilla
cinnamon	Marsala	
coconut	oranges	

Chocolate Brioche Custard Bread Pudding with Chocolate Sabayon —Bradley Ogden

Chilled Pineapple-Moscato Zabaglione—Michael Romano

Banana Crème Brûlée—Lindsey Shere

Caramel Rice Flan—Nancy Silverton

Truffle Custard with Asparagus and Lobster Sauce—Jeremiah Tower

Smoked Salmon Custard with Fennel Juice—Jean-Georges Vongerichten

DANDELION GREENS (Spring)

bacon	lemon	onions
cheese	mustard	vinegar, especially red
garlic	olive oil	wine

DATES (Fall)

almonds	cinnamon	pecans
apricots	**cream**	rum
bacon	**cream cheese**	vanilla
brandy	ginger	walnuts
caramel	**nuts**	
chocolate	orange	

DUCK (Fall)

anchovies
apples
apricots
Armagnac
artichokes
basil
blackberries
blood oranges
bourbon
brandy
cabbage
cabbage, red
Calvados
cherries, fresh or dried
   tart
chiles
chocolate, bittersweet
cider
cloves
Cognac
Cointreau
coriander leaves
corn
cranberries

currants, black
curry
duck livers
figs
garlic
gin
ginger
Grand Marnier
hoisin sauce
honey
juniper berries
kumquats
lemon
lentils
mangoes
mint
molasses
mushrooms
mustard
nutmeg
olive oil
olives
onions
oranges, bitter
paprika
parsley
peaches
pears
peas
pepper, black, green
  and pink
peppers, hot and red
pineapple

pistachios
plums
plum sauce, Chinese
pomegranate
port
prunes
quinces
rhubarb
rice
rosemary
sage
sauerkraut
scallions
shallots
sherry
soy sauce
spinach
star anise
stuffing
tarragon
thyme
tomatoes
turnips
vinegar
walnuts
wines, red (especially
  Burgundy and pinot
  noir) and white

braise
roast
spit-roast

Wild Mushroom and Duck Risotto with Butternut Squash and White Truffle Essence—Terrance Brennan

Duck-Leg Confit with Pear Ginger Chutney—Gary Danko

Crispy Duck with Star Anise Sauce—Susanna Foo

Roasted Colvert Duckling with Glazed Chestnuts and Cranberries—Gray Kunz

Molasses-Tabasco Grilled Duck Steak with Braised Greens and Cornbread—Mark Miller

Grilled Duck Escalope *with Preserved Figs, Crisp Leg "Beignet," and Ginger-Citrus Essence Sauce*—Charlie Palmer

(continued on facing page)

Chinese Style Duck with Blood-Orange Sauce and Shiitake Mushroom Salad
—Mark Peel

Duck Rubbed, then Roasted, with Skin of Tangerine and Clove—Lydia Shire

Salad of Duck Breast with Bitter Greens, Chestnuts, Grain Mustard, and Pomegranate Seeds—Joachim Splichal

Duck Breast Roasted with Carmelized Pear, Pommery Mustard Sauce, and Red Cabbage—Jean-Georges Vongerichten

Duck Leg Confit with Green Lentils, Braised Endives, Roasted Vegetables, and Wild Mushrooms—Alice Waters

EELS   (Fall)

aïoli
anchovies
bacon
bay leaves
brandy
crayfish
cream
dill
eel blood
garlic
leeks

lemon
mushrooms
nutmeg
olive oil
onions
parsley
pepper
prunes
raisins
shallots
soy sauce

tomato sauce
vinegar, especially bal-
    samic
wine

broil
grill
poach
sautee
stew

EGGPLANT   (Summer)

aïoli
anchovies
bacon
basil
béchamel sauce
bread crumbs
capers
cheese, especially goat,
    Gruyère, Mozzarella,
    Parmesan, and
    Ricotta
chervil
cream
cumin
garlic
ham
lamb
lemon

mint
mushrooms
olive oil
olives
onions
oregano
paprika
parsley
**peppers, especially
    green**
pesto
pignoli
rice
rosemary
salt
shallots
shrimp
soy

tarragon
thyme
tomatoes
vinegar, especially bal-
    samic
walnuts
yogurt
zucchini

bake
braise
broil
fry
grill
roast
sauté
stew

(continued on next page)

EGGPLANT *(continued)*

Soy-Braised Chinese Eggplant with Zucchini and Mushrooms—Susanna Foo

Grilled Eggplant with Shallot and Olive Oil—Mark Miller

EGGS

anchovies
asparagus
bacon
bread
butter
capers

caviar
cheese
chicken livers
chives
crab
cream
croutons
fines herbes
ham
herbs
hollandaise sauce
morels
mushrooms
onions
Parmesan cheese

parsley
pepper
peppers, green
potatoes
ratatouille
salt
scallions
shallots
shrimp
smoked salmon
sorrel
spinach
tomato
truffles
watercress

ENDIVE   (Winter)

apples
bacon
beans, white
beets
blue cheese
bread crumbs
butter
cheese, especially
  Gruyère or Parmesan
cream
figs

ham
kumquats
lemon
Mornay sauce
mushrooms
orange
pears
Roquefort cheese
scallops
smoked fish, especially
  salmon or trout

sugar
tangerines
thyme
vinaigrette
walnuts
watercress

braise
raw
sauté
stew

Our Salad of Endive and Watercress with Walnuts, Bacon, Pears and Iowa Blue Cheese—Patrick O'Connell

Vivien's Endive Sauté with Swiss, Apple and Cress—Lydia Shire

Endive, Watercress, and Blue Cheese with Hot Apple Fritters—Jasper White

ESCAROLE   (Winter)

apples
bacon
capers
cheese, especially
  Fontina, Mozzarella,
  and Roquefort
chiles
currants
eggs
garlic
olive oil
olives
onions
vinegar
walnuts

braise
raw
sauté

FENNEL   (Fall)

butter
celery root
cheese, especially goat,
  Gruyère, and
  Parmesan
chestnuts
coriander
cream
fruit
garlic
hearts of palm
lemon
mushrooms
olive oil
olives
onions
oranges
pancetta
Parmesan cheese
peppers
Pernod
potatoes
sherry
thyme
tomatoes
truffles
vinaigrette

braise
raw
sauté

Braised Fennel with Prosciutto and Parmesan—Norman Van Aken

Shaved Fennel and Parmesan with Summer Truffles—Alice Waters

FIDDLEHEAD FERNS   (Spring)

bacon
butter
hollandaise sauce
leeks
lemon
nutmeg
olive oil
onions
shallots
vinaigrette

deep-fry
steam

FIGS   (Summer–Fall)

almonds
anise
brown sugar
caramel
cheese, especially blue
  and goat
chocolate
cinnamon
cinnamon basil
citrus peel, candied
coconut cream
Cointreau
cornmeal
cream
cream cheese
crème anglaise
crème fraîche
Curaçao
ginger
honey
lavender
lemon
Marsala

(continued on next page)

FIGS (continued)

mint
molasses
nuts (except peanuts)
orange
Parma ham
peaches
pears
pepper, black
port wine

praline
prosciutto
quince
raspberries
rosemary
sherry
sour cream
strawberries

thyme
vanilla
walnuts
wine, red

poach
raw
roast

Chilled Spiced Red Wine-Fig Soup—Michael Romano

Warm Figs with Gorgonzola and Walnuts on Greens—Anne Rosenzweig

Fresh Figs with Beaumes-de-Venise Ice Cream and Peach Caramel Sauce—Lindsey Shere

Walnut Crêpe with Honey Ice Cream and Roasted Figs—Lindsey Shere

Crisp Galette of Roasted Figs and Honeyed Devonshire Cream—Lydia Shire

Beaujolais Sorbet with Marinated Figs in Phyllo Pastry—Jeremiah Tower

FISH (See also specific fish)

almonds
anchovies
basil
butter
Champagne
cider
cilantro
coriander seeds
cream
cucumber
curry
fennel
Florentine sauce

gin
guava
horseradish
kiwi fruit
leeks
lemon
lime
mace
marjoram
mint
Mornay sauce
mushrooms
mustard

nutmeg
oranges
oysters
rosemary
saffron
shellfish
tarragon
thyme
tomatoes
vermouth
vodka
wine, especially white

I still use the recipe for fish mousse I learned at L'Auberge de l'Ill. It's very simple: 2 pounds of fish, 6 eggs, a quart of cream. But many chefs have their own recipe, and like to say things like, "The secret is a half egg yolk" or "a half egg white" or some other variation on the basic recipe. If there's a secret, it's in how the ingredients are treated and combined. For example, one technique emphasizes the proper chilling of the cream so that it's the same temperature as the fish.—Hubert Keller

FISH, SMOKED

avocados	cucumbers	lemon
capers	eggs, hard-boiled	onions
cream cheese	horseradish	

FLOUNDER

butter	mustard	*grill*
Cognac		*poach*
lemon	*braise*	*sauté*
mushrooms	*broil*	

Flounder is really, really mild. I think you've got to be very careful when you cook flounder. You've really got to keep it very, very simple. You can really mask it quickly.—Jasper White

FOIE GRAS   (Fall)

allspice	garlic	pomegranates
apples	grains	port wine
artichoke hearts	**grapes**	quinces
blood oranges	greens	raisins
brandy	lemon	salt
cabbage	lobster	shallots
celery root	Madeira	star anise
cèpes	mushrooms	tarragon
cherries	nutmeg	**truffles**
cinnamon	nuts	turnips
cloves	onions	vinegar, especially sherry
Cognac	peaches	walnuts
currants	pepper, black	wine, especially
custard	pistachios	Sauternes
daikon	polenta	

The fattiness of foie gras is complemented by fruits which add a tart or acidic component. I've served it with toasted panettone, which has candied rind in it.—Lydia Shire

Sautéed Foie Gras Au Poivre with Organic Grain Salad, Carrot and Pomegranate Vinaigrette—Terrance Brennan

Seared Foie Gras with Fuji Apples, Carmelized Onions, Verjus Sauce—Gary Danko

New York State Foie Gras in Fresh Herb and Black Pepper Gelée served with Toasted Brioche—Hubert Keller

(continued on page 124)

Sautéed Foie Gras with Quince Confits

Gray Kunz
LESPINASSE
New York, New York

Very often when I create a dish it is spurred by the best ingredients I can find. I came up with this dish one day based on the seasonal ingredients I had at hand, and it was a dish that worked instantly. I had the picture so clearly in my mind of how the lentil salad would work with the quince, and how the *foie gras* would blend with the Sauternes and the lemon juice and the cooking liquid of the quince. I was convinced that it would work even before I tried it—and it did. In fact, it was so good the first time I tried it that it was just a matter of making a few minute adjustments. The richness of the *foie gras* needed a tart balance, and although quince is not typically used this way, it provided the right balance. There are three or four very exciting flavors in your mouth at once—then it goes into richness and then a little sour and then you have the wine also picking it up. All of that comes together, making a very interesting dish, and then the lentil salad makes it a little homey and more robust and adds a nice softness.

1/2 quince

2 ounces Sauternes

1/2 ounce honey

1/2 ounce lemon juice

sugar to taste

3 ounces *foie gras*

1/2 ounce butter (*beurre noisette*)

1/4 ounce rice vinegar

1/4 ounce veal stock

2 teaspoons Calvados

1 ounce green lentils

1/2 ounce leeks, blanched

beet greens

1/4 ounce walnuts, roasted in butter

1/4 ounce brioche, cut in lozenges and roasted in butter

2 teaspoons walnut oil

1/4 ounce chives

1. Cut the quince in round-shaped form; cook the slices in Sauternes, honey, and lemon juice. When ready, take the quince out, reduce the liquid, and put the quince back in.
2. Cook the trimmings of quince with water, sugar, and lemon juice for 1 hour. Pass through a chinois; add some Sauternes, honey, and lemon juice. Adjust to taste.
3. Sauté the *foie gras* in *beurre noisette*, deglaze with vinegar, add some veal stock, and finish with a splash of Calvados and quince stock.

Vegetables

1. Make a lentil salad with a purée of lentils; season with vinegar, olive oil, salt, and pepper.
2. Marinate the blanched leeks with vinegar, olive oil, salt, and pepper.
3. Place the beet greens upside down with the red stems facing up, forming a circle. Place the *foie gras* in this basket.

Topping

Roasted walnuts with croutons of brioche, walnut oil drizzled along the base of the plate, topped with vinegar and chives.

FOIE GRAS *(continued)*

Sautéed New York State Foie Gras *on Roasted Shallots with Truffle-Potato Coulis and Smoked Duck*—Hubert Keller

Hot Seared Foie Gras *"Nacho" with Fresh Fig Glaze, Grilled Cabbage Salad, and Fresh Corn Tamale*—Mark Miller

A Slab of Goose Foie Gras *with Poached Pears, Virginia Riesling Jelly, and Pear Butter Toasts*—Patrick O'Connell

Seared Foie Gras *Escalope with Roasted Plums, Wild Mushroom Crêpe and Baby Arugula*—Charlie Palmer

Seared Foie Gras *Sandwich with Pear-Cranberry Chutney*—Anne Rosenzweig

Cider-Spiked Foie Gras *with Crisped Pork Jowls in Warm Cabbage Salad*—Lydia Shire

Duck Liver with Granny Smith Apples Three Ways: Frozen, Raw, and Caramelized—Joachim Splichal

Salad of Figs, Walnuts, and Garden Lettuces with Foie Gras *and Chanterelles*—Alice Waters

(See also Gray Kunz's recipe for Sautéed Foie Gras *with Quince Confits on pages 122–123.)*

FROGS' LEGS   (Spring–Summer)

basil	**garlic**	truffles
brandy	**lemon**	vinegar
bread crumbs	lime	wine, white
butter	**mushrooms**	
Champagne	**onions**	*braise*
chiles	paprika	*deep-fry*
chives	**parsley**	*fry*
crayfish	pepper	**sauté**
cream	risotto	*simmer*
crème fraîche	shallots	
curry	tarragon	
fennel	**tomatoes**	

GAME

cherries	grapes	squash
chocolate, bittersweet	**Madeira**	tomatoes
currants	mushrooms	

GOOSE

apples
barley
cabbage
cèpes
chestnuts
garlic
ginger
hollandaise sauce
honey

horseradish
lemon
mustard
onions
oranges
pepper
plums
potatoes
prunes

rice
sauerkraut
soy sauce
stuffing
turnips
wild rice

roast

GRAPEFRUIT (Winter)

bananas
brussels sprouts
Campari
cashews
Champagne
cheese, soft
chicory
cabbage, napa
citrus fruits, other
Cointreau

coriander
Curaçao
fish
gin
Grand Marnier
honey
melon
mint
offal
orange

pineapple
pomegranate
raspberries
rosemary
rum
shellfish
sherry
strawberries
sugar, especially brown
vodka

Citrus Compote with Ruby Red Grapefruit Granite—Bradley Ogden

Grapefruit and Pomegranate Tart—Jimmy Schmidt

Pink Grapefruit and Champagne Sherbet—Lindsey Shere

Grapefruit-Campari Granite—Jean-Georges Vongerichten

GRAPES (Summer–Fall)

brandy
brown sugar
cheese, especially soft
    white (e.g., Brie)

lemon
melon
mint
raspberries

sour cream
strawberries
walnuts
wine

GREENS

bacon
butter
cream
garlic
ham
lemon

mint
mushrooms
mustard
onions
pancetta
pepper, black

salt pork
sausage
soy
vinegar
walnuts

GROUPER   (Spring)

garlic	spinach	*grill*
honey	wine, white	*poach*
lemon		*sauté*
mustard	*braise*	*steam*

GUAVAS

bananas	honey	**pineapple**
cinnamon	lemon	sugar
cloves	lime	**vanilla**
cream	mangoes	wine, white
cream cheese	nutmeg	
fish	papayas	*bake*
ginger	pears	*purée*

Guava, by itself, is a flat flavor. But if you combine guava and a white wine like Gewürtztraminer, the whole flavor is completely different. I found that out because once I was drinking a glass of Gewurtztraminer and there was some guava purée on the same table, and I decided to make a spritzer out of it—and it tasted so good!—Dieter Schorner

GUINEA HENS

apples	Madeira	**wine**
bacon	mushrooms	
beans, white	**olives, black**	*bake*
brussels sprouts	onions	*braise*
cabbage	thyme	*roast*
Champagne	tomatoes	*sauté*
lemon	watercress	

Roast Guinea Hen and Pheasant Sausage served with Apples and Brussels Sprouts—Gray Kunz

Grilled Guinea Fowl with Morel and Bacon Risotto—Alice Waters

HADDOCK

bananas
butter
capers
celery seeds
crab
curry
dill
fennel
lemon

Mornay sauce
mushrooms
mustard
nutmeg
parsley
saffron
shrimp
tomatoes
Worcestershire sauce

bake
boil
broil
fry
poach
sauté
smoke

HALIBUT   (Spring–Summer)

anchovies
bacon
basil
butter
cabbage
chives
cucumbers
fennel
garlic
horseradish
leeks
lemon
lime

mangoes
mushrooms
mustard seeds
onions
parsley
potatoes
rosemary
saffron
scallions
shallots
shrimp
tarragon

thyme
tomatoes
vinegar
wine, white
zucchini

braise
grill
poach
roast
sauté
steam

Halibut with Scallion Sauce—Jasper White

Halibut Braised in White Wine with Shallots and Wild Mushrooms
—Jasper White

HAM

apples
bananas
barbecue sauce
basil
bay leaves
bourbon
bread crumbs
brown sugar
Champagne
cheese, especially
    Gruyère
cherries
cider

cloves
cola
cranberries
cream
Dijonnaise sauce
figs
garlic
honey
horseradish
juniper berries
lemon
Madeira
mushrooms

mustard
onions
oranges
oregano
paprika
parsley
peaches
pineapple
port
raisins
rosemary
sherry

(continued on next page)

HAM (continued)

sour cream	truffles	*bake*
sweet potatoes	vermouth	*boil*
thyme	**wine**, red or **white**	*fry*
tomatoes		*grill*

Attic-Aged Country Ham Steak with Scrambled Eggs, Garlic Cheese Grits, Wilted Greens—Gary Danko

Country-Cured Ham with Grilled Pancetta-Wrapped Figs and Watercress Salad—Bradley Ogden

HAMBURGER

cheese, especially Cheddar	ketchup	onions
chili sauce	Maggi seasoning	shallots
garlic	mushrooms	tomato sauce
	mustard	Worcestershire sauce

HARE (See also RABBIT)   (Fall)

bay leaves	lavender	**thyme**
blood	mushrooms	tomatoes
Burgundy	mustard	vinegar, especially red
chocolate	onions	wine
cream	oranges	walnuts
cumin	parsley	**wine, especially red**
currants, red	pignoli	
garlic	**port**	*roast*
juniper berries		

(See also Terrance Brennan's menu featuring hare on the next page.)

HEARTS OF PALM

bacon	shellfish	vinaigrette
lime		

Terrance Brennan

PICHOLINE
New York, New York

There is a group of Filipino foodies that visits some of the better restaurants around Manhattan and enjoys tasting menus. I came up with this menu for them one afternoon in the winter of 1995, incorporating a couple of the dishes I was running as specials at the restaurant, as well as a game dish. This is a group of very adventurous eaters, so I enjoyed serving them dishes that are usually too "out there" to include on the restaurant's regular menu. The hare with chocolate sauce was a perfect dish for this group—but would probably never sell to the average customer!

Menu for the Ambassador to the Philippines

Amuse-Gueule
Fresh Sardines and Caponata

• • •

*Fricasee of Pemmaquid Oysters
with Leeks, Salsify, Fingerling Potatoes, and Osetra Caviar*

• • •

*Sautéed Foie Gras au Poivre
Organic Grain Salad and Pomegranate Vinaigrette*

• • •

*Roasted Line-Caught Sea Bass
with Savoy Cabbage, Fresh Porcini, and Lobster Bordelaise*

• • •

*Main Diver Sea Scallops
Larded with Black Truffles, Artichokes Barigoule, and Truffled Poultry Broth*

• • •

*Wild Scottish Hare
with Gratin of Acorn Squash and Prune with Bitter Chocolate Sauce*

• • •

Selection of Artisan Cheeses

• • •

Trio of Blood-Orange Desserts

• • •

Petits Fours and Housemade Chocolates

HERRING

apples	oatmeal	sour cream
bacon	olive oil	**vinegar**
chives	onions	wine, white
cream	parsley	
hollandaise sauce	potatoes	*bake*
lemon	shallots	*grill*
mustard		

HONEYDEW (See also MELON)   (Summer–Fall)

ginger	lemon	lime

ICES   (Summer)

apricots	grapefruit	passion fruit
bananas	grapes	peaches
Champagne	kiwi fruit	persimmons
cherries	lemons	pineapples
cider	limes	raspberries
coffee	mangoes	strawberries
cranberry	melons	tangerines
currants, black	mint	wine
Grand Marnier	oranges	

ICE CREAM   (Summer)

	buttermilk	oranges
	Camembert	passion fruit
	caramel	peaches
	cherries	persimmons
	chocolate	pistachios
	coffee	praline
	cream, clotted	raspberries
	ginger	rum
	honey	strawberries
apples	maple syrup	vanilla
apricots	mangoes	walnuts
bananas	nuts	

JERUSALEM ARTICHOKES　　　　　　　　(Winter–Spring)

béchamel sauce	hollandaise sauce	*bake*
butter	lemon	*boil*
cream	Mornay sauce	*fry*
garlic	Parmesan cheese	*purée*
ginger	parsley	*steam*
hazelnut	scallions	

JÍCAMA　　　　　　　　　　　　　　　　　(Winter–Spring)

cayenne	**lime**	*pan-fry*
chiles	mangoes	*raw*
cilantro	oranges	
citrus, especially lime	**salt**	
cucumbers	vinaigrette	

Ensalada de Jícama: *Jícama Salad with Cucumber, Pineapple and Tangy Orange Dressing*—Rick Bayless

Watercress and Jícama with Lime & Olive Oil
—Susan Feniger & Mary Sue Milliken

JOHN DORY

basil	lemon	thyme
bay leaves	lemon thyme	**tomatoes**
butter	mushrooms	wine, especially white
caviar	parsley	
chives	peppers, red and yellow	*poach*
cream	sage	*sauté*
garlic	shallots	*steam*

KALE　　　　　　　　　　　　　　　　　　　(Winter)

bacon	garlic	onions
cheese	lemon	potatoes
cream	olive oil	

KIDNEYS

brandy	**Madeira**	shallots
butter	Marsala	sherry
cayenne	morels	sour cream
cèpes	**mushrooms**	vermouth
Cognac	**mustard**	**watercress**
cream	nutmeg	**wine, red or white**
curry	onions	
gin	pancetta	*broil*
horseradish	**parsley**	*fry*
juniper berries	rice	*sauté*
lemon	salt	

KIWI FRUIT (Winter)

apples	**lime**	proscuitto
bananas	nuts, especially cashews,	strawberries
cucumbers	hazelnuts, and	tamarillos
honey	macadamias	
Kirsch	oranges	*poach*
lemon	passion fruit	*raw*

Easter Basket of Sorbets: Kiwi, Passion Fruit, Blood Orange and Meyer Lemon-Banana, served with Spun Sugar and Cookies—Joyce Goldstein

Cold Kiwi Soup—Jean-Georges Vongerichten

KOHLRABI (Winter)

béchamel sauce	lemon	*bake*
butter	nutmeg	*boil*
cream	parsley	*steam*
hollandaise sauce		

KUMQUATS (Fall–Winter)

apples, green	gin	vanilla
aquavit	pineapples	vodka
crème anglaise	rum	

LAMB   (Spring)

almonds
anchovies
aniseed
apples
apricots
artichoke hearts
bacon
basil
bay leaves
beans, especially flageo-
    lets, green or white
blueberries
bread crumbs
capers
cardamom
cayenne
cheese, especiall Feta
    and Parmesan
cherries, dried sour
chestnut purée
chiles
chives
cilantro
cinnamon
cloves

couscous
crab
cream
cumin
currants
curry
daikon
dill
eggplant
endive
fennel
foie gras
garlic
ginger
grapefruit
gremolata
hazelnuts, toasted
honey
juniper berries
lemon
Madeira
mint
morels
mushrooms
mustard
mustard seeds
olive oil
olives
onions
oranges
oregano
parsley
pecans
pepper, black

pignoli
pimientos
pineapple
plums
pomegranates
prunes
red peppers
rhubarb
rice
rosemary
rum
sage
soy
star anise
tamarind
tarragon
thyme
tomatoes
truffles, especially black
veal kidneys
vinaigrette
vinegar, especially red
    wine
walnuts
wine, especially red
yogurt
zucchini

bake
braise
broil
grill
roast

American lamb is the best in the world. New Zealand or Australian lamb has a much gamier flavor. Nothing can touch real Colorado lamb. And I think you need strong flavors to bring out the best in lamb.—Lydia Shire

Roasted Rack of Lamb Pagnol with an Herbed Pine-Nut Crust and Provençal Vegetable Fricassee—Daniel Boulud

Moroccan Spiced Loin of Lamb with Vegetable Couscous, Mint, and Yogurt —Terrance Brennan

Truffled Rack of Lamb with Napoleon of Leeks and Potato—Gary Danko

(continued on next page)

LAMB *(continued)*

Carpaccio of Baby Lamb on Arugula with Tabouli and Rosemary-Mustard Sauce—Patrick O'Connell

Boneless Rack of Lamb in a Pecan Crust with Shoestring Sweet Potatoes—Patrick O'Connell

Grilled Lamb with Brazilian Relish of Tomatoes, Peanuts, and Coconut Milk—Chris Schlesinger

Smoked Lamb Sirloin with Pearl Couscous, Zucchini, and Curry Sauce—Jeremiah Tower

Lamb Rack Dusted with Seven Spices, Haricots Verts, *and Cucumber-Mint Relish*—Jean-Georges Vongerichten

A lot of people have the tendency to crank their oven up to 500 degrees and blast the living bejeezus out of their meat. Look at Art Culinaire—*how many of those dishes with lamb have got a raw center like that? That is an improperly cooked piece of meat, to me. Although the layer that's cooked is going to be tender, the rare part is just raw, and it's like eating lamb carpaccio. The aging process starts to break down the connective tissues. Aging has to be done on the bone with the fat cap on. So if you start with a tender cut of meat, and then if you cook at a more moderate temperature, pull it out and let your meat rest so that the juices distribute, then you have a perfectly cooked lamb all the way through, and it's beautifully tender. In meat, if you don't get it to a certain temperature and the connective tissues don't break down, you're basically chewing on sinewy connective tissue that is just gross and raw in your mouth.*—Gary Danko

(See also Patrick O'Connell's lamb recipe on pages 135–137.)

LAMB CHOPS (See also LAMB)   (Spring)

aïoli	**garlic**	**tarragon**
anchovies	ginger	tomatoes
baby artichokes	mushrooms	vinegar, balsamic
basil	mustard	yogurt
bay leaves	onions	
brandy	oregano	*braise*
caraway	parsley	*broil*
caul fat	pepper	*grill*
celery root	pignoli	*sauté*
cèpes	pomegranates	
curry	**shallots**	

Sautéed Lamb Chop and an Eggplant Tart in a Light Curry-Carrot Juice—Gray Kunz

Oak Oven-Roasted Lamb Chop Salad with Roasted Peppers, Onions, and Goat Cheese Vinaigrette—Bradley Ogden

Lamb Chops in Pomegranate Marinade—Mark Peel & Nancy Silverton

Boneless Rack of Lamb in a Pecan Crust with Barbecue Sauce and Shoestring Sweet Potatoes

Patrick O'Connell

THE INN AT LITTLE WASHINGTON
Washington, Virginia

You can't exactly serve a pulled pork barbecue for ninety-eight dollars, much as we might love to. So, you have to do the next best thing. I love barbecue and cole slaw, and I think people—especially those coming in from New York or California—crave to have some of the regional flavors come through. Rack of lamb is pretty ubiquitous, and this preparation was an attempt to bring it into the scope of the South and Virginia and to create a sense of place with it. Through the years, this has been one of our most popular versions of rack of lamb. The racks are brushed with barbecue sauce, grilled, boned, rolled in more sauce, and then rolled in crushed pecans. The meat is then sliced into medallions and served with crispy shoestring sweet potatoes and sautéed fresh green beans.

SERVES 6

Lamb

3 racks of lamb, about 1 1/2 pounds each, with 8 rib bones

salt and freshly ground pepper to taste

1/2 cup coarsely chopped pecans, toasted

Barbecue Sauce

1 cup ketchup

1 medium-size onion, quartered

1/2 cup white wine vinegar

1/4 cup Worcestershire sauce

2 teaspoons dry mustard

1 teaspoon Tabasco

1/2 cup firmly packed brown sugar

(continued on next page)

(continued from preceding page) ### Red Wine Sauce

1 tablespoon vegetable oil

1/3 cup chopped white mushrooms

1 carrot, peeled and coarsely chopped

1/2 onion, coarsely chopped

1 shallot, coarsely chopped

1/4 cup all-purpose flour

1 clove garlic, minced

2 tablespoons chopped fresh parsley

2 teaspoons fresh rosemary

2 teaspoons fresh tarragon

2 bay leaves

2 quarts chicken stock or water

2 cups red wine, such as Cabernet Sauvignon

2 tablespoons tomato paste

1 tomato, peeled, seeded and chopped

salt and freshly ground pepper to taste

sautéed fresh green beans

To make barbecue sauce

In the bowl of a food processor fitted with a steel blade, purée the ketchup, onion, vinegar, Worcestershire sauce, mustard, Tabasco, and brown sugar. Set aside. (Note: This sauce may be made several days in advance and kept refrigerated.)

To make the red wine sauce

1. In a 6-quart heavy-bottomed stock-pot, heat the oil over medium-high heat. Add the mushrooms, carrot, onion, and shallot and cook until the vegetables are a deep golden brown.

2. Add the flour and cook for 5 to 6 minutes, stirring to prevent sticking.

3. Add the garlic, parsley, rosemary, tarragon, bay leaves, stock or water, red wine, tomato paste, tomato, and salt and pepper. Simmer for 1 1/2 hours, stirring occasionally, until reduced by half. Adjust the seasoning and strain.

4. For each cup of strained wine sauce, add 2 tablespoons of the barbecue sauce. This sauce may be made several days in advance and kept refrigerated.

To cook lamb

1. Preheat the oven to 400°.
2. Season the lamb with salt and pepper and brush each side with the basic barbecue sauce.
3. Grill or broil the lamb enough to crisp and lightly char the exterior on all sides.
4. Place the lamb in a roasting pan and finish baking for about 14 to 15 minutes (for medium rare).
5. Remove the lamb, place on a cutting board, and let rest for 5 minutes. Lay the blade of a sharp knife against the bone and slip the meat off in one piece.
6. Roll the boneless loins first in the basic barbecue sauce, then in the pecans. Slice each loin into 6 medallions.

To serve

1. Reheat the barbecue-flavored red wine sauce.
2. Place 3 medallions on each of 6 hot serving plates. Dribble the wine sauce over the plate. Garnish with sautéed green beans.

Shoestring Sweet Potatoes

1 large sweet potato, peeled
2 quarts peanut or vegetable oil

1. Heat the oil to 350°.
2. Using a mandoline or sharp knife, cut the potatoes into very fine julienne matchsticks.
3. Sprinkle the julienned potatoes into the hot oil and stir, allowing them to cook for 20 to 30 seconds.
4. Using a mesh dipper or slotted spoon, remove the potaotes from the oil and drain on paper towels.
5. Sprinkle with salt to taste.

LAMB SHANKS

flageolets	lemon	*braise*
garlic	wine, red	

LAMB'S LIVER

butter	parsley	shallots
cream	salt pork	

LAMB'S TONGUE

artichokes	fennel	tomatoes
basil	garlic	vinaigrette
curry	olives	

LEEKS (Fall)

bacon	hollandaise sauce	tomatoes
béchamel sauce	lemon	**vinaigrette**
beets	mousseline sauce	wine, red
bread crumbs	mustard	
butter	olive oil	*boil*
cheese, especially	Parmesan cheese	*braise*
Cheddar, goat, and	parsley	*purée*
Gruyère	peas	*steam*
cream	potatoes	*stew*
fish	thyme	

LEMON (Spring)

almonds	currants, black	poppy seeds
cardamom	honey	raspberries
chocolate	lime	strawberries

I think the combination of chocolate and lemon is so refreshing. In England, I even tasted a yogurt flavored with chocolate and lemon. Sounds weird, tastes great!—Dieter Schorner

Sardinian Lemon and Sheep's Milk Cheese Fritters with Honey
—Michael Romano

(continued on facing page)

Lemon Curd Mousse with Fresh Summer Berries in Almond Tuiles
—Anne Rosenzweig

Lemon Ice—Chris Schlesinger

A Light Lemon Mousseline with Native Strawberries and Whisked Cream
—Lydia Shire

LENTILS (Winter)

bacon
bay leaves
cheese, Feta and goat
foie gras
garlic
ham
lemon
mint
olive oil

onions
parsley
peppers
pork fat
prunes
radishes
sausages
scallions
sorrel

spinach
thyme
tomato sauce
tomatoes
vinegar, especially sherry or wine

purée
simmer

Pasta with Lentil and Prosciutto Sauce—George Germon & Johanne Killeen

Savory Lentil, Tomato, and Lobster Salad, served with Cucumber Vinaigrette
—Hubert Keller

LETTUCES (Spring)

anchovies
avocados
cheese
egg yolks
garlic
lemon
mayonnaise

mustard
oil, especially hazelnut, olive, peanut, and walnut
onions
pepper
salt

vinaigrette
vinegar, especially balsamic, cider and red wine

braise
raw

"The lettuce ever was and still continues to be the principal foundation of the universal Tribe of Salads, which is to cool and refresh."—John Evelyn

Field Lettuces with Spanish Sherry Vinegar, Roasted Garlic, and Roquefort Cheese Croutons—Hubert Keller

Salad of Seasonal Lettuces and Herbs with Citrus-Dijon Vinaigrette
—Charlie Palmer

Warm Sonoma Goat Cheese with Kona Kai Farm Lettuces—Alice Waters

LIME   (Summer)

bananas	lemon	rum
coconut	raspberries	

LITCHI NUTS   (Summer)

coconut	cream	kiwi fruit

LOBSTER

anchovies
anisette
apples
asparagus
avocados
bacon
basil
bordelaise
bourbon
brandy
bread crumbs
butter
caviar
cayenne
cheese, especially
  Vacherin
chervil
chiles
chives
cider
cilantro
coconut
Cognac

coral
coriander
corn
couscous
cream
crème fraîche
curry
endive
fennel
foie gras
garlic
ginger
grapefruit
hollandaise sauce
horseradish
leeks
lemon
lemon basil
lemongrass
lime
Madeira
mayonnaise
Mornay sauce
mushrooms
mustard
olive oil
onions
oranges
oysters
paprika
parsley
pepper, black

Pernod
porcini
port
portobellos
quinoa
rice
saffron
seaweed
shallots
sherry
star anise
tarragon
thyme
tomalley
tomatoes
truffles, black
vanilla
vinaigrette
vinegar, especially
  white wine
wine, white

bake
boil
broil
grill
pan-fry
poach
roast
sauté
steam

The best six months of the year for hard-shell lobsters are May and June, and October through January. At that point, they can be pan fried, grilled, roasted, steamed, boiled, made into salad or soup—they're almost as versatile as chicken.—Jasper White

(continued on facing page)

First, I'd parboil the lobster whole in a really spicy court bouillon to add a little more flavor, or with some white wine, chiles, herbs—maybe a little cilantro— and bay leaves. I'd cook it seven-eighths of the way, and then finish roasting it in the wood-burning oven.—Bradley Ogden

Maine Lobster in Cilantro Broth served with Black Chanterelles and Flageolets—Hubert Keller

Maine Lobster with Grapefruit, Orzo, and Citrus Butter Sauce —Patrick O'Connell

Seaweed Salad with Maine Lobster and Ginger Emulsion—Jean-Louis Palladin

Wood-Grilled Maine Lobster with Fragrant Truffle Oil, Tiny Green Beans, and Basil Essenced Potato Purée—Charlie Palmer

Lobster-Sweet Corn Chowder—Michael Romano

Chimney-Smoked Lobster with Tarragon Butter and Summer Squash and Potato Fritter—Anne Rosenzweig

Slow-Baked Lobster with Tomatoes—Jimmy Schmidt

Winter Lobster Flamed in Cognac, with a Surrounding Spoon of Vacherin Cheese—Lydia Shire

Warm Lobster Salad with Roasted Quince, Shiitake Mushrooms, and a Vanilla-Bean Coulis—Joachim Splichal

Pan-Roasted Lobster with Chervil and Chives—Jasper White

(See also Jimmy Schmidt's lobster recipe on pages 142–143.)

MÂCHE (Also known as LAMB'S LETTUCE)   (Winter)

anchovies	oils, especially nut and	Parmesan cheese
beets	olive	

MACKEREL

anchovies	horseradish	soy sauce
béarnaise sauce	**lemon**	spinach
béchamel sauce	lime	tomato sauce
bread crumbs	Mornay sauce	tomatoes
butter	**mustard**	**vinegar**, especially sher-
carrots	onions	ry or wine
caviar	paprika	**wine, white**
chiles	Parmesan cheese	
chives	parsley	*bake*
coriander	rosemary	*boil*
currants	scallops	*broil*
garlic	sorrel	**grill**
ginger	sour cream	*sauté*
gooseberries		

Lobster and Quinoa Risotto

Jimmy Schmidt
META RESTAURANTS
Detroit, Michigan

The quinoa adds some great earthy flavors to this dish, and is unusual. Quinoa is high in protein, which makes the dish very nutritious. It also produces a starch gel, similar to that of risotto, which gives it kind of a silky texture. The combination of lobster and quinoa is one that I really like—the mineral and earthy components of the lobster and the quinoa are very complementary. From a taste point of view, they tend to "cancel each other out" somewhat, so that each one on its own doesn't seem as strong.

SERVES 4

2 red bell peppers

2 (1–1 1/2 pound) live lobsters

2 cups quinoa

4 cups homemade vegetable broth
or low-sodium vegetable broth from bouillon cubes

2 tablespoons extra virgin olive oil

1 cup diced red onion

2 cloves garlic, peeled and minced

1 tablespoon New Mexican ground chiles or mild Hungarian paprika

kosher salt (optional)

freshly ground black pepper

1 cup corn kernels, cut from the cob (2–3 ears corn)

1/4 cup chopped fresh basil

4 sprigs fresh basil or other herb

1. Roast the peppers by placing them whole on an open gas flame or outdoor grill, or under the broiler. Cook, rotating on all sides, for about ten minutes, until the skins are black. Put the peppers in a bowl and cover with plastic wrap. Allow to cool for 15 minutes. Using your hands, peel off the charred skin. Discard the cores, stems, and seeds. Dice the roasted peppers and set aside.

2. Plunge the lobsters headfirst into a large pot of boiling water and cook for 5 to 6 minutes. Transfer them to a colander and cool under cold running water. Cut the lobsters in half lengthwise and remove the meat from the tails, legs, and claws. Keep the lobster claw meat intact in large pieces and reserve for garnish. Cut the tail meat into 3 to 4 pieces each. Cover the lobster meat with plastic wrap and set aside.

3. Put the quinoa into a fine strainer and rinse under cold running water to remove any residue of its bitter husks. Drain thoroughly.

4. Bring the vegetable broth to a boil in a medium saucepan. Meanwhile, heat the olive oil in a large saucepan over medium-high heat. Add the onion and garlic and cook for 4 to 5 minutes, until tender. Add the chile powder and quinoa and cook for about 2 minutes until hot, stirring to prevent sticking.

5. Remove the pan from the heat and carefully pour the boiling broth over the quinoa. Return to heat and bring to a simmer, stirring. Season to taste with salt and a generous dose of black pepper. Cook for about 8 minutes, stirring frequently, until most of the liquid is absorbed but the quinoa is still moist.

6. Add the corn, roasted peppers, and lobster to the quinoa and cook for about 3 minutes, until heated through. Add the basil and cook the risotto gently for about 2 minutes longer, until the risotto is slightly moist and creamy. Stir often.

7. Place a generous serving of risotto in the center of each plate. Take care to divide the lobster evenly among the plates and top each serving with a piece of claw meat. Garnish each with a sprig of basil and serve.

MAHIMAHI

avocados	ginger	tomatoes
chiles	grapefruit	
cilantro	lime	*bake*
coconut	olive oil	*broil*
cumin	papaya	**grill**
fruits, especially	parsley	*sauté*
tropical	pineapples	*sear*
garlic	soy sauce	*steam*

Baked Ecuadorian Mahimahi Stuffed with Shredded Crab and Rock Shrimp Salpicon and Served with Roasted Tomatoes, Capers, Olives, and Herbs —Rick Bayless

Mahimahi with Pineapple-Coconut Sauce—Susanna Foo

Grilled Mahimahi with Summer Bean Salad and Tomato Vinaigrette —Bradley Ogden

Sautéed Mahmahi with Cucumbers, Mangoes and Cilantro—Jeremiah Tower

MANGOES (Summer)

almonds	**lime**	shellfish
blackberries	papayas	star anise
cloves	passion fruit	
coconut	pineapples	*bake*
fish	**raspberries**	*freezing*
ginger	**rum**	*poach*
Kirsch	Sauternes	*sauté*
lemon		

Mango by itself is very simple, with a little peppery flavor. But if you sprinkle some lime on the top, the flavor wakes you up! And it wakes up the mango, making it taste even more 'mango-y' than before. It's a beautiful combination. —Dieter Schorner

MARROW

artichoke hearts	eggs	lemon
cayenne		

MASCARPONE

brandy liqueur	mushrooms	sugar
fruit, especially **strawberries**	polenta	

Fresh Fruit Gratin with Mascarpone Custard
—George Germon & Johanne Killeen

Puff Pastry Strawberry Tart with Mascarpone Cheese—Joyce Goldstein

Creamy Polenta with Mascarpone—Michael Romano

MELON   (Summer)

basil	ice cream	**port wine**
berries	ices	**prosciutto**
Champagne	Kirsch	**raspberries**
chiles	**lemon**	salt
Cognac	**lime**	sherry
Cointreau	Madeira	**strawberries**
cucumber	mint	**vanilla**
Curaçao	muscat	wine, especially sweet
ginger	nuts	
grapefruit	oranges	*freeze*
Grand Marnier	pear	*raw*
honey	pepper	

A melon that was perfect yesterday may be too ripe today, so we wouldn't serve it simply sliced on a plate—we'd make it into a sherbet.—Alice Waters

Thai Melon Salad with Cilantro and Lime—Susan Feniger & Mary Sue Milliken

Fresh Melon-Basil Salad with Habanero—Mark Miller

Charentais Melon with Beaumes-de-Venise Sabayon—Lindsey Shere

MONKFISH   (Winter)

aïoli	cider	Marsala
artichokes	coriander	**mushrooms**
asparagus	cream	olive oil
bacon	curry	olives
butter, especially brown	fennel	parsley
cabbage	**garlic**	peas
capers	ginger	peppers
carrots	leeks	rosemary
chervil	**lemon**	saffron
chives	**lemongrass**	*(continued on next page)*

MONKFISH *(continued)*

sage	**tomatoes**	*grill*
shallots	**wine**	*roast*
sherry, dry		*sauté*
soy sauce	*bake*	*steam*
thyme	*braise*	

Monkfish in Lemongrass and Coconut Broth
—Susan Feniger & Mary Sue Milliken

Roasted Monkfish with Cauliflower Served with Caper-Raisin Emulsion Flavored with Nutmeg—Jean-Georges Vongerichten

MORELS (Spring)

asparagus	onions	shallots
bread crumbs	Parmesan cheese	sour cream
butter	parsley	tarragon
chervil	peas	tomatoes
chicken	pepper	truffles
chives	potatoes	watercress
cream	poultry	
custard	rosemary	*bake*
eggs	salt	*cream*
garlic	Sauternes	*fry*
lemon	scallops	*stew*

MUSHROOMS (Fall)

almonds	*crème fraîche*	nutmeg
anchovies	dill	nuts
bacon	eggplants	olive oil
barley	eggs	**onions**
basil	fish	oranges
bordelaise sauce	**garlic**	oregano
bread crumbs	grapes	oyster sauce
butter	gremolata	pancetta
caraway seeds	ham	paprika
cayenne	**lemon**	**parsley**
cheese, especially	**Madeira**	pasta
Gruyère and	**marjoram**	peas
Parmesan	marrow	pepper, black
chervil	mascarpone	pineapple
chives	mint	pistachios
coriander	Mornay sauce	potatoes
cream	mustard	*(continued on facing page)*

rosemary
sausages, especially
 smoked
Sauternes
shallots
shellfish
sherry
sorrel
sour cream

spinach
stock
tarragon
thyme
tomatoes
vinegar, especially wine
walnut oil
walnuts
wine, red or white

bake
broil
fry
grill
purée
raw
sauté
steam

A Portobello Mushroom Pretending To Be a Filet Mignon with a Roasted Shallot and Tomato Fondue—Patrick O'Connell

Wild Mushroom Tarts—Anne Rosenzweig

Potato and Forest Mushroom Lasagna with Chive Sauce—Joachim Splichal

Mushroom Caps with Bone Marrow—Jeremiah Tower

MUSSELS (Fall–Winter)

aïoli
anchovies
aniseed
bacon
basil
bay leaves
beans, white
bread crumbs
butter
cayenne
chervil
chives
cilantro
Cognac
cream
curry

fennel
garlic
leeks
lemon
lime
mayonnaise
mushrooms
olive oil
onions
orange
pancetta
parsley
pepper, black
Pernod
pesto
rice

saffron
shallots
snails
spinach
thyme
tomatoes
vinaigrette
vinegar
wine, white

broil
grill
pan-fry
steam

Farm-Raised Canadian Mussels in Tabasco-Style Escabèche *(Extra Virgin Olive Oil, Fruit Vinegar, Garlic, Sweet Spices, and Aromatic Vegetables)*—Rick Bayless

Mussels with Green Garlic, Thyme, and Toasted Rye Bread—Mark Peel

Grilled Mussels with Garlic and Tomatoes—Jimmy Schmidt

Fedelini Pasta with Prince Edward Island Mussels, Mirepoix, *Saffron Mayonnaise, and Crouton*—Alice Waters

Mussels Steamed with White Wine, Garlic, and Fresh Herbs—Jasper White

MUTTON

Calvados
capers

mushrooms
tarragon

thyme

NECTARINES (See also PEACHES)   (Summer)

almonds
berries
blackberries
blueberries
caramel
Champagne

cherries
cinnamon
figs
ginger
nuts

orange
peaches
pepper, black
raspberries
vanilla

NOODLES, EGG

bread crumbs

poppy seeds

tomato sauce

OCTOPUS

basil
bay leaves
chervil
garlic

lemon
parsley
vinegar
wine, red

grill
stew

OKRA   (Summer)

basil
butter
garlic
hollandaise sauce
lemon

onions
parsley
pepper, black
peppers, especially
   green

tomatoes
vinaigrette

sauté
stew

ONIONS   (Fall)

apples
bacon
butter
cheese sauce, especially
   Cheddar or Gruyère
cinnamon
cloves
cream

mushrooms
nutmeg
paprika
Parmesan cheese
parsley
pepper, black
raisins
salt

sherry
sorrel
thyme
tomato sauce
vinegar
Worcestershire sauce

(continued on facing page)

bake	*fry*	*roast*
boil	*grill*	*sauté*
braise	*raw*	*steam*

In Mexico, you use raw onions but you always wash them really well after you cut them, or you let them soak for five minutes in acidulated water made with lime or vinegar, or you douse them real heavily with sour orange juice and you let them sit for two hours, or you blanch them for thirty seconds in water. There are all these different variations on working with raw onions and still keeping the fresh, raw crispness to them. On the other hand, we do a number of dishes where we throw whole onions down into the fire and let them blacken on the outside, because there's a sort of steaming that happens on the inside, which is very different from trying to grill it or cook it on a flat top or something like that already sliced.—Rick Bayless

Cream of Five Onion Soup—Joyce Goldstein

Wood-Roasted Onion filled with Spoon of Silky Macomber Turnip—Lydia Shire

ORANGES (Winter)

Armagnac	cinnamon	mangoes
basil	coconut	olives
brandy	Cointreau	pecans
cardamom	ginger	sherry
chipotle peppers	Grand Marnier	strawberries
chocolate	Kirsch	vanilla

Orange and Armagnac Sherbet—Lindsey Shere

Grand Marnier Soufflé with Orange Custard Sauce—Jeremiah Tower

ORANGES, BLOOD (Winter)

citrus fruit, especially grapefruits and tangerines	pomegranates

OXTAILS

garlic	onions	wine, red especially Burgundy
grapes	pepper, black	
gremolata	prunes	
Madeira	shallots	*braise*
mustard	**tomatoes**	*stew*

OYSTERS (Fall–Spring)

ale, beer, or stout
allspice
anchovies
artichokes
bacon
bay leaves
beurre blanc
bread, brown
bread crumbs
caviar
cayenne
Champagne
chiles
chives
cilantro
cream
cucumbers
curry
eggs

fennel
foie gras
garlic
ginger
horseradish
ketchup
leeks
lemon
lime
mace
marjoram
mignonette sauce
mint
mustard
nutmeg
onions
pancetta
paprika
Parmesan cheese
parsley
pepper, black
Pernod
potatoes
saffron
salsify

salt
sauerkraut
scallions
sea urchin roe
shallots
sherry
shrimp
snails
spinach
Tabasco sauce
thyme
vinegar, especially
   champagne
wine, white
Worcestershire sauce

bake
broil
deep-fry
grill
poach
raw
roast
sauté
stew

Fricasee of Pemmaquid Oysters with Salsify, Leeks, Fingerling Potatoes, and Pancetta (with or without Osetra Caviar)—Terrance Brennan

Glazed Oysters with Leek Fondue and Osetra Caviar—Gary Danko

Fanny Bay and Point Reyes Oysters with Malt Vinegar Dressing and Homemade Cocktail Sauce—Bradley Ogden

Kumamoto Oysters with Champagne Mignonette and Pumpernickel Toast—Mark Peel

Oysters Poached in Champagne—Jimmy Schmidt

Hog Island Oyster Chowder with New Potatoes and Smoked Bacon—Alice Waters

PAPAYAS (Spring; Fall)

avocados
cayenne
chicken

chiles
coconut cream
coriander

cumin
ginger

(continued on facing page)

grapefruit	Parma ham	strawberries
lemon	passion fruit	sugar
lime	peaches	vanilla
mangoes	pineapple	
oranges	port	*raw*

Spinach, Avocado, and Papaya Salad with Orange-Cumin Dressing
—Chris Schlesinger

Napoleon of Strawberry and Papaya with Passion Fruit and Raspberry Sauces—Jimmy Schmidt

PARSNIPS (Winter)

almonds	lemon	tarragon
butter	Madeira	walnuts
chives	nutmeg	
cinnamon	**parsley**	*boil*
curry	pepper, black	*deep-fry*
garlic	potatoes	*grill*
hazelnuts	sorrel	*purée*

PARTRIDGES (Fall)

almonds	juniper berries	shallots
apples	**lemon**	tarragon
bacon	lentils	**truffles**
cabbage	mushrooms	wine
cèpes	onions	
chocolate	oysters	*braise*
cream	parsley	*poach*
curry	peppercorns, green	*roast*
foie gras	sage	*sauté*
garlic	sauerkraut	

Wild Partridge with a Red Cabbage Confit and Fall Fruit Chutney
—Daniel Boulud

Young Roasted Partridge with Christmas Pears of Muscat and Spice
—Lydia Shire

Roasted Partridge with Cabbage, Pearl Onions, Apple-Smoked Bacon, and Fried Parsnips—Joachim Splichal

Roast Partridge with Tarragon and Green Peppercorns—Jasper White

PASSION FRUIT   (Winter)

Champagne	coconut	orange
chocolate	kiwi fruit	papaya

Passion fruit is a flavor that wakes you up.—Dieter Schorner

PASTA

basil
beans, especially can-
nellini

butter
cheese, especially
   Parmesan
chiles
cream
garlic
herbs
lobster
mascarpone
mushrooms
olive oil
pancetta

pepper, black
pesto
pignoli
potatoes
ricotta
Romano cheese
tomatoes
**truffles, especially
   white**

PEA PODS   (Spring)

almonds	mushrooms	*steam*
butter	peanuts	*stir-fry*
chicken	sage	

PEACHES   (Summer)

almonds
apricots
basil
berries
blackberries
blueberries
bourbon
brandy
brown sugar
Calvados
caramel
Cassis
Champagne
cherries
cinnamon
cinnamon basil
cloves

coconut
Cognac
Cointreau
cream
currants, red
framboise
ginger
Grand Marnier
hazelnuts
honey
Kirsch
lemon
lime
Madeira
maple syrup
Marsala
Melba sauce

oranges
pecans
plums
port
praline
raspberries
rum
sherry
sour cream
strawberries
sugar
vanilla
wine, especially
   Burgundy

poach
raw

(continued on facing page)

At the Savoy [Hotel, in London], we had a dessert that I thought was absolutely great. It was white poached peaches, stoned, and filled with chestnut mousse with a light Grand Marnier sauce served with lemon sherbet. It was refreshing, and it tasted like fall. I'll never forget it!—Dieter Schorner

Individual Peach and Almond Galette Served Warm with Caramel Ice Cream
—Joyce Goldstein

Peach Tart with Peach Liqueur Coulis and Apricot Sherbet
—Jean-Louis Palladin

Honey-Lavender Ice Cream with Peaches—Lindsey Shere

Peaches and Sweet Cream Ice Cream on Bitter Chocolate Wafers
—Lydia Shire

PEARS   (Fall)

almonds
anise
Armagnac
Beaujolais
blackberries
bourbon
brandy, especially pear
  brandy
brown sugar
Calvados
caramel
Cassis
chablis
cheese, especially Brie,
  Cantal, Feta,
  Gorgonzola, and
  Roquefort

chocolate
cinnamon
cinnamon basil
cloves
Cognac
cream
crème anglaise
crème fraîche
Curaçao
currants, black
figs
ginger
Grand Marnier
grappa
hazelnuts
honey
ice cream, especially
  caramel, pistachio,
  and vanilla
kirsch
lemon
lingonberries
mace
maple
Marsala
Melba sauce

Muscat
nutmeg
nuts
oranges
pecans
pepper, black
pineapple
prunes
quinces
raisins
raspberries
Riesling, Late Harvest
spinach
star anise
vanilla
vinegar, balsamic
walnuts
wine, especially
  Burgundy
zabaione

poach
raw

One of the loveliest of fall fruit compotes is made of white poached pears, dark figs, and fresh red raspberries, with quinces and their pink syrup.
—Lindsey Shere

(continued on next page)

PEARS *(continued)*

Baked Caramel Pears with Gingerbread and Nutmeg Ice Cream—Gary Danko

Poached Seckel Pear, Forelli Pear Tart, and Chocolate-Pear Ice Cream
—Gray Kunz

*Broiled Trio of Virginia Seckel Pears served with Caramel-Brittle Ice Cream
and Tossed Huckleberries*—Mark Miller

Feuilleté of Pears, Pear Ice Cream, and Caramel of Pears—Jean-Louis Palladin

Pear Timbales with Sticky Caramel Sauce and Sugar Biscuits
—Anne Rosenzweig

Baked Pears with Espresso-Chocolate Sauce—Jimmy Schmidt

Pear Salad with Baby Greens, Frisée, *Walnuts, Shaved Parmesan, and
Balsamic Vinaigrette*—Jimmy Schmidt

Pears Poached in Sauternes and Honey with Crème Fraîche—Lindsey Shere

Warm Pear Tart with Zabaione and Spiced Nuts—Nancy Silverton

Pears Poached in Beaumes-de-Venise and Honey

Lindsey Shere
CHEZ PANISSE
Berkeley, California

SERVES 6–8

A half bottle of Beaumes-de-Venise wine
1 1/2 cups of water
1/2 cup honey
About 2 pounds firm, ripe pears, preferably Bartlett or Bosc

1. Combine the wine, water, and honey in a non-corroding saucepan and bring to a simmer. Meanwhile, peel the pears neatly with a vegetable peeler, keeping the stem but removing the blossom end. Drop each pear into the simmering wine as you peel it, and lay a piece of parchment directly on the surface of the pears to keep them basted.

2. Cook at just under a simmer until the pears are barely tender when tested with a knife in the blossom end, about 10 to 40 minutes, depending on the pears.

3. Remove the pears to a container to cool in a single layer. Cook down the remaining syrup to about 3/4 of its original volume and cool separately. Add the pears when cool and chill, preferably overnight. Serve with *crème fraîche* and *ossi dei morti* or some other crisp cookie.

PEAS
(Spring)

almonds
artichokes
bacon
butter
carrots
chervil
chives
cream
fennel
garlic
ham

leeks
lemon
lettuce
mint
mushrooms
nutmeg
onions, especially tiny
parsley
prosciutto
rice
risotto

rosemary
sage
salt pork
savory
shallots
sugar
vinegar

boil
purée
steam

PECANS

bourbon
brown sugar
butterscotch

caramel
chocolate
corn syrup

molasses
oranges
rum

Butter Pecan Ice Cream with Hot Caramel Sauce—Patrick O'Connell

Pecan Tart with Caramel Sauce and Vanilla Ice Cream—Jimmy Schmidt

Pecan Puff Pastry with Chocolate Sauce and Sabayon—Jeremiah Tower

PEPPERS, BELL
(Summer–Fall)

anchovies
basil
chiles
coriander
corn
garlic
lemon

meat, especially chicken, lamb and veal
olive oil
onions
rice
tomatoes
vinegar

bake
broil
grill
par-boil
roast
stew

PERSIMMONS
(Fall)

brandy, especially pear
brown sugar
caramel
cinnamon
cloves
cream
custard
ginger

grapefruit
honey
ices
Kirsch
nutmeg
pecans
pork

sweet potatoes or yams
vanilla
yams

freeze
purée
raw

(continued on next page)

PERSIMMONS *(continued)*

Persimmon Pudding with Coffee and Caramel Sauces—Gary Danko

Warm Persimmon Pudding with Creme Chantilly—Lindsey Shere

PHEASANTS   (Fall)

apples
bacon
blackberries
brandy
cabbage
Calvados
chestnuts
chicory
chiles
cider
cream
crème fraîche
endive
foie gras
garlic
horseradish

juniper berries
lemon
Madeira
Marsala
mushrooms
olives
onions
orange
oysters
pecans
pepper
pheasant liver
pomegranate
port
rice
sage

sauerkraut
sausage
shallots
sour cream
stuffing
tangerines
thyme
truffles
vinegar
walnuts
whiskey
wine

braise
broil
roast

Garlic-Marinated Roasted Pheasant in Crema Poblana *(Poblano Peppers Blended with Homemade Sour Cream) with Braised Swiss Chard*
—Rick Bayless

Wild Scottish Pheasant with Roasted Chestnuts, Savoy Cabbage, and Foie Gras—Terrance Brennan

Chile-Orange Braised Pheasant Salad with Hearty Greens and Smashed Butternut Squash—Mark Miller

Braised Pheasant with Chanterelle Risotto, Roasted Cipollini Onions, and Sauce of Ximenez Sherry—Charlie Palmer

Hunter's Style Breast of Pheasant with Wild Mushrooms, Pearl Onions, Country Bacon, and Tomatoes—Jasper White

PIGS' EARS

butter
cloves
lentils

mustard
onions
parsley

simmer

PIGS' FEET

béarnaise sauce
bread crumbs
cabbage
capers
garlic
hollandaise sauce
mayonnaise

mustard
onions
pepper
sauerkraut
tartar sauce
thyme
tomato sauce

vinaigrette
vinegar, especially wine
wine, white

braise
broil
stew

PIKE   (Fall–Winter)

bacon
crayfish
cream

hollandaise sauce
sorrel

tomatoes
vinegar

PINEAPPLE   (Winter)

apricots
avocados
bacon
bananas
brandy
coconut
cucumbers
grapefruits
hazelnuts

liqueur, especially
    Cognac, **Cointreau,**
    Grand Marnier, and
    Kirsch
lime
mangoes
melon
mint
oranges

papayas
raspberries
rum
strawberries
sugar
vanilla

A winter compote made with slices of pineapple, kiwi fruit, mango, and papaya, with a little passion fruit flesh and a few of its dark seeds for contrast, needs only a grating of lime peel and a sprinkling of rum or Kirsch.
—Lindsey Shere

Warm Pineapple Tart Tatin with Coconut Ice Cream—Patrick O'Connell

Caribbean Coconut Wafer filled with Fresh Pineapple and Piña Colada Sauce—Francois Payard

Pineapple Sherbet Bombe with Kirsch Mousse—Lindsey Shere

PLANTAINS

bacon
beans, black
butter
cinnamon
nuts, especially almonds

and walnuts
pineapples
rum
sour cream

deep-fry
sauté
simmer

(continued on next page)

PLANTAINS *(continued)*

Plantanos con Crema: *Sweet Fried Plantains with Homemade Sour Cream and Fresh Cheese*—Rick Bayless

Black Bean Dip with Fried Sweet Plantains—Chris Schlesinger

PLUMS   (Summer)

almonds	ginger	Sauternes
apricots	grapefruits	vanilla
bananas	honey	**walnuts**
brandy	**lemon**	wine, red
brown sugar	Muscat	
caramel	nectarines	*poach*
cherries	nuts	*raw*
cinnamon	**oranges**	*stew*
custard	peaches	
fruits, especially citrus	rhubarb	

Gingersnap Ice Cream Sandwiches with Plum Ice Cream—Lindsey Shere

Plum Sherbet Bombe with Grand Marnier Mousse—Lindsey Shere

Walnut Tart of Warmed Plums with Mascarpone Soufflé—Lydia Shire

POLENTA

butter	escarole	pepper
cheese, especially	garlic	tomato sauce
Cheddar, goat,	mascarpone	
Gorgonzola, Monterey	milk	
Jack, and Parmesan	**mushrooms**	

Bowl of Creamy Polenta with Wild Mushroom and Goat Ricotta
—Bradley Ogden

Matzo Polenta with Sautéed Mushrooms—Michael Romano

POMEGRANATES   (Fall)

bananas	chocolate	grapefruit
blood oranges	cream cheese	yogurt

For one dessert, we squeezed the juice from the pomegranate seeds and made it into a sauce for a flourless chocolate cake served with bananas.
—Susanna Foo

POMPANO   (Winter)

basil	lemon	shrimp
bread crumbs	lime	*bake (in paper)*
coconut	mustard	*sauté*

PORCINIS   (Summer)

butter	olive oil	thyme
garlic	parsley	truffles, white
Marsala	sage	
Muscatel wine	sherry	*grill*

The combination of porcini and garlic is a perfect combination—when it's done perfectly. That's when the garlic is not overpowering the mushroom, and the mushroom is well caramelized and meaty at the same time, and the garlic is bringing up all the flavor so that it's not just plain and bland.
—Daniel Boulud

PORK   (Fall)

apples	**ginger**	quinces
apricots	hoisin sauce	**rosemary**
bay leaves	**honey**	**sage**
beans, black	juniper berries	sauerkraut
beer	lemon	soy sauce
brandy	lime	star anise
cabbage	Marsala	tarragon
Calvados	molasses	**thyme**
cherries, dried sour	mustard	**vinegar**
clams	onions	walnuts
Cognac	**orange**	whiskey
coriander	parsley	wine, white
cream	**pepper, black**	
cumin	pineapple	*brine*
fennel	plum sauce, Chinese	*grill*
fruit	plums	*roast*
garlic	prunes	

Pork and apples is a classic combination that has been served together for hundreds of years. Apples cut the fattiness of pork. —Lindsey Shere

Tacos al Pastor: *Red-Chile-Marinated Pork, Wood-Grilled, Thin-Sliced, and served with Charcoaled Pineapple, Guacamole, and Black Beans*
—Rick Bayless

(continued on next page)

PORK *(continued)*

Grilled Pork Tenderloin with Mustard, Sage, and Rosemary—Joyce Goldstein

Pork Tenderloin with Black-Eyed Peas, Braised Onions, and Tomatillo Salsa
—Jeremiah Tower

PORK CHOPS (Fall)

apples	leeks	thyme
bay leaves	mint	tomato sauce
beer	**mustard**	
bread crumbs	onions	*bake*
cabbage	oranges	*braise*
cream	parsley	*broil*
curry	**pepper, black**	*grill*
fennel	**rosemary**	*pan-fry*
garlic	**sauerkraut**	*sauté*
ginger	sour cream	
juniper berries	soy sauce	

Grilled Double-Cut Pork Chop with Braised Cabbage, Boiled Potatoes, and Stone-Ground Mustard Aïoli—Bradley Ogden

Pork Loin Chop Grilled with Gâteau of Apple and Caramelized Red Onion, with Rosemary Cider Sauce—Jimmy Schmidt

Double-Thick Pork Rib Chop with Sage and Apples, with Roasted Sweet Potatoes—Jasper White

POTATOES (Fall–Winter)

	chard	horseradish
	cheese (especially	juniper berries
	Cheddar, goat,	kale
	Gruyère, and	**leeks**
	Parmesan)	lemon thyme
	chervil	**lovage**
	chicory	mint
	chives	mushrooms
anchovies	**cream**	mustard
bacon	*crème fraîche*	nutmeg
basil	dill	olive oil
butter	duxelles	olives
caviar	fennel	onions
cayenne	fenugreek	paprika
celery root	**garlic**	**parsley**
cèpes	ham	

(continued on facing page)

parsley root	squash, winter	*deep-fry*
pepper	sweet potatoes	**fry**
pork	thyme	*purée*
salt	truffles	*roast*
savory	turnips	*steam*
smoked salmon		**stew**
sorrel	**bake**	
sour cream	**boil**	

PROSCIUTTO

beans, lima	**figs**	papayas
bread	kiwi fruit	peaches
butter	**melons**	pears

Pasta Salad with Prosciutto and Peas—Susan Feniger & Mary Sue Milliken

Veronese Grilled Polenta with Soppiessata and Proscuitto
—George Germon & Johanne Killeen

Prosciutto with Arugula and Blood Oranges—Jeremiah Tower

Parma Prosciutto with Melons and Marsala—Alice Waters

Proscuitto with Warm Wilted Greens—Alice Waters

PRUNES

almonds	**lemon**	sugar
apricots	nuts, especially almonds,	vinegar, balsamic
Armagnac	hazelnuts, pistachios,	**walnuts**
brandy	and walnuts	**wine**, especially
chestnuts	oranges	Burgundy and sweet
cinnamon	pears	
cream	port	*stew*
currants	rum	
Kirsch	sherry	

Baked Salmon with Prune Sauce—Joyce Goldstein

Baked Red Wine Tart with Prunes, Poached Pear, and Prune-Armagnac Ice Cream—François Payard

Poached Prunes in Darjeeling Tea and Sauternes—Lindsey Shere

Prune Soufflé with Armagnac—Lindsey Shere

PUMPKIN (Fall)

apples
bacon
bourbon
brown sugar
butter
caramel
cinnamon
cloves
coconut
Cognac
cream
duck, including confit
garlic
ginger

Gruyère cheese
honey
leeks
mace
maple syrup
mint
molasses
mushrooms
nutmeg
nuts
olive oil
onions
pecans
pepper, black

pumpkin seeds
rum
sage
sherry
sour cream
sugar
thyme
vanilla
vinegar, especially
　white wine
walnuts
yogurt

bake

Pumpkin and Potato-Filled Free-Form Lasagna with Black-Olive Butter
—George Germon & Johanne Killeen

Pumpkin Ice Cream with Caramel Pecan Sauce—Jimmy Schmidt

QUAIL (Fall)

anchovies
apples
bacon
basil
bay leaves
beets
chiles, red
cider
Cognac
cranberries
currants, especially black
curry
figs
foie gras
garlic
gin
ginger
grapes
honey
juniper berries

leeks
lemon
lime
maple syrup
molasses
mushrooms
mustard
onions
orange
pancetta
parsley
pears
pecans
pepper
persimmons
pignoli
pineapple
port wine
potatoes

prunes
quail eggs
quail liver
quinces
risotto
sage
salt
scallions
shallots
thyme
truffles, especially white
watercress
wine, white
Worcestershire sauce

broil
fry
grill
roast

Quail with Pomegranate, Orange and Marsala—Joyce Goldstein

Grilled BBQ Quail with Duck Sausage and Grilled Figs—Bradley Ogden

(continued on facing page)

Crisp Flattened Quail with Shallots, Dried Figs, and Baby Spinach
—Mark Peel

Roast Quail with Savoy Cabbage and Kasha—Anne Rosenzweig

Spit-Roasted Quail on a Flaky, Delicate Moroccan Pie of Toasted Almonds
—Lydia Shire

Roast Quail with Pumpkin Seed Sauce—Jeremiah Tower

*Grilled Quail with Pancetta and Sautéed Chino Ranch Corn, Beans, and
Squash Blossoms*—Alice Waters

QUINCES   (Fall)

apples	honey	vanilla
brown sugar	lemon	
butter	nuts	*bake*
Cognac	pears	*broil*
cream	raspberries	
foie gras	sugar	

*Quinces, if you eat them alone, don't taste great. But if you broil and
caramelize them, they do.*—Dieter Schorner

Sautéed Foie Gras *with Quince Confits*—Gray Kunz

Quince and Apple Tarte Tatin—Lindsey Shere

RABBIT (See also HARE)   (Fall–Winter)

almonds	cream	saffron
apricots	*foie gras*	sage
bacon	garlic	shallots
basil	grapes	sour cream
bay leaves	horseradish	spinach
beer	juniper berries	tarragon
blood, especially rabbit	lemon	**thyme**
and pork	Marsala	tomatoes
brandy	mole sauce	vinegar
bread crumbs	**mushrooms**	walnuts
carrots	**mustard**	**wine, especially red**
cherries	**onions**	
chervil	oranges	*braise*
chives	**parsley**	*fry*
chocolate, bitter	pistachios	*grill*
cider	**prunes**	*roast*
cloves	rosemary	*sauté*
coriander		

(continued on next page)

RABBIT *(continued)*

Braised Rabbit with Pappardelle Pasta and Sage—Daniel Boulud

Our Homemade Rappahannock Rabbit Sausage with Lentils and a Tangle of Tart Greens—Patrick O'Connell

Rabbit Pâté with Warm Grappa, and Italian Prune Plum Conserve—Lydia Shire

Rabbit Sausage with Mustard Oil—Jean-Georges Vongerichten

Rabbit Salad with Browned Shallots—Alice Waters

Warm Terrine of Rabbit with Prunes and Apples—Jasper White

RADICCHIO (Fall–Winter)

anchovies	**garlic**	**vinegar, especially balsamic**
bacon	lemon	
butter	olive oil	watercress
cheese, especially Parmesan	pancetta	

RADISHES (Spring; Fall)

chives	parsley	**vinegar**, especially rice wine and sherry
lemon	**salt**	
oranges		

RASPBERRIES (Summer)

almonds	**chocolate**	melons
apricots	Cognac	peaches
bananas	**cream**	pears
brandy, especially raspberry	cream cheeses	pepper, black
brown sugar	**currants, especially red**	pineapple
buttermilk	fruits, especially citrus	pistachios
caramel	Grand Marnier	sour cream
Cassis	**Kirsch**	sugar
Champagne	**lemon**	vanilla
	mangoes	wine, red

The acidity of lemon will bring out the flavor of raspberry.—François Payard

Raspberry No-Cholesterol Soufflé with Raspberry Sauce—Gary Danko

Raspberries with a Grand Marnier Sauce—Patrick O'Connell

(continued on facing page)

Dark Chocolate and Brandied Raspberry Ice Cream Bombe—Lindsey Shere

Russian Raspberry Gratin—Jeremiah Tower

Raspberry goes with a lot of different kinds of fruit. I like it with pear, and raspberry ice cream with chocolate is nice.—Lindsey Shere

RED SNAPPER

anise
basil
bay leaves
bordelaise sauce
butter
capers
celery
cilantro
cloves
curry, especially red
dill
fennel
five-spice powder
garlic
ginger
honey
leeks

lemon
lime
mustard
olives, black
onions
oranges
parsley
pepper, black
peppers, especially
   green
potatoes
romesco sauce
Parmesan cheese
rosemary
saffron
scallions
sesame

shallots
tarragon
thyme
tomatoes
vinegar, especially sherry
vinaigrette
wine, especially white

bake
braise
broil
grill
poach
roast
sauté
steam

Auntie Wu's Braised Red Snapper with Garlic and Ginger—Susanna Foo

Braised Sashimi of Red Snapper and Yellowfin Tuna with Tart Herbal Dressing and Mixed Lettuces—Norman Van Aken

RHUBARB   (Spring)

apples
berries, especially
  strawberries
brandy
brown sugar
butter
cinnamon

cream
fruit, especially citrus
ginger
oranges
pepper, black and pink
plums
sour cream

sugar

bake
poach
stew

Chilled Rhubarb Soup with Fresh Berries and Passion Fruit Sorbet
—François Payard

Rhubarb and Strawberry Sherbet—Lindsey Shere

Rhubarb-Plum Crisp—Nancy Silverton

RICE, WHITE

almonds
basil
brown sugar
cardamom
cherries, dried
cinnamon
coconut
cream
curry

custard
garlic
ginger
lemon
mushrooms
nutmeg
nuts, especially
 almonds, walnuts,
 pecans, and pistachios

oranges
parsley
pignoli
pineapples
raisins
saffron
tomatoes
vanilla
yogurt

Warm Rice Pudding with Coconut Cream Sauce—Susanna Foo

Curried Rice Salad—Joyce Goldstein

Caramel Rice Flan—Nancy Silverton

RICE, WILD

almonds
butter
hazelnuts

mushrooms
oranges

pepper
pignoli

RICOTTA CHEESE

almonds
chocolate
cinnamon
cloves
cream cheese
garlic

graham crackers
lemon
nutmeg
nuts
pepper
pignoli

salt
spinach
sugar
vanilla

RISOTTO

artichokes
asparagus
crab
mushrooms
Parmesan cheese
peas
saffron
shallots

shellfish
truffles
veal
wine

(continued on facing page)

I think a great risotto is a dish to be savored. It should be about eight bites of fabulous flavor, where you almost hate to take that last bite—and any more than that would be gross.—Lydia Shire

Risotto of Lobster, Mussels, and Clams with Sweet Pimientos, Scallions, and Saffron—Daniel Boulud

Risotto of Black Truffle and Fall Vegetables, with Parmigiano-Reggiano—Gary Danko

Risotto with Butternut Squash, Greens and Prosciutto—Joyce Goldstein

Fricassée of Mushrooms and a Parsley Risotto—Gray Kunz

Risotto with Mussels and Fresh Herbs—Mark Peel & Nancy Silverton

Risotto with Fresh Bay Leaves, Peas, and Pea Shoots—Alice Waters

ROMAINE

anchovies	chives	olive oil
cheese, especially Parmesan and blue (Gorgonzola and Roquefort)	**garlic** lemon	**pepper, black**

Ensalada Frontera: Hearts of Romaine with Wood-Grilled Onions, Radishes, Fresh Cheese, and Roasted Garlic Dressing—Rick Bayless

Moroccan Orange, Romaine, Walnut, and Watercress Salad—Joyce Goldstein

Hearts of Romaine with a Creamy Garlic Dressing and Oven-Roasted Tomatoes—Patrick O'Connell

Young Romaine with Green Goddess Dressing and Garlic Croutons—Alice Waters

RUTABEGAS (Winter)

butter	parsley	*bake*
cream	pepper, black	*boil*
ginger	sage	*deep-fry*
lemon	sour cream	*purée*
nutmeg	thyme	*roast*

SALMON

aïoli
anchovies
aquavit
artichokes
avocados
bacon
basil
beans, fermented black
béarnaise sauce
beurre blanc
bordelaise sauce
bread crumbs
capers
caviar
Champagne
chervil
chives
citrus
clams
Cognac
coriander
corn

crab
cream
crème fraîche
cucumber
cumin
curry
dill
fennel
five-spice powder
garlic
ginger
hollandaise sauce
horseradish
juniper berries
leeks
lemon
lime
Madeira
maple syrup
mayonnaise
mint
mousseline sauce
mushrooms
mustard
olives, black
parsley
pepper, black
peppers
pomegranates
raisins

salmon caviar
sesame
shallots
shrimp
snow peas
sorrel
spinach
tarragon
tomato
truffles
vermouth
vinaigrette
vinegar, especially
   white wine
walnuts
watercress
wine
Worcestershire sauce
zucchini

bake in parchment
braise
broil
grill
pan-fry
pan-roast
poach
sauté
sear
steam

Salmon is such a fatty, flavorful fish. It can handle a big flavor; I do it in a horseradish crust. And acid goes well with it, to cut the richness of the fish, like some kind of citrus.—Terrance Brennan

I love to cook a whole salmon on the grill and then cover it completely, from head to toe, with about one inch of dill, and then finish it either on the grill or in the oven this way, with some lemon slices and cracked pepper and olive oil. It's like cooking it in a forest of dill. The inside is very well flavored and moist.—Daniel Boulud

Salmon en Mole Verde: Farm-Raised Atlantic Salmon with Classic Green Pumpkin-Seed Mole, Roasted Potatoes, and Mexican Vegetables
—Rick Bayless

Tournedos of Salmon with Horseradish Crust, Cucumbers, and Salmon Caviar—Terrance Brennan

(continued on facing page)

Fresh Atlantic Salmon Baked in a Tender Corn Pancake Topped with Golden Caviar and Watercress Sauce—Hubert Keller

Flash-Seared Atlantic Salmon with Horseradish-Black Pepper Sauce, Oyster Pan Stuffing, and Sesame Asparagus—Mark Miller

Salmon Five Ways: Home-Smoked, Pastrami-Cured, Cilantro-Gravlax, Tartare, and Poached—Patrick O'Connell

Pan-Roasted Salmon with Braised Lentil Salad and Red Wine Vinaigrette—Bradley Ogden

Pepper-Seared Salmon Fillet with Grain Mustard, Braised Asparagus, and Roasted Creamer Potatoes—Charlie Palmer

Pasta with Mint-Cured Salmon, Cucumbers, Lemon, and Cream—Anne Rosenzweig

Lemon Pasta with Smoked Salmon and Caviar—Jimmy Schmidt

Smoked Salmon and Watercress Omelet—Jimmy Schmidt

Grilled Salmon with Roasted Beets, Leeks, and Horseradish—Jeremiah Tower

SALMON, SMOKED

artichokes	dill	melon
avocados	eggs	plums
capers	ginger, pickled	pepper, black
caviar	grapefruit	potatoes
celery root	horseradish	radishes
cream	leeks	
cucumber	lemon	

SALMON TROUT

avocados	dill	lemon
cream	herb mayonnaise	

SALSIFY   (Winter)

béchamel sauce	hollandaise sauce	tomatoes
bread crumbs	**lemon**	vinegar
butter	mayonnaise	walnuts
celery root	nutmeg	Worcestershire sauce
cheese, especially	onions	
Gruyère or Parmesan	parsley	*boil*
chives	salt	*sauté*
cream	shellfish	

SALT COD

bacon	mayonnaise	parsnips
caviar	mustard	**potatoes**
cream	**olive oil**	tomato
garlic	onions	truffles

There are three foods that must never be overcooked lest they become tough: eggs, calf's liver, and salt cod.—Paula Wolfert

SARDINES (Spring–Summer)

anchovies	paprika	thyme
arugula	parsley	tomatoes
butter	**pepper**	vinegar, especially balsamic
garlic	pignoli	
lemon	potatoes	wine, white
mint	raisins	
mustard	salt	*broil*
olive oil	savory	*grill*
olives	spinach	*sauté*
onions		

Fresh Sardine Fillets with Arugula—Jasper White

Grilled Fresh Sardines from Maine with Olive Vinaigrette—Jasper White

SAUERKRAUT

apples	dill	pork
bacon	**juniper berries**	potatoes
beer	mushrooms	**sausages**
brown sugar	onions	shallots
caraway seeds	pheasant	tomatoes
cream	pineapples	wine, white

SAUSAGES

apples	tomatoes
cabbage	wine, white
cider	
grapes	*boil*
lentils	*grill*
mustard	*pan-broil*
onions	*roast*
sauerkraut	*sauté*

(continued on facing page)

Chinese Sausage Salad Served in Red Onion Cups
—Susan Feniger & Mary Sue Milliken

Roasted Sausages and Grapes—George Germon & Johanne Killeen

Homemade Sausages with Grain Mustard, Five-Onion Slaw, and Stewed White Beans—Mark Miller

Our Homemade Boudin Blanc *(White Sausage) with Sauerkraut Braised in Virginia Riesling on Apple Coulis*—Patrick O'Connell

Curried Lamb Sausage with Compote and Pecan Pancakes—Jimmy Schmidt

Duck Sausage with Prunes—Norman Van Aken

Lobster Sausage with Savoy Cabbage—Jasper White

SCALLOPS (Spring–Fall)

almonds
anise
asparagus
avocados
bacon
basil
bay leaves
brandy
bread crumbs
butter, especially brown
cabbage
cabbage, napa
capers
carrots
caviar
cayenne
celery
cheese, especially
  Gruyère or Parmesan
chervil
chives
cilantro
coriander
crab
cream
cucumbers
curry
dill

endive
fennel
foie gras
garlic
gin
ginger
hollandaise sauce
Jerusalem artichokes
leeks
lemon
lemongrass
lemon thyme
lime
marjoram
mint
Mornay sauce
mushrooms
mustard
olive oil
onions
oranges
paprika
parsley
pepper, black
peppers, red and hot
Pernod
porcinis
potatoes

pumpkin
rosemary
saffron
salsa
salt
shallots
sorrel
soy sauce
spinach
Tabasco sauce
tarragon
thyme
tomatoes
truffles
vanilla
vermouth
vinaigrette
vinegar, especially cider
wine, white

broil
deep-fry
grill
marinate
poach
sauté
steam

(continued on next page)

SCALLOPS *(continued)*

Maine Sea Scallops Layered with Black Truffles in Golden Puff Pastry
—Daniel Boulud

Black Truffle-Larded Maine Diver Sea Scallops with Artichokes Barigoule, Braised Lettuce, and Truffle Broth—Terrance Brennan

Diver Scallops Wrapped in Bacon Pastrami on Sweet Potato Latkes
—Lydia Shire

Seared Maine Scallops with Sevruga Caviar, Crème Fraîche, *and Diced Potato*—Joachim Splichal

Scallops Broiled and Served on Celeriac Rémoulade with Osetra Caviar
—Jean-Georges Vongerichten

Scallops in their Shells with American Sturgeon Caviar Butter—Alice Waters

Cape Scallops Sautéed with Garlic and Sun-Dried Tomatoes—Jasper White

SEA BASS   (Winter–Spring)

anchovies	**mushrooms**	**tomatoes**
basil	nutmeg	truffles, black
bay leaves	**olive oil**	vinegar, especially bal-
chervil	olives	samic and white wine
chives	oranges	**wine**
coriander	pepper	
cumin	**peppers**	*bake*
curry	rosemary	*braise*
fennel	seaweed	*grill*
garlic	**shallots**	*poach*
ginger	star anise	*roast*
lemon	tarragon	*sauté*
Madeira	thyme	

American sea bass is probably the best fish in the United States.
—Susanna Foo

Roasted Black Sea Bass in a Crisp Potato Shell on a Bed of Leeks with a Red Wine Sauce—Daniel Boulud

Pan-Fried Sea Bass with Fried Basil and Richard Olney's Eggplant Gratin
—Alice Waters

SEAFOOD

aïoli	**lemon**	pepper, hot red
avocados	lettuce	pignoli
citrus	lime	smoked meats
currants, red	olive oil	
grapefruit	parsley	

SEA URCHIN   (Winter)

lemon   lime

SHAD   (Spring)

butter	parsley	*bake*
lemon	sorrel	*broil*
mustard	watercress	*roast*
onions		

SHAD ROE   (Spring)

anchovies	Mornay sauce	**watercress**
bacon	mushrooms	wine, white
basil	mustard	
butter, especially brown	onions	*bake*
capers	Parmesan cheese	*broil*
chervil	**parsley**	**grill**
chives	pepper, white	*par-boil*
cream	shallots	*poach*
lemon	tarragon	*sauté*
lime		

Grilled Shad Roe with Smoked Bacon, Roasted Morels, and Lemon Linguine
—Bradley Ogden

Shad Roe Wrapped in Bacon and Grilled with Wilted Spinach, Red Onions, and Oranges—Jasper White

SHELLFISH

bacon	lemon	vermouth
gin	mushrooms	vodka
ham	saffron	wine
leeks	truffles	

SHIITAKES

butter	game	*bake*
cabbage, napa	garlic	*sauté*
chicken	olive oil	*steam*
eggplant	parsley	*tempura-fry*
fish	shallots	

SHRIMP

allspice
anchovies
artichokes
bacon
basil
bay leaves
beans, white
beer
brandy
butter
buttermilk
carrots
caviar
chervil
chiles
chives
cocktail sauce
coconut
Cognac
corn
cream
cucumbers
curry, especially red

dill
eggplant
garlic
ginger
lemon
lemongrass
lime
Madeira
mangoes
mayonnaise
mint
mushrooms
mustard
olive oil
onions, especially red
oranges
parsley
peanuts
pepper, black
Pernod
pineapple
pomegranates
rice

rosemary
saffron
Sauternes
scallions
shallots
soy sauce
Tabasco sauce
tarragon
thyme
tomatoes
vinaigrette
vodka
wine, especially rice or
    white
Worcestershire sauce

boil
broil
deep-fry
grill
pan-fry
poach
tempura-fry

Fresh Florida Pink Shrimp in Red Chile Escabèche with Grilled Red Onions, Peas, and Garlicky White Rice—Rick Bayless

Sautéed Rock Shrimp with Toasted Ancho Chiles, Slivered Garlic, and Lime, served with Seared Greens and Rice—Susan Feniger & Mary Sue Milliken

Coriander-Crusted Grilled Shrimp with Pineapple Salsa and Lime
—Chris Schlesinger

Shrimp Dusted with Orange Zest, Artichoke, and Basil
—Jean-Georges Vongerichten

Saffron Noodles with Maine Shrimp, Country Bacon, and Pine Nuts
—Jasper White

SKATE

aïoli
butter, including brown
capers
coriander
garlic
hazelnut
hollandaise sauce

mayonnaise
mint
olive oil
parsley
pepper
thyme
truffles

vinegar, especially red
    wine
wine, especially white

poach
roast
steam

SNAILS

anchovies
anise
bacon
basil
bay leaves
bread crumbs
butter
chervil
cream

fennel
garlic
lemon
mushrooms
nutmeg
parsley
pepper, black
pignoli
rosemary

salt
shallots
thyme
wine, white

bake
braise
broil
simmer

SNAP PEAS

butter

olive oil

vinegar, balsamic

SNAPPER

bread crumbs
endive

ginger
mustard

roast
sauté

SOLE

almonds
anchovies
béarnaise sauce
béchamel sauce
butter
capers
carrots
cayenne
Champagne
chives
coriander leaves
cream
garlic
hollandaise sauce
leeks
lemon
lobster
Marsala

mint
morels
mushrooms
mussels
mustard
nutmeg
olive oil
onions
oranges
oysters
paprika
Parmesan cheese
parsley
pepper, black
peppers
port wine
salt
scallions

shallots
shrimp
Tabasco sauce
thyme
tomatoes
truffles
vinaigrette
vinegar
wine, especially white

braise
broil
fry
grill
poach
sauté
steam

SOLE, DOVER (See also SOLE)

basil

mustard

vermouth

wine, especially red

grill

SORREL

(Spring)

butter

celery root

chard

chervil

cream

crème fraîche

eggs

fish

lentils

mustard

olive oil

pepper, black

potatoes

salt

spinach

sugar

tarragon

blanch

purée

sauté

SOUFFLÉS, SWEET

chocolate

coffee

fruits, especially apples,
  apricots, blueberries,
  peaches, pears,
  pineapple, quinces,
  raspberries, and
  strawberries

hazelnuts

liqueurs, especially
  anisette, Cointreau,
  Curaçao, Grand
  Marnier, Kirsch,

Madeira, Marsala,
  port

vanilla

SPAETZLE

butter

pepper, black

poppy seeds

SPARERIBS

barbecue sauce

garlic

ginger

honey

lemon

pepper

plum sauce

rosemary

sauerkraut

soy sauce

wine, rice

vinegar

bake

barbecue

boil

broil

par-boil

SPINACH

anchovies
bacon
brains
butter
cardamom
carrots
cheese, especially feta,
    goat, Parmesan, and
    ricotta
chiles
chives
cream
cumin
curry
eggs
fish
garlic

ginger
ham
hollandaise sauce
horseradish
leeks
lemon
lemongrass
mint
mushrooms
mustard
nutmeg
nuts (especially
    almonds and walnuts)
olive oil
olives
onions
oranges

pepper, black
peppers, especially red
raisins
sorrel
sour cream
soy
sugar
tarragon
tomatoes
vinegar, especially red
    wine
yogurt

boil
purée
sauté

The thought of spinach is pleasure. French cooks, Chinese cooks, Italian cooks, Indian cooks would all rate spinach the best of leaf vegetables.
—Jane Grigson

SQUAB

apricots
bacon
basil
beer
brandy
butter
cabbage
cherries
chestnuts
chives
chocolate
cider
Cognac
cranberries
cream
cumin
currants
eggplant
figs

foie gras
garlic
grapes
huckleberries
juniper berries
lemon
lime
mushrooms
olive oil
olives
onions
oranges
paprika
parsley
peaches
peas
pepper, black
raspberries
rhubarb

rice
rosemary
sage
shallots
sour cream
soy
stuffing
tarragon
thyme
vinegar
truffles
wine, especially red

braise
broil
grill
roast

SQUASH, ACORN (See also SQUASH, WINTER)   (Fall–Winter)

bacon	maple syrup	*bake*
brown sugar	nutmeg	*boil*
butter	Parmesan cheese	*steam*
garlic	pepper, black	
honey	sage	

SQUASH, BUTTERNUT (See also SQUASH, WINTER)   (Fall–Winter)

ancho chiles	cinnamon	rosemary
apples	curry	sage
butter	nuts	sherry
celery root	oranges	
Cheddar cheese	Parmesan cheese	*bake*
chestnuts	pears	
chorizo	pecans	

SQUASH, SPAGHETTI

butter	pepper	*bake*
cream	salt	*boil*
nutmeg	tomato sauce	
Parmesan cheese		

SQUASH, SUMMER (See also ZUCCHINI)   (Summer)

bacon	lemon	pepper
basil	lemon thyme	saffron
butter	nutmeg	
cinnamon	olive oil	*bake*
cream	onions	*deep-fry*
curry	paprika	*sauté*
ginger	Parmesan cheese	*steam*

SQUASH, WINTER   (Fall–Winter)

bacon	garlic	onions
brown sugar	ginger	oranges
butter	leeks	parsley, especially Italian
cheese, Gruyère and Parmesan	maple syrup	pineapples
	mint	potatoes
chiles	nutmeg	raisins
cinnamon	nuts	sage
cream	olive oil	

(continued on facing page)

sherry
thyme

truffles, white
vanilla

bake
purée

SQUASH BLOSSOMS   (Summer)

butter
cheese, especially goat
forcemeats

garlic
olive oil

bake
deep-fry
sauté

SQUID   (Winter)

anchovies
basil
bay leaves
bread crumbs
cilantro
garlic
ginger
lemon
lime

mayonnaise
mint
olive oil
onions
parsley
rosemary
salsa
squid ink
tomatoes

vinaigrette
wine, especially white

bake
cook briefly
fry
braise slowly
grill
sauté

Squid Salad with Five-Flavor Vinaigrette—Susanna Foo

Marinated Tomatoes and Arugula with Fried Squid—Jasper White

STEAK

avocados
basil
béarnaise sauce
bordelaise sauce
bourbon
brandy
butter with anchovies,
   chives, garlic, parsley,
   tarragon
cayenne

chives
Cognac
coriander
garlic
ginger
horseradish
juniper berries
leeks
lemon
Madeira
mushrooms
mustard
olive oil
onions
parsley
pepper, black
peppers, especially green
pizzaiola sauce
potatoes
rosemary

scallions
shallots
sherry
sour cream
soy
Stilton cheese
tomatoes
truffles
vinegar, especially bal-
   samic and red wine
wine, red or white
whiskey
Worcestershire sauce

broil
grill
pan-broil
pan-fry

(continued on next page)

STEAK *(continued)*

Carne Asada: *Charcoal-Grilled, Butterflied Coleman Natural Rib Eye Marinated in Red Chile, with Black Beans and Fried Plantains with Sour Cream and Guacamole*—Rick Bayless

Grilled Hanger Steak with Roasted Bone Marrow, Fondant of Winter Vegetables, and Crisp Shallots—Terrance Brennan

Charcoaled Filet Mignon *with Roasted Shallot and Pinot Noir, Country Potato,* Foie Gras-*Stuffed Morels, and Crisp Parsnip*—Charlie Palmer

Grilled Adobo-Rubbed Sirloin Steak with Pickled Corn Relish, Tamarind Ketchup, and "Damn Good Fries"—Chris Schlesinger

Hot Roquefort-Broiled Rib Steak with Chilled Layered Tomato Salad and Beet Fries—Lydia Shire

Grilled Rib Steak with Yellow Finn Potatoes, Mushrooms, and Green Peppercorn Butter—Jeremiah Tower

STRAWBERRIES   (Spring)

coconut
Cognac
Cointreau
cream
cream cheese
crème fraîche
Curaçao
currant, black
figs
Grand Marnier
grapefruits
guavas
Kirsch
kiwi fruit
lemon
lime
maple syrup
mascarpone
nuts

almonds
apricots
bananas
basil
brown sugar
caramel
Cassis
Champagne
cinnamon
clotted cream

oranges
passion fruit
peaches
pepper, black or pink
pineapple
port
raspberries
rhubarb
sambuca
sherry
sour cream
sugar
vanilla
vinegar, balsamic
violets
wine, especially red (e.g.
    Beaujolais and claret)
yogurt
zabaione

Strawberry Shortcake with Crème Chantilly—Lindsey Shere

Strawberries in Beaujolais Sauce—Nancy Silverton

Sautéed Rhubarb with Strawberries and Vanilla Syrup
—Jean-Georges Vongerichten

STUFFING

apples
bacon
Brazil nuts
bread crumbs
carrots
celery
chestnuts
cornbread crumbs
garlic
liquor, especially bourbon, Cognac, whiskey

liver
mushrooms
nutmeg
onions
oysters
pancetta
parsley
pecans
prunes
rice
rosemary

sage
sausages
savory
shallots
tarragon
thyme
walnuts

STURGEON

mayonnaise
oysters

braise
grill

sauté

SUCKLING PIG   (Spring)

garlic
myrtle

onions
rosemary

roast

SWEET POTATOES   (Winter)

apples
apricots
bacon
bananas
brown sugar
butter
cilantro
cinnamon
cloves
coconut
cream
garlic
ginger
honey

lemon
lime
maple syrup
nutmeg
oranges
paprika
pears
pecans
pepper, black
pineapple
raisins
rum
salt
sherry, dry

sour cream
sunflower seeds
thyme
vanilla
walnuts

bake
boil
deep-fry
purée
roast
sauté

SWEETBREADS

apples
bacon
brandy
bread crumbs
butter, especially brown
capers
carrots
cherries
chervil
citrus
clove
corn, puréed
cream
crème fraîche
curry
eggs

garlic
hazelnuts
hollandaise sauce
lemon
Madeira
Marsala
morels
mushrooms
mustard
onions, especially red
oysters
Parmesan cheese
parsley
peas
peppers, red
port

savory
shallots
sherry
spinach
tarragon
thyme
tomatoes
truffles
walnut oil
watercress
wine, white

braise
broil
poach
sauté

"Jump in the Mouth" Sweetbreads Sautéed with Fresh Fig and Summer Savory—Lydia Shire

Sweetbread Club Sandwich with Apple-Smoked Bacon, Foie Gras, *and a Good Sauce*—Joachim Splichal

Sweetbread and Potato Salad in a Shallot and Hazelnut Dressing
—Jean-Georges Vongerichten

SWISS CHARD   (Summer)

chiles
garlic

lemon
tarragon

tomatoes
vinegar

SWORDFISH

basil
Beaujolais
beet juice
butter
capers
caviar
chanterelles
chives
coconut
coriander
cream

curry
ginger
grapefruit
lemon
mustard
olive oil
parsley
pineapples
rosemary
tarragon
tomatoes

vinaigrette
vinegar, balsamic
wine, especially white

bake
broil
grill
roast
sauté

(continued on facing page)

Cold Swordfish Salad with Basil—Daniel Boulud

Grilled Swordfish with Scallion Vinaigrette—Susan Feniger & Mary Sue Milliken

Sautéed Swordfish and Osetra Caviar Cake with Caviar Sauce
—Jean-Louis Palladin

Grilled Swordfish with Tomato and Roast Pepper Compote—Michael Romano

Swordfish with Ginger and Grapefruit—Jimmy Schmidt

Grilled Swordfish with Rosemary Mayonnaise—Jeremiah Tower

Roasted Swordfish with Herbs, Smoked Bacon, and Red Wine Butter
—Norman Van Aken

Grilled Swordfish with Basil Butter and Tomato Sauce—Jasper White

TOMATOES   (Summer)

anchovies
arugula
basil
bread crumbs
Champagne
cheese, especially Feta,
    goat, Mozzarella, and
    Parmesan
chiles
chives
cucumbers
eggs
garlic
lemon
lovage

marjoram
mint
mushrooms
olive oil
olives
onions
oregano
parsley
pasta
pepper, black
peppers, especially red
saffron
salt
seafood
shallots

sugar
tarragon
thyme
vinegar, especially bal-
    samic, sherry and
    wine

bake
broil
fry
grill
raw
sauté
stew

Summer Crostini with Native Tomatoes, Little Compton Corn, Red Onion, and Basil—George Germon & Johanne Killeen

Vine-Ripened Tomato Salad with Mozzarella and Roasted Sweet Onions
—Bradley Ogden

Spicy Cold Tomato and Pepper Soup Barcelona-Style—Alice Waters

TONGUE

anchovies
capers
cherries
chervil
chives
garlic
horseradish
lemon
mushrooms
mustard
olive oil
parsley
pepper, black
port
rosemary
tarragon
thyme
tomatoes
vinegar, especially red
   wine

bake
boil

TRIPE

allspice
bacon
brandy
bread crumbs
Calvados
chickpeas
cider
cloves
cumin
garlic
lemon
marjoram
mushrooms
mustard
nutmeg
onions
pancetta
paprika
Parmesan cheese
parsley
pepper, black
prunes
saffron
Sauternes
thyme
tomatoes
truffles
vinaigrette
vinegar, especially red
   wine
wine
Worcestershire sauce

braise
fry
poach
sauté
simmer

TROUT

almonds
anchovies
bacon
beans, especially flageo-
   lets
**butter, especially
   brown**
capers
cèpes
chervil
chiles
chives
cream
garlic
horseradish
lemon
mushrooms
parsley
pears
pepper, black
Pernod
port
scallions
sorrel
Tabasco sauce
tomatoes
vinegar, especially wine
walnuts
wine, white

bake
broil
grill
poach
roast
sauté
sear
steam

(continued on facing page)

Roasted Maine Brook Trout Stuffed with Winter Greens, Tomato Confit, and Country-Cured Bacon, with Fingerling Potatoes and Wild Mushrooms with Sage—Daniel Boulud

Sautéed Trout Stuffed with Garlic, Chile, and Toasted Pecans with Garden Tomato Relish—Chris Schlesinger

TROUT, SMOKED

bacon	horseradish	olive oil
cream	lemon	sour cream

House-Smoked Trout with Apple-Chive Fritters and Horseradish Cream
—Bradley Ogden

Grapefruit and Smoked Trout with Pickled Onions and Pepper Cress
—Alice Waters

TRUFFLES (See also BLACK and WHITE) (Fall–Winter)

	chicken	onions
	Cognac	Parmesan cheese
	cream	pasta
	eggs	pepper
	foie gras	**port**
	garlic	**potatoes**
	ham	poultry
	leeks	poultry fat
	Madeira	risotto
butter	meats	salt
Champagne	morels	sweetbreads

(See also Gary Danko's Truffle Menu on page 186.)

TRUFFLES, BLACK (Winter)

chicken	pâté	veal
eggs	**potatoes**	wine, white
fish	poultry	
foie gras	turkey	

TRUFFLES, WHITE (Fall)

butter	**eggs**	**risotto**
cheese, especially	**pasta**	salads
Fontina or Parmesan		

Gary Danko

THE DINING ROOM AT THE RITZ-CARLTON HOTEL
San Francisco, California

We've had three or four promotions a year where we've developed special menus—around caviar, cheese, or truffles, for example—in order to increase our business. Each would be kicked off with a press luncheon about three weeks before the menu debuted. For example, we'd serve truffle hors d'oeuvres, bring in an expert on truffles from France to provide a slide or video show and talk about truffles, and then bring the journalists into the kitchen where they could watch the preparation of the special menu and ask questions.

With a menu like this, you want to have the truffle speak—not anything else! I started backwards, with a truffle dessert and a truffled cheese course. Since these were both heavy on the cream, I aimed for lighter preparations of the other courses.

Truffle Menu

Truffle Soup
La Gitana, Manzanilla

• • •

Seared Scallops with Spring Vegetables and Truffles
Domaine Ostertag 1990, Pinot Blanc

• • •

Lamb Medallions with Wild Mushrooms and Truffled Lamb Essence,
Gratin Potatoes
Tinto Pesquera 1989, Ribera del Duero

• • •

Truffled Brillat-Savarin
Chateau de Trignon 1985, Rasteau

• • •

Truffle Ice Cream

TUNA   (Summer)

aïoli
anchovies
artichokes
avocados
bacon
bay leaves
beans, especially black
   and white
beets
capers
carrots
caviar
chives
cilantro
daikon
dill
garlic
ginger
leek

lemon
lemongrass
lime
mayonnaise
mint
mushrooms
olive oil
onions
parsley
pepper, black
peppers, especially red
   bell
pineapple
potatoes
saffron
scallions
seaweed
sesame
soy sauce

tamarillos
teriyaki sauce
thyme
tomato sauce
tomatoes
vinaigrette
vinegar, especially wine
wasabi
wine, especially white

bake
braise
broil
grill
raw
roast
sauté
sear

Roasted Tuna with Black Pepper, Parsnip Purée, and Shallot Confit in Port Wine—Daniel Boulud

Seared Rare Ahi Tuna with Avocado and Soy-Lemon Herb Dressing —Gary Danko

Grilled Marinated Tuna with Roasted Peppers, Bok Choy, Shiitake Mushrooms, Soy, and Ginger—Gary Danko

Grilled Tuna au Poivre with Cracked Black Pepper and Lemon Butter served with Shoestring Potatoes and Spinach—Joyce Goldstein

Ahi Tuna with a Crust of Pink and Black Peppercorns Enhanced with Lime, Orange, and Lemon—Hubert Keller

Lemon-Dijon Tuna Tartare with Rye Toast and Scallion Oil—Mark Miller

Filet Mignon of Rare Tuna Capped with Duck Foie Gras on Charred Onions and a Burgundy Butter Sauce—Patrick O'Connell

Grilled Tuna Steak with Pickled Ginger, Soy, Wasabi, Liang Pan, and Jasmine Rice Cakes—Chris Schlesinger

Tuna Tartare Mixed with Cucumbers, Onions, Capers, and Wasabi Vinaigrette—Jimmy Schmidt

Yellowfin Tuna Braised with Anchovies, Tomatoes, Onions, Garlic, and Bay Leaves—Alice Waters

TURBOT

anchovies
béarnaise sauce
butter
capers
cayenne
Champagne
chives
cream
cucumbers
hollandaise sauce

horseradish
leeks
lemon
mousseline sauce
mushrooms
mustard
mace
nutmeg
olive oil

parsley
shallots
shrimp
tomatoes
wine, white

broil
poach
sauté

TURKEY   (Fall)

celery
celery root
cheese, especially
  Parmesan
chestnuts
chocolate, bitter
ham
lemon
Madeira

maple syrup
Marsala
mole sauce
mushrooms
parsley
prunes
raspberries
sage
stuffing

tarragon
thyme
truffles, white
vinegar
wine, white

broil
grill
roast

Grilled Breast of Turkey, Peppered and Vinegared, served with Sweet Potatoes and Seared Greens—Susan Feniger & Mary Sue Milliken

TURNIPS   (WINTER)

apples
bacon
butter
carrots
cheese, Gruyère and
  Parmesan
chives
cider
cinnamon
cream
fat, animal (e.g., chick-
  en, lamb, pork)
garlic

lemon
lemon thyme
maple syrup
mushrooms
mustard
onions
paprika
parsley
potatoes
salt
sherry
sugar
sweet potatoes

tarragon
thyme
vinaigrette
vinegar

boil
fry
purée
sauté
simmer
steam

VEAL

anchovies
apples
artichokes
arugula
bacon
basil
bay leaves
bread crumbs
butter
capers
carrots
cèpes
cheese, especially
  Gruyère and
  Parmesan
chervil
cider
cloves
corn, puréed
cream
dill
endive

foie gras
garlic
ginger
grapefruit
ham
leeks
lemon
lime
Madeira
Marsala wine
morels
Mornay sauce
mushrooms
mustard
olive oil
onions
paprika
Parma ham
parsley
pepper, black
peppers
pistachios

potatoes
rosemary
sage
salmon
shallots
sorrel
sour cream
spinach
sweetbreads
tapenade
tarragon
thyme
tomatoes
truffles, especially white
tuna
verbena
vermouth
wine, especially white

braise
roast
sauté

Everything goes with veal. Like chicken, it's a meat with a neutral flavor, so you can take it in a lot of different directions. A very earthy direction would be combining it, grandmère-style, with bacon, mushrooms, potatoes, and pearl onions. Or you can take it in a bitter direction, with caramelized endive. Or you can make the dish sharp by pairing the veal with capers or mustard sauce. Veal's pretty bland on its own, so you need something to give it a little bit of life.—Terrance Brennan

Sautéed Veal Medallions with Chestnuts, Celery Root, and Apples with Potatoes Fifi—Gary Danko

Pan-Roasted Veal Steak with Yukon Gold Potatoes, Peppers, and Garlic—Gray Kunz

"Sandwich" of Veal and Veal Sweetbreads with Oyster Mushrooms, Country Ham, and Onion-Plum Confiture—Patrick O'Connell

Veal Medallions with Wild Mushroom Canelloni, Tomato Confit, and Essence of Fresh Sage—Charlie Palmer

Sautéed Veal Steaks with Rum, Plantains, and Creole Mustard Cream—Norman Van Aken

VEAL CHOPS (See also VEAL)

anchovies
bacon
basil
bay leaves
bread crumbs
capers
chervil
Cognac
garlic
ginger
lemon
Madeira
morels

Mornay sauce
mushrooms
olives
onions
paprika
Parmesan cheese
parsley
pepper, black
peppers
potatoes
rosemary
shallots
sorrel

tarragon
thyme
tomato sauce
vinegar, especially rasp-
   berry and wine
watercress
wine

braise
broil
roast
sauté

Roasted Veal Chop and Sweetbreads with Rosemary, Winter Root Vegetables, and Sweet Garlic—Daniel Boulud

Seared Veal Chop with Parmigiano-Reggiano Spinach and Soft Polenta—Gary Danko

Veal Chops with Shitake Mushrooms—Mark Peel

VEAL KIDNEYS (See also KIDNEYS)

bacon
beans, especially white
brandy
butter
Cognac
cranberries
cream
curry
garlic

gin
juniper berries
lemon
morels
mushrooms
mustard
nutmeg
onions
paprika

parsley
shallots
wine

bake
broil
grill
sauté

VEAL SHANKS   (Winter)

carrots
garlic
gremolata
honey

lemon
onions
parsley
pepper, black

rosemary
sage
thyme
wine, white

VEAL SWEETBREADS (See also SWEETBREADS)

brandy
Cognac
crayfish

mushrooms
onions
tomatoes

braise
broil
sauté

VENISON   (Fall)

apples
bacon
bananas
barley
bay leaf
béarnaise sauce
brandy
cherries, especially black
chestnuts
chiles, especially ancho
   and poblano
cider
coriander seeds
cream
currants, red

garlic
goat cheese
horseradish
huckleberries
juniper berries
Madeira
marjoram
mushrooms
mustard
onions
oranges
parsnips
pears
pepper, black
pomegranates

port
prickly pears
prunes
rosemary
sweet potatoes
tarragon
thyme
vinegar, especially red
   wine
wine, especially red

braise
grill
roast
sauté

Honey and Cumin Glazed Loin of Venison with Foie Gras, *Endive, Kohlrabi, Orange Zest, and Pine Nuts—*Daniel Boulud

Medallions of Venison with Purées of Parsnip, Sweet Potato, and Mushrooms —Terrance Brennan

*Cervena Venison Pepper Steak with Mushroom Spaetzle, Butternut Squash Flan, and Caramelized Parsnip—*Charles Palmer

*Venison with Mustards and Chiles—*Jimmy Schmidt

*Roasted Racks of Venison, One of Sweetened Chestnut, the Other of Bitter Chocolate—*Lydia Shire

(See also Charlie Palmer's venison recipe on pages 192–193.)

WALNUTS   (Fall)

caramel
cèpes
cheeses, especially
   Roquefort and
   Stilton

fish
mushrooms
pork
port
raisins

salads
sherry
zucchini

Mignons of Cervena Venison

Charlie Palmer
AUREOLE
New York, New York

This recipe, I think, represents my style of food—complementary, big flavors; a bit complex in its preparation in some ways, but really a concentration of big, strong flavors. It's robust. It's solitude. It's the kind of dish that makes you sit up and take notice. That's what I really try to do with every kind of recipe I create.

SERVES 4

For the squash

3 tablespoons butter

2 shallots, peeled and minced

2 medium butternut squash, peeled, seeded, and cut into 1/2-inch dice

3 1/2 cups chicken stock

1/2 teaspoon nutmeg

1/2 teaspoon mace

salt and pepper to taste

Place the butter in a medium sauté pan and melt over medium heat. Add the shallots and sauté 2 minutes. Add the squash and toss together. Next, add all the remaining ingredients and cook slowly for about 12 to 15 minutes, stirring occasionally. Hold warm after almost all the stock is absorbed.

For the portobellos

2 large portobello mushroom caps

2 tablespoons extra virgin olive oil

1 tablespoon balsamic vinegar

1 clove garlic, sliced thin

1 tablespoon salt and cracked pepper

Brush mushrooms with olive oil and vinegar. Top with garlic slices, season, and roast in an oven preheated to 500° for 7 to 8 minutes. Hold warm.

For the venison and sauce

2 cups Beaujolais wine

2 finely minced shallots

1 herb sachet including thyme, bay leaf, peppercorns

1 1/2 cups good venison *glace* or veal *glace*

8 3-ounce mignons of Cervena venison (cut from the Denver leg),
1–1 1/4 inch thick

salt and pepper

2 tablespoons canola oil for searing

1/4 cup sun-dried currants (reconstituted in warm water)

4 tablespoons cassis for deglazing

1. Begin by reducing the wine, shallots, and sachet to 1/2 cup of liquid. Add the *glace* and reduce by 1/2 (about 20 minutes at a medium simmer). Skim the sauce and strain into a bowl. Reserve.

2. Season the Cervena venison with salt and pepper. In a very hot sauté pan, heat the canola oil. Place the mignons in the pan and sear for about 2 to 3 minutes or till almost crusty. Turn the mignons and sear the other side for an additional 1 1/2 to 2 minutes. Remove from the pan to a platter and drain any grease. Add the cassis to the pan along with the drained currants. Finally, add the base sauce and bring to a boil. Adjust the seasoning and hold warm.

3. Reheat the squash and spoon into the center of 4 warm dinner plates. Set 2 mignons atop each bed. Slice the warm portobellos and lay a few pieces over each mignon. Bring the sauce back to a boil and spoon generously over the meat. Serve very hot.

WATERCRESS   (Spring)

beets	oranges	walnuts
chicory	oregano	
eggs	**parsley**	*purée*
endive	thyme	*raw*
mustard	**vinaigrette**	

YAMS (See also SWEET POTATOES)   (Winter)

apricots	persimmons	maple
butter		

YOGURT

apples	honey	radishes
bananas	mint	raspberries
blueberries	nuts, especially hazel-	strawberries
carrots	nuts	watercress
coconut	oats	
cucumbers	onions	
granola	peaches	

ZUCCHINI

anchovies
basil
bread crumbs
butter
cayenne
cheese, especially Feta,
Gruyère, **Parmesan,**

and Ricotta
cilantro
cinnamon
cloves
cream
dill
eggplant
garlic
hazelnuts
lemon
marjoram
mint
mushrooms
olive oil
onions
oregano

(Spring–Summer)

parsley
pesto
pignoli
rosemary
sage
salmon
tarragon
thyme
tomatoes
vinegar
walnuts

bake
fry
sauté

Tinga de Verduras: *An Earthenware Casserole of Grilled Zucchini and Woodland Mushrooms with Smoky Roasted Tomato Sauce, Fresh Cheese, Avocado, and White Rice*—Rick Bayless

Sautéed Zucchini with Sun-Dried Tomatoes—Susanna Foo

Baked Eggplant, Zucchini and Parmigiano Tortino—Michael Romano

Parmesan-Fried Zucchini with White Bean Hummus—Lydia Shire

SEASONING MATCHES MADE IN HEAVEN

ACHIOTE

chicken	meat, white	rice
fish	pork	

ALLSPICE

beef	grains	spinach
beets	lamb	squash
cabbage	meats	stews
carrots	onions	sweet potatoes
corned beef	pumpkin	tomatoes
fruit pies	rabbit	turnips
game	soups	

ANCHOVY

Caesar salad	pizza	puttanesca
pissaladière	potatoes	tapenade

ANISEED

beets	cauliflower	melon
breads	desserts	sauerkraut
cabbage	fish	seafood
carrots		

BASIL

cheese, especially Mozzarella and Parmesan	onions	shellfish, especially crab and shrimp
	pasta sauces	soups
	pesto	sweet peppers
chicken	pimientos	**tomatoes**
duck	pizza	turtle soup
eggplant	pork	veal
eggs	potatoes	vegetables, especially Mediterranean
fish	rabbit	
lamb	salad greens, especially dandelion and rocket	vinegars
liver		zucchini
olive oil		

If I had to choose just one plant for the whole herb garden, I should be content with basil…Basil enhances almost anything with which it is cooked.
—Elizabeth David

BAY LEAF

beans	*pâtés*	soups
game	potatoes	stews
grains	risotto	terrines
lentils	shellfish	tomatoes

BEANS, FERMENTED BLACK

fish	poultry	shellfish

CAPERS

fish	onions	tomatoes

CARAWAY

bread, especially rye	pork	soups
cabbage	potatoes	turnips
cheese, especially	sauerkraut	
Muenster	sausages	

CARDAMOM

chicken	lentils	rice
coffee	meat	squash
curries	oranges	sweetmeats
duck	peas	

CASSIA

apples	couscous	peas
chocolate	lentils	stewed fruit

CAYENNE

cheese sauces	fish	pototoes
corn	lobster	rice
crab	onions	sardines
eggplant	peppers	tomatoes

CELERY SEEDS

eggplant	peas	stuffings
eggs	potatoes	tomatoes
fish		

CHERVIL

asparagus	**fish**	soups
carrots	peas	spinach
cheese	potatoes	tomatoes
chicken	**salads**	veal
eggs	sauces	venison

CHILES

bananas	corn	pineapple
beans	fruit, especially citrus	rice
chutneys	ketchup	

CHIVES

eggs	**salads**	sole
fish	shellfish	soups
potatoes		

CHOCOLATE, BITTER

desserts	poultry	seafood
game	rabbit	

CILANTRO (CORIANDER LEAVES)

avocado	mayonnaise	salsas
chicken	peppers	shellfish
fish	pork	tomatoes
ice cream	rice	yogurt
lamb	root vegetables	
lentils	salads	

I've used fresh leaf coriander, which is vaguely anisey, in ice cream, to serve with a fig tart. It's a very nice combination.
—Lindsey Shere

CINNAMON

apples	coffee	oranges
avgolemono	custards	pears
berries	fruit compotes	rice
chicken	lamb	tea
chocolate	mulled wine	zucchini

CINNAMON BASIL

crème anglaise	fruit	veal

I use cinnamon basil to flavor poaching liquids for fruit.—Lindsey Shere

CLOVES

apples	lamb	tea
beets	mincemeat	tomatoes
game	pumpkin	walnuts, candied
ham	sausage	wine, especially mulled

COCONUT

chicken	fruit	shellfish
custard	oranges	

CORIANDER

curry	lamb	stuffing
fish	lentils	tomatoes
ham	pork	turkey

CUMIN

beans	lamb	potatoes
chicken	lentils	rice
couscous	peas	sausages
curry	pickles	soups
eggplant	pork	stews
fish		

(continued on next page)

CUMIN (continued)

Anyone who loves the food of Mexico loves cumin, which is usually combined with chiles and peppers in that country. In Colombia and other parts of South America, you'll see cumin combined with cilantro and scallion. In Morocco, you'll see it with cinnamon, red peppers, and saffron. And in India, you'll see it combined with cardamom and coriander.

So one spice can take you to many countries, depending on what you do with it. It becomes a question of where you want to be, what country you want to be in, when you cook with that spice.—Lydia Shire

DILL

beets	cream sauces	scallops
breads	eggs	seafood
cabbage	**fish**	sour cream
carrots	lamb	tomatoes
chicken	pickles	veal
crayfish	**potatoes**	
cucumbers	**salmon**	

Dill is not an herb I'm crazy about, so I don't like chopped dill in a dish. But I'll cook something like salmon on a bed of it, and the fragrance it imparts is enough.—Daniel Boulud

FENNEL

bouillabaisse	herring	sauerkraut
cabbage	lentils	**sausage**
chicken	pork	sea bass
cucumbers	mackerel	**seafood**
duck	olives	soup
eggs	pork	suckling pig
figs	poultry	tomatoes
fish	red mullet	veal
goose	salami	

FENUGREEK

chicken	legumes	rabbit
curries	potatoes	

GARLIC

beans
beef

beets
cabbage
chicken
eggplant
fish
lamb
lentils
mushrooms
pasta
pork
potatoes

rice
shellfish
spinach
tomatoes
zucchini

GINGER

carrots
chicken
chocolate
fruit
gingerbread

ham
ice cream
melon
onions
pork

pumpkin
rice
tomatoes

Each ingredient does a different dance. Each dish does a different dance. A crème anglaise with ginger does a soft, dreamy waltz. When I think of a spicy pork stir-fry with ginger, I get an image of a big dance floor with lots of ingredients doing a real energetic dance, with the garlic and chiles spotting each other, and suddenly breaking out into their own riveting lambada!
—Norman Van Aken

HORSERADISH

apples
beef
beets
chicken
chives
cream

crème fraîche
eggs
fish
pork
salmon
sausages

shellfish
smoked fish
sour cream
trout
walnuts
yogurt

JUNIPER BERRIES

beef
cabbage
game
game birds
ham

lamb
liver
kidneys, especially veal
mutton
pâtés

pork
stuffings
sauerkraut
veal
venison

LAVENDER

fruit	lamb	stew
ice creams	rabbit	

LEMON

chicken	fish	shellfish
desserts	oysters	veal

LEMONGRASS

chicken	pork	soups
fish	shellfish	

LEMON THYME

carrots	potato purée	stews
eggs	rabbit	stuffings
lamb	salads	

LEMON VERBENA

dessert soups	lamb	mushrooms
ice cream		

LOVAGE

chicken	haricot beans	soups
cream cheese	pork	stews
fish soups	potatoes	veal
greens	rabbit	

MAPLE SYRUP

carrots	ham	pumpkins
desserts	onions	ribs
fruit		

MARJORAM

brains
carrots
chicken
corn
cucumber
duck
eggs
fish
goat cheese
halibut

lamb chops
meats
mushrooms
mutton
peas
pork chops
potatoes
rabbit
ravioli
salads

soups
spinach
squash, especially sum-
    mer
stuffings
tomatoes
tuna
zucchini

MINT

beans, black
carrots
chocolate
cream sauce
duck
eggplant
fish soups and stews
fruit salads
goat

ices
ice creams
lamb
lemon sauce
lentils
mushrooms
oranges
peas
peppers

pilafs
pork
potatoes
rice
salsas, especially tomato
tomatoes
vegetable salads
vegetables
yogurt dressings

Mint is one of the cleanest tasting of herbs.—Elizabeth David

MOLASSES

apples
baked beans

brown bread
gingerbread

walnuts

MUSTARD

avocado
beef
beets
cabbage
chicken
crab

fish
lamb
mussels
pigs' feet
pork
rabbit

salmon
sauerkraut
sausages
steaks
vinaigrette

NUTMEG

broccoli
cabbage
carrots
cauliflower
cheese
custards
eggs
fruits

lamb
mutton
pasta
potatoes
pumpkin
raisins
ricotta cheese
rice

sausages, especially
  blood and pork
soufflés
spinach
stuffings
veal

OREGANO

artichokes
beans
chicken
eggplant
fish and fish soups
lamb

mushrooms
pasta
peppers
pizza
pork
potatoes

quail
rabbit
sausage
tomatoes
veal
zucchini

PAPRIKA

cauliflower
chicken
crab
fish stew

goulash
lamb
potatoes
rice

shellfish
stroganoff
veal

PARSLEY

chicken
eggplant
eggs
fish
game
lentils

mushrooms
mussels
pasta
peas
potatoes
poultry

rice
seafood
snails
tomatoes
zucchini

PEANUTS

beef
chicken

noodles

shrimp

PEPPER, BLACK

cheese
eggs
fish
game
lamb
pfeffernüesse

pork
poultry
roast beef
salad
sausages
soup

steaks
strawberries
tomatoes
veal

PISTACHIOS

asparagus
chicken
ice cream

leeks
pasta
pâtés

rice
sausages

POMEGRANATE SYRUP

beef
duck

game
lamb

walnuts

POPPY SEEDS

breads
curries

fruit
noodles

rice

ROSEMARY

beans, especially dried
  and fava
chicken
fish, oily (e.g., mackerel, sardines)
game
grains

lamb
mushrooms
onions
oranges
peas
pork
potatoes

poultry
salmon
spinach
steaks
veal
suckling pig

I remember making a rosemary and muscat wine sherbet almost twenty years ago.—Lindsey Shere

ROSEWATER

cream cheese
custards

fruit salad
ices

ice creams
strawberries

SAFFRON

bouillabaisse
chicken
curries
fish
lamb

mussels
paella
rice
risotto
sauces

shellfish
soup
tomatoes

SAGE

duck
eggplant
fish
game
goose
liver

offal
peas
pork
poultry
ravioli

roasts
stuffings
tomatoes
tuna
veal

SAVORY

beans
chicken livers
eggs
goat cheese

lamb
legumes
lentils
meats, grilled

peas
poultry, grilled
rabbit
soups

SESAME SEEDS

breads
chicken
chickpeas
eggplant

fish
halvah
lamb
noodles

shellfish
tahini

SORREL

eggs
fish
lentils

meats
poultry
shellfish

soups
stuffings

SOUR CREAM

borscht
caviar

fruit

potatoes

STAR ANISE

chestnuts
duck
eggs
fish

leeks
pastry
pears
pork

poultry
pumpkin
scallops
shrimp

SUMAC

chicken
fish

kebabs

lentils

TAMARIND

chicken
curries
fish

lamb
lentils
peaches

pears
poultry
rice

TARRAGON

artichokes
béarnaise sauce
carrots
chicken
crustaceans, especially
   lobster
eggs

fish, especially salmon
lobster
meats, white
mushrooms
onions
potatoes
rabbit

salads
sole
spinach
stuffings
tomatoes
veal

THYME

beef
carrots
chicken
figs
fish

goat cheese
lamb
lentils
onions
peas

pork
potatoes
soups
tomatoes
venison

TURMERIC

beans
chicken
curry

lamb
lentils
meats, white

paella
rice
shellfish

VANILLA

apples	fish	plums
apricots	fruit	shellfish
chocolate	ice cream	soufflés
custards		

VINEGAR, BALSAMIC

steaks	strawberries	tomatoes

You can get tired of balsamic vinegar—it's one of those overused ingredients. Many trendy restaurants use a lot more balsamic vinegar than any Italian restaurant ever would.—Mark Peel

WASABI

sashimi	sushi

AROUND THE WORLD WITH FLAVORS

If you'd like to cook with flavors and ingredients inspired by a certain part of the world, refer to this list:

AFRICAN

chiles	garlic	peanuts
cumin	grains of paradise	

ARGENTINIAN

beef	chorizo	cumin
chiles	corn	rice

ARMENIAN

parsley	yogurt

AUSTRALIAN

fish	shellfish	tropical fruits and
meats		vegetables

AUSTRIAN

cream cheese	paprika	poppy seeds
onions		

BRAZILIAN

beans, black	garlic	rice
chiles	limes	scallions
cilantro	pineapples	

CAJUN

chiles	hot sauce	tomatoes
crayfish	seafood	

CANADIAN

maple

CANTONESE

ginger	pork	shark skin
mushrooms	scallions	soy sauce
nuts		

CARIBBEAN

allspice	ginger	pineapples
avocados	guavas	plantains
bananas	jerk	pork
beans, especially red	limes	rum
chiles	mace	seafood
cilantro	mangoes	sugar
cinnamon	mint	sweet potatoes
cloves	nutmeg	tomatoes
coconut	okra	vanilla
curry	papayas	
garlic	passion fruit	

CHILEAN

cilantro	onions	seafood
corn	oranges	tomatoes
garlic	pimientos	
meats	rice	

CHINESE

basil	**ginger**	shrimp
bean sprouts	hoisin	snow peas
bok choy	mushrooms	**soy sauce**
cardamom	rice	star anise
cassia	scallions	tofu
coriander	sesame	vinegar, rice wine
garlic	shiitakes	wine, rice

In Americanizing her Chinese cuisine, Susanna Foo learned to make substitutions of readily available ingredients that were in many cases of better quality and flavor than the authentic ingredients available.

Ingredient	Substitution/Enhancement
bamboo shoots	artichoke hearts
dried leaf cabbage	sun-dried tomatoes
hoisin sauce	hoisin sauce enhanced with brandy
oyster sauce	oyster sauce enhanced with onions
peanut or sesame oil	soybean or corn oil; olive oil (in salads)
rice vinegar	balsamic vinegar (in salads and stews) cider vinegar (in sauces)
rice wine	brandy (with pork) gin (with fish) Madeira (with red meat and game) vermouth (with fish, shellfish, and white meat) vodka (with fish, shellfish, and white meat) whiskey (with pork)
Szechuan peppers	Mexican ancho chiles
soy sauce	Kikkoman soy sauce

COLOMBIAN

coconut	onions	tomatoes
corn	pimientos	

CORSICAN

Broccio cheese	olives	tomatoes
citrus fruits		

CREOLE

alcohol	okra	seafood
bananas	pineapples	spices
chiles	rum	tomato

DANISH

butter	cream	potatoes
chives	dill	tarragon

DUTCH

fish	seafood

EAST INDIAN

aromatics	curry	saffron
coconut	mint	turmeric
coriander		

ENGLISH

bacon	fish	potatoes
cheese	game	Worcestershire sauce
cucumbers	mustard	
dill	oats	

EUROPEAN

caraway	ginger	saffron
cinnamon	juniper berries	sesame
cloves	mustard	vanilla
coriander	nutmeg	
fennel	poppy seeds	

FINNISH

milk	mushrooms

FRENCH

apples	**cream**	parsley
butter	eggs	stock
cheese	garlic	**tarragon**
chervil	herbs	truffles
chives	olive oil	**wine**

White wine, cream, and the delicate herb known as tarragon are three of the foundations for classic French cuisine.—Craig Claiborne

GERMAN

caraway seeds	mustard	sorrel
dill	pepper	thyme
juniper berries	poppy seeds	vinegar

GREEK

cinnamon	marjoram	parsley
clove	mint	rice
garlic	**olive oil**	spinach
goat cheese	**olives**	thyme
honey	**oregano**	tomatoes
lemon	**ouzo**	yogurt

HUNGARIAN

bacon	mushrooms	sour cream
beets	onions	spaetzle
caraway seeds	paprika	
dill	parsley	

INDIAN

anise	fennel	peas
cardamom	fenugreek	pepper
cassia	garlic	pomegranates
chiles	ginger	poppy seeds
cinnamon	lemon	saffron
cloves	lentils	sesame
coconut	mint	spinach
coriander	mustard	tamarind
cumin	nigella	turmeric
curry	onions	yogurt
dill	peanuts	

INDONESIAN

basil
brown sugar
chiles
cilantro
cinnamon
coconut

cumin
curry
garlic
ginger
lemongrass
lime

mint
peanuts
rice
soy sauce
sugar

IRANIAN

almonds
aromatics

rice
saffron

yogurt

IRISH

cabbage
oats

oysters
potatoes

rye

ITALIAN

basil
**cheese, especially mas-
  carpone, Mozzarella
  and Parmesan**
garlic

olive oil
oregano
pancetta
pasta
rosemary

spinach
tomatoes
vinegar, especially red
  wine

JAMAICAN

allspice
ginger

jerk

pepper

JAPANESE

garlic
ginger
rice
sake

scallions
sesame
shiitakes
soy sauce

sugar
vinegar, rice
wasabi
wine, rice

JORDANIAN

marjoram	oregano	peanuts

KOREAN

brown sugar	sesame	soy sauce
chiles		

LATIN AMERICAN

achiote	corn	potatoes
beans, red	garlic	rice
chiles	plantains	

LEBANESE

bulgur	sesame oil

MALAYSIAN

cardamom	chiles	lemongrass
coconut		

MEDITERRANEAN

anchovies	garlic	parsley
coriander	olive oil	tomatoes

MEXICAN

avocados	**corn**	pork
beans	cumin	rice
chiles	*epazote*	scallions
chocolate	garlic	tomatoes
cilantro	**lime**	vanilla
cinnamon	peppers	

MIDDLE EASTERN

anise
chiles
cilantro
cinnamon
coriander
cumin
dill
eggplant
fennel

fenugreek
garlic
honey
lemon
mint
olive oil
oregano
parsley
pignoli

pomegranates
poppy seeds
saffron
sesame
sumac
tahini
tamarind
tomato
yogurt

MOROCCAN

almonds
chickpeas
cilantro
cinnamon
coriander
couscous

cumin
eggplant
fruit
ginger
harissa
lemon, dried

mint
olives
onions
saffron
tomato

NORTH AFRICAN

coriander
cumin
fenugreek

garlic
grains of paradise
lemon

mint
ras el hanout
saffron

NORWEGIAN

cod
dill

herring
salmon

sour cream

PAKISTANI

fruit
legumes

rice

spices

PERUVIAN

chiles
corn

lime
onions

tomatoes

PHILIPPINE

garlic
rice

soy sauce

vinegar

POLISH

dill
fish
kielbasa

mushrooms
potatoes

sauerkraut
sour cream

PORTUGUESE

cabbage
chiles
chorizo
cilantro

cod
eggs
garlic
olive oil

potatoes
rice

PUERTO RICAN

achiote
ginger

lime

plantains

ROMANIAN

garlic

root vegetables

tomatoes

RUSSIAN

beets
cabbage
caraway seeds

dill
mushrooms
parsley

potatoes
sour cream

SCANDINAVIAN

butter
chives
cream

dill
horseradish
mushrooms

pepper
potatoes
vinegar

SCOTTISH

oats	potatoes

SINGAPOREAN

chiles	coconut	scallions
cinnamon	onions	turmeric

SOUTH AMERICAN

allspice	chorizo	fruits, especially tropical
beans	coriander	garlic
chiles	corn	rice

SOUTH SEAS

coconut	ginger	red curry

SOUTHEAST ASIAN

chiles	ginger	scallions
curry leaes	lemongrass	turmeric
garlic	nutmeg	

SOUTHWESTERN UNITED STATES

chiles	clove	nuts
anise	cumin	rice
cajeta	fruits, especially tropical	sage
cinnamon	juniper berries	

SPANISH

almonds	coriander	oranges
anchovies	cumin	paprika
beans	**garlic**	parsley
capers	nuts	**peppers**
chiles	**olive oil**	pork
chocolate	olives	rice
cinnamon	onions	

(continued on facing page)

saffron   sweet peppers   turmeric
seafood   tomatoes   vanilla

SRI LANKAN

cardamom   cinnamon

SWEDISH

dill   juniper berries   reindeer
gravlax

SWISS

bacon   chocolate   sausages
cheese   meats

SYRIAN

peppers, especially red   pistachios   pomegranates
pignoli

SZECHUAN

chiles   ginger   peanuts
fish sauce   leeks   Szechuan pepper
garlic

THAI

basil   cumin   mint
cardamom   **curry**   peanuts
chiles   **fish sauce**   pepper
cilantro   garlic   sugar
coconut   lemongrass   tamarind
coriander   lime   turmeric

Fifty percent of Thai cooking is Indian—not Chinese.
—Jean-Georges Vongerichten

TUNISIAN

cinnamon	garlic	mint
couscous	honey	pistachios
cumin	lemon	

TURKISH

allspice	olive oil	rice
bulgur	onions	thyme
garlic	oregano	walnuts
lamb	parsley	yogurt
lemon		

UKRANIAN

dill   sour cream

VENEZUELEAN

bananas	beef	rice
beans, especially red	corn	

VIETNAMESE

basil	garlic	lime
chiles	ginger	mint
cilantro	**lemon**	shallots
fish sauce	lemongrass	star anise

"Hitting the right notes" in terms of the flavors within a single dish is one thing; coming up with a harmonious sequence of dishes is quite another. The focus here is on what makes a meal work and how culinary artists are able to compose a menu that flows from one course into the next—like the sentences of a paragraph of prose, like the movements of a symphony—making the whole greater than the sum of the individual parts.

Composing a Menu

A menu is not a moment of inspiration, as a single dish might be. It's not a single painting but rather the entire show; it's not

a single song but rather the entire concert. Still, a menu is more than merely a list of dishes. At its best, it communicates a chef's personality and point of view, and offers a significant opportunity for artistic expression. The writing of a menu can be approached as poetry or literature, with the aim of choosing words that impart meaning to the experience of the dish, or heighten diners' expectation of it, or amuse them with a humorous or clever twist on looking at it. A menu should excite the palate, starting with the very words chosen to describe the dishes. A menu can tell a story, just as a theater or opera performance can, such as the story of an ingredient, a region of the world, or a time in history. The physical menu itself should also be aesthetically pleasing. Menus in history, in fact, have served as showcases for the artistic talents of the likes of Manet and Picasso.

However, the art of composing a menu is too often overlooked. For example, the food media frequently place much more emphasis on the recipe for and presentation of a single dish than on its place in the procession of a menu that spotlights it. And consumerism has resulted in "have-it-your-way" expectations on the part of restaurant diners who now count on having the freedom to order whatever they want whenever they want it. Unfortunately, diners have thereby robbed themselves of the experience of culinary artists' full expression of their talent through the composed menus which are the best exemplars of their cuisines. Chez Panisse is alone among leading restaurants in its policy of offering a single menu—without choices—to all its diners, although other restaurants may offer a chef's tasting menu that is determined at the chef's discretion.

The principles of composing a menu stem from the desire to maximize the impact on both the palate and the person over a continuum of time. How can they best enjoy a series of tastes and textures? The ideas of grading and sequence—progressing in a meal from lighter to heavier dishes and from white to red wines, for example—evolve from this desire. What the palate has experienced in the previous dish will in fact affect its enjoyment of the current one. (A sweet dish eaten after a sweeter one won't taste as sweet as when the dishes are served in the reverse order, for example.) And how can a gastronomic experience be best enjoyed? Certainly it helps to have a gracious environment that is appealing to all the senses, with the food served on pleasing dishes and china, in beautiful surroundings, perhaps with appropriate music. Of course, chefs and restaurateurs together serve as the controlling forces who ensure that the diner's total experience is as pleasurable as possible.

Just as a frame will have a subtle but appreciable impact on how we view the painting within it, so do the accoutrements of a meal affect our aesthetic experience of it. The appointments of the table—from the centerpiece to the glassware—affect our reception of the food that is served in its presence, as do even the eating utensils, which may range from polished silver to lacquered chopsticks. (We were once pleasantly and memorably served just a sip each of a fragrant broth in flat Chinese-style white spoons as an *amuse-gueule* by Manhattan chef Ed Brown!)

This is not to say that composing a menu applies only to twelve-course tastings in fine surroundings. Imagine the same level of thought and care applied to a lunch break or a weekend picnic! The art of composing a menu has to do with making the most of the food experience, no matter how brief or modest. It has to do with designing the overall food experience—not only through a series of dishes but through thoughtful attention to each component of a menu (which may also include such items as wines, specialty teas and coffees, bread, and cheese) as well as its presentation (whether in a picnic basket or on Bernardaud china!). The purpose of providing some of the principles of menu composition is not to put chefs into straitjackets of rule-following but to liberate their creative imaginations through a more complete understanding of culinary cause and effect.

The Menu as Shared Experience

"We've lost that sense of the menu as a composition," says Mark Miller. "The idea of a holistic experience, a shared perceptual experience, as opposed to 'ordering something'—I think that's part of what food has lost. It's become commercial. Women chefs in particular are much more attached to menus. They are, I believe, much more concerned with creating a sense of family, the bonding of food and the social process, and the menu itself and how things flow from one thing to the other. There's an emotional quotient in food that I think women understand better than men."

In the early days of Chez Panisse, Miller recalls, "It was nice because everyone came for

a meal, without the ability to order. There was this feeling of shared antici-
pation—110 people coming in to something where they didn't actually know
what they were going to get," he says. "Looking across the room, you'd see
everyone eating the same thing, and everyone being surprised, and everyone
being a part of a 'Chez Panisse experience' rather than their own experience—their own date, their own family, their own business meeting. They
were part of a larger whole."

Menu Planning in World History

China	cold ⟶	hot dishes
France	entree ⟶	salad
	cheese ⟶	dessert
Germany	few or no	hors d'oeuvres
Great Britain, U.S.	dessert ⟶	cheese course
Italy, U.S.	salad ⟶	entrée
Japan	mild ⟶	spicy dishes

The Principle of the Thing

The principles behind menu composition are useful to understanding how to design a meal for maximum effect. Even if doing so involves
breaking the rules put forward, at least it's being done with conscious intention instead of haphazard whim, with the hoped-for result being the maxi-
mization of pleasure on the part of the diner.

Some of the key factors underlying menu composition include the
season, both for its impact on the *ingredients* that are at their peak and the
usual daily *weather/temperature*; the *guests*; the *occasion* or theme; and the
availability of *time* and other resources. *Grading* (an ascension of flavors and
textures from lighter and milder to heavier and stronger), *contrasts* (in
color, texture, and temperature, for example), and the *non-repetition* of
ingredients and garnishes (unless for conscious effect) are all important.
Guests should leave the table satisfied, never hurriedly rushed nor uncom-
fortably full.

Examples of Grading Principles in a Menu

light   ⟶   *rich textures*

delicate   ⟶   *full-bodied consistencies*

subtle   ⟶   *strong flavors*

complex   ⟶   *simple flavors*

white   ⟶   *brown meats*

white   ⟶   *dark breads*

white (simpler)   ⟶   *red (more complex) wines*

light   ⟶   *dark chocolates*

'Tis the Season

"Menu planning is something that people do at home, for themselves and when they're cooking for family and friends," notes Alice Waters. "It's very, very important to understand the principles, I think. And a complex thing to do." For Waters, there's no question where the process starts. "Obviously, it's what's in the market, what's seasonal. That's number one," she says. "I just go and look, and I really don't decide before I look. What if what I wanted wasn't ripe, or wasn't there? I have some ideas, of course; when you get used to doing this, you look through books and get ideas, and then go to the market.

The first factor in putting together a menu is the season. With its particular produce and style of cooking, the season provides the keynote for the whole meal.
—Curnonsky

"When I'm doing a menu, I'm thinking about what kind of day it is, what I feel like eating. If it's cold, do I feel like eating some warm soup, or if it's hot outside, do I crave something very simple like a tomato salad? Then immediately I think about what else needs to be with that," says Waters.

The Audience

Once chefs know the larder of ingredients that are available and of the best quality, they must strive to present them in ways that will best please their customers. "The composition of a menu should reflect who you are aiming the menu for," says Daniel Boulud.

Charlie Palmer believes that chefs should understand how their clients feel and know what they like, and not assume that everyone in the same party has similar preferences. "For example, one of our good customers loves to start out with *foie gras* and Sauternes. It's perfect for him," says Palmer, "but his wife would prefer a simple salad, served with something acidic. Our job is to please each customer."

CHEFS ON THE ORDER OF A MENU

Carême	Curnonsky	Escoffier	Japanese kaiseki meal	George Germon and Johanne Killeen	Terrance Brennan	Terrance Brennan's comments
	cold entrée (or salad)	oysters or caviar or smoked salmon or hot hors d'oeuvres	mukozuke (an assortment of tiny elaborate delicacies) served with sake	amuses-gueules, such as passed hors d'oeuvres or "cappuccino soups"	amuses, e.g., smoked salmon or scallops, hearts of palm salad	*You want it to be interesting, but not to take their breath away.*
vegetable soup	hot entrée or soup	soup	soup	antipasto, e.g., a salad	soup or appetizer, e.g., oysters	
				the lighter preparation of pasta or risotto	*foie gras*	
roasted or braised fillet of beef with glazed vegetables or rice and jus				the heavier preparation of pasta or risotto		
poached or gratinéed fish or fish stew	fish	fish	sashimi		fish, light (sea bass, halibut) to heavy (cod, salmon, tuna)	*You want to progress with flavors, serving the more delicate fish first, followed by the stronger fish. You could start with sea bass in a vinaigrette, followed by scallops with black truffles, followed by salmon with horseradish.*
	sorbet	relevés				

roasted fowl with vegetables	main course of poultry, meat or game	entrées	grilled meat	main course, e.g., meat	meat or game	*If possible, I like to leave it up to the guest to select what they want—beef, lamb, or game.*
pastries		roast meat or game				
salad	(salad)	salad				
		vegetable	rice dish e.g., sushi			
	entremets		miso soup			
	cheeses				cheeses	
					sorbet	*May be served in a fruit soup.*
dessert	dessert (pâtisserie, ice cream or fruit)	dessert	fruit	dessert	dessert	
	coffee, petits fours, and chocolates		tea		coffee / petits fours	*You want guests to have something sweet with their coffee.*
					chocolates	*At the very end of the meal, it's another little surprise that allows you to surpass all expectations.*
	liqueurs and spirits					

Joyce Goldstein agrees that chefs should try to know who they're cooking for. "Because then you can seduce them!" she laughs. "If you know they took a wonderful trip to Greece last year, you can reawaken their memories by serving a Greek-inspired menu. Or you can simply cook them a favorite dish that you know turns them on, and set it in front of them without saying a word. Feeding people is like sending them a love letter."

What does Goldstein hope for in response? "When a plate is set down in front of them, I want their eyes to light up and for them to say, 'Oooh!'" she says. "And once they taste it, I want them to smile and say, 'Ahhh!'"

Menu Themes

Sometimes a particular ingredient serves as the theme for an entire menu. Alice Waters was particularly inspired by a meal she'd had in a Japanese restaurant. "I had a fish that was alive, that they killed on the spot," she remembers. "They took the filet off one side and grilled it, and the other side was sliced for sashimi right on the counter. And the bones were deep-fried. It was a great idea for sort of understanding that fish, and an inspiration for a menu.

Rick Bayless

FRONTERA GRILL and TOPOLOBAMPO
Chicago, Illinois

My menu works well, I believe, because it unveils snapshots of personalities, histories, and emotions from a single place. There is a vivid Oaxacan melody that runs through the whole, starting with the brash and smoky *chiles pasillas oaxaquenos*, stuffed with shredded pork, nestled into tangy greens, and soothed with soft and saucy black beans. All the fire and tang resolve into the comfort of creamy, luxurious squash blossom soup, then the flavors begin to swell with the charcoaled shrimp, roasted vegetables, and tender little dumplings, all doused with the concentrated verdant herbiness of the classic Oaxaca green *mole*. Black *mole* captivates all the senses with its inky rich complexity over the savoriness of roast lamb and the sweetness of nut-crusted *plantain torta*, giving two backgrounds against which to enjoy it. Dessert, I feel, after this thrill of flavors, should bring you to a restful spot—but not one that is totally recognizable. The homey, comforting texture of the trifle is perfumed with orange and the almost-known tropical flavor of mamey. Springing from a pool of crimson prickly-pear sauce, the dessert combines both what we're hoping for and where we'd like to be.

Oaxacan Fiesta
Dinner at the Beard House in April 1996

Coctel Marimba—*A blend of mezcal, grapefruit juice, sangrita, and lime,
featuring Oaxacan Mezcal from Encantado*

Pass-around appetizers

Empanadas de Amarillo—*Crusty, fresh masa turnovers filled with classic yellow* mole,
shredded chicken, and hoja santa

Cluyadas en Miniatura—*Tortillas crisped over an open fire,
topped with Oaxacan string cheese, chorizo, and guacamole*

Tostadas de Chileajo—*Crispy tortillas piled with red chile vegetables and dusted with aged Mexican cheese*

Dinner

Chile Rellenos—*Smoky Oaxacan pasilla chiles filled with shredded pork picadillo,
served with black beans and young lettuces*

Sopa de Flor de Calabaza—*Delicate squash-blossom soup with fresh corn, zucchini, epazote and thick cream*

Camarones en Mole Verde—*Grilled shrimp with classic herby green* mole,
fragrant with cilantro, epazote, and hoja santa

Borrego en Mole Negro—*Crawford Farm leg of lamb in homemade black* mole *(made from chilhuacle chiles
and two dozen other ingredients), served with plantain torta*

Dessert

Ante de Mamey—*Tropical "trifle" of mezcal-laced cake and ripe mamey,
served with caramel, prickly pear, and praline*

Joachim Splichal

PATINA
Los Angeles, California

Both special menu offerings were designed with the tastes and desires of Patina's Los Angeles clientele in mind. When we first opened for lunch, we had a lot of people who came constantly—they'd have three lunches here in a row. When you do that on a day-to-day basis, you want to eat light. You can't just eat things full of butter and calories.

Some customers see angel hair pasta with tomato and basil as light. I think of broiled fish or vegetarian dishes as definitely light, and maybe more satisfying. The Garden Menu was developed to highlight the best available produce, while the Crustacean Menu was a way to offer a lighter menu which did not rely on vegetables alone.

I've been a consultant to Canyon Ranch, a spa in Tucson and the Berkshires, and when you're trying to come up with three meals for 1000 calories, that's a big challenge. There's no dairy, no salt, no high-fat dishes. Most of the meals are chicken, and most of the time you enhance the food from a spa standpoint with onions, leeks, scallions, lemongrass, vinegar, mustard, and a lot of different herbs.

When you're cooking for a spa, everything you think about cooking you can't think anymore. But at Patina, I do whatever I want. There are no restrictions, so we often enhance the natural flavor of ingredients with a little butter and cream.

"I guess that's a lot of what we do at Chez Panisse—celebrate one vegetable or meat or another," says Waters. "With spring lamb, you'll think about a menu that goes around that lamb. I'll think about what's growing at the same time that that little lamb was, and probably end up with asparagus and spring onions. I always look up classic preparations of lamb and how people cook it in the spring—baking it in the hay, for example—to inspire what we might do."

Other menu themes are inspired by a sense of place. Daniel Boulud recalls a wild game dinner he served, that evolved from consommé to *pâté* to a small game bird to a larger game bird to a main course of "some hairy stuff." "To continue the theme, dessert needed to include 'fruit of the forest,' like chestnuts—things that a hunter would find when he's out hunting. It keeps dessert related to the experience," says Boulud. "Or you could serve grapes with game, since birds love to eat grapes. Then whatever the birds eat becomes the relation."

Joachim Splichal, who collects black-and-white photography, believes outside interests can inspire one's cooking. "I once did a black-and-white dinner, featuring black and white truffles, squid, and black trumpet mushrooms," he recalls.

Crustacean Menu

Seared Maine Scallops with Sevruga Caviar, Crème Fraîche, and Diced Potatoes

• • •

Pistou Stew with Little Cockles, Rice Beans, Orzo, and Basil

• • •

Fresh Oysters with Spinach, Cream, and White Truffle Oil

• • •

Lobster with Tot Soi, Arugula, and Garlic-Chive Mashed Potatoes

• • •

Chocolate Sea Shell Filled with a Pistachio Cream and Orange Sorbet

Garden Menu

*Salad of Roasted Chestnuts, Bitter Greens, Grain Mustard,
and Pomegranate Seeds*

• • •

Big Ravioli with Grilled Fennel, Rosemary, and a Fresh Tomato Jus

• • •

Gratin of Rice Beans with Roasted Garlic, Artichoke Hearts, and Spinach

• • •

*Chausson of Cèpes and Portobello Mushrooms with Spanish Onions, Marjoram,
and Balsamic Vinegar*

• • •

Warm Potpourri of Winter Fruit with a Spice Bouquet and Gingerbread

Joyce Goldstein says, "Right now, I have to plan four show-stopping menus for clients; I'm doing an Indian menu, a Moroccan menu, a Spanish menu, and an Asian-inspired menu. Today I'm going to try to zero in on the last one with the client, and to find out where he wants to be. Pan-Asia? Thailand? China? Where's his palate? And then where am I going to go with it? I always look at the whole meal as a composition, not just each dish."

"In any menu, I'm definitely going to want to work with this region's bounty," says Norman Van Aken. "We definitely cross all racial and language barriers, and celebrate what is here with-

out worrying whether or not it's going to be culturally correct. It turns out that it is, because here at the table we can break down these fearful sort of barriers among us. It's the most common remark I hear about my menu. People say, 'This is unlike any menu I'm used to seeing, and I can't make up my mind.' And I'll say, 'Good! Come back again.' "

The Pacing of Courses

To begin a menu, Daniel Boulud likes to begin with a soup. "I love soup," he says. "In the summer, I'll start with a cold soup, and in the winter, a hot one. My restaurant menu will typically have two or three soups on it, and sometimes I run as many as two or three soups as daily specials." Next, typically, might come a salad. "Salads offer an opportunity for different compositions and styles," says Boulud. "In the spring I like doing a crab salad with mango and cucumber served with mint and coriander dressing and crushed peanuts. It's healthy and refreshing."

The palate should be kept fresh, teased, surprised, excited throughout a meal.
—Richard Olney

"I certainly have the French and Italian way of looking at a menu," says Alice Waters. "I like a little something to begin. I'd put fish before a meat course, probably. But I'm not rigid about that. I could imagine putting an appetizer of sliced prosciutto and melon before a grilled piece of fish with an olive sauce or something. And I would eat a salad before the entrée as a first course, or if I were having a little longer meal, I'd eat it after. And sometimes I eat it with, these days. I kind of like the idea of salad with a meat dish. It helps to provide a little contrast and cut the richness of the meat, to have a salad with vinaigrette.

"I like small portions. Or I like people to be able to help themselves from a platter and take what they would like; that's ideal for me," says Waters. "I don't want people to end up being full—satisfied, yes, but not full."

Lydia Shire agrees that the size of portions can be very important. "Certain things should be served in delicate amounts," says Shire. "Often, when I order head cheese, it comes in too thick a slice and loses its appeal. Or when I've had rabbit *pâté* on my menu, sometimes a cook would slice it too thick, which is horrible.

"On the other hand, I love things that are *meant* to be huge," she counters. "Like the New York steak houses that grill three-pound lobsters when they know you'll never be able to finish them, or the big steaks they serve. And [the Manhattan restaurant] Christ Cella used to serve a whole head of broccoli!"

Some chefs control portion size through the number of courses served. "Our gourmand menu has an extended format—it's nine courses—which allows more freedom and flexibility in the construction of each of the dishes," says Wayne Nish. "The problem with three-course formats is that you're basically jamming all of the food groups into those three courses. When you have an extended tasting menu, you can spread those food groups out over five, six, nine courses, and make each individual course more special as a result of being able to simplify. It's also a nice parade, in a luxury environment, of luxury ingredients that can be displayed in an almost Japanese presentation fashion.

Sometimes a dinner will have so many courses that it's overwhelming. It's like you're being set for slaughter.
—Mark Peel

"What I mean is that if you get in, say, fresh langoustine, to serve it as an entrée, you've probably got to put several on the plate and add a sauce and a starch. And it all takes away from the specialness of that langoustine. But in a multi-course format, you put that langoustine on a plate in its unadorned beauty, the specialness that it has, that God gave it, and maybe it only requires a little sauce to complement it, or some herbs. You're no longer forced to crowd the plate with really extraneous things that are demanded by the customer," says Nish.

Contrasts

Gary Danko says, "Sometimes I'll get teamed with other chefs to prepare a meal for a special event. In accepting, I say I'll do so on the condition that we really work on the menu so that it flows beautifully. I don't want to have a spicy rooster gumbo opening up that meal when I'm planning to serve a delicate fillet of sole, because you're not going to taste the sole. Your palate is going to be anesthesized by all those spices."

Daniel Boulud believes it's important that dishes on a menu not overlap in flavor, taste, or texture. "Each one should have its own identity, its own character and taste," he says.

When designing a menu, Lydia Shire sets the goal of achieving a balance: "I look to see what can play off the other elements, whether it's spicy versus sweet, hot versus cold, crunchy versus soft, astringent versus fatty. In transitioning from one course to another, you probably wouldn't want to serve two meat courses in a row, or two rich courses in a row. You want one sensation and flavor to play differently against the next."

Because her eclectic cuisine incorporates such disparate influences, she adds, "I don't think I'd do a menu that took you from France to Japan to South America, for example—at once, that can be too much. I think you should carry through with a whole regional theme. But that doesn't mean you

Examples of Contrasts
Between Courses in a Menu

brown meat/white meat

cold/hot

cooked/raw

creamy/crispy

dry/sauced

heavy/light

mild/spicy

savory/sweet

can't modernize it! For example, you might serve one Japanese dish, and the next Indian or Thai—but we wouldn't serve any dishes using cream (which is not native to Asian cuisine) as part of that menu."

Alice Waters believes that combining multicultural influences within a single menu is difficult. "I think it's very hard to put a menu together when you have dishes all over the menu that are from different cuisines," says Waters. "They all may be tasty in and of themselves. But I keep trying to push the cooks [at Chez Panisse], telling them, 'If you're in Italy, stay in Italy. Make dishes in the spirit of the Italians.'"

Waters feels strongly about integrating different textures within a menu. "I don't like everything to be sort of pureed. If one dish is very smooth, like a silky fish with a sauce, I'd make the next course contrasting, like little fried potatoes served with grilled duck. I like juxtapositions. And always something refreshing at the end.

"I always think about texture and color. I think that's one thing I bring to the menus still—when I'm critiquing the menus here, it always ends up being a color consideration. I pick that up, whereas other people don't as much," says Waters. "And I want them to be very aromatic. Other people are thinking about other things, like taste, but I like a kind of liveliness to the food from one course to another."

Rick Bayless believes that creating a menu should be an exercise in balance and parameters. "You want a variety of textures, from crispy to soft, as well as some fresh components punctuating the entire meal," he says. While nearly every sauce he serves in his restaurants has chiles in it, some are heavier or lighter in texture, and they have varying degrees of heat. "You want to build a crescendo of flavors, or maybe start out with

something that's very hot, and then cool down with something that has almost no chile in it, before coming back up to something hot again. And it's important to never put too many flavors on the table—there shouldn't be more than four courses served," says Bayless. "You want people to leave with a vivid memory of the meal. Because these flavors are very bold, more than that is too much for the palate."

Rules are sometimes meant to be broken, which explains the appeal of a menu that features the same ingredient in more than one course or, in special or whimsical cases, in every course—whether potatoes, or tomatoes, or truffles. "While classically you'd never repeat any item in a menu, if an ingredient is in season, I don't mind having or serving it more than once," says Terrance Brennan. "In corn season, one might serve two dishes featuring corn, or an all-corn menu."

I think that the repetition of certain tastes within a menu—corn in the hors d'oeuvres and corn in the soup, and the grilled flavor of peppers recalled by grilled fish—can be surprisingly effective and unifying as a recurring theme.
—Alice Waters

"It's possible to create a real array of tastes with one ingredient," attests Daniel Boulud, whose restaurant now offers a selection of such tastings with advance notice. "At the Beard House, I once cooked a seven-course menu based on tomatoes. Sometimes customers will ask me to come up with a truffle menu during truffle season. It's part of the excitement of a great menu to be able to achieve this."

A Way With Words

While it's fine to have fun, one of the most important things on a menu can be accuracy. Think of the times you've been excited to order a dish, only to have the reality of it provoke disappointment. "When you write a menu, you want to deliver the food that you promise," says Terrance Brennan.

Mark Peel adds, "I like for people to get a little more than they expect. And I've read many menus where something sounds great, and you get it and it's not quite what it sounded like. Or it's less than it sounded like. And that's very disappointing. And I would rather that there be a little more, that there's a little surprise there. I don't like menus that read like shopping lists."

But Nancy Silverton points out that there are things that you can't leave off: "For example, you would never surprise somebody with walnuts. You'd never surprise somebody with onions, I don't think." Peel adds, "Or things like scallops or mussels."

Lydia Shire believes it's important to bring humor into a menu. "The way you describe a dish on the menu should be fun!" she says. "I'm proud that we were the first to put on our menu such-and-such a dish 'with expensive caviar.' People should have a playful attitude toward food." Her menu at Biba has featured lamb's tongue paired with lamb's lettuce, a play on both words and flavors.

"Chefs shouldn't hesitate to play with words on their menus," encourages Joachim Splichal. As a case in point, his menu features a dish of Chicken Wings with Unorthodox Chicken Liver. Splichal says, "If every menu read 'Broiled Chicken with...,' it would be unbearably boring."

While humor can be an effective device, the goal of menu descriptions should be to get the customers excited about the food. "Anything on the menu must sound attractive," says Charlie Palmer. "It should make the customer think, 'I've *got* to try this dish!'"

George Germon & Johanne Killeen

AL FORNO
Providence, Rhode Island

Lageder was a vegetarian, so we used very little meat on his menu. Also, the wines had extremely clean, clear flavors, so we knew they'd be perfect with vegetables. In the first course, the white beans add a creamy texture to the salmon, while the grapefruit picked up the acidity of the wine. The antipasto was a series of different things, including eggplant and zucchini and a rich, creamy cheese that went well with the wine. Asparagus, which is usually a tough match with wine (although not as hard as artichokes), was good with the grassiness of the wine; the Parmesan and béchamel of the lasagna again added a creaminess and balance that rounded out the grassiness of the wine and asparagus. The vegetables were prepared in different ways in the next dish; some were steamed and some were roasted to give crunchiness and texture. Plus, there was a little butter and wine in the dish and a creamy crust to balance the crunchy vegetables. The mushroom was meaty, to go with the wine, and garlic and herbs added contrast and depth of flavor, while the polenta provided a creamy contrast. Because a sweeter dessert would have overwhelmed the wine, we used tart flavors for the dessert, which showed off the wine instead.

On the Table

Even if the table is a stage, and the food and wine play starring roles, the performance of a meal would not be the same without its supporting players. If any of the players are out of sync, they can ruin the effect of an entire performance. An ill-chosen first course—one that is too spicy, for example—can ruin a delicate entrée. Mismatched wine and food ruin our enjoyment of them both.

In planning menus, it's important to consider the special role of various courses and accompaniments. While clearly not every menu one writes will be a long, multiple-course feast, coming to recognize the flow of well-written menus—of any length—is critical to mastering the art of composition.

Wine

The progression of wines served during a meal should provide its own parallel, harmonious symphony to that of the food. Wines should complement the food with which they are served, as well as the reverse.

Winemaker Dinner with Alois Lageder
Wines of Alto Adige/Sudtirol
April 29, 1993

Smoked Salmon with White Beans and Grapefruit Vinaigrette
Pinot Grigio 1991
• • •
Vegetable Antipasto with Robiolo Cheese
Pinot Bianco "Haberlehof" 1990
• • •
Roasted Asparagus Lasagna
Sauvignon Terlaner 1991
• • •
Ten-Vegetable Stew with Chicken
Chardonnay 1991
Chardonnay "Lowengang" 1989
• • •
Grilled Portobello Mushroom with Garlic and Herbs
Creamy Polenta
Lagrein Dunkel 1990
• • •
Strawberry-Rhubarb Tart
Dried Cranberry Shortbread Cookies
Pisoni Vino Santo 1985

"It's important to pair food to wine, and not vice versa," says Jeremiah Tower. "A bottle of wine can change like that, but ingredients are more stable."

Joyce Goldstein agrees. "I always ask for the wines before coming up with a menu for a wine dinner, so that I can taste them first," she says. "My son is a sommelier, and wine is important in our family. Wines surprise you; wines can change, even over the course of a year.

"Too many chefs don't taste the wines before creating a menu for a wine and food dinner. I was recently preparing a menu for a special event and was planning to serve lamb. But after tasting the red wine that was going to be accompanying it, which was pruney, I realized it would have made the lamb taste too muttony," she said. "In the end, I decided to revise my menu to serve beef instead, which was a much better match with the wine. In another case, one wine I tasted was over-oaked, and I could only pair it with potatoes, which helped to neutralize that. Other chefs' egos are sometimes too big, thinking that the food is more important. But wine and food should make each other look good."

Jimmy Schmidt concurs that when creating a menu for a wine dinner, the wine themselves are the starting point; he also develops dishes that make the most of their pairing with the particular wines. "The personality of the wine will give you direction to shape the dish in a way that will enhance the flavor of the wine," he says.

François Payard recalls being asked to create a dessert to be served with Château d'Yquem. "It would have been a crime to serve it with a chocolate dessert," he says. Because of the fruitiness of the Château d'Yquem, Payard decided to serve a mango soup made with fresh mango purée and coconut milk. "If you know wine, you know it won't go with chocolate, which is bitter and powerful," says Payard. "But sometimes port can go with chocolate, because it's aged and spicier."

A fruit compote can be served with a great dessert wine, as long as the compote is not too sweet. "If it's too sweet, the wine will taste sour," notes Jeremiah Tower. Tropical fruits best lend themselves to pairing with dessert wines, he adds.

On the other hand, "a rich, sweet chocolate dessert will obliterate the wine," according to Tower. "So with chocolate, coffee should be served—or nothing."

Jimmy Schmidt on Cooking with Wine

Working with wine is the best because in matching food with wine, you do a lot of cancellation and reinforcement of flavors. For example:

- If you have a wine that has a lot of *tannin* in it, you want fats and salts to kind of take the edge off the tannin.

- If you've got a lot of *herbaceous* qualities, which I'm not terribly fond of in wine, you can use green things like parsley or greener-flavored herbs swirled into the sauce at the last second to strip away a lot of those herbaceous qualities in the wine. You'll associate the herbaceousness as coming more from the parsley than from the wine.

- If the wine is high in *acid*, your sauce can come up right to that acid level; then there wouldn't be much contrast between the two acidity levels, so it's not going to seem very acidic. On the other hand, if you go higher in acid on the sauce, then the wine will seem kind of flat. If you go too low on acid in the sauce, then the wine will seem very acidic.

- In terms of *body* and *flavor*, if it's really a very light wine, the concentration of the sauce can kill it if becomes so powerful that the wine seems watery.

- In terms of *fruit* levels, if you've got a lot in the wine and there's none in the sauce, the sauce will be flat. So you've got to bring up some of the red flavors in the sauce—red wine reduction, the addition of red fruit purée like cranberry. The wine will taste fruitier if you've got lots of red flavor in the sauce than if you don't. Your mind will read the red in the sauce as part of the wine, when really it's part of the sauce.

- There are some wines that have a lot of good *earthy* characteristics— they're flinty and such. You can use the drier spices like coriander that seem to come off as more of an earthy-type flavor or mineral-type flavor.

So you can either build dishes to reinforce them, which is to get those flavors close, or you can separate them quite a bit for contrast and strip them. You can kill a wine really easily, or you can really parallel up next to it. With a wine, you have a perceived taste—then you take out of the wine your own perception of the taste of the wine's different flavors, and then you design the dish around it, with flavors that will coordinate really well.

Jimmy Schmidt

THE RATTLESNAKE CLUB
Detroit, Michigan

This was a real seasonal menu that really captured all the first ingredients of spring—the asparagus, the wild mushrooms, the scallops and oysters. There was a real seasonal-regional approach, although obviously not all of the ingredients come out of Michigan. The sauces were really attuned to the wines. That's what really made the dinner something special. The flavors in the dishes tended to enhance the wines by cancelling any of their rougher characteristics and allowing the real fruit and balance in the wine to come forward. Food and wine harmony is not all just trying to pair ingredients together, but to match certain flavors in the wine—whether herbaceous or earthy or flinty—with similar characteristics in the food, depending on which you want to be more predominant. You can use food and wine pairing to reinforce flavors that you want to accentuate or highlight, as well as cancel out things that you want to get rid of.

This particular preparation of salmon involves running the potato through a mandoline that makes almost potato *cappellini* (a type of pasta noodle), and wrapping the salmon with it. The salmon actually has had horseradish and other seasonings rubbed on it prior to being wrapped. It's sautéed over a very high heat in a non-stick pan, which makes the potato very crispy while allowing the salmon to retain its moisture. It gives it the crunchy exterior that we like, while letting the full flavor of the salmon come through and not interfere terribly with the texture of the fish.

The pistachio and the peppercorn was really the combination I was after in the tenderloin of beef dish. The nuttiness and kind of spicy flavors of the pistachio allow me to use it more as a spice here than as a nut per se. The pistachio tends to not make the peppercorn overwhelming—it kind of cuts the strength of the peppercorn while adding a certain richness of its own.

Wine does work well with desserts, and I like red wine with chocolate. The pear and the red wine work real well together—some fruits are a little tougher in combination with red wine, which is why I chose the pear, which is filled with a chocolate ganache. It's actually roasted and then filled, and then covered with chocolate on the outside. You get a really crunchy, really bittersweet chocolate on the exterior, and then more of a silky, smooth chocolate ganache on the inside. The pear offers this kind of silky texture that lies between the mousse and the exterior chocolate that offers a nice contrast so that your palate can pick up all three textures.

May 15, 1996

Hors d'Oeuvres

Chilled Oysters in a Ginger Salsa
Spicy Tuna with Seaweed Slaw
Heated Asparagus and Caramelized Onion Flatbread
Smoky Chicken Quesadillas

1995 Chenin Blanc, Yountville Cuvée

• • •

Dinner

Seared Scallops and Roasted Mussels with Coriander
and Saffron Ginger Cabbage Salad

1993 Chardonnay, Kollside Cuvée
1994 Chardonnay Stags Leap District

• • •

Potato-Skinned Salmon with Mustard and Red Wine Essence
Leek and Cippolini Compote

1994 Merlot, Selected Cuvée

• • •

Grilled Tenderloin of Beef with Pistachio-Peppercorn Crust
Wild Mushrooms and Cabernet Essence

1993 Cabernet Sauvignon, Napa Valley
1993 Cabernet Sauvignon, Rutherford
1992 Cabernet Sauvignon, Stags Leap District

• • •

Dessert

Roasted Pear Entombed in Chocolate

Coffee or Tea

Alice Waters

CHEZ PANISSE
Berkeley, California

This menu was composed to celebrate the arrival of the 1971 vintage of the Domaine Tempier wines. The look of the wild rice with the tiny green peas was a wonderful accompaniment to the quail. It was at this meal that we decided that *crème fraîche* is ideally suited for serving with stewed figs.

The Bandol Wine Dinner

Fresh Delicacies from the Sea

• • •

A Bouillabaisse of Salt Cod made with Garlic, White Wine, Tomatoes, Onions, Potatoes, Fresh Basil, Orange Rind, Olive Oil and Fish Broth
1973 Bandol, Domaine Tempier

• • •

Fresh Quail Roasted Provençal Style with Branches of Fresh Thyme and Olive Oil Served with Wild Rice and Fresh Peas
1971 Bandol, Domaine Tempier

• • •

Goat Cheeses from the South of France
1974 Bandol, Domaine Tempier

• • •

Figs Cooked with Honey and Bandol Wine Served with Crème Fraîche

Bread   In addition to wine, bread is often the only constant within an entire meal. "However, I don't like the way bread is treated in most American restaurants," says Alice Waters. "When you get served a big pile of bread with a plate of butter the minute you are seated in a restaurant, it takes away the appetite. And people use it to clean up the plate. I think for the most part we need to get back to a light baguette being served with a meal. And I do love things like tandoori breads served with Indian dinners, where they seem to play an integral role in the meal."

"I always forget the bread," admits Jeremiah Tower. "But then I'll visit Richard Olney, who couldn't have a meal without it. For a while, I'll adopt his habit—but then I'll find myself eating a loaf of bread a day! Bread fills in the gap in meals, and American diners, some of whom have the attention spans of three-year-olds, need something to fill the gaps. But I'm never quite sure where it belongs. To eat with the cheese? To sop up the meat juices? Maybe that's why I forget it."

Lindsey Shere believes that bread is an important accompaniment to a meal. She observes that "large flavors often need a background to hold them in place. And I happen to like the flavor of flour and yeast. I don't have a lot of interest in things like cheese bread, because I don't think they work well with dinner menus."

In Shere's definition, a perfect bread is "the levain bread at Acme Bread," she says. "It's got a gutsy flavor, and is good with cheese, butter—or nothing!" Even leftover bread excites Shere. "I think a delicious crouton can add a really special touch to a dish," she says. Alice Waters echoes this: "A lot of our food is served with croutons, whether it's a garlic crouton with a fish soup, or a crouton topped with grilled leeks served as part of an antipasto."

Shere believes butter or olive oil is the perfect accompaniment to good bread. To heighten the experience of enjoying La Brea Bakery's wonderful breads, at Campanile Mark Peel and Nancy Silverton offer customers an opportunity to order one-ounce portions of various extraordinary olive oils, ranging from $1 to $2.50 per ounce, to accompany them.

Silverton believes that there should be a progression of flavors in bread throughout the course of a meal. "White sourdoughs are appropriate for starting out, to be followed by heavier breads like ryes," she says.

Silverton also gives careful thought to pairing bread with other courses. She once had to come up with a bread to pair with a *foie gras* dish by Jean-Louis Palladin at an event. "I selected a fruit and nut bread, which will work with the dish if it's sliced very, very thinly," she says. "Duck is great with sour dried cherries, pecans, candied orange, and these flavors also work well with *foie gras*." Similarly, she's teamed a mushroom bread made of farro with a risotto with chanterelles, and paired a Normandy rye made with fermented apple cider with hearty food, like cabbage. While Silverton thinks that few foods can hold up to the strength and the sourness of a pumpernickel, she finds both oysters and smoked fish equal to the task.

Even sandwiches can be enhanced by the selection of the right, complementary bread. "I think a seeded sourdough goes well with turkey, and a French baguette is delicious with prosciutto and butter," Silverton says. "And

President and Co-founder
The Acme Bread Company
Berkeley, California

As a busboy and cook at Chez Panisse in the mid-1970s, self-described bread fanatic Steven Sullivan started baking bread for the restaurant. His inspiration? "The book *English Bread and Yeast Cookery* by Elizabeth David," says Sullivan, who went on to open Acme in 1983. Acme has supplied Bay Area restaurants, including Chez Panisse, Stars, and Zuni Cafe, with their daily bread. Sullivan's lead has been an inspiration to other top bakers, including Nancy Silverton, who dedicates her 1996 book *Breads from the La Brea Bakery* to him. Sullivan says, "I'm proud of being involved in 're-presenting' the possibility for bread and its potential in America." He judges the bread he eats on three distinct qualities, which he believes must "resolve themselves" within the bread:

1) Intrinsic technicality—time, temperature, texture, and taste
Sullivan points out that basic white bread is made from only four ingredients—water, flour, salt, and yeast—in standard proportions. But approaching these ingredients from the point of view he gained through reading David's book, he learned that flavor could be maximized through fermentation. "This also gives the bread its texture and its pleasing visual characteristics," he says. "When acids are left in contact with protein, it modifies not only the flavor but the underlying structure. The byproducts of fermentation are these little animals that consume sugars and give off acids and alcohol. Their level in a dough determines the bread's flavor."

Bread, without which no good, honest feast, no meal, is possible!
—Chatillon-Plessis

egg salad goes well on *pain de mie*, while tunafish is complemented by something like a potato-dill bread."

Lydia Shire, whose restaurant Biba bakes Indian *naan* bread in a tandoori oven in the dining room to top off a basket already piled high with crusty sourdough bread and oniony focaccia, says, "I'm proud that we've got what I think is the best bread basket in Boston." Her restaurant Pignoli's signature bread is a crispy two-ply bread called *ciacci*, which is made with ricotta salata and served with fava bean purée, basil oil, and pignolis. The striking—and widely copied—bread "basket" at Pignoli is actually a piece of white butcher paper rolled into a cone, which is then inserted into a metal coil.

Hors d'Oeuvre/Amuse-Bouche

Alice Waters notes that the first food tasted in a meal should be enticing, in order to awaken the palate. "With the first bite, you want

2) Theatre—both in the bread itself, and within the restaurant context

Sullivan has enjoyed experimenting with different shapes of bread. "If bread is different in one way, a customer will pay more attention to all of its characteristics," he argues. "And it's enticing to be able to say 'We baked it ourselves'—especially when I was a busboy at Chez Panisse and could tell customers, 'I made this.' It's theatrically effective."

3) Heart and soul—what the baker brings to the bread

"You can tell when someone brings an energy and exuberance to bread. In fact, sometimes a funky bread can work if there is enough theatre and soul in the bread to overcome less-than-perfect technique."

With regard to pairing bread with food, Sullivan cites a few of his favorite combinations. "We served rye bread with oysters in the Café [at Chez Panisse], which is a traditional combination," he says. "I like peanut butter on toasted whole wheat bread, and toasted cheese sandwiches on levain bread. And I like walnut bread with goat cheese. I don't know if that's a traditional combination or not, but on our honeymoon my wife Susie and I really enjoyed it." Does Sullivan prefer butter or olive oil on his bread? "I think both are really, really good ways to get your USRDA of fat," he deadpans. "I recommend both heartily."

Does Acme bake the best bread in the world? At first, Sullivan humbly dodges the question by using it as an opportunity to relate how Keith Richards of the Rolling Stones was once asked to name the best rock-and-roll band in the world, and Richards' reply that on any particular night, anywhere in the world, at some bar, you can find the best rock-and-roll band in the world.

But after further prodding, Sullivan finally admits, "Sometimes the bread we bake is *awfully* good."

---

to help the diner feel happy that they're there," agrees Joachim Splichal. "The first bite should be amusing, like a corn blini with marinated salmon and caviar [an *amuse* Splichal sends out to Patina's special customers]. Caviar is not cheap, so it's a nice surprise to welcome the guest to the restaurant and say hello."

Jeremiah Tower's preferred way of welcoming a guest is with something salty and champagne, which together serve to cleanse the palate. "It can be caviar, but it doesn't have to be—ham, pork, or air-cured beef can all be delicious. I don't like to serve anything with butter, because it dulls the palate....But I wouldn't turn down blini with caviar!"

In some cases, the first course served is a soup. "Even if people only want a few courses, I always give them soup," says Jean-Louis Palladin.

Out of respect for Mexican tradition, Rick Bayless feels the same. "You would never have a meal in Mexico where soup was not served," he explains.

The hors-d'oeuvre *is the first magisterial movement of a culinary symphony that continues to the very end without a false note. Just when you've reached the ultimate with a particular course, another follows to surpass it.*
—Fernand Point

A particular favorite at his restaurants is one of fresh corn and roasted poblanos, with a handful each of *epazote* (a fragrant, anise-flavored, light-green herb which "gives the soup a light mouthfeel") and raw *masa* (the dough used for tortillas, which gives the soup its creaminess). "This soup is tangy and tart, light and crunchy," says Bayless. "These are soul-satisfying flavors."

On the other hand, Alice Waters argues, "I'm a soup-as-main-dish person. Soup is too filling, and I find it hard to fit into a menu, unless it's a consommé."

Cheese

Nancy Silverton knows exactly what she likes in terms of cheese after a meal. "Always a blue cheese," she says, "and always a goat cheese. If the blue cheese is Stilton or gorgonzola, then a fresh goat cheese. If it's a mild blue, then I like an aged goat cheese. And I always like a strong-tasting cheese—even a Parmesan."

If only serving one bread with cheese, Silverton would like to see it be a white bread, such as a sourdough bâtard, while Lindsey Shere might opt for a whole wheat/walnut bread offering. "It's so good with cheese," Shere says.

And wine is a must to properly enjoy cheese, according to Charles Palmer. "I don't understand when people don't drink wine with cheese," he says. "It's hard to intrude on someone and risk making them feel stupid in the restaurant by not ordering it. But sometimes I'll send over a little glass of port if I see people eating cheese without red wine or port."

"I think that cheeses like dried Jack, Gruyère, and hard sheep's-milk cheeses are the best to be served with wine," says Jeremiah Tower. "Triple-crèmes are much too strong for red wines."

Even Palmer, who is a partner in a dairy, admits that "cheese is often too much for most people. It's too much for me half the time! At Chanterelle [in New York City], they have an incredible cheese display. But after that, dessert becomes an afterthought."

Cheese is like the apotheosis of a good meal.
—Curnonsky

Serving cheese with a meal usually calls for a simple dessert, like a sherbet, according to Lindsey Shere. Or in Alice Waters' case, "I like cheese instead of dessert—maybe with a little candy at the very end. I love cheese and fruit. Or cheese and salad. Or cheese by itself with a few nuts and dried fruits. But I really like cheese," she says.

Dessert Terrance Brennan admits that until he visited three-star restaurants in France, "I was not much of a dessert person. But there, I saw how sublime it could be." Brennan fell in love with "the perfect *mille-feuille*" and other desserts he was served, which he found the perfect finale to a great meal. "Too often before that time, I was disappointed with desserts. But now I believe that a great meal should end with a great dessert," says Brennan. "It also inspired me to make sure I worked every station during my *stages*—including pastry."

One of the best desserts Brennan ever had was at Le Bacon, an all-seafood restaurant in France famous for its bouillabaisse where the windows opened out onto the Mediterranean. "I was served a perfect *fraise de bois* (wild strawberry) tart. It was just *sablé*, a light, crispy, airy sugar crust—and a little pastry cream, and *fraises des bois*," Brennan remembers. "It was sublime."

The key to a great dessert? "Flavor. The marriage of perfect ingredients. Getting the best chocolate you can buy and the best fruit you can buy," says Brennan. "Not having too many different things on the plate. Preparing the dessert *à la minute* as much as possible, so it's as fresh as possible. And it should be focused; it has to make sense."

"Dessert should be an equal part of the meal," says Charles Palmer. "And it should be built around cravings. People tend to have definite feelings about dessert. Even if I told a customer, 'This dessert is perfect with what you're having,' I'd worry about disappointing them! Sometimes you feel like eating a specific thing for dessert."

Despite its popularity in desserts, cravings are not always for chocolate. "I'll go through phases when I don't eat chocolate," says Palmer. "In the winter, nothing will taste as good as a caramelized apple dessert." On the other hand, "seventy-five percent of customers love chocolate," says Dieter Schorner. "And they will be disappointed if there's not a chocolate dessert on the menu."

A pastry chef has the unique challenge of making desserts that complement a chef's creations. Lindsey Shere has faced that challenge under a long line of chefs at Chez Panisse, from Jeremiah Tower to the restaurant's current chef, Jean-Pierre Moulle. "I still create based on my own inspirations, but I also try to keep up with them and to understand where they're coming from," she says. "Jean-Pierre is the most classic chef we've had in a while, probably since Jeremiah. His interest is more French-oriented, and since he started out in pastry, it's great because he knows the kinds of things he'd like to see with a particular menu as dessert, whether it's a cake or pastry or sherbet. That's a big help!"

Shere contrasts his style with that of former Chez Panisse chef Paul Bertolli: "Paul was more interested in Italian cuisine and simple desserts. But he liked fireworks—he once came back from New York City, where he'd eaten at Le Cirque, and was talking about a dessert he'd had with planets and swirling sauces. He loved that. And I do think that dessert is the one place where you can have fun and occasionally do a whimsical garnish that is silly."

Too often, dessert is a sugar fix rather than a little touch of sweetness as a change from the savory, the salty, or the piquant.

—Alice Waters

Shere uses chocolate when the chef suggests that it's appropriate. "Jean-Pierre knows the richness of his menus," says Shere. Getting the green light recently inspired her to serve a trio of chocolate desserts: a flourless chocolate cake, a chocolate-orange sherbet, and chocolate-almond bark. "Some people like chocolate any time," she admits, "but after something rich, I prefer clean and light flavors. A tangerine sherbet with liqueur poured over it can be the best. Citrus sherbets and pear sherbets are desserts I always like. And they're always served here with accompaniments like cookies."

While Shere thinks it "impossible" to name the best dessert she's ever had, one particular dessert does stand out in her memory. "*Timbales Elysées*— a dessert with a cookie cup, a scoop of ice cream, berries, and sauce in a caramel cage," she says. "It is such a wonderful combination of textures and flavors."

But an extraordinary dessert can also be quite simple. Alice Waters recalls, "One of my favorite, favorite desserts ever was after a kaiseki meal in Kyoto. We had had seventeen fantastic courses, with ten people in the kitchen cooking for five people at the counter. It was an amazing experience. And at the very end, we were offered a little glass of the most sweet and delicious tangerine juice that was not too cold or too warm— just the perfect temperature. And you just drank it, and that was it. It was 'the end'—and just so nice to be able to punctuate the meal properly."

Very rich desserts should follow only the simplest of meals; on most menus, something light and playful in spirit is best. Lots of air, in the form of a soufflé or a mousse, is usually appreciated; ices are refreshing.
—Richard Olney

In Susanna Foo's opinion, traditional Chinese desserts "aren't very good. They're typically either very heavy, based on puréed walnuts or red beans, or just fresh fruit. Even there, Western-style bakeries are popular." Foo takes some liberties from tradition with her desserts, such as serving poached pears flavored with star anise and ginger, or *crème brûlée* flavored with ginger.

If he chooses to serve multiple desserts to end a meal, François Payard might start out with a small fruit soup—"just two or three bites," he says— before serving a tiny fruit dessert, perhaps followed by a chocolate dessert. "I don't make smaller chocolate desserts, because they're a lot of work," explains Payard. "And dessert is like food—you have to take the time to appreciate it."

Charles Palmer enjoys presenting a table of six with a combination of desserts. "I'll send two, two, and two of three different desserts. People love passing them back and forth, trading tastes—it becomes party time!" says Palmer. "Dessert is the time to festively finishing things off in a meal."

Susan Feniger and Mary Sue Milliken agree. They recall a $250-a-head dinner for which they were asked to provide the dessert. "We served ice cream sandwiches made with mocha chip ice cream," Milliken remembers with amusement.

Some chefs make a point of extending the pleasure at the end of an elaborate meal through *petit fours* and chocolates. "I love *petit fours*," says Terrance Brennan. "In the European style, espresso should be served after dessert, and it's nice to have a sweet to go with your espresso. I serve a plate of *petit fours* with the coffee, followed by a plate of chocolates to send you on your way."

François Payard believes there should even be an order to the service of the chocolates. "They should be consumed from the lightest to darkest, just like wine," he says.

Coffee, Tea?

Joachim Splichal, whose restaurant Patina already offers chamomile and thyme-lemongrass "infusions" after a meal, is now experimenting with estate coffees, to be served in individual plunger-style coffeepots. "Our coffee is a blend of four different types of coffee we came up with six years ago after trying more than fifty different coffees," he says, "and we've learned that now people know their coffee. Coffee has taken on the importance of the valet parking guy who opens the door for the customer—it can be a customer's last impression of a restaurant."

Dieter Schorner recalls the standards for tea at one of the finest restaurants where he once worked. "There was never granulated sugar served with it—only brown sugar cubes or crystal sugar. The tea flavor comes out better with raw sugar, as opposed to pulverized, bleached sugar," says Schorner.

Writing a Restaurant Menu

As opposed to writing a set menu for a single meal, writing a restaurant menu is all about giving one's customers choices—ones that are likely to please them, and ones that the restaurant will be able to fulfill, in most cases, for an entire season.

It's mostly the latter constraint that prompts Daniel Boulud to confess, "If it were up to me, I would not have an *à la carte* menu. I would just cook every day whatever I could buy, and have a limited menu of maybe four appetizers, four main courses, and four desserts—and have them change all the time." The varied demands of Restaurant Daniel's customers, however, dictate a much longer menu. "There's a difference between this dream and reality," Boulud admits.

Chris Schlesinger on Menu Development

What I teach my cooks when we do menus is to think in terms of three columns:

1) The first is the *availability of ingredients*. I'll have everyone call around to the vegetable, meat, and fish purveyors and compile a list of raw ingredients that are available at that time.

2) Then we have a list of different *geographic regions*, because we're somewhat international and we try to balance the menu. So someone will mention that they've been to Tuscany, and they know that I just got back from Spain. If a particular country is mentioned—say, Korea—it brings up all these ingredients, all these techniques, all these key words and dishes, all this Korean 'stuff.' And I think that's helpful when they think of the food, in my system.

3) Finally, we'll have *cool stuff* that we've found in books—cool combinations, like pickled grapes, or something unusual found in the market, like persimmons.

So you have all those columns, and then you kind of mix and match. You figure out what works

No matter how long a restaurant's menu, "A chef cannot be everything to everybody," says Michael Romano. "A restaurant has a certain style, a certain feeling. And that's true whether it's Italian, French, or Thai. Here [at Union Square Café], we're loose; we've got an Italian spirit, especially in our appetizers,

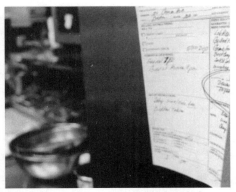

but we're a little bit all over the place. One of our more popular dishes is a tuna dish that's actually very Asian. And right now we've even got an Indian dish on the menu—made with grilled shrimp, coconut, and *paratha* [an Indian bread]."

Unlike other chefs, who might spontaneously cook new dishes to serve to special guests on a particular night, Rick Bayless says he never serves anything that's not on his restaurants' menus. "Our menu represents our best work," he explains. "We work on dishes over and over and over again before we put them on the menu in the first place. I wouldn't want to serve a guest anything that had been tested any less."

together, and what other ingredients you need to tie in. Then the cooks will come up with dishes based on them, and they'll have them critiqued.

Before cooks are allowed to participate in the menu development process, they are required to have read two books: Raymond Sokolov's *Why We Eat What We Eat* (Touchstone Books, 1991), which talks about the evolution of food, and Elisabeth Rozin's *Ethnic Cuisine* (Penguin, 1992).

I have them read Sokolov so they understand things like what the Spanish cooks were faced with when Christopher Columbus came to Puerto Rico. They'd lived in Spain their whole lives, and dealt with Spanish ingredients, and now all of a sudden they're in Puerto Rico. They're still Spanish cooks, but all of a sudden they have this whole new larder of ingredients. Likewise, the first Spanish cooks that went to the Phillippines created the original East-West food. And real cuisines grew out of these travels. Mexican cuisine, you could argue, is fusion food—fusion between Aztecs and Spaniards.

Of course, *nouvelle cuisine's* influence got everybody off just duplicating the classics. And now we're at a new point where all the lines are just totally blurred. I've got six different nationalities living in my neighborhood. I've got people who've never traveled who have an intimate knowledge of Thai food. I think the cross-cultural aspects of people's tastes and their ideas about adventurism have changed, and for me, as a cook, that opens everything up.

1) When we're putting together a menu, we'll make a roster of *sauces* first. We work very definitely from the sauce as the starting point.
2) Like most restaurants, we have the sort of *protein* categories pretty well fixed. You've got to have poultry, you've got to have fish dishes and crustaceans and that kind of stuff.
3) A few days after we've come up with that, we'll sit down and talk about the way we're going to put it on *the plate*. That usually will dictate or give rise to a number of ideas for accompaniments and garnishes and that sort of thing.
4) After we've got that sort of sketched out, we'll live with that for a few days, and then we'll come back and really *fine-tune* it. We're just getting ready to make a menu change at Topolobampo next week. We'd gone through this whole process and last night I was doing the final re-write on the menu, and I realized that we had too many things coming from one station. We'd been thinking more in terms of all the flavors in the dishes, but we didn't get it right in terms of the logistics on our line, so we had to go back and re-vamp some things this morning.

And the testing process should be thorough. "Before you put something on a menu, you shouldn't just taste it with your finger," says Jean-Georges Vongerichten. "You must eat a whole plate of it first."

"I could write a menu in an afternoon," says Lydia Shire. "But to do it right, we spend weeks developing and testing ideas, reading, talking, researching ingredients, and making sure each dish is great. We could just put a curry dish on the menu and leave it at that. But instead, we go to the Indian market and get some edible silver leaf to put on the plate. And Susie [Regis, Shire's second-in-command at Biba] will develop a *poori*—a puffed Indian bread—to serve with it. Now she makes the best *pooris* in the world!"

Seasonal Ingredients and Techniques

Writing a restaurant menu is a process that leading chefs typically undertake seasonally—or even more frequently. "We will change the menu twice a season in order to incorporate ingredients at their peak in the late versus the early season," says Daniel Boulud.

"I cook seasonally, so my menu changes a lot," says Terrance Brennan. "I serve a lot more stews in the fall and winter, along with a lot more slow

cooking and rustic cooking. It lightens up in the spring, and in the summer it goes really light—more geared toward fish and lighter preparations."

Brennan points out that it's produce that changes the most from season to season. So while he has certain non-seasonal dishes, such as risotto with wild mushrooms, that are always on the menu, he'll change the garnish with the seasons. "The same risotto dish I serve with a pumpkin garnish in the fall might be served with a squash garnish in the winter, an asparagus-and-fava-bean garnish in the spring, and a corn garnish in the summer," he says.

The starting point? Daniel Boulud says he gathers books, prior restaurant menus from the same season, and a list of previously-run specials from the same season in order to come up with a "repertoire" of ingredients for that season.

"The most important thing here is to focus on the products I know and the quality and reliability of the suppliers I use to get them in. When there are ingredients that I can only get in sporadically, I'll feature them as daily specials instead of putting them on the menu," says Boulud. "Things like frog legs, which I can only get in on Mondays or Thursdays—if I'm going to put a dish on my menu, then I have to be certain that the supply and quality I can get is consistent."

Johanne Killeen says that seasonality is probably the most important thing when coming up with a menu. "In the summer, our menu is just loaded with corn and tomatoes. In the fall, we go into squashes. In the winter, cabbages and sweet potatoes and a lot of pumpkin, and now [in the spring] we're beginning to see some green again," she says. "But going to the market is a big influence. We market every day, and when we visit our wholesaler occasionally we come back loaded with stuff to experiment with."

Variety

Once the basic menu has been established, chefs double-check to ensure that their offerings include enough diversity. "I like to give my customers a broad variety," says Joachim Splichal. "You have to have beef, chicken, and veal on the menu; it's expected at a place like this. About four years ago, we added vegetarian and seafood offerings to the menu. And a couple of years ago we added the category of 'Odd Things,'" which includes Splichal's beloved offal.

With one week's advance notice, Restaurant Daniel offers special tasting menus and classic dishes that can be ordered for the entire table. These include:

Les Menus sur un Thème

New York State Apple Menu

Black and White Truffle Menu

North Atlantic Seafood Menu

Wild Mushroom Menu

Wild Game Menu

Les Plats Classiques

Pot au Feu Served in Five Courses

Roasted Whole Sea Bass Stuffed with Shellfish (for 4–6 people)

Whole *Foie Gras* with Grapes, Hazelnuts, and Spinach (for 4–6)

Free-Range Chicken Roasted in a Sea Salt Crust with Herbs (for 2)

Roasted Pheasant Stuffed with *Foie Gras* and Black Truffles (seasonal, for 2)

Wild Game Pie (seasonal, for 4–6)

Terrance Brennan also likes to offer a well-balanced menu featuring pheasant or chicken, steak, lamb, duck, and four or five fishes which change seasonally, except for salmon, which is offered year round. And he won't repeat garnishes on various dishes, except perhaps for tomatoes, but then he'll vary the preparation.

Joyce Goldstein takes the diversity of her customers into consideration when planning her menu. "I'll have some things on the menu that are comforting, for people who aren't there to think about the food. Things that are recognizable—classic dishes like chicken and mashed potatoes. Other people want to be stimulated and transported. They come into the restaurant thinking, 'Dazzle me!' So I'll offer them something Moroccan. Others are middle-of-the-roaders, and I have Italian dishes on the menu for them."

In terms of writing a dessert menu, François Payard says, "I try to make everyone happy. I make a lot of fruit soups here, which our women customers like, especially in the summer. And I'll ask good customers what they'd like to eat for dessert."

Signature Dishes

Much as some chefs might like to get away from them, there are certain dishes they've become known for that they can't eliminate from their restaurant menus without causing an uproar among their customers. Such dishes have come to be known as "signature dishes."

At Patina, Joachim Splichal can't take off his famous shrimp or gratin of lamb dishes. At Picholine, Terrance Brennan counts as the staples always on his menu his salmon in horseradish and Moroccan lamb. One of Anne Rosenzweig's signature dishes at Arcadia even became the name of her new restaurant: The Lobster Club.

"That became a jail for me after twelve years—the fact that there were dishes that could never come off the menu," says Jasper White. "A restaurant, over time, becomes greater than the person who started it. Every time you serve a dish in the restaurant, you reinforce what that restaurant is. And there's a point when you grow away from your restaurant. That's why chefs open other restaurants—because it's not wise to keep changing your restaurant. Restaurants tend not to evolve that much; they tend to become more of what they are. And that's what people love about them.

"People don't go to your restaurant seven nights a week; they go once every three months or whatever, especially in fine dining and especially in cities where you have a lot of choices. Even though they might absolutely adore it, it doesn't mean they'll be back [right away]. You might not go back for six or eight months, and when you do go back, you're going to remember what you had the last time, and if it was that great that you still have a memory of it, you're going to start looking for it. Especially non-food people. People in the business are always looking for new things, because they're always looking for new ideas. But regular people were going to Jasper's for the pan-roasted lobster. If I'd ever taken that off the menu, it would have been death. They're going to Coyote Café for Mark [Miller]'s *chile rellenos*, or going to Dean Fearing for his crabmeat tacos. Those dishes become larger than the restaurant, and the restaurant becomes bigger than the chef.

"That's what people want from restaurants, is that familiarity," says White. "And restaurants that fight it tend to fail, I've noticed, because they don't establish a real identity. To be successful, I think there has to be something, when people ask themselves, 'What am I in the mood for?', they say,

CHEZ PANISSE

Berkeley, California

Sometimes a single menu can be a turning point in the evolution of a cuisine. Jeremiah Tower's 1976 Northern California Regional Dinner menu represents the first time Chez Panisse made a conscious effort to serve the ingredients indigenous to the Northern California area, which set a precedent the restaurant has followed ever since. This is the now-infamous menu:

Northern California Regional Dinner

Tomales Bay Bluepoint Oysters on Ice
Schramsberg, Cuvée de Gamay 1973

Cream of Fresh Corn Soup, Mendocino Style, with Crayfish Butter

Big Sur Garrapata Creek Smoked Trout Steamed over California Bay Leaves
Mount Eden, Chardonnay 1973

Monterey Bay Prawns Sautéed with Garlic, Parsley, and Butter
Mount Eden, Chardonnay 1973

Preserved California-Grown Geese from Sebastopol
Beaulieu, Cabernet Sauvignon, Private Reserve 1970

Vela Dry Monterey Jack Cheese from Sonoma
Ridge, Zinfandel, Fiddletown 1974

Fresh Caramelized Figs
Harbor Winery, Mission del Sol 1974

Walnuts, Almonds, and Mountain Pears
from the San Francisco Farmers' Market
Feast Side Winery, Tawny Port

'Remember that dish we had at…?' Can you imagine if Al Forno took grilled pizza off their menu? I would cry. When I go to Al Forno, I'm having grilled pizza. I have two pizzas, and it's great and that's part of the identity of the restaurant. But you can be sure that George has got to be a little tired of making those pizzas!"

When It's Right

"The best compliment you can get is when a customer is leaving the restaurant after a several-course meal and says, 'I feel so good!'" says Hubert Keller. "The food doesn't lie."

As we've seen, how chefs accomplish that feat is through applying basic principles of menu composition to achieve their desired affect on a customer, just as great composers and playwrights can hit the right buttons that they know will make us laugh or cry.

Joyce Goldstein believes that as a chef, you must design the way a menu will affect the customer. "You have to figure out, with finger food and a three-course meal plus dessert, how many orgasms do you have in a meal? You don't want to have four! Nothing will have any meaning, because they'll all be the same," she says. "So it's, How do you want to play it? Do you start quiet and build to the second course, and then lay low and build to the third? Do you start quiet, quiet, quiet, and build? Do you hit them the first time, and let them recover? You have to choose where you think your big gun is, or the one that's going to cause silence at the table. And you can't do it at every course. So you just have to plot your attack. Which dish is the killer? Which is nice? Which is another little crescendo? And where's the surprise?"

Norman Van Aken says, "During a wine dinner there's an inherent probability of going from light to rich, interposing it occasionally with a little preview of a little bit of richness before you get down to the very rich, and then a relief somewhere in the middle.

"I think of composing a menu as a lot like putting together a four-act play," Van Aken says, before providing examples of the roles various ingredients and dishes can enact. "Every now and then, the villain's got to jump out of the closet and scare the shit out of everybody. The 'villains' are only in the wording, in the 'costuming.' I might describe something 'chile-rubbed and roasted breast of squab on a habañero salsa'—but when it's eaten, it's not going to be villainous. And at the end, the little girl comes out with a flower in her hand. She's safe, we're all safe—we've had chocolate!"

COMMON ACCOMPANIMENTS TO ENTRÉES[*]

Over time, certain accompaniments have become familiar companions to various entrées—liver and onions, meat and potatoes, pork chops and applesauce, turkey and stuffing. This list includes other combinations that, while perhaps not as well known, are similarly time-tested matches.

Given that today vegetables are commonly incorporated as part of a dish itself rather than simply served as a side dish, there is some ambiguity as to whether the match should be included under "Composing a Dish" or here. Readers may wish to refer to both lists, whether composing a dish or a menu, for different inspirations.

While this list provides suggested matches, a chef's point of view will inspire how they will be applied (or whether they will be reinterpreted or ignored!). For example, the classic combination of meat and potatoes is open to interpretation as:

- *Pot-Roasted Beef Fillet with Mashed Potatoes*
  —George Germon & Johanne Killeen

- *Grilled Fillet of Beef with Cracked Black Pepper and Cognac Mustard Cream, served with Shoestring Potatoes and Glazed Carrots and Beets*
  —Joyce Goldstein

- *Braised Short Rib of Beef, Leeks, and Potato Mousseline*—Gray Kunz

- *Grilled C.A.B. Rib-Eye Steak with Red Sage Steak Sauce and Twice-Baked Potato Skins*—Mark Miller

- *Patina Smoked Beef Tenderloin with Horseradish-Glazed Potatoes and Spinach*—Joachim Splichal

BASS

broccoli	endive	potatoes
eggplant		

BEEF

artichoke hearts	morels	ratatouille
brussels sprouts	**mushrooms**	red cabbage
celery root	parsnips	spinach
escarole	**potatoes**	tomatoes
fennel		

[*] Many of these combinations are classics; these are indicated in **boldface** type.

BEEF BRISKET

beets   parsnips   potatoes
cabbage   pasta   sauerkraut

BEEF SHANKS

polenta   potatoes, especially
                             mashed and roasted

BRAINS

rice   tomatoes   watercress
salad

BUFFALO

cabbage   carrots   potatoes

CAPON

celery, puréed   onions   potatoes, especially
chestnuts, puréed   parsnips   puréed
mushrooms   stuffing

CATFISH

cole slaw   potatoes   tomatoes
hush puppies

CAVIAR

blini   eggs, hard-boiled   sour cream
bread, dark   lemon   vodka
Champagne   onions, raw

CHICKEN

artichoke hearts	celery root	parsnips
asparagus	crayfish	peas
beans, fava	dumplings	**potatoes**
beans, green	egg noodles	rice
beans, lima	eggplant	spinach
broccoli	**mushrooms**	turnips
brussels sprouts	onions	wild rice
carrots	orzo	zucchini

COD

beans, green	escarole	potatoes
broccoli	kale	tomatoes
eggplant		

CORNED BEEF

beets	carrots	potatoes
cabbage	onions	turnips

CRAB

asparagus	pea greens	radicchio
cabbage		

CRAYFISH

cole slaw	rice

DUCK

apples	chestnuts	potatoes
apricots	corn	rhubarb
barley	endive	rice
beans, fava	escarole	rutabagas
beans, white, puréed	figs	sauerkraut
bok choy	greens	scallion pancakes
broccoli	grits	spaetzle
brussels sprouts	lentils	spinach
bulgur	**mushrooms**	squash, butternut
cabbage	parsnips	**sweet potatoes**
cabbage, red	passion fruit	turnips, especially baby
carrots	pears	**wild rice**
celery	peas	
celery root	polenta	

EGGS

bacon	ham	sausage
corned beef hash	potatoes	toast

FISH

artichokes	chips	pasta
asparagus	coleslaw	ratatouille
beans, fava	cucumbers	rice
broccoli	endive	spinach
cabbage	**fennel**	
cèpes	leeks	

FISH, WHITE

cole slaw	potatoes	sorrel
parsnips		

FOIE GRAS

cèpes	grapes	toast
compote	lentils	

FROGS' LEGS

celery root	mushrooms

GAME

apples	grapes	pears
cabbage	hominy	potatoes
cabbage, red	lentils	sweet potatoes
celery root, puréed	parsnips	turnips
chestnuts, especially puréed		

GOOSE

apples	chestnuts, especially puréed	sauerkraut
brussels sprouts		wild rice
cabbage, red		

GOULASH

noodles	rice	spaetzle

GUINEA HEN

apples	carrots	risotto
brussels sprouts	lentils	sausage
cabbage	potatoes	

HALIBUT

beans, green	cabbage	potatoes
broccoli	eggplant	spinach

HAM

apples	corn pudding	sauerkraut
apricots	gnocchi	spinach, especially
beans	lentils	puréed
biscuits	**peas,** especially puréed	spoon bread
cabbage	**potatoes,** especially	**sweet potatoes**
carrots	creamed or puréed	turnips
chestnuts		

HARE

chestnuts	porcini	squash
cranberries		

HERRING

apples	leeks	**potatoes**
cabbage		

KIDNEYS

cèpes	mushrooms	potatoes
coleslaw	noodles	salad

LAMB AND MUTTON

aïoli	**beans, flageolets/white**	brussels sprouts
apricots	**beans, green**	bulgur
artichokes	**beans, white**	carrots, especially
asparagus	broccoli	creamed

(continued on facing page)

cauliflower
chard
chestnuts, especially
   puréed
chick peas
couscous
eggplant

escarole
fennel
lentils
peas
peppers, bell
potatoes
ratatouille

rhubarb
rice
spinach
turnips, especially baby
watercress, especially
   puréed

LAMB CHOPS

asparagus
beans, green
brussels sprouts
couscous
eggplant
fiddlehead ferns
mushrooms, especially
   broiled

noodles
onions, especially
   puréed and fried
peas
potatoes
rice
salad
spinach, especially

   puréed
tomatoes, especially
   broiled
watercress
zucchini

LAMB, CROWN ROAST

brussels sprouts
chestnuts, puréed
lamb kidneys

mushrooms
peas

rice pilaf
tomatoes

LAMB SHANKS

apples
beans

fennel
pasta

potatoes
rice

LIVER

mushrooms
mustard greens
onions

pasta
potatoes
rice

salad
truffles
vegetable purées

LOBSTER

artichokes
chanterelles

couscous
pea greens

radicchio
rice

MACKEREL

apples	gooseberries	potatoes
eggplant		

OXTAILS

noodles	parsnips	rice
onions	potatoes	

OYSTERS, FRIED

coleslaw	potatoes

OYSTERS, RAW

ale, beer, or stout	toast	wine, white and dry
bread, dark (e.g., pumpernickel, rye, wheat)		

PARTRIDGE

endive	polenta	scrapple
fritters	potatoes	watercress
greens	rice	
pasta	sauerkraut	

PHEASANT

apples	gnocchi	pumpkin
brussels sprouts	hominy	rice
cabbage	lentils	salad
cabbage, red	**mushrooms**	sauerkraut
carrots	noodles	squash, especially butternut
celery root, especially puréed	onions	turnips
celery	orzo	watercress
chestnuts, especially puréed	parsnips	**wild rice**
	peas	
foie gras	polenta	
	potatoes	

(See also Jeremiah Tower's menu featuring pheasant on page 267.)

Jeremiah Tower

STARS and J.T.'s
San Francisco, California

The reason I think this menu works so well is that the flavors of the dishes are very direct, but subtle and clean, so that it is possible to have a menu with three sauced courses.

The consommé is the real break between two sauces, as I deplore the continued use of sorbet to cleanse the palate. If the menu is composed properly, why should you have to cleanse your palate? The consommé here is to warm your stomach and invigorate your appetite.

This menu celebrates the quality of ingredients available to us today, and the menus at J.T.'s are written to reconfirm, as when we opened Stars, that the ingredients are the engine of the menus and recipes, more than ideas or preconceived notions.

Stars' Happy New Year to Urania and Brunno

Black Truffle Custard, Jerusalem Artichokes, and Chervil Sauce
Cordon Rouge, Brut, Mumm

• • •

Quinault River Steelhead Salmon with Mussel Mousseline Sauce
Corton-Charlemagne, Bonneau du Martray, 1992

• • •

Consommé

• • •

Pheasant with Sugar-Pie Pumpkin and Watercress
Cabernet Sauvignon, Napa, Ristow

• • •

Stars Strawberry Soufflé
Nivolé, Moscato d' Asti, Chiarlo, 1994

• • •

Friandises
El Rey Carenero Superior Chocolate Cigars and Digestifs

PORK

apples
beans, fava
beans, lima
broad beans
brussels sprouts
cabbage
cabbage, red

cèpes
chestnuts, especially
  puréed
lentils
pears
potatoes, especially
  mashed

quinces
rice
salad
sauerkraut
snow peas
sweet potatoes
turnips

PORK CHOPS

apples
beans, especially pinto
  and refried
beets
cabbage, red
coleslaw

endive
hominy, especially fried
potatoes
rice
salad
sauerkraut

spinach
squash, especially
  mashed
watercress

POT ROASTS

carrots, especially braised
dumplings
endive
onions

potatoes, especially
  baked or pancakes
salad
spinach

tomatoes
turnips

POULTRY

apples
beans, fava
brussels sprouts
cabbage
cauliflower

chestnuts, especially
  puréed
fennel
figs
grapes

polenta
potatoes
ratatouille
spoon bread

QUAIL

arugula
beans, green
brussels sprouts
cèpes
chestnuts
corn
mâche
mushrooms

pears
polenta
potatoes
quinces
rhubarb
rice
scrapple
stuffing, especially corn

bread
sweetbreads
sweet potatoes
Swiss chard
watercress
wild rice

RABBIT

barley
cabbage, especially red
celery root
chestnuts, especially
    puréed

greens
noodles
pasta
potatoes

rice pilaf
spinach
turnips

RED SNAPPER

broccoli
cabbage

eggplant
fennel

zucchini

ROASTS

broccoli
brussels sprouts
carrots
celery root

corn, especially creamed
grits
onions
parsnips

potatoes
salsify
shallots
turnips

ROAST BEEF

bean, green
brussels sprouts
cabbage

onions
peas
potatoes

turnips, mashed
Yorkshire pudding

SALMON

asparagus
beans, fava
cabbage, red
corn
couscous

cucumbers
eggplant
Jerusalem artichokes
lentils
mushrooms

onions
peas
potatoes
quinoa
spinach

SAUSAGES

apples
beans
brussels sprouts
cabbage
cabbage, red
cauliflower
celery

chestnuts
fennel
leeks
lentils
onions
peas
polenta

potatoes, especially
    mashed
rice
sauerkraut
tomatoes, especially
    fried

SCALLOPS

escarole	radicchio	watercress
kale	**rice**	
potatoes, especially mashed		

SEA BASS

beans, black, fava, and white	fennel	potatoes, especially new

SHANKS

noodles	rice
polenta	root vegetables, especially puréed
potatoes, especially mashed or roasted	

SHELLFISH

fennel	peas	rhubarb
grains		

SHORT RIBS

beans, puréed	coleslaw	potatoes
beer	leeks	rice
broccoli	noodles	sauerkraut
brussels sprouts	pasta	tomatoes
cabbage	peas	

SHRIMP

grains	pea greens	rice
pasta	radicchio	salad

SKATE

beans, especially white	eggplant	sweet potatoes

SMOKED SALMON

blini	rye bread	toast

SOLE

broccoli	pasta	rice, especially pilaf
fennel	radicchio	risotto

SPARERIBS

beer	pickles, dill	sauerkraut
bread, especially rye	potatoes, especially	tomatoes
cabbage	boiled or mashed	
coleslaw	rice	

SQUAB

artichokes	eggplant	mashed
barley	**lentils**	rice
beans, especially fava	mushrooms	salad
brussels sprouts	onions	squash
cabbage	**peas**	tomatoes
chanterelles	polenta	wild rice
corn	potatoes, especially	

SQUIRREL

peaches, especially pickled	pears, especially pickled	sweet potatoes, especially baked

STEAK

artichoke	onions	salad
broccoli	onion rings	shallots
carrots	parsley	spinach
corn, especially creamed	peas	tomatoes
custard	peppers, bell	watercress
iceberg lettuce	**potatoes**	
mushrooms	**rice**	

SUCKLING PIG

apples	corn	stuffing
cabbage	onions	sweet potatoes
chestnuts	rutabagas	turnips

Bradley Ogden

THE LARK CREEK INN
Larkspur, California

This was a very creative and festive holiday menu. Thanksgiving is the ultimate meal when looking at American cuisine. It reflects family, American heritage, and the goodness of holidays.

Thanksgiving Dinner
Thursday, November 28, 1991

Platter of American Antipasto

• • •

*Field Lettuce Salad with House-Cured Gravlax and
Herbed Potted-Cheese Toast*

• • •

*Baked Quilcene Oysters with Peppers, Onions, Bacon,
and Garlic Bread Crumbs*

• • •

*Roasted Butternut Squash and Apple Soup
with Lemon Crème Fraîche*

• • •

*Spit-Roasted Quail with Braised Lentil Salad
and Truffle Aïoli*

• • •

Whole Barbecue Suckling Pig Cassoulet

• • •

*Oak-Roasted Turkey with Sage amd Corn Stuffing,
Mashed Red Potatoes, Giblet Gravy, Homemade
Jellied Cranberry Sauce, Candied Yams*

• • •

*Prime Rib of Beef with Scalloped Turnips and Potatoes,
Roasted Vegetables*

• • •

*Pan-Roasted Atlantic Salmon with Corn Spoon Bread
and Chervil Tomato Broth, Sugar Snap Peas*

• • •

*Pumpkin Pie
Lemon Pudding Cake with Tangerine Compote
Apple and Cranberry Crisp with Vanilla-Bean Ice Cream
Apple Cider Sherbet, Pomegranate Ice, Persimmon Sherbet
Banana Layer Cake with Butter Pecan Ice Cream
Chocolate Espresso Custard with
Burnt Sugar Topping*

SWEETBREADS

asparagus	lentils	rice
beans, fava	morels	sorrel
cauliflower	mushrooms	spinach
cèpes	noodles	tomatoes
chicory	peas	

TUNA

beans, black and green	oranges	radishes
eggplant	plantains, especially fried	turnips

TURKEY

brussels sprouts	giblets	squash, winter
cabbage, red	gravy	stuffing
chestnuts	parsnips	sweet potatoes or yams
corn	potatoes	turnips
cranberries	sauerkraut	watercress

(See also Bradley Ogden's Thanksgiving menu on page 272.)

VEAL

asparagus	dumplings	rice
beans, green	eggplant	sorrel, especially puréed
beets	morels	**spaetzle**
carrots	mushrooms	**spinach**
cauliflower	noodles	tomatoes
celery	peas	turnips
chestnuts, especially puréed	potatoes	watercress, especially puréed
	prunes	

(See also Charlie Palmer's menu featuring veal on page 274.)

VEAL CHOPS

eggplant	peas	spinach
mushrooms, especially creamed and shiitake	polenta	watercress
	potatoes	zucchini
noodles	rice	
onions, especially red	shallots	

Charlie Palmer

AUREOLE
New York, New York

The reason I thought it was really neat to do this menu is that I have huge respect for Michael Graves (the dinner's guest of honor) as an architect. He's been one of my idols in the sense of design, so the opportunity to construct a menu around what I thought matched his architectural design and thought process in general was very exciting. Some of the dishes were architecturally sculpted to coincide with both the house where the dinner was held and the plateware, both of which he'd designed.

The New York Public Library's
100th Birthday
December 6, 1995

Osetra Caviar and Lobster "Coupe"
with Smoked Salmon and Chive-Citrus Oil
Iron Horse, Brut, Late Disgorged 1989

• • •

Roasted Butternut Squash
and Duckling Soup
Chardonnay, Marcassin, Gauer Ranch Upper Barn 1993

• • •

Proscuitto Crusted Veal Rib-Eye
Potato Turnip Press and Chanterelles
Iron Horse, Cabernet Sauvignon 1984

• • •

Fantasy in Caramel
Study in Nougatine
Muscat Canelli, Bonny Doon, Vin de Glacière 1994

• • •

Coffee and Petits Fours
Iron Horse, "Vrais Amis" 1989

VEAL KIDNEYS

noodles
potatoes, especially
   chips
rice
watercress
veal stew
peas
spaetzle

VENISON

apples
brussels sprouts
cabbage, red
celery root, especially
   puréed
chard
chestnuts, especially
   puréed
celery salad

cranberries
French beans
hominy
lentils
mushrooms
orange salad
pears, poached
potatoes
quinces

root vegetables
red cabbage
spaetzle
squash
sweet potatoes
tomatoes
wild rice

The menus on the pages that follow were shared by the chefs, whom we asked for samples of some of their favorites from among those they've created. They also share their comments as to why they believe the menus "work" so well.

Joyce Goldstein

SQUARE ONE
San Francisco, California

This was one of the best dinners we ever did. A lot of it was food that would ordinarily be a hard-sell on an *à la carte* menu. It was sort of funky food that people practically fell over—they were so impressed with it. But if we had put some of these dishes on our menu—like the pigeon soup, or the whipped salt cod on soft polenta—they'd be murder to try to sell. But as part of a set menu, we didn't have to "sell" them; everyone was served all of these things. And they were in heaven—they were moaning and groaning with pleasure!

The antipasto we always do as sort of an ice-breaker and a family-style thing is sort of nice to get people talking to each other. Now, it's hard to do gnocchi every day, because it ties up six people standing around a table for three or four hours. So it's economically stupid to have it on a restaurant menu—but for a special event dinner it was very nice. The *sopa coada* is an unusual main course, but it's incredibly sexy, and all the desserts came together on a plate.

I love when people put themselves in your hands and say, "Feed me, take care of me!" Then you don't have people saying, "What's in it? Can you leave that out?" You know, the Burger King school. It's very nice to have people say, "I trust you!" And they loved it.

Veneto Dinner at Square One
Wednesday, October 11, at 6:30 P.M.

Fish Appetizers:
Whipped Salt Cod on a Bed of Soft Polenta
Mixed Fry of Squid and Stuffed Zucchini Blossoms
Marinated Filet of Sole with Sweet and Sour Onions
Shrimp with Garlic, Lemon, and Olive Oil
Onion and Rosemary Bread
1994 Gini Soave Classico Superiore
• • •
Potato Gnocchi with Crab, Shallots, and Tomatoes
1994 Vignalta Pinot Bianco, Colli Euganei
1993 Il Podere dell'Olivos, Tocai Friulano Central Coast
• • •
Sopa Coada—Baked Bread "Soup" with Squab, Aromatic Vegetables,
and Parmesan Cheese
1993 Vignalta Rosso, Colli Euganei
1993 Qupe "Los Olivos Cuvee," Santa Barbara
• • •
Radicchio Salad with Anchovy Garlic Vinaigrette
and Croutons with Gorgonzola Brandy Butter
• • •
Pound Cake, Zabaglione, and Baked Figs with Lemon
Marco De Bartoli Inzolia di Samperi

Gray Kunz

LESPINASSE
New York, New York

I wanted to start with a simple lobster salad, but put a lot of emphasis on the sauce. We made a reduced lobster sauce from the lobster bodies and combined it with one egg yolk and olive oil, and drizzled that around the lobster salad, and added quite a lot of chopped orange and made it a bit spicy with cayenne, salt, and pepper.

Truffle dishes have become somewhat of a signature, as I have a small farm in the Périgord region which provides me with fresh truffles. We serve the cassolette side by side with about three teaspoons of risotto, the black truffles right next to the white.

When we grill the daurade, we top it off with kind of a mini-cut ratatouille and then undercook the fish. The daurade is a very simple fillet, served sizzling on a heated marble slab placed on a silver tray. There is something very rustic yet elegant in this presentation.

The venison is from upstate New York, and we coat the medallions with a special combination of spices which include juniper, coriander, and black pepper before sautéeing them. We blanch the cabbage and finish it with a little bit of butter, and add chestnuts which have been roasted and caramelized. The *salmis* sauce is made from roasted venison bones.

On the longer menus, before the main dessert, we serve a cold fruit soup, which has become a signature part of the restaurant. During the summer, we have elderflower or cherry or peach—whatever is in season. Lemongrass soup is a distinctive dish made from simply milk and a split vanilla bean and sugar, and infused with chopped lemongrass. You simply bring it to a boil, cover it, then chill it. You'd be amazed how good that tastes, especially garnished with all the tropical fruits you can find—I like it with mango and pineapple. It makes an incredibly refreshing soup, especially after the venison, which is pretty hefty.

After the lemongrass soup, which is so fragrant and flavorful, I think you need something which balances out your palate again that is pretty rich. It's a matter of going from one extreme to the other. The warm chocolate tartlet is a basic dark chocolate dough topped with a rich ganache, baked for seven minutes so it arrives at the table with a liquid center. We serve it with seasonal fruit—such as a coulis of passion fruit, a sesame *tuile*, and some white chocolate ice cream.

Chef's Menu

Salad of Crisped Lobster, Spiced Orange-Crustace Rémoulade

• • •

Cassolette of Fresh Périgord Truffles, Risotto of White Truffles

• • •

Grilled Daurade Served Sizzling with Shallots and Bell Peppers

• • •

Sautéed Venison Medallion with Confits of Chestnuts, Cabbage, and Salmis Sauce

• • •

Chilled Soup of Lemongrass, Yogurt Lime Sorbet

• • •

Warm Chocolate Tartlet

Gray Kunz

LESPINASSE
New York, New York

Generally when I compose vegetarian menus, I look at the first dish as either a soup or a salad—and something that really sets the tone for the menu right away. This carrot soup is quite pungent, as there are quite a lot of spices in there. It really awakens you. In fact, we used to name the menu "Vegetarian and Spice Tasting Menu," because there are so many spices that it's become a signature of what I'm doing.

This menu begins with basically a carrot soup. The base is finished with yogurt, and we sprinkle a fairly complex spice mix, based mainly on roasted coriander seeds, around the soup. Basil seeds are available in Indian stores; we soak the black seeds in water until they "pop" and turn transluscent. That inside the soup gives it a little bit of that texture. Then we add a strip of crispy potatoes going all the way across the soup, and sprinkle on the top some julienne of carrots and coriander.

I would follow a liquid course like this with something very crunchy. We make a kind of Indian bread and put rice flakes on top, and pan-sear them so they come out really, really crunchy. The saffron-yogurt emulsion provides a very simple sauce around it.

Napa cabbage is a little bit more complex, and we add pearl onions and julienne of peppers—almost like a stir-fry in the pan. We make a curry sauce from all the trimmings of the vegetables, and de-glaze the pan with that. We spice it with Thai basil and kaffir leaf and other Oriental flavors. It sits in a bowl, but we add a cloche or a "dome" on top which is made from a Middle Eastern dough, run through a machine to make it very thin and then bake it on top of a salad bowl. You have to crack into the crust to get to the napa cabbage, and then it releases all the aromas of the flavors and spices.

The pineapple gratin is very simply a wedge of baby pineapple that we have broken down into small pieces and marinated in rum and brown sugar before placing back into the quarter. We spread it with a little egg white, vanilla and sugar mixture, and we gratinée it under the broiler. The pineapple comes out warm with a little reduced coconut juice as a sauce, next to a *quenelle* of coconut sorbet garnished with a julienne of lime zest.

We serve a small wicker basket filled with chocolates and small cookies and things like that, and on the side we serve lemon curd and *tuiles*—all served on a silver tray. And it's a bit intriguing because you have to open the small basket to really see what's in there!

Winter Vegetarian Tasting Menu

Carrot Potage, Roasted Coriander, and Rösti

• • •

Crispy Rice Cake with Saffron-Yogurt Emulsion

• • •

Napa Cabbage Stew, Thai Basil, and Curry

• • •

Pineapple Gratin and Coconut Sorbet

• • •

Coffee, Espresso, Cappuccino, or Tea

• • •

Petits Fours

Mary Sue Milliken and Susan Feniger

BORDER GRILL
Santa Monica, California

We offer a family-style menu to groups of eight or more at Border Grill. It's smart from a business standpoint because that way people don't spend a lot of time trying to decide what to order, but it's also the way we love to eat. This way, you get to sample all kinds of different tastes.

When we eat out, we don't like to be burdened with too many decisions, and we like to taste as much as possible. You see more family-style eating when you travel a lot outside America. For example, when [Mary Sue] lived in Paris, even tiny bistros would have family-style seating. Buttered new potatoes would be placed in the middle of the table that you'd share with friends, even strangers—and it brought people together. When you travel, you're often seated with other people in your table—even in places like Chinatown in New York City. It's a nice thing. We always meet people that way. We're big proponents of sharing around the table—it's a great way to get the conversation flowing.

When we first opened Border Grill, we had two huge long tables that seated forty people, and we designed menus around eating communally. We kept the one in the bar area—people come in all night long and might sit next to a stranger and strike up a conversation. It's really nice.

The shared appetizers cater to people's whimsies, while they get to choose their entrées. At dessert time, everyone likes to share because no one can decide what to order and no one wants to miss anything! *Pastel Rufina*—"Ruth's Cake"—is named after Mary Sue's mother, and is based loosely on a *Gâteau St. Honoré*. She was our pastry chef when we opened Border Grill, and ended up working for us for seven years until she had to retire. She's seventy-three now!

Family-Style Menu

Appetizers

Green Corn Tamales with sour cream and salsa

• • •

Guacamole mashed to order

• • •

Quesadillas with Cheese and Poblano Chilies

• • •

Platano Empanadas Stuffed with Black Beans

Choice of Entrée

Border Vegetarian Plateful of Assorted Steamed, Grilled, and Roasted Vegetables

• • •

Grilled Skirt Steak Marinated with Garlic, Cilantro, and Cracked Pepper

• • •

Sautéed Rock Shrimp with Toasted Ancho Chilies, Slivered Garlic, and Lime

• • •

Grilled Pork Chop with Apple Tamarind Sauce

• • •

Breast of Chicken al Carbon Citrus Marinade, with Onion Orange Salsa

Dessert

An Assortment of Our Homemade Pastries
Pastel Rufina
Oaxacan Chocolate Cake
Mexican Chocolate Cream Pie
Lime Pie
Vanilla Flan

"La Vida Es Muy Grande"

Lydia Shire and Chef de Cuisine Daniele Baliani

PIGNOLI
Boston, Massachusetts

With this menu, we didn't look at a particular region of Italy so much as we tried to do things that were both seasonal and based on traditional foods served during the winter in Italy. Using classic ingredients more than actual recipes, we came up with our own dishes and interpretations of them that were rooted in tradition—with a little twist.

The Antipasto Giuliano was a combination of about a dozen plates of all sorts of marinated vegetables and calamari—typical Venetian grilled seafood and marinated vegetables.

Next, we served a mini-*panettone* (Italian Christmas brioche bread), filled with a potato soup laced with oxtail and beef marrow. The soft and rich marrow just melted into the soup and gave added richness to the soup, as the potatoes were just a clear and simple base. It's very Italian to serve double starches like the bread and potato here. In fact, a lot of the pasta courses in Italy—especially in Tuscany—feature double starches like pasta with chickpeas or beans or lentils. That's very common, actually.

Normally in Italy, *baccala* or salt cod, is whipped with potatoes, the way the French do a *brandade*. But in this case, we chilled and sliced it paper-thin, carpaccio-style, and served it with a beet salad and beet vinaigrette. Beets are sweet, and contrast nicely with the saltiness of the *baccala*.

Garganelli are quill-shaped pasta found in Emilía-Romagna, while *stracci* is the Italian word for rag, so this is pasta cut into sheets. The sea urchin reflects our desire to use both Italian ingredients as well as what's local and pristine from our waters.

Snapper is the closest thing to the Italian *bentice*—the fish most commonly used in Italy, sort of a cousin of our red snapper. The idea was to pair that with something that was kind of hot and spicy. Mustard fruits are just that—they're typically summer fruits like peaches and apricots that are preserved in a mustard syrup. The Parmesan has sort of a saltiness to it, and the mustard fruits are sweet and spicy, so it's still a matter of trying to achieve a balance with the brininess of the fish, for example. *Crespelle* are little crepes, which were stuffed with the mustard fruits, rolled, and baked with a little cheese on top like canneloni.

We basically "Frenched" the rabbit the way you would a rack of lamb—and a rack of rabbit is about the size of a quarter, so it was a very painstaking process. We marinated them in garlic and thyme, roasted them, and served them with medallions of seared *foie gras* and rabbit livers. "Rich and poor" is what the Italians call a combination like this—rabbit livers are typically the offal that are left from the carcasses that are eaten by the peasants, and the *foie gras* gives the dish a sort of regal touch. This dish keeps to our theme of using the whole animal, because in high cuisine a lot of the time we tend to disregard those lower-caste cuts, which actually have a lot of flavor. For the sauce, we did a classic rabbit *jus* with port and *foie gras* melted in at the end. I think we served it with some fried polenta.

Strozzapreti—or priest's stranglers—are typically served in Italy right before Lent. They're little pastry dough tied in the form of a knot or a noose and fried. The Italians call them "priest's stranglers" because typically in Italy, the church is known to eat very well, so there's always a bit of a sarcasm and resentment toward the fact that people of the cloth are supposedly living a life of humble existence, and yet they're known as having the best meals and the most sophisticated palates. In Italy, there are a number of dishes like that which refer sarcastically to the Church. We wanted to pair the pastry with a creamy and rich frozen mousse, which serves as something to dip the hot fried dough into. I believe we served it with a little blackberry sauce.

We did a lot of work on this menu, preparing it for more than 100 guests. But they told us that it was one of the better Chaine dinners that they'd had.

La Confrérie de la Chaine des Rôtisseurs
Bailliage de Boston
February 5, 1995

Antipasto Giulliano
Bellavista, "Franciacorts" Cuvée Brut 1988

• • •

Oxtail and Marrow Soup in Roasted Bread
De Bartoli, "La Vigna Miccia," Marsala Superiore

• • •

Carpaccio of Baccala
Cinque Terre, Cinque Terre D.O.C., Liquria 1992

• • •

Hand-Rolled Garganelli and Stracci with Fresh Maine Sea Urchin
Livio Felluga Pinot Grigio 1992

• • •

Silk Snapper, Parmesan Sauce, and Mustard-Fruit Crespelle
Jermann, Chardonnay, "Piccolo Sogno," Friuli 1991

• • •

Rack of Rabbit with Two Livers
Marchesi di Barolo, Barolo, "Cannubi" 1992

• • •

Hot "Priest's Stranglers," Chilled Mascarpone Soufflé
Remo Farina, Recioto della Valpolicella Classico 1992

Norman Van Aken

NORMAN'S
Coral Gables, Florida

This was a menu for my wife, Janet, and Charlie Trotter and his wife, Lynn, as a celebration of love conquering all adversity in opening up a restaurant [Norman's].

The first courses had textures, with the conch and the deep-fried sushi. The second courses were to show regionality—the *paellita* was a mini-version of *paella*. The *foie gras* was a regional, down-island interpretation. The salad platter was fun, because I got to use the words "dressed and ripped." The main course addressed the necessary issue of drinking red wine. The style of desserts was what I'd call Carib-Asian, because Asian-style food goes well with the cuisine of Florida. And the dessert course was the positive apocalypse of the entire meal!

A "Love Conquers All" Dinner for Janet, Lynn, and Charlie

Various Amusées and Tapas

First Plates

Creamy Cracked Conch Chowder with Saffron, Toasted Coconut, and Oranges

• • •

*Spicy Steamed Clams with Deep-Fried Sushi,
Asian Black Beans, and a Hot Sesame-Cumin Drizzle*

• • •

*Yucca-Stuffed Shrimp with a Sour Orange Mojo
and a Scotch Bonnet Tartar Salsa*

Second Plates

*Grilled Tuna with Preserved Lemon Couscous, Harissa,
and a Cucumber-and-Yogurt Raita*

. . .

*Seared Wafers of Curaçao-Scented Foie Gras on a Cuban Bread Shortstack
with Exotic Fruits Caramel*

. . .

A Paellita with Petit Gris and Crabmeat en Pimiento

A Shared Salad Platter

*Crispy Chinese Chicken Salad with Passion Fruit
Dressed and Ripped Lettuces*

. . .

Main Plates

*Roast Pork Tenderloin with Haitian Corn Grits, "21st–Century Molé"
and a Red Onion, Black Bean, and Sweet Corn Salsa*

. . .

*Rioja-Braised Lamb Shank Stew and Grilled Double-Cut Lamb Chop
on a Rioja Red Wine Reduction with Truffle-Buttered Potatoes*

. . .

*Palomilla Strip Steak au Poivre with a Cabrales Crema, Blistered Bell Peppers,
a Stacked Sweet Tater Torta, and West Indian Pumpkin*

Dessert Plates

A New World Banana Split with Macadamia-Nut Crunch Ice Cream

. . .

A Little Venezuelan Chocolate Love Triangle

. . .

Asian Tea-Spiced Sorbet with Ginger Snap "Dragon" Cookies

Some painters are so well known for their characteristic styles that even the occasional museum-goer can identify a Picasso or a Mondrian. Similarly, certain writers, such as the poet e.e. cummings or the novelist John Irving, have unique styles which distinguish their writing from that of other writers. But do chefs have recognizable signature styles of their own?

"It would be interesting to blindfold ten food critics and ask them to taste the dishes of ten leading chefs to see if they could identify the chef," says Daniel Boulud.

Does Boulud believe they could? "Yes, I

Evolving a Cuisine

Cuisine: The food prepared, as at a restaurant; the style of cooking or manner of preparing the food.

think so, if the dishes were ones they'd tasted before," he says. "The critics would have to know the traditional dishes of the chefs."

Boulud cites as examples his own dishes of scallops, pea soup, and tuna tartare with radish and curry as ones that would likely be recognizable to experienced critics as his and his alone. "And they'd know Jean-Georges Vongerichten's shrimp in carrot juice at Jojo, or Gray Kunz's braised short ribs at Lespinasse. In order to recognize the dish, it would have to be a very distinct dish—not a complex dish with a lot of fried stuff on top. Sometimes the most memorable dishes are the simplest.

"I believe you can recognize the subtle nuances in other chefs' cooking. Some cook with more acidity, others with more saltiness, and others with more sweetness. You get to know these styles after a while," says Boulud.

Jasper White also believes that critics could pass the test. "But I think you'd have to let them see the dishes, because I think the look of the plate has something to do with personal style as well," he says. "In my own personal style, I like food to taste great, and I like textures. The entire focus is on taste and textures, not on looks. The look that I want happens naturally. I don't want food to look artificially beautiful; I want it to look like it tastes good. That's my point of view. How does it look like it tastes good? It has little specks of pepper and chopped herbs, and kind of a rustic style to it. It's something that looks like the whole focus was making something that tastes really good."

What Distinguishes a Chef's Style?

Through the myriad decisions a chef makes, including those related to the composition of flavors and dishes and menus, a personal style evolves, reflecting a chef's particular point of view.

> My cuisine is not intellectual. I want it to have a more soul-satisfying emphasis. I think my women colleagues are less interested in pyrotechnics. Our heart lies in finding the most delicious combinations of things. Flavor is key, and presentation is definitely secondary. While presentation is fun to play with, it's never the starting point.
>
> —Anne Rosenzweig

Mark Miller distinguishes between two prominent schools. He says, "Just as there are writers who use words very creatively and are masters of language, and other writers who are better at telling stories, I think there are chefs who are masters of the language of flavors and other chefs who can tell great stories.

"I would say that the technical people, the ones who strive for dramatics, are sometimes the ones who understand the words and the use of the words. The chefs who think about menus and carrying out compositions are more interested in the interplay between the words themselves and the overall feeling of a story rather than just the effect. You have to be careful here because form, style, and meaning get so integrated, and yet they are so separate in some sense.

"Certain chefs have a great style; Jeremiah [Tower], Alice [Waters], Joachim [Splichal], Charlie Trotter—they all have a lot of personal style in their food. Sometimes a chef who has a lot of style is seen as a more important chef, because he does dishes that have a flair. Personally, I would rather eat Rick Bayless's food. He understands and can interpret the culture, in a way, through the technique—and he also creates something in his own right. Rick creates Mexican meals, and his restaurant is a reflection of Mexican hospitality and the way he thinks about life—his artwork is in the room. He represents to me an integrity in food."

As for Bayless, he agrees that a chef's cuisine tastes of more than its raw ingredients. "Flavor, commitment—customers taste all of this in the food," says Bayless. "They're tasting the fact that I spent years in Mexico learning from really great cooks how to do all of this, and that I was able to pull it together into the cooking that we do here. I think they taste culture and history, basically, in dishes that have been refined—which I don't mean in a negative sense, but in a good sense—over generations. That's the flavor that I think is on our plates here."

So what is it that creates a chef's style? "Chefs' cuisines are a result of their lives," explains Gary Danko. "And it's important for chefs to be honest with themselves. If you're honest with yourself, there will be revealed to you a path in life, and cooking happens to be my manifestation of this life. I describe a pyramid that represents the heart, mind, and hands of cooking. The heart needs to be the base emotion—then you need the mind to conceive the dish and the hands to execute it. It's that pyramid that I try to reflect in my food, and my cooking is a direct result of my life.

A chef should be free to express his own individuality.
—Edouard Nignon

"That's why it's so critical for chefs to travel and to study history, art, and culture," says Danko. "The result of this journey is sometimes the lesson that life is really so simple, and that simple things—in cooking, simple flavors—can be very rewarding."

Gray Kunz agrees. He encourages chefs to understand their own personal "food context." "How you've been eating at home all your life will 'haunt' you in your life as a chef," he says. "You'll have images and feelings built in from all your experiences."

Charlie Palmer says he tells his young cooks to concentrate on what they feel and what they know when they cook. "I tell them not to just do a version of what I'm doing or Mark Miller's doing or anyone else is doing," he says. "I tell them, It's got to be you. It can't be me."

"Developing a personal style has to do with developing a point of view," Jasper White explains. "I think it takes years to develop that. And it never really stays quite the same. But I think at a certain point you know what it is and you become yourself."

"There are many different ways to do things," Danko says. "You need to go out and see everybody's style, and then look inside yourself and ask, 'What feels and works best for me?'"

Influences on Chefs' Styles

Because chefs' cuisines are a direct result of their experiences, their use of certain ingredients or offering of particular dishes can often be traced back to specific culinary influences.

After opening her first restaurant with partner Susan Feniger, Mary Sue Milliken admits, "For a few months, we basically just copied things that we'd done before that we'd liked the most. Mostly, they were the more peasanty, country-style dishes." Feniger adds, "When we first opened, we were doing

---

Mark Miller on the Influence of Richard Olney

When we talk about my own heightened consciousness, the events or people or chefs that have been influences in my life—it's people like Richard Olney. He is not a chef; he is basically a cook. He's a painter. And his knowledge of cuisine is unparalleled, even in France. He is respected as the most knowledgeable person in food and wine probably in the English or French language today. Whenever you mention Richard Olney in that circle, he's revered and he's respected—and this is amazing, because he's American and comes from Iowa!

Here's a person who influenced James Beard. He was probably one of the greatest influences on Alice Waters, myself, Jeremiah Tower. Certainly *The French Menu Cookbook*, but more importantly *Simple French Cooking* when it came out, really did revolutionize California cuisine. From Elizabeth David through Richard Olney through Alice Waters, you can see there's a direct descendency of philosophy.

The French Menu Cookbook—I think we cooked everything in that book at Chez Panisse. And you know what? The public liked every single dish, whether it was the squid or the Provençal lamb. The food itself reflects a certain spirited mentality. It is the honesty of the ingredients that people wanted. It was coming out of the 1960s, when people wanted a change—more connection with their own lives and their own bodies and their own environment. It was that kind of consciousness.

cassoulet, confit of duck, *pot-au-feu*, lamb stews—all that kind of stuff. That was influenced a lot by the restaurant where we met [Le Perroquet in Chicago]."

While Hubert Keller can immediately point to two dishes he learned in his first job which he continues to serve to this day (an onion tart, and *foie gras* terrine with toasted brioche), he believes that young chefs shouldn't waste their time in top restaurant kitchens trying to get the restaurant's recipes. "It's more important to understand their message, their philosophy," he says. "You want to try to understand the underlying concept and organization that makes the restaurant successful. Because if it's successful, there's something behind it—and it's not likely to be simply a recipe for fish sauce."

Keller credits his time cooking at L'Auberge de l'Ill in France as improving his technique and teaching him the details of execution. "And the time I spent in the south of France with [French chefs Roger] Vergé and [Jacques] Maximin was a real eye-opener," he says. "Having grown up in Alsace, it followed me more, and I was more receptive to it. In the south of France, we cooked with olive oil and basil, which we'd never used at L'Auberge." (Joachim Splichal is another Maximin alumnus who cites the French chef as the single person who's had the

Cuisine has the image of he who made it.
—Charles Barrier

His food has such an intensity and such a simplicity. The perfection of it is unparalleled. The meals I've had at Richard's house were meals that are memorable because you could not maximize the taste or the dish any more. A grilled lamb with Provençal herbs, a pasta with sorrel, a salad with rocket flowers in it, some cheeses, a great old Bordeaux, some white Burgundies, some figs—I remember the meal like it was yesterday, and it was twenty years ago. It was those flavors.

What Richard Olney did was look at French cuisine in the countryside and say, "It isn't just this French classic cuisine existing in restaurants; really the basis of it, underneath it, is this great spirited food and the simple food that came from ingredients that were pure, strong ingredients." The analogy would be that he brought about California cuisine through his interpretation of regional, simple foods with strong flavors—with salads, an emphasis on herbs. Without that, there probably would not have been California cuisine.

Richard Olney is one of those geniuses who really changed the way French people think about their own food, taught Americans about food, and created what we think of as modern food. I would say James Beard is the founder of regional American food, but certainly not modern American food. Olney, more than anybody else, is the person most responsible for changing a lot of what we eat today—everything from Alice and Jeremiah to California Pizza Kitchen.

With Richard, the ripples of his influence on everyone from leading chefs to bread bakers to wine distributors go very far. These people are at the top of their careers, and then underneath it all, there's some commonality. And that's Richard Olney.

most influence on his style. "He was very Mediterranean in his use of olive oil and fresh herbs," Splichal remembers.)

Opening the restaurant Cuisine de Soleil in Brazil for Roger Vergé, while serving to expand his cuisine in new directions, was, Keller says, a little like cooking in the south of France. "Again, we were cooking with olive oil, garlic, onions, and tomatoes," Keller recalls. "And cilantro, which we used there, had never been used in any of the French three-stars. I found myself putting coconut into fish stew, and using coriander. Just tasting all the local dishes, plus a class I took in Brazilian cuisine while living there, was a real education of my eye and palate."

Rick Bayless recalls that he taught cooking classes in his early twenties during graduate school at the University of Michigan. "My whole world was academics, and because I pored over cookbooks, I fancied that I knew a lot about cooking," says Bayless. "Someone once said to me, 'If you travel with all the knowledge you have in your head, you'll probably bring back almost nothing. But if you go with a clean slate, then you'll probably bring back mountains of information.' I remembered that the following year when I was able to take six weeks and go to Mexico to just study food, and I took that advice with me when I went.

"A lot of times, I see that in my fellow chefs when they travel to Mexico—especially the ones who want to learn a little bit about Mexican flavoring and so forth to incorporate into their own version of whatever cuisine they're working in, or their own cuisine—and they go with their minds all full of information, and they're looking for anything that they can kind of slip in between the cracks of information that they already have. So frequently I think that they miss all of the big stuff, the really good stuff, when they do that.

"There were a number of times that I was traveling through Mexico doing research for our first book that I would just stop, because I realized that I was just fitting everything into my framework. I would say to myself, 'I don't understand anything about what this person is really doing. But I'm just going to watch, and I'm just going to taste, and I'm going to write it all down. And then I'm going to make this dish, just this way, over and over again until I can figure out why the person was doing it that way, in terms of flavor.'"

This was the way Bayless managed to learn so much about Mexican cuisine. "The real cuisine of Mexico is not a cuisine of restaurants and chefs," argues Bayless. "It's really the cuisine of the women who have been in the kitchen for centuries doing this stuff. There's a name for them—they're called the *majordes*, and they're the holders of the whole tradition. Unfortunately, many of the male chefs, when they go into that role in the hotels, go in with this attitude that if they cook the cuisine of the *majordes*, they're cooking 'girl food.' So they want to show that they know what 'real' cuisine is all about. Unfortunately, I think that they generally miss the mark, because they're not willing to open their eyes and say, 'This is it—this is what tastes good, this is what it should be. I understand what the cuisine is all about, and I'm going to work with it instead of trying to somehow dominate the scene.'

"Similarly, I like [French] *cuisine bourgeoise* much better than I do most of the *haute cuisine*. In fact, when I eat *haute cuisine* that is really satisfying to me in France, I always think that it tastes very much like good home cooking. It satisfies in that same way," Bayless says.

How Have Their Cuisines Evolved?

Bayless describes his current food as being "much more confident" than the food he cooked when he first opened Frontera Grill. "Now I'm much more willing to really listen to my own heart and do what I know is right. This is in spite of the fact that with every issue of *Art Culinaire* I get, I go into some immediate panic or depression because I can't cook food that looks like that. I usually can come out of it very quickly and say, 'You know, my food is the food that really satisfies me.' And I'm thankful that other people react to it and can relate to it and seem to really like it, too—that it doesn't have to be all that fancy, fussy stuff to be good.

"I think the strong flavor profile of a dish makes it satisfying from the first bite to the last. In Mexican food, it's much more of a homogeneity of flavor; you're looking for this round, rich flavor that speaks of one thing, and it's the name of that dish, whatever it would be. I think when you eat one of our dishes from beginning to end now, you will notice that all of the components on the plate are in harmony, that we've got the right accompaniments, the right garnishes, that everything just seems right about it. That has always been spurred on by my confidence in the fact that when you get everything taken away from a dish and still have a perfect dish—then it's right," says Bayless. "It's not a matter of how much can you put on, but how much can you take away from it that is the question you should always ask."

Norman Van Aken describes his own process of evolution as a chef: "I only did what I was told I was supposed to do as a chef, until there was a certain little part of me that said, 'No way am I going to do that!' That was 1977, and I'd been cooking since 1971. Then I needed to educate myself. So the biggest change has been the process of self-education and growing up and learning so much more about food."

Even Alice Waters admits that when she first opened Chez Panisse in 1971, "I didn't know anything about seasonality. I really thought the season for green beans lasted from the spring to the fall! But there's a moment for those, and everything else—and you have to catch it. And you have to resist using those ingredients at other times of the year."

Waters believes, "We've uncovered a whole range of ingredients, a whole range of tastes, that we didn't know anything about twenty-five years ago. That's significant. I think we were sort of working with the primary colors when we opened. We had a little fennel—something so exotic as that, at

Mark Miller on the Importance of Pushing

People say they're pushing the envelope, but I don't really think they are. I see us turning away from food and becoming more selective about what we eat and why we eat it and when we eat it and with whom we eat it. And young chefs aren't pushing their own palates past the point of where they're automatic.

I wonder if chefs are doing enough for themselves to actually understand what they should be doing for others. Or do they always go to the new hot restaurant thinking that they should create the new hot restaurant, or the new hot dish? Or do they just want to be in *Art Culinaire?* Is that their only goal? If these are their role models, if that's what they want to do, then that's where food is going in America.

I think a lot of chefs are really on that road today. But at Chez Panisse, we would always go to the countryside and do big dinners and Thanksgiving parties together. I remember cooking a turkey in the fireplace. I don't think the young cooks do that today. If I go to someone's party, they usually get a bunch of pizzas or empanadas and put them on the table with a bunch of beer. When I was in California, I would do a Moroccan meal, or an Algerian meal, or an Indonesian meal—I would do the whole thing, I would spend days on it. And I was living on two or three hundred dollars a month! I don't see kids doing that today. Where is the new generation of chefs and restaurateurs taking food in the future? It's what they're doing today, it's what their experiences are, it's who their role models are.

the time. And we put nasturtiums [edible flowers] in a salad, and that was exotic. But now we have seventeen kinds of wild mushrooms, and an equal number of heirloom tomatoes, and turnips that I could never have imagined the shapes and colors of. Same for beets. And, of course, all the potatoes—russet

potatoes and red ones were as much as I knew about potatoes back then. Now, we cook with yellow fins and ruby crescents and fingerlings. It's just fantastic, the possibilities. To have watercress back then was exotic, and now we have upling cress and ancho cress and tiny little watercress—a whole world of tastes. I think at Chez Panisse we've learned a lot of things about putting together a menu, but even more in terms of ingredients."

Gary Danko believes his food at The Ritz-Carlton Dining Room (San Francisco) was much different from the food he served prior to that at Chateau Souverain in Napa Valley. "And my next restaurant will again reflect a different style of food," he says. "A lot of the principles and techniques will stay, such as how I make my stocks or fish *fumés*. But say my next kitchen has fifty burners and is a Mercedes-Benz of kitchens—like Gray Kunz has!—then my style of cooking is going to change because I'm in a different environment.

"Say, for example, I left San Francisco and moved to New York. There would be an additional change as I went into a new city and adopted to what the specifics are—serving dinner later, looking at different produce. Although people say we have better produce in California, I think New York has a whole new league of produce because it has Europe as its market and California has Asia. Very little fresh produce comes in from Asia—quite frankly, California is not going to let any citrus in from any part of the world—whereas New York gets oranges from Spain or clementines and that kind of thing. And I think the fish and the selection of fish is better in New York. So I'd have a very different market basket," says Danko.

Evolving as a chef over the course of a career has its challenges. "It's never been an easy process," says Patrick O'Connell. "You're continually frustrated with wanting to be more inventive and more creative and have more ideas than you do. And you have dry periods, too, when you feel you're in a terrible rut. What I've learned is that after you dig the rut deep enough, at the point where you feel where there's no way out, ever, you just kind of keep going and then you end up exploding out of it."

That's why even the most seasoned chefs keep pushing themselves. "With every menu, we try a new technique," says Lydia Shire. Inspired by other leading chefs like Jean-Louis Palladin, Shire and her chef at Biba, Susan Regis, have prepared many specialty foods from scratch. "We've air-dried our own beef and made our own prosciuttos," Shire reports with pride. "And I recently made a wonderful *cotechino* sausage with a recipe I got from Lidia Bastianich of Felidia restaurant in Manhattan."

"If you stand still, it becomes boring," agrees Joachim Splichal. "And we are not factory workers—we are artists."

The Chef as Owner

For culinary artists whose passion for cooking is greater than their passion for running a business, it can be difficult to balance the two. "If you're a chef without your own business, then you can concentrate more on the cooking. But if you have your own restaurant, then you have to be more of a collaborator," says Daniel Boulud. "I won't let my business or my cooking go entirely into others' hands. I have a lot of people working with me, but I am the epicenter of all of it."

Norman Van Aken points out the differences in his style since becoming a chef-owner, as opposed to serving as the chef of someone else's restaurant. "Norman's is a much bigger restaurant. [At A Mano], I cooked sometimes out of a sense of escape; it had a stranglehold on me because I wasn't the owner and I was trying so much to become the owner of the restaurant. There were times when it was more edgy, I guess. Whereas now, it's like being in my own home, and I feel much more comfortable with my food. It's more balanced, overall.

"When you're not the owner, you're going to take the opportunity to reach beyond where you should reach sometimes because you're hell-bent on finding out exactly all that you want to find out in the creative process. As the owner, there's a certain sort of a calmness that comes in that allows you to feel more balanced about everything," says Van Aken.

Rick Bayless found that the pressures of restaurant ownership initially had an undeniable influence on his food. "When you put your entire savings and your parents' retirement money on the line opening your restaurant, it's a hard thing to say, 'I'm just going to do what I'm going to do, and the hell with all the rest of the world,'"

says Bayless. "When I opened, I wasn't quite sure where we were going to have to end up for financial reasons, although I was very much committed to trusting my own gut and instincts about what good food really is. I think that after we were open for six or eight months, I relaxed into my own style and I knew that it was something that people could appreciate."

A chef's cuisine swings on what Gray Kunz calls "the dot on the i" factor. "Getting every detail right is what gives cuisine its greatness," says Kunz. "Otherwise, it's just good."

Other aspects of a chef's cuisine may likely change over time. Jean-Georges Vongerichten clearly moved consciously toward a less formal cuisine when he left his hotel kitchen at the Lafayette to open his own French bistro, Jojo. "In the beginning, the menu was a lot like it was at Lafayette, incorporating vegetables juices. It was a lower-key restaurant, but the same food. We had the same cooks, the same waiters, but at a more casual price and atmosphere," he says. "But five years later, the menu is totally different. There are more natural flavors, and far fewer ingredients—in some cases, only three—on a plate." Vongerichten describes Jojo's cuisine today as "very loose. We might serve something one way one day, and it might be as much as ten percent off the next day."

Still, Vongerichten admits that he misses the style of cooking demanded of a high-end restaurant. "I miss the preciseness of things," he says. "At a high-end restaurant, the customers expect even more. And the more pressure you have, the better the recipes." Vongerichten announced plans to return to this style of cuisine with his next restaurant, scheduled to open in Manhattan's Lincoln Center area.

Another one of his goals is bringing back grand service. "Like the 1930s," he says. "When you're in the kitchen, you have all these great smells, but the customer doesn't. I want the customer to be able to hear the sizzle, to see the food as it is cut into." He credits as inspiration a dinner at Taillevent in Paris, to which his parents took him for his eighteenth birthday. "It was very sensual," he remembers. "Everyone was so excited before a dish arrived. I think the appetite develops more when you eat this way."

Vongerichten says he plans to serve half the dishes tableside at his next restaurant. "If we have a lobster salad on the menu, a technical cook will cook the lobster, but it will be cut at the table and tossed with spinach," he says. "And then the people at the next table will see the lobster, or the duck being carved. I'm not talking about having flambés or putting on shows. We're just going to bring aromas back into the dining room and have people participate more in the food experience."

Lydia Shire describes Biba as an eclectic American restaurant "where we're free to do anything we want," she says. "Pignoli, on the other hand, is an Italian restaurant, period. And we don't bastardize or Americanize. Italians don't eat pasta as a first course, so we don't offer it as one.

Americans are used to having an appetizer and an entrée, but Italians eat three smaller courses: antipasto, then risotto or pasta, then a small entrée. It's the best way in the world to eat—that way, you get to try three things instead of two!"

Shire adds, "Our customers are paying us to put some interesting flavor combinations on a plate. They want to see things that they can't recreate at home."

Hubert Keller agrees. "When customers come into Fleur de Lys, they are expecting a gastronomical experience," he says. "Very simple dishes can be very good, but I believe that if an average customer can recreate the same dish at home, then the restaurant and the chef have missed something. And I know that there are many chefs who don't agree with me on this. But I think we should go beyond what a home cook would do. After all, this is our profession."

Vongerichten recounts how Picasso once gave a demonstration on how to make a lot of money in a short time: "He slapped some paint on a canvas and signed his name to it, and claimed he'd created five million dollars in minutes. 'It's bullshit, but it sells,' was his comment," says Vongerichten. "In food, that used to happen more and more—but there's no bullshit anymore. You can't get away with it. People recognize flavor and freshness now."

Often evolution results in simplification. Jean-Louis Palladin believes that customers won't be able to "find the tastes" on the plate if there are too many ingredients crowding it. "Now, I'm trying to be as simple as possible," says Palladin. "I don't like to put more than three elements on a plate."

Norman Van Aken agrees. "Every year, I know that it's going to be a further stripping away and peeling back and finding out what's essential," he says. "It may be simpler, or what we feel to be truer. And that's the ultimate goal."

Global Cuisine

Cuisine is constantly being shaped and reshaped by ever-changing influences: customer demands, the availability of ingredients, chefs' experimentation, even media play. "Unfortunately, the cooking of a lot of countries is disintegrating," observes Alice Waters. "It's hard to get those really simple and perfect dishes anymore. Everybody's embroidering all kinds of things all over."

Michael Romano has observed that all the Michelin three-star restaurants seem to have become very French—even those in Italy. "It's probably all part of the drive for Michelin stars," he speculates. Johanne Killeen also notices that, "the more [Michelin] stars an Italian restaurant has, the more Frenchified it is. It's tragic. Michelin ought to take each cuisine on its own merit and judge every restaurant accordingly." George Germon agrees: "It's

difficult to find food that's pure. A lot of Italian food has become muddled, with no clear flavors, no focus. There are too many acrobatics, too much jumping through hoops."

Rick Bayless says he "bristles" at the new-style cuisine in Mexico. "There are a few people who are doing a fine job with it. But most of them are hotel-trained chefs, and when they start doing this modern version of Mexican food, it comes out looking like bad *nouvelle cuisine*—there's little tiny bits of stuff all over the plate. And sometimes they try to tone it down. When they do that, I feel like they're taking out the guts of the dish and all you're left with is a kind of hollow shell," he says.

"Mexican cuisine is a robust and very elegant cuisine, but it's elegant in its simplicity, its naturalness, its spontaneous feel. When you start making a dish with sixteen garnishes and little things dropped around the plate, it's not Mexican. It's missed the point of Mexican food, in my book," says Bayless. "That's why my food is much more immediate and much more straightforward. We work with big, bold strokes. We don't put too much food on the plate, because I feel like it interferes with our guests' ability to really appreciate what's there, because your palate can get confused really quickly with strong flavors like the ones we work with."

"Even French cooking is changing," notes Daniel Boulud. "The French cooks are learning more about Italian food. Italians have been learning about French food. Even Spanish chefs went to France to learn, and when they returned they created a cuisine that was sophisticated and refined enough to be noticed by the French."

Cosmopolitan Cuisine?

The exchange of ideas and ingredients globally has, needless to say, also had a marked effect on American food.

Keeping his focus on French cuisine when the world's pantry is available to him in New York City requires Daniel Boulud to focus. "I have to try hard to 'think French' when I am in the kitchen," Boulud admits. "Besides, it's too boring if everyone cooks the same!

"American chefs are now traveling the world and returning home to create a cuisine worth noticing and appreciating. It is an interpretation. It may not be totally French or totally Italian or totally Asian. But wonderful things are being created. On my own menu, I feature a dish of ravioli with nine herbs and tomato coulis. I'm proud of it, and people love it. And I don't think there's an Italian who could make it as good!

"And I love risotto, and like to offer it to my customers. Risotto is wonderful for providing a stage for the flavor of ingredients, which can give many dimensions to it. For example, I'll serve a lobster risotto made with lobster stock, or a squab risotto made with squab broth, or a shellfish risotto made with the juice and water of shellfish. I like to 'French-ize' my risotto.

"One of the last risottos I came up with was inspired by my vacation in the Pays Basque [near the border of Spain and France] last year: a seafood risotto with a purée of pasilla peppers and a saffron broth," says Boulud. "I love this dish very much—it's like French Tex-Mex."

Some chefs are well respected for their ability to merge a wide array of culinary ingredients and techniques. Lydia Shire describes her cuisine as having both eclectic (involving a mixing and matching of courses with varying influences) and fusion (representing a melding of the ingredients and/or techniques of two or more regions) elements. She hastens to add, "But with restraint! I won't do things just for shock value; there are certain things we'd never, ever do." She cites as an example a fish dish served with couscous and wasabi, which she was once taken aback to see on another restaurant's menu.

Norman Van Aken on New World Cuisine

One of the torches that I carry is one that tries to illuminate the type of cooking that has not been so well known yet in most of North America, which is the regional cuisine of the Caribbean, Central and South America, and the mother countries that affected the cuisines that were brought to those areas, such as Africa and to a lesser degree France and Italy, of course. So even though I might read about or taste a great dish in New York made by Gray Kunz or someone like that, I have to tell myself, "That's not my story. My story is a regional story that needs to echo the immigrant patterns that are south Florida." So that's a very important factor behind why I cook what I'm going to cook.

People ask if the New World cuisine I cook means the same thing to me as it does to other chefs. Well, I don't think rock and roll meant the same thing to Jerry Lee Lewis as it did to Elvis Presley. However, there's a certain reference that's shared, a parenthetical opportunity to express a certain sort of probability. And I welcome the fact that there are different definitions that would be espoused by the various people who would say that they're practitioners of New World cuisine.

I coined the term *fusion cuisine* as a response to the melding together of disparate cultures, although I was not so much initially talking about marrying French and Thai, for example, as I was talking about marrying rustic cuisine, with its boldness and gutsiness, to classic cuisine, with its intellectuality. That to me is what I was describing when I first talked about fusion.

But fusion is a very large umbrella. And fusion cuisine can take place everywhere from Hong Kong

Gray Kunz says, "A good friend told me, 'What you're doing is taking the rough edge off ethnic cooking.' I knew what he was trying to say. I do see myself as incorporating flavors and fragrances, but in a very subtle way. Doing so successfully has a lot to do with finesse. You want to make sure that the context is still approachable and not go overboard and shock customers."

To keep cuisine from going "overboard," Jean-Georges Vongerichten believes there should be boundaries in food. "The 1990s should not be a melting pot," he asserts. "Now everyone has ginger in their kitchen. In twenty years, I don't want to see 'universal cooking.' I think people should go back to their roots and keep traditions going. Daniel Boulud is from Lyons, and you can still find things like tripe and pork with lentils, which he grew up with, on his menu.

"I will never put star anise in my *choucroute*. If someone else finds something new to do with cabbage, great. But it hurts me to see things on a menu like 'Thai Bouillabaisse.' They should call it a "Thai Fish Soup' instead of ruining something great."

Norman Van Aken believes that it's important for chefs in various parts of the world to honor their regional bounty. "As much as possible, they

to Vancouver to New York to Florida, because of chefs taking disparate cuisines and welding them together in hopefully a harmonious wedding.

New World cuisine was the term that I came up with to describe what takes place in southeastern Florida and to a degree will begin to take place in other places as well, much the same way as the Southwestern food movement took and married classical technique and methodology with Mexican produce and, eventually, Mexican methodology or pre-Columbian Indian methodology. With us here in south Florida, the various influences are Latino to a great degree, with all the different *patois* of the Caribbean offering all these wild twists and turns.

If you go into a market or a little grocery store or a little café, whether it's Jamaican or Nicaraguan or Argentinian or Cuban or Bohemian, you'll see the differences in the cuisines. It'll take a while to understand the differences, but as you spend more and more time you'll begin to understand the nuances among them. Being from none of these traditions, I don't have any allegiance to a particular cuisine. It allows me the freedom to go in and visit and put my own quilt together.

Some of my coworkers are natives of these places; they respond to my experimentation by being sort of startled and happy and sometimes a little shy about it. If I say to them, "How does your grandmother work with this particular tuber?" or whatever, once I've gotten through enough of the language barrier, I think they feel a part of it—it makes them feel happy. It makes me feel happy, because it certainly is just as important to me as reading books by people who have perhaps lived in these places themselves.

should glorify and celebrate the cuisines of their regions, so that as we travel from city to city, and suburb to suburb, and little hick town to little hick town, that there still is a great regional opportunity."

In a graduation speech Van Aken delivered at Johnson & Wales University a few years ago, he says he told students, "Don't go back to Virginia and cook New World cuisine. Don't go home to southern California and do that either. I think what you should do is go back and find out really what your strongest sense is of the people who are in that community at that point in time.

"And I don't mean cook 'museum food,'" Van Aken says he emphasized. "If you're in Dallas now, I think you should embrace some Vietnamese flavors, because there's a strong Vietnamese community. But I hope that other chefs will do what I did in terms of reacting to where I live by reacting to where they live. That would be honoring it—honoring the tradition but also being able, through creativity and the natural inclination we have as people, to move ahead."

Communicating Their Point of View

Driven by their great love for particular ingredients, some leading chefs have taken steps to encourage the development or production of products of the highest possible quality. Former Chez Panisse cook Steven Sullivan's passion for bread led him to develop his own artisan breads for the restaurant and, eventually, leave to found the Acme Bread Company in Berkeley (see pages 246–247). Chef Charlie Palmer partnered with cheesemaker Jonathan White in Peekskill, New York, to develop artisan cheeses through Egg Farm Dairy, whose motto is "Setting the Dairy Industry Back 150 Years." Even chef Daniel Boulud is a partner in a venture to bring La Ratte potatoes—"they're rich and buttery, and the most beautiful potatoes in the world"—to the United States.

Is playing a role in the development of higher-quality products a trend? "It's not a trend—it's a necessity, to grow and help to develop the best products," says Boulud. "In New York City, we have wonderful farmers' markets. Every year, they're getting better. But we need to do even more." It is through such individual efforts that chefs can collectively elevate American cuisine as they in turn distinguish their personal style of cuisine.

We've forfeited our culinary and gastronomic heritage by letting big business determine our eating habits—including crazy, perverse things like Olestra. Chefs need to be the guiding light to bring it back. The family isn't, especially in urban environments.

— Michael Romano

For example, Charlie Palmer arranged the purchase of some baby partridges and had them raised to his specifications for the restaurant. "We wanted them raised semi-wild and fed wild watercress and apples, so that they had a lot of flavor," says Palmer. "The wife of

Chefs' Styles Personified in Their Menus

Various leading chefs around France created dinners honoring the centenary of the birth of the renowned gastronome Curnonsky. Twelve examples were classified as reflecting the personalities of their creators as follows:

Fernand Point: Classicism

Charles Barrier: Harmonious Simplicity

François Bise: Tradition Revived

Paul Bocuse: Vitality and Generosity

Alain Chapel: Supreme Inventiveness

Michel Guérard: Subtleties of Taste

Paul Haeberlin: The Strength of Tradition

Louis Outhier: A Delight for the Eyes

Jacques Pic: A Spread of Independent Creations

Raymond Thuilier: Epicurean Delights

Troisgros Brothers: Flavors Close to the Land

Roger Vergé: Exuberant Originality

the man who cared for the birds had a garden with herbs like garlic chives and wild onions, and I truly believe it brought a lot of flavor to them."

The partridges were killed and bled and hung with the guts in as well. Because of all the trouble he'd gone to making sure the partridges had flavor, Palmer didn't want to destroy their taste during the cooking process. "I made a *jus* from the bones, which was finished with *glace de viande* and herbs that played on what the partridges had been eating, and then, in the traditional manner, thickened the sauce with the partridges' blood," says Palmer. The partridges were then roasted rare and served with the sauce, the finely minced liver and gizzard of the partridges, chanterelles, and some caramelized turnips, along with a pinot noir. "A Bordeaux would have been too overpowering," notes Palmer. "The intense fruit of the pinot noir was perfect."

Palmer points out, "The knowledge and technology in the United States is light-years ahead of where it is in other countries. We're not stuck in tradition, so in this country we have the capacity for the best ingredients in the world." After all this trouble for one ingredient, did his customers appreciate it? "About 70 percent of them didn't get it," Palmer admits. "But the other 30 percent thought it was one of the best dishes they'd ever eaten in their life. Chefs should strive to do something special."

For the customers who appreciate subtle distinctions, "we need to keep pushing," says Boulud. "Today, we have very good spices. But I know we can find even better ones. People have to learn more about the wilderness, and what's available. Are there herbs we've forgotten? And why couldn't we grow truffles in America someday? Things are changing fast—and we'll see all this and more in the next century."

And to the very best ingredients, only the most careful techniques must be applied. "We must remember the purity of the woman who made only one apple pie from her perfect apples, and bring that spirit to whatever quantity of food we cook," says Jeremiah Tower. "We need to remember the time we caught a fish and cooked it on the beach, squeezing a lemon over it.

"The closer we can stay to this in our cooking," adds Tower, "the better off we'll be."

How have the cuisines of some of America's leading chefs changed over time? Through comparisons of actual restaurant menus created by the chefs, we examine some of the ways in which their restaurants and their cuisines have evolved. We'll take a look at the cuisines of:

George Germon and Johanne Killeen
AL FORNO
Providence, Rhode Island
1980/1996

Joyce Goldstein
SQUARE ONE
San Francisco, California
1984/1996

Charlie Palmer
AUREOLE
New York, New York
1988/1996

Chris Schlesinger
EAST COAST GRILL
Cambridge, Massachesetts
1985/1996

Jimmy Schmidt
LONDON CHOP HOUSE/THE RATTLESNAKE CLUB
Detroit, Michigan
1984/1996

Jeremiah Tower
STARS/J.T.'s
San Francisco, California
1984/1996

Alice Waters and Lindsey Shere
CHEZ PANISSE
Berkeley, California
1971/1995

The Evolution of Leading Chefs' Cuisines

George Germon and Johanne Killeen

AL FORNO
Providence, Rhode Island

Food, like any other cultural phenomenon, is a living thing. It naturally goes through a seamless, almost imperceptible evolution. Perhaps there are more choices on our present menu—and the choices are continually being refined and simplified—but our basic philosophy has the same clarity of vision. Our palate is acute, aggressively clean in taste, and our style is grounded in reality. It seems our signature is clear, bold, and large. We guess that's the reason our food is presented on platters, not plates, and in celebratory mounds and not wimpy servings.

1980
[as written on a small chalkboard]

Roasted Rosemary Chicken with Roasted Potatoes
Sliced Sausage Roasted with Potatoes and Onions
Clams Al Forno
Roasted Clams and Sausage
Pasta Al Forno
Roasted Vegetables of the Day

Salad Al Forno
Green Salad
Squid Salad

Snail Salad
Cannellini Beans with Tuna

Pissaladière
White Pissaladière with Potatoes and Rosemary
Pissaladière with Eggplant Caponata

Tartufo Cake
Fresh Apple Tart

1996

Appetizers—Salads—Side Plates

Tuscan Fettunta
Garlic-Roasted Rapini
Spring "Cappucino" Soup
Clams Al Forno
Grilled Pizza Capri
Vegetarian Antipasto
Grilled Pizza Margarita
Antipasto Al Forno
Fresh Mozzarella with Imported White Anchovies
  and Tuscan Olive Oil

Mixed Green Salad with Lemon and Capezzana
  Olive Oil
Mixed Baby Greens with Grilled Prosciutto Cotto
  and Honeyed Onions
Mixed Baby Greens with Sardinian Pecorino,
  Cracked Black Pepper, and Tuscan Olive Oil
Apple and Arugula Salad with Lemon and
  Capezzana Olive Oil
Arugula and Shaved Cheese with Tuscan Olive Oil
  and Balsamic Vinegar
Endive Caesar Salad with Grilled Crouton
Caesar Salad with Grilled Crouton

Salad Al Forno
Sweet and Spicy Crispy Pork

Pasta

Pasta Baked in the Pink with Fresh Herbs, Cream,
and Five Cheeses
Pasta Baked with Mushrooms, Pancetta, Rapini,
Cream, and Five Cheeses
Tagliatelle with Mascarpone and Oven-Cured Pink-
Prosciutto Cotto
Spaghetti with Tuscan Meat Ragu
Pumpkin and Potato-Filled Free-Form Lasagna with
Black Olive Butter
Rolled Mushroom Lasagna with Béchamel, Tomato,
and Parmigiano

Grills, Roasts, and Braises For Little Appetites

Small Plate of Roasted Seasonal Vegetables
Pepper-Grilled Chicken Paillard with Mixed Greens,
Shaved Parmigiano, Caramelized Onions, and
Spiced Olives
Tuscan Veal Stew with Butternut Mashed Potatoes
Tuscan Roasted Sausages and Grapes with Mashed
Potatoes
Mahogany Duck Legs with Rice and Mesclun Salad

Grills, Roasts, and Braises for Al Forno Appetites

Grilled and Roasted Veggie Entrée with Mashed
Potatoes
Grilled Chicken Breast with Wood-Roasted Stuffing
and Mixed Greens
Grilled Chicken Breast with Grilled Portobello
Mushroom and Roasted Potatoes

Roasted Half-Chicken on a Nest of Vermicelli with
Mixed Greeens
Oven-Roasted Pork Tenderloin with Herbed Crust,
Roasted Potatoes, and Pear Mostarda
Pot-Roasted Beef Fillet with Mashed Potatoes
Vintner's Steak
Grilled Veal Tenderloins with Grilled Polenta, Pan
Drippings, and Fennel-Infused Onion
Clam Roast with (HOT!) Spicy Sausage, Endive,
Tomato, and Mashed Potatoes
Grilled Veal Chop with Gremolata-Mashed Potatoes
and Pickled Onions
Grilled Brine-Cured Pork Chops with Mashed
Potatoes and Mixed Greens
Rosemary-Infused Veal Spareribs with Aged
Balsamic Vinegar and Roasted Garlic-Potato
Cake
Fresh Little Compton Tilefish in Aqua Pazza
Fresh Little Compton Cod Roasted in a Caper
Mayonnaise with Roasted Potatoes

Desserts (all, except first two, made to order)

Tiramisu
Fresh Fruit with Cannoli Cream
Tartufo Gelato with Baby Baci
Orange and Fresh Fig Gelato
Lemon Granita with Hazelnut Biscotti
Coffee Granita with Whipped Cream
Toasted Coconut Ice Cream Sandwich
Grand Cookie Finale
Fresh Plum Tart
Fresh Blueberry Tart
Fresh Blackberry Tart
Black Mission Fig and Blueberry Deep-Dish Pie
Fresh Blueberry Gratin
Fresh Plum Gratin
Fresh Black Mission Fig Gratin

Joyce Goldstein

SQUARE ONE
San Francisco, California
(1984–1996)

Since the time Square One opened, our cuisine came to show a deeper understanding of the traditional cuisines. Rather than being simplified for Americans, we tried to give them greater authenticity. Also, as our skills and our sense of organization improved, we were able to take on a little bit more and have the plates be a little more complex. But I think the key really is that rather than giving customers a short-hand version of the Mediterranean, we gave them the long-hand—we really tried to give it to them as if they were there. We eliminated a lot of international things and things from other cultures as people wanted to know what kind of food we prepared. So with the word "international" terrifying and bewildering them, and not wanting to call it "California cuisine," whatever the hell that is, we became more and more Mediterranean and more and more true to the source. That's my story…Tonight's our last night…(July 13, 1996)

Daily Specials
May 15, 1984

Fedelini with Tuna, Onions, Capers, and Olives
Fettuccine alla Genovese with Spinach, Pinenuts,
    Lemon Rind, Golden Raisins, and Cream
Grilled Veal Chop with Zucchini and Eggplant Gratin
Pork Scalloppine with Marsala, Vinegar, and Cream
    served with Red Swiss Chard and Corn Fritters
Chicken Fricassee with Meatballs, Mushrooms, and
    Thyme served with Rice

Almond Cake with Ganache and Rum Buttercream
Puff Pastry Strawberry Tart with Mascarpone
    Cheese
Mango Sorbet served with Tegole Cookies
Pineapple Ice Cream served with Tegole Cookies

Daily Specials
Weekend of May 17, 1996

Paella—Saffron Rice with Lobster, Prawns, Clams, Chicken, Chorizo, Artichokes, Favas, Peppers, and Tomatoes

Veal Scaloppine with Mushrooms, Shallots, and Hazelnuts, served with Tagliarini with Asparagus, Prosciutto, and Peas

Roast Halibut with an Armenian Sauce of Roasted Peppers, Roasted Onions, Basil, Allspice, and Cayenne, served with Cracked Wheat Pilaf, Grilled Eggplant, and Sautéed Spinach

Greek Mixed Grill—Lamb in Souvlaki Marinade, served with Tzatziki, Quail with Oregano, Thyme, Garlic, and Lemon, wrapped in Vineleaves, and Loukanika (Pork Sausage with Marjoram, Coriander, Orange Zest, Allspice, and Wine), served with Rice Pilaf with Eggplant, Tomatoes, and Pinenuts, Spanakopita, and Zucchini with Tomatoes and Dill

Grilled Fillet of Beef with Red-Wine-Glazed Shallots, served with Potato and Celery Root Gratin, and Green Beans with Chives

Grilled Sonoma Squab in a Moroccan Marinade of Cumin, Cinnamon, Honey, and Sesame Seed, served with Couscous with Raisins and Orange, and Carrots and Beets with Orange, Mint, and Ginger

Grilled Swordfish alla Puttanesca with Tomatoes, Capers, Olives, Garlic, Hot Pepper, and Basil, served with Oven-Roasted Potatoes and Broccoli and Cauliflower Gratin

Tagliarini with Asparagus, Mushrooms, Favas, and Gremolata (Lemon, Garlic, Parsley)

Vegetarian Paella with Artichokes, Favas, Green Beans, Zucchini, Peppers, and Tomatoes

Charlie Palmer

AUREOLE
New York, New York

What's changed since we opened Aureole? In two words, we do "progressive cooking." I think our food has progressed, it's changed, it's constantly gotten better and more refined over the years. It's obvious when you just look at the menus.

Opening Week Menu
1988

Appetizers

Warm Mozzarella "Lobes" with Basil Oil, Thin Strips of Ham, and Roast Eggplant and Tomato Salad

Terrine of Veal Shank and Foie Gras with Marinated Mushrooms and Toasted Brioche

Salad Of Lettuces and Herbs, Olive Oil, and Champagne Vinegar

Composed Salad of Squid and Frisée on a Mild Bed of Marinated Vegetables, Rice-Vinegar Sauce

Warm Porcini Salad with Tea-Smoked Squab and Cabernet Vinegar

Ravioli of Smoked Grouper and Porcini in Brown Butter and Cèpes

Warm Smoked Grouper with Sevruga Caviar Butter and a Savory Leek Ragoût

Savory Partridge Soup

Abalone Escalopes Sauté Couscous and Vegetables Tossed in Lemon Oil

Sea Scallop Sandwiches in Crisp Potato Crusts, Citrus Juices

Sauté Foie Gras and Crisp Corn Cakes with Caramelized Onion Conserve

Main Course

Pan-Braised Halibut with Chanterelles and Roast Sweet Garlic

Roast Saddle of Monkfish and Sweet Garlic with Crisp New-Potato Tart

Poached Steak-Cut Salmon with Basil Butter and Hand-Cut Semolina Noodles

Grilled Beef Tenderloin and Chanterelles with Barolo Natural Sauce

Roast Lamb Rib-Eye with Ginger Essence and Crisp Potato Tartlet

Sauté Veal Loin Steak with Oregon Cèpes, Glazed Sweetbreads, and Root Vegetables

Seared Mignon of Venison with Zingara Currants and Celeriac Cakes

Tea-Smoked Squab with Stewed-Leek Risotto and Beaujolais Sauce

Apple-Wood-Grilled Mallard Duck with Roast Shallots and Fresh Spaetzle

1996

First Course

Hot Lobster Vichyssoise
   with Melted Leeks and Potato Crisps
Open Ravioli of Smoked Capon and Wild
   Mushrooms in Sweet Garlic-Infused Pan Broth
Trio of Mullard Duck Preparations
   Foie Gras Roulade, Confit and Chicory, Smoked
   Duck Sausage
Sea Scallop Sandwiches
   in Crisp Potato Crusts and Citrus Juices
A Service of Petrossian Ossetra Caviar
   in the Traditional Fashion
Salad of Seasonal Lettuces and Herbs
   Citrus-Dijon Vinaigrette
Savory Celery Root Flan and Vegetables à la Grecque
   Essence of Sweet Garlic and Kalamata Olives
Market Select Oysters Over Shaved Ice
   with Shallot Mignonette and Caraway Crisps
Oak-Smoked Salmon with Vegetable-Citrus Salad
   Smoked Salmon Mousse and Michael's Sourdough
   Toasts (or served naturally)
Seared Foie Gras Escalope with Roasted Plums
   Wild Mushroom Crêpe and Baby Arugula

Main Course

Eggplant-Crusted Maine Cod with Bay Shrimp,
   Thyme-Roasted Vegetables and Port-Wine
   Essence
Pepper-Seared Salmon Fillet with Grain Mustard,
   Braised Asparagus, and Roasted Creamer
   Potatoes or Simply Grilled with Select Steamed
   Vegetables
Sesame-Glazed Tuna Steak with Roasted Fennel,
   Braised Baby Bok Choy, and Potato-Onion Cake
Wood-Grilled Maine Lobster with Fragrant Truffle
   Oil, Tiny Green Beans, and Basil-Essenced
   Potato Purée
Garlic-Crusted Chicken with Slow-Roasted
   Artichoke, a Purée of Barlitto Beans, Tomato
   Oil, and Fresh Rosemary
Veal Medallions with Wild Mushroom Cannelloni,
   Tomato Confit, and Essence of Fresh Sage
Cervena Venison Pepper Steak with Mushroom
   Spaetzle, Butternut Squash Flan, and
   Caramelized Parsnip
Braised Pheasant with Chanterelle Risotto, Roasted
   Cipollini Onions, and Sauce of Ximenez Sherry
Grilled Duck Escalope with Preserved Figs, Crisp
   Leg "Beignet" and Ginger-Citrus Essence Sauce
Charcoaled Filet Mignon with Roasted Shallot and
   Pinot Noir, Country Potato, Foie Gras Stuffed
   Morels, and Crisp Parsnip

Chris Schlesinger

THE EAST COAST GRILL
Cambridge, Massachusetts

I traveled to diverse places—from Mexico to Thailand—and found that I really liked a lot of the aspects of the food. When I opened the East Coast Grill, I tried to come to an understanding of what things all these diverse foods had in common. When I look at my cooking, I think there are three major themes:

1) My love of *live fire*—wood-burning stuff. The dynamic of going into the kitchen every day and cooking with something that is as uncontrollable as fire, as opposed to just going in and turning the oven on to 350 or 375, is a constant challenge to me. Roasting whole pigs, grilling fish, or trying to keep something from sticking—that dynamic is so soulful and extends so much character into the food.

2) My other love as a cook that I developed while cooking with Jimmy Burke at the Harvest [in Cambridge, MA] is discovering and learning about *new things* all the time—getting a new food in and learning about it and reading about it.

3) The other aspect developed out of my travels is a desire for *deeply-flavored food*. What I started to work out was that, for a lot of different reasons, cuisines that are closer to the equator are more flavorful; they have deeper flavors or clearer flavors or use more spices.

There are different mutations at the East Coast Grill versus The Blue Room. The Grill is more straight-ahead equatorial cuisine—warm-weather cuisines tied together by their concentration of flavors—with a slight barbecue orientation. The Blue Room had some of that, but was probably grounded more in live fire, and looking at live fire, from rôtisserie to hot stones to hearth to smokers, as a commonality among cuisines.

Original Menu Items
September 1985

Spicy Black Bean Soup with Sausage, Sour Cream, and Scallions

Seared Raw Sirloin with Ginger, Soy, and Wasabi

Green Salad with Cold Marinated Vegetables

Cold Grilled Eggplant Salad with Ginger and Scallions, Sesame Vinaigrette

Skewered Grilled Monkfish with Smithfield Ham and Clementine Relish

Cold Pickled Tiger Shrimp with Chipotle Mayo and Black Bean Salad

Grilled Tuna with Green Chili Sauce

Ginger Pasta with Shrimp and Monkfish

Missouri Barbecued Pork Spareribs

Shredded North Carolina Pork Barbecue

Hickory-Smoked Duck with Grilled Pineapple and Tangy Citrus-Cilantro Glaze

Grilled Lamb with Grilled Vegetables and Grilled Sweet Potatoes

86-Proof Chocolate Cake

Apple Strudel

Mississippi Mud Cake

Bread Pudding with Pear Brandy

Coriander-Crusted Grilled Shrimp with Pineapple
    Salsa and Lime
Fettuccine Pasta with Oven-Dried Tomato Sauce,
    Fresh Herbs, and Asiago Cheese
Buttermilk-Fried Chicken Livers with Apple-Raisin
    Chutney, Spinach, and Warm Bacon Dressing
Grilled Sausage from Hell and Cornbread Salad with
    Hell Sausage, Lava Soaked Pineapples, and Lime-
    Guava Dressing
Middle Eastern Sampler Plate with Grilled Eggplant,
    Raisin Couscous, Olives, Feta, Orange Cumin
    Dressing, and Grilled Pita
House Green Salad
Arugula Salad with Smoked Pears, Spiced Pecans,
    and Stilton Cheese
Lime and Chicken Soup with Corn Tortillas

Grilled Salmon Fillet with White Grape-Garlic
    Sauce, Lime Tomato Rioja, and Spanish Rice
Caribbean-Style Spit-Roasted Pork Loin with West
    Indies Beans and Rice, Jamaican Slaw, Grilled
    Fennel, and Mango Marmalade
Grilled Tuna Steak with Pickled Ginger, Soy,

Wasabi, Liand Pan, and Jasmine Rice Cakes
Grilled Skewered Leg of Lamb with Baba Ganoush,
    Roasted Red-Pepper-Cucumber Salad, Preserved
    Lemon, Pomegranate Dressing, and Grilled Pita
Grilled Adobo-Rubbed Sirloin Steak with Pickled
    Corn Relish, Tamarind Ketchup, and "Damn
    Good Fries"
Spit-Roasted Herb and Lemon-Rubbed Chicken with
    Mashed Sweet Potatoes and Seared Kale

Sides

Apple-Raisin Chutney
Spanish Rice
"Damn Good Fries"
Seared Kale
Vegetarian Rice and Beans
Grilled Banana
Grilled Pineapple
Pineapple Salsa
Fried Plantains with Banana-Guava Ketchup
Cordito
Mashed Sweet Potatoes

Jimmy Schmidt
Detroit, Michigan

I think my cuisine has actually become more intricate, but more subtle. In years past, I did like to combine wild tropical flavors with more staid, standard-type dishes. However, I never really got into stuff like "blueberry vinaigrette on sweetbreads" or things like that. But now, I really work on a lot of contrasting flavors and textures and such that add a certain depth and complexity. At the same time, it's a little more subtle, so that you kind of get the overall flavor and then if you really like food and really want to delve in more, you can pick out all the components. It's more rounded, more subtle—although I don't know if I should use the word "subtle," because it still kind of jumps out at you! I'm much more careful about combining ingredients than I was ten years ago. Over the course of time, I've come to the realization more and more that I need to make all of the ingredients tie together—that the flavors have to work together. I don't just combine ingredients to shock or to create controversy, but to enrich the palate and to enrich the dining experience.

Selected Entrées-Specialties
London Chop House
May 25, 1984

Medallions of Norwegian Salmon
  with Caviar, Dill and Sherry Wine, Julienne of
  Vegetables
Grilled Atlantic Swordfish
  with Beaujolais-Butter Sauce, Julienne of
  Vegetables, New Potato
Atlantic Soft Shell Crabs
  Sautéed with Capers and Lemon-Butter, Shoe
  String Potatoes
Rack of Milk White Veal
  with Morels, Fiddleneck Ferns and Cattails
Mancelona Rainbow Trout
  with Mousseline of Perch, Champagne Sauce,
  Julienne of Vegetables
Duck and Pheasant Ravioli
  with Sweetbreads, Morels, and Cattails
Fettucini Primavera
  with Asparagus, Mushrooms, Artichokes, Peppers,
  Basil, Spinach Noodles, Parmesan Cheese
Air-Flown Fresh Fillet of Dover Sole Grilled in
  Butter, Vegetable Panache

A Mess of Lake Erie Perch Sautéed in Butter
Fresh Air-Flown Whole Maine Hard Shell Lobster
  (1 1/4 lbs), Broiled or Steamed with Drawn
  Butter, Shoe String Potatoes, Cole Slaw
Broiled Baby Chicken with Lemon-Butter Sauce,
  Snow Pea Pods, Parsleyed New Potaoes
Double Thick Baby Rib Lamb Chops with Bacon
Sautéed Veal Oskar II with Maine Backfin Crab,
  California Asparagus, Béarnaise
Roast Prime Ribs of Beef Au Jus,
  Creamed Horseradish, Garlicked Potatoes
Chateaubriand Bouquetiere
Chopped Beef Steak with
  Warm Pancho Sauce, Relish Garnish (request
  with or without garlic)
Beef Tenderloin Pepper Steak with Cracked
  Peppercorns, Mushrooms, and Brandy Sauce
Beef-Steak Tartare
Gulf Shrimp Papaya and Kiwi with Lime Sauce
Maryland Back-Fin Crab Lumps with Avocado,
  Chive Mustard Sauce

Selected Main Courses
The Rattlesnake Club
Spring, 1996

Capellini (Thin Angel Hair Pasta) with Tomatoes, Garlic, and Basil or with Sautéed Rock Shrimp

Crawfish Risotto with Roasted Red Pepper, Garlic, Sweet Corn, and Basil

Collection of Vegetables and Grains Grilled or Steamed as a Main Course

Herb-Crusted Mahi Mahi, Oven-Baked with Fennel and Tomato, Saffron, and Balsamic Essence

Freshwater Pickerel with Pinenut Crust, Lentils, and Tomato Sauce or Broiled with Fresh Herbs and Lemon

Crab and Salmon Cake with Maine Crab Spring Roll, Yellow Pepper Cream, and Spiced Chile Oil

Escalope of Sterling Salmon Crispy-Wrapped in Potato Crust with Sherry Mustard Sauce and Potato Crisps

Striped Sea Bass Pan Seared with Oriental-Style Vegetables and Chile Mashed Potatoes

Lobster and Mixed Grain Risotto—Barley, Arborio Rice, and Quinoa with Saffron, Basil, and Red Pepper Sauces

Breast of Free-Range Chicken, Garlic-Mashed Potato, Crimini Mushrooms, and Roasted Pepper Herb Glace

Medallions of Veal with Roasted Vegetables and Gorgonzola Polenta

Black Angus Filet of Beef Grilled with a Rhubarb and Cipollini Onion Compote, Red Wine Essence or Grilled with Garlic-Peppercorn Butter

Rack of Lamb Roasted with a White Bean, Asparagus, and Eggplant Ragout

Jeremiah Tower

STARS and J.T.'s
San Francisco, California

So-called California cuisine at its worst, made by the people who'd imitate it without understanding it in the first place, just got incredibly confusing. At Stars, we've always tried to fight against that "starch and three vegetables on every plate" mentality. There's certainly an instinct for chefs and cooks to want to do that all the time. At J.T.'s, since it's small and it's got my name on it, I can really do my vision of what I like to do with food—which is to take the "with" off the menu. So, it will be lobster, braised lamb shanks and black truffles. I don't say "with," "with," "with"—I've taken everything else off the plate. So it's a perfect sauce, perfectly braised lamb shanks, some big slices of spring garlic, some black truffles—and that's enough. I'm tired of seeing so many ingredients on the plate. That's where I came from in the first place, so I think I've come around full circle.

Stars
July 1984

Specials of the Day

First Courses

Texas Ham with a Japanese Eggplant Salad
Smoked Salmon with Grilled Herb-Oil Bread
Malpeque Oyster Stew with Ancho Chili Butter and
  Chervil Purée

Main Courses

Pasta with Alaskan Blue Prawns, Red Bells,
  Tomatoes, Basil, and Garlic
Grilled Salmon with Vegetable Brochettes and
  Rosemary Mayonnaise
Fillet of Beef in Broth with a Horseradish, Mustard,
  Tarragon Cream

Appetizers

Iced Oysters with Spicy Lamb Sausage
Rillettes of Smoked Fish with Bitter Greens Salad
Fish Paillard with Tomatoes, Cilantro, and Chives
Brioche with Marrow, Lobster Sauce, Poached
  Garlic, and Chervil
Snails with Ham, Shallots, Tarragon, and
  Chardonnay

Salads and Soup

Mixed Green Salad with Vinaigrette and Tomatoes
Mixed Green Salad with Blue Cheese Vinaigrette
Santa Fe–Balboa Café Garden Mixed Salad with
  Hazelnut Oil
Garlic Soup with Sage Leaves and Herb Profiteroles

Pasta and Fish

Subject to the Whims of the Chef, Prices, Weather,
  and Fishing Conditions

Grills and Main Courses

Chicken with Tarragon, Cream, Mushrooms, and
  Radicchio
Grilled Sweetbreads with Artichokes and a Wild
  Mushroom Butter
Grilled Aged New York Steak with Fries and a
  Tarragon Colbert Butter
Blanquette of Veal with Summer Vegetables and
  Crayfish Sauce

J.T.'s
Week of February 27–March 2, 1996

Hors d'Oeuvre

....

Choice of First Course

Black Truffle Custard with Sunchokes
Limestone Lettuce with Maytag Blue Cheese and
  Brioche Croutons
Warm Foie Gras Sandwich
Osetra Caviar Service with Iced Vodka
Crab Ravioli with Black Truffles
Steamed Mussels in a Shellfish Tarragon Sauce

Choice of Main Course

Boned American Snapper with Herb Vegetable Salad
Prime Fillet of Beef with Duxelle Potatoes and
  Pecan-Herb Salad
Capon Breast with Morels and Lobster Essence
Braised Lamb Shank with Fava Beans and Spring
  Garlic
Saddle of Venison with Truffled Celery Root and
  Cippolini Onions

....

Choice of J.T.'s Desserts

Alice Waters and Lindsey Shere

CHEZ PANISSE
Berkeley, California

Week of November 14, 1971

Sunday

Hors d'Oeuvres Variés
Daube d'Agneau
Salade
Lemon Mousse

Monday

Hors d'Oeuvres Variés
Manicotti and Meatballs
Salade
Biscuit Tortoni

Tuesday

Hors d'Oeuvres Variés
Pork Roast with Plums
Salade
Vanilla Bean Custard

Wednesday

Hors d'Oeuvres Variés
Lapin Sauté Provençal
Salade
Fruit and Cheeses

Thursday

Hors d'Oeuvres Variés
Steak au Poivre
Salade
Profiteroles

Friday

Tartelettes aux Poissons
Carrot and Orange Soup
Ris de Veau or Stuffed Lamb
Salade
Frozen Chocolate Marquis

Saturday

Pâté Maison
Cream of Watercress Soup
Poulet Vallé d'Auge
Salade
Fruit à l'Occitanienne

À la Carte

Dessert, Coffee, Espresso, Steaks and Chops

Monday

Patricia Wells' Salad à l'Ail: Garden Greens and Chicories with Garlic Croutons, Bacon and Mustard Dressing

Lulu Peyraud's Whole Gulf Snapper Stuffed with Garlic, Wild Fennel, and Savory à la Provençale

Sierra Beauty Apple Tart with Vanilla Ice Cream and Lavender Honey

Tuesday

Duck Breast "Proscuitto" Salad with Frisée and Chanterelles

Pasta with Artichokes and Black Olives

Grilled Lobster with an Olive Oil and Lemon Sauce, Young Spinach and Cabbage, Steamed Fingerling Potatoes with Fleur de Sel

Strawberry Feuilleté with Champagne Sabayon

Wednesday

Celery Root and Mâche Salad with Rabbit Rillettes and Toast

Roasted Atlantic Cod with Shell Beans, Fennel, and Chanterelles

Spit-Roasted Watson Farm Pork and Sausage with Cabbage and Chestnuts; Apple and Onion Marmalade, and Garden Greens

Key Lime Meringue Tartlet

Thursday

Artichoke and Watercress Salad with Black-Olive Vinaigrette

Freshly Salted Cod Bouillabaisse with Fennel and Herbs

Grilled Quail with Grapes and a Warm Salad of Chestnuts, Potatoes, Pancetta, and Chanterelles

Biancomangiare: Almond and Citron Bavarian Cream

Friday

An Apéritif

Mâche and Bay Scallop Salad with Black Truffle Vinaigrette

Sautéed Northern Halibut with Spinach and Sea Urchin Butter

Grilled James Ranch Lamb with Mustard and Mustard Greens, Potatoes Lyonnaise, and Chino Ranch Vegetables

Rum Baba à la Creole

Saturday

An Apéritif

Grilled Sea Bass with Red Pepper Oil and Fried Leeks

Sautéed Duck Foie Gras with Capers and Watercress

Roasted Goose Breast and Leg Confit with a Fig and Balsamic Sauce, Sautéed Apples and Potatoes, Garden Salad, and Roasted Vegetables

Pink Grapefruit, Meyer Lemon, and Passion Fruit Sherbets with Champagne

Most of our produce and meat comes from local farms and ranches that practice ecologically sound agriculture.

Substitutions of particular fish varieties may have to be made.

How is it possible to characterize the cuisine of a particular chef? Labels such as "Californian," "French," or "Mediterranean" are only somewhat useful in categorizing a chef's efforts, as even within those parameters there is a personal interpretation being expressed.

In our hope to capture a "snapshot" of how the chefs we interviewed approach food and cooking, we posed a dilemma: If they were asked to choose only ten ingredients to take with them to a proverbial desert island to cook with for the rest of their lives, which of their favorites would they choose? Which ingredients and flavors do they feel they couldn't live without? How do these ingredients and flavors "color" their cuisine? Similarly, we asked them which three cooking techniques they would choose if limited to cooking with those three for the rest of their lives.

We asked for answers to these questions on the spot, not giving in to requests to "get back to us" on these toughies. In doing so, it was fascinating to observe how chefs' minds worked. Their answers reflected their resourcefulness as well as their passion for certain ingredients. Running out of choices and not being able to take along a favorite ingredient seemed to pain them almost as much as learning they couldn't bring a favorite pet—or perhaps more so.

Collectively, the chefs' most popular choices of ingredients to bring along with them were: tied for (1) salt and tomatoes; tied for (3) olive oil, wine/grapes, and greens/spinach; and then (6) citrus (lime, lemon, orange); (7) potatoes; (8) bread/wheat; (9) garlic; and tied for (10) pig/pork/bacon and chicken/eggs.

And their favorite techniques were quite clear: (1) grilling; (2) sautéeing; and (3) braising.

But even more interesting than their collective choices are the chefs' individual lists that follow, and in certain cases, recipes inspired by their choices.

Desert Island Lists

Rick Bayless

FRONTERA GRILL and TOPOLOBAMPO
Chicago, Illinois

INGREDIENTS:

1. **Beans.** In my cooking, that's kind of my meat. I live on them.

2. **Dried corn.** I couldn't live without making tortillas, so I'd really need that.

3. **Ancho chiles.** Ancho has a deep sweetness to it.

4. **Guajillo chiles.** Guajillo has a really bright spiciness and high acidity to it.

5. **Poblano chiles.** Poblano is my favorite of all the green chiles; it's got a tremendous complexity of flavor, and I can turn it inside and out, doing everything from using it as a flavoring to using it as a vegetable.

6. **Greens.** I like greens in just about any way, and if I chose something like chard, I could use it raw, braised, or mixed in with the corn or the beans and cooked that way.

7. **Garlic.** Garlic gives me a lot of different options for flavor, whether it's raw or cooked or roasted. That is one of the things that is absolutely essential with the chiles, to add a lot of depth.

8. **Onions.** I could do away with onions before I could garlic, but I wanted some fresh flavors and to be able to add crunch and liveliness to a dish, so that's where the onions come in.

9. **Sugar.** I love sweets, so I have to have sugar. And I could even turn some of these things into sweet dishes that would really satisfy my sweet tooth. I could make cornbread-like things with the corn. There are even sweet bean dishes in Mexico as well.

10. **Salt.** Mexican food tends to be fairly high in sodium, because the corn and the beans really need a fair amount of salt to get them to a place where they're really tasty.

TECHNIQUES:

1. **Grilling.** It's one of those things I couldn't live without. I love smoky flavors. And they go really, really well with the rest of this stuff.

2. **Boiling.** You've got to cook corn and beans a long time.

3. **Shallow-frying.** I'm referring to when you cook something slowly for a long time, in just a tiny bit of oil, and it kind of gets crusty and you scrape it all up.

Veracruz-Style Greens and Beans with Red Chile and Dumplings

by Rick Bayless

MAKES ABOUT 10 CUPS, SERVING 6 AS A MAIN COURSE

1 pound (about 2 1/2 cups) dry black beans

4 stemmed, dried chipotle chiles (or canned chipotle chiles *en adobo*)

3 medium (1 1/2 ounces total) dried ancho chiles, stemmed and seeded

3 garlic cloves, peeled and roughly chopped

1/2 small white onion, sliced

4 tablespoons olive or vegetable oil or rich-tasting lard

1 cup (8 ounces) fresh masa for tortillas
OR a generous 3/4 cup dried *masa harina* mixed with 2/3 cup hot water

salt, about 2 1/2 teaspoons

3/4 cup chopped cilantro

1 1/2 cups (6 ounces) crumbled Mexican *queso fresco* or pressed salted farmer's cheese

6 cups stemmed, thickly sliced sturdy greens (such as lamb's quarters–*quelites*, chard, collard,
or practically any other—if you're cooking in Mexico, try the Veracruz *xonequi* or *quintoniles*
or Yucatecan *chaya*)

1. *The beans.* Rinse the beans, then scoop them into a large (6-quart) pot (preferably a Dutch oven or a Mexican earthenware *olla*), and add 2 quarts of water and remove any beans that float. Bring to a boil, reduce heat to medium-low, and simmer, partially covered, until the beans are thoroughly tender (they will taste creamy, not chalky), about 2 hours. You'll need to stir the beans regularly and add water as necessary to keep the level of the liquid a generous 1/2 inch above the level of the beans.

2. *The chiles.* While the beans are cooking, make the chile purée. On an ungreased griddle or heavy skillet over medium heat, toast the dried chipotles, turning regularly and pressing flat with a spatula, until they are very aromatic and a little toasty smelling, about 30 seconds. (Canned chipotles need no preparation.)

On the same hot surface, toast the anchos: open the chiles out flat and, one or two at a time, press flat for a few seconds with a metal spatula until they start to crackle, even send up a faint wisp of smoke, then flip and press down to toast the other side. In a small bowl, cover both kinds of toasted chiles with hot water and let rehydrate 30 minutes, stirring frequently to ensure even soaking. Drain and discard the water.

(continued on next page)

(continued from preceding page)

In a food processor or blender, purée the chiles with garlic, onion, and about 1/2 cup water (you may need a little more water to get everything freely moving through the blades). Press through a medium-mesh strainer into a bowl. In a large saucepan, heat 2 tablespoons of the oil or lard over medium-high. Add the purée all at once and stir nearly constantly as it sears and thickens for about 5 minutes. When the beans are tender, scrape the chile purée into them, stir well, and simmer 30 minutes longer.

3. *The masa dumplings.* In a large bowl, knead together (your hand works best here) the fresh or reconstituted masa with the remaining 2 tablespoons of oil or lard, 1/2 teaspoon of the salt, 1/4 cup of the chopped cilantro, and the cheese until uniformly mixed. Form into about 48 balls, each the size of a large marble. Cover and set aside.

4. *Finishing the dish.* Check the consistency of the black bean stew; there should be a good amount of broth in the beans (you have to add the dumplings and greens and still come out with a stew-like consistency, so add additional water if necessary) and the broth should be as thick as a light sauce. (If it's not as thick as you'd like, purée a cup of the beans in a food processor or blender and return to the pot as thickening.) Liberally season the stew with salt, usually about 2 teaspoons (the beans themselves will continue to absortb the salt for quite a while after you season them).

With the pot simmering over medium, add the dumplings one at a time, nestling them into the gurgling broth as they go in. Simmer 5 minutes, then add the greens; stir gently so as not to break up the dumplings, and simmer until the greens are fully cooked (about 7 minutes for tender greens like chard, 10 to 12 minutes for tougher ones like collard and lamb's quarters).

Ladle into warm bowls, sprinkle liberally with the remaining chopped cilantro, and serve with plenty of steaming tortillas for a really satisfying meal.

Daniel Boulud

RESTAURANT DANIEL
New York, New York

INGREDIENTS:

1. **Onions.** They come into many dishes in my hometown…if I'm thinking about survival, I'd go back to my roots.

2. **Tomatoes.** I can eat them every day.

3. **A whole pig.** It would carry me a while—I love ham, saucisson, confit, boudin! (See Daniel Boulud's recipe for Braised Spiced Pork Belly on pages 328–329.)

4. **Two rabbits, one male and one female.** In a few months, I'd have five hundred rabbits! And I could live on just pig and rabbit.

5. **Olive oil.** You can cook anything with it; you can barbecue or stir-fry or make a dressing with it, and it always tastes great.

6. **Sea salt.** I use *fleur de sel,* which is the top of the crust when the sea dries. It's the most sophisticated and refined salt—I use it more for finishing dishes.

7. **Potatoes.** I love potatoes—the variation in cooking potatoes is endless.

8. **Truffles, white and black.** If life is going to be tough, you might as well have it with truffles. And you can do anything with truffles. You could put the black truffles with a baked potato....

9. **Cheese.** Aged goat cheese. I'd want it to be the kind I ate growing up in Lyons, like my grandmother used to make.

10. **Wine.** Red wine, like a great Burgundy or Merlot.

TECHNIQUES:

1. **Steaming.** It's healthy, and can always be prepared with simplicity. When you steam something, the idea is to flavor what you steam in order to preserve the purity of the dish. I'd use this for seafood, fish, shellfish.

2. **Braising.** I'd use this for roasts and meat mostly, serving them with a basic *jus.*

3. **Grilling.** That's how I live and cook in the summer. I love vegetables and whole fish, like salmon, cooked on the grill.

Braised Spiced Pork Belly

by Daniel Boulud

The ingredients list may appear long, but any unavailable herbs and spices can be omitted or replaced with others.

SERVES 6-8

one 4 lb. slab fresh, very lean pork belly

Spices

1 teaspoon coriander seeds
1/2 teaspoon fennel seeds
2 teaspoon black peppercorns
1/4 teaspoon whole cloves
2 pieces star anise
1 three-inch long cinnamon stick

Herbs

6 sprigs rosemary
2 bay leaves
6 sprigs sage
6 sprigs thyme

1 cup coarse salt

1/4 cup sugar

1 teaspoon finely chopped garlic

1 large carrot, peeled and diced

1 large onion, peeled and diced

1 branch celery, diced

2 gallons chicken stock

1. Preheat oven to 400°. Toast the spices about 5 minutes. Using a mortar and pestle or a food processor, crush the toasted spices and combine with salt, sugar, garlic, and herbs. Score the skin of the pork belly and rub well with the herb and spice mixture. Cover and refrigerate for 1 to 2 days.

2. Preheat the oven to 350°. Scrape the surface of the pork belly lightly to remove the excess herb, spice, and seasoning rub. Discard the excess herb and spice mixture, and place the pork in a large braiser along with the carrot, onion, and celery. Add the chicken stock to cover and bring to a boil. Cover with lid and place in the oven for 2 1/2 to 3 hours or until the pork is tenderly cooked. Remove the pork carefully from the braising liquid and place it in a shallow roasting pan. Roast approximately 1 hour, basting occasionally with cooking juices, until the pork is nicely glazed.

3. Serve with braised potatoes or lentils. Either of these may be cooked using one part of the cooking liquid reserved from the pork and one part water.

Terrance Brennan

PICHOLINE
New York, New York

INGREDIENTS:

1. **Olive oil.** That's what I cook with—it reigns in the kitchen! It's healthy and tasty.

2. **Garlic.** I love garlic—it's very gutsy.

3. **White truffles.** Especially over pasta.

4. **Porcini.** The greatest mushroom, in terms of flavor and texture.

5. **Tomatoes.** I love tomatoes, but only during the summer. (See Terrance Brennan's recipe for Poached Halibut with Tomato Confit on pages 331–332, which he says he devised "in order to extend the tomato season!")

6. **Bread.** A good, crusty *campagne* bread.

7. **Cheese.** With bread, cheese, and wine, you'd have a nice lunch. I'd want to take a basket of cheeses— Brin d'Amour, Cabralles (a Spanish blue cheese), Reblouchon, and Parmesan, which is arguably the greatest cheese in the world. It's the only cheese with an entire cuisine behind it.

8. **Wine.** I love wonderful, big, nicely aged red wines.

9. **Peaches.** Perfectly vine-ripened peaches—they're perfect with blueberries.

10. **Chocolate.** I love chocolate.

TECHNIQUES:

1. **Sautéeing.** It's the medium for about 80 percent of my cooking.

2. **Roasting.** I like the texture it gives, like the crispy skin on chicken.

3. **Grilling.** For the flavor it gives through the woods used, and for its lightness.

Poached Day-Boat Halibut with Tomato Confit and Aged Balsamic Vinegar

by Terrance Brennan

I came up with this dish in the early fall, in order to extend the tomato season a little more—I like keeping tomatoes on the menu as long as possible, since we are a French-Mediterranean restaurant. Provençal flavors are evident throughout the dish—olive oil, balsamic vinegar, eggplant. While halibut is fine sautéed, I think poaching is one of the better ways of cooking it and that it results in the best texture. This dish is representative of my style of cuisine, in that it's light yet flavorful and respectful of the fish itself.

SERVES 6

2 large eggplants (about 3 pounds),
split lengthwise

1 whole egg

1/3 cup all-purpose flour

1/4 teaspoon finely chopped garlic

salt and pepper to taste

6 ounces extra virgin olive oil

1. Brush cut surface of eggplants with olive oil.
2. Place cut surface down on roasting rack; place in a roasting pan.
3. Roast in a 325° oven for 1 hour and 15 minutes, or until eggplant skin collapses when touched; remove from oven.
4. When cool enough to handle, scoop flesh out of eggplant into fine mesh strainer; allow to drain one hour.
5. Place drained eggplant in food precessor, purée, and remove to a mixing bowl.
6. Add egg, flour, garlic, salt, and pepper.
7. Blend together.
8. Place 1 ounce olive oil in 10-inch teflon pan and heat.
9. Place 1 tablespoon of eggplant mixture in a medium-hot pan and sauté until edges begin to brown.
10. Turn over, lower heat, and cook through.
11. Remove and drain on paper towel, place on baking sheet, and continue until all the mixture is gone. You should have 18 to 20 pieces.
12. Place on a baking sheet and heat them in a 325° oven when you are ready to serve.

(continued on next page)

(continued from preceding page)

Court Bouillon

1 1/2 cups white wine

6 cups water

1 medium onion, sliced

2 celery ribs, sliced

1 head of garlic, split

6–8 branches fresh thyme

1 teaspoon white peppercorns

2 bay leaves

1 lemon (peel only)

salt and pepper to taste

1. Place all ingredients in a non-reactive saucepot and bring to a boil.
2. Lower heat and simmer for 30 minutes.
3. Strain and reserve.

Tomato Confit

2 pounds fresh plum tomatoes, peeled and seeded

4 cups extra virgin olive oil

2 branches thyme

2 peeled garlic cloves

1. Cook tomatoes over low heat (just under a simmer) in olive oil with garlic and thyme until there is no texture, about 1 1/2 hours.
2. Cool in oil.
3. Strain and chop tomatoes fine.
4. Heat to serve.

For Plating

six 7-ounce halibut fillets

1. Divide court bouillon between two 10-inch sauté pans. Place 3 halibut fillets in each. Bring to a simmer and cook for approximately 3 minutes on one side; turn over and cook for 3 more minutes.
2. Divide hot eggplant pancakes among 6 plates. Place halibut on top. With 2 tablespoons, make 6 quenelles from the tomato confit to place on top of each plate. Drizzle each with 1/2 ounce each of olive oil and 25-year-old balsamic vinegar.

Gary Danko

INGREDIENTS:

1. **Salt.** It's the basis of life. It would satiate my palate.

2. **Olive oil.** It's the healthiest oil in the world.

3. **Wheat.** I love the flavor of bread.

4. **Maple syrup.** I even eat it with yogurt. It's a childhood thing.

5. **Yogurt.** I eat it every day. I love a good yogurt, like Nancy's (which is made in Oregon).

6. **Basil.** I love basil.

7. **Tomatoes.** Another childhood thing—I love tomatoes.

8. **Duck.** It's plain, flat-out simple and delicious. There is no comparison to a beautifully roasted duck that you've rubbed with salt and lemon juice—to me, that is like heaven.

9. **Raspberries.** I love them, and they've typically got more flavor than strawberries.

10. **Butter.** It's one of the gifts of nature—and no animals died to make it.

TECHNIQUES:

1. **Roasting.** It's simple and efficient and delicious. Some of the best foods are done that way—from duck to vegetables.

2. **Braising.** It's another way of developing flavor, and a streamlined way of preparing a dish and sauce at the same time.

3. **Grilling.** Proper grilling is done when the flames are simply glowing embers, not big licking flames that leave carbon deposits on the meat.

Duck Prosciutto

by Gary Danko

This is a delicious dish, made with an ancient method of preservation. You can hang it for 15 to 30 days, depending on how dry you want it. I make them 40 at a time! I like serving it in the traditional manner—with half of a peeled ripe fig, some melon or slices of pear, shaved fennel and arugula, or drizzled with fennel oil.

1 tablespoon kosher salt

1/2 teaspoon thyme

1 bay leaf, ground

1 teaspoon whole coriander seeds, cracked

1 teaspoon black peppercorns, cracked

1 large Barbarie or moulard duck breast, about 1 pound

1. Combine salt with spices and herbs.

2. Trim duck breast of excess skin, tenderloin, and sinews. Rub spice mix into breast. Place on a plate and wrap with plastic wrap. Cure for 24 hours or longer. Brush off excess rub, wrap in cheesecloth and hang in cooler for 15 days. Trim excess fat. Slice very thin. The prosciutto may be frozen and cut on a meat slicer.

Susan Feniger

BORDER GRILL
Santa Monica, California

INGREDIENTS:

1. **Olive oil.** I love the flavor of a really strong, fruity olive oil—over cheese, over vegetables, on bread.

2. **Vinegar.** I'd need an acid of some sort. I love vinegar with olive oil, and when I make stews, I like to finish them with an acid.

3. **Cheese.** A great feta. I love a great cheese—I can always eat it.

4. **Avocados.** Really satisfying to eat again and again, like artichokes. (See Susan Feniger's recipe for Avocado Corn Relish on page 336.)

5. **Tomatoes.** As a side. I need some balance—everything so far is too rich.

6. **Green beans.** I need a vegetable. I'm thinking of combinations of things. I could stew them with tomatoes and feta, or have them with olive oil and vinegar.

7. **Salt.** Avocado, olive oil, and salt. I can't think of a more perfect dish.

8. **Bread.** A great bread, like a great sourdough, with a lot of crust.

9. **Olives.** Dry-cured black olives of some sort. I like snacking food, I like to pick like that—some olives, some feta...

10. **Chocolate.** Sometimes you need something sweet, even just a little bit. I'd take a high-quality semi-sweet chocolate.

After being told which of their ingredients were the same, Susan Feniger went on to correctly guess each of the rest of her partner Mary Sue Milliken's list!

TECHNIQUES:

1. **Grilling.** You can do anything on a grill. I like to grill; you can bake in the charcoal, you can grill or sauté or boil on a grill.

2. **Sautéeing.** I would want to be able to cook things quickly.

3. **Stewing.** I love soups—I think they're comforting. A one-pot meal is easy and can last for days.

Avocado Corn Relish

by Susan Feniger

In this refreshing relish, corn kernels are lightly cooked just to develop their flavor and then mixed with chunks of smoky roasted chiles, luxurious avocodo and crunchy sharp scallions. Such a fabulous relish can easily take the place of a cooked sauce with casual foods liked grilled skirt steak or fish, and it is a boon on buffet tables since it complements so many foods. We have been known to eat this relish off the spoon or with nothing more than tortillas and be quite content.

MAKES 6 CUPS

3/4 cup olive oil

4 cups fresh corn kernels (about 5 ears)

1 tablespoon salt

3/4 tablespoon freshly ground black pepper

2 avocados, peeled and seeded

1 large red bell pepper, cored and seeded

4 poblano chiles, roasted, peeled, and seeded

4 scallions, white and light green parts, thinly sliced on the diagonal

1/2 cup red wine vinegar

1. Heat 1/2 cup of the olive oil in a large skillet over medium heat. Sauté the corn with the salt and pepper, about 5 minutes. Transfer to a large mixing bowl and set aside to cool.

2. Cut the avocados, bell pepper, and roasted poblanos into 1/4-inch dice. Add to the sautéed corn along with the scallions, red wine vinegar, and remaining 1/4 cup olive oil. Mix well and let sit 20 to 30 minutes to blend the flavors.

3. Serve at room temperature. Corn relish can be stored, tightly covered, in the refrigerator up to a day. To make 2 to 3 days in advance, mix well all the ingredients except the avocado and store in the refrigerator. Add the avocado shortly before serving.

George Germon and Johanne Killeen

AL FORNO
Providence, Rhode Island

INGREDIENTS:

1. *George* = **rice,** *Johanne* = **onions.** *George:* I'd take Uncle Ben's converted rice. *Johanne:* I loves onions in everything, and the underlying structure of a lot of my food starts with onions—whether stuffing onions into a chicken for roasting or making an onion base for soups.

2. **Pasta.** We couldn't live without pasta. We'd bring a string pasta, like linguini. There's something sexy and satisfying about string pasta.

3. **Olive oil.** We'd bring Capezzana or Provençal oil. We couldn't live without the flavor; we use it in rice, and to sauté garlic.

4. **Wine.** We'd bring Italian red wine to drink and to turn into vinegar. We love the balance of acid in food, and vinegar is important to bring out flavor.

5. **Salt.** It's important—it can perk things up and bring out their flavor.

6. *Johanne* = **chicken,** *George* = **pork.** *Johanne:* I favor chicken because you can do so much with it. (See their Roasted Chicken recipe on page 338.) *George:* I like the flavor of pork; there are very few cuts of meat that have good flavor anymore.

7. **Tomatoes.** For sauces! In our wedding vows, Johanne has to make red sauce once a week.

8. **Greens.** *George:* Whether before or after or with a meal, I always crave a salad. *Johanne:* I even like a salad instead of dessert!

9. **Sugar.** *George:* I use sugar a lot in my cooking; it gives a vibrancy and sparkle to otherwise dull things. Just a pinch of it, say, in a chicken dish will make the few ingredients in the dish come alive. And I use it for carmelization—when you brown food in caramel instead of oil, it gives a depth of flavor you can't get any other way.

10. **Garlic.** It's important in pasta, and it tastes very different depending on how you cook it. You can use it sparingly when raw, or sauté it slowly and use it golden or brown. You can boil it in milk to get the mildest flavor, or roast it to bring out the flavor of caramel.

Germon and Killeen were aghast to discover they'd forgot to mention bread. "It's a staple," they insisted.

TECHNIQUES:

1. **Boiling.** *George:* You'd have to be able to boil to have pasta and rice. *Johanne:* For pasta—and boiled chicken is one of my favorite meals.

2. **Sautéeing.** *George:* When you cover the pan, you can get the same effect as roasting. *Johanne:* For sauces, and onions.

3. **Grilling.** *George:* For the flavor, and for the immediacy of it. *Johanne:* Especially over an open fire. It's clean and simple.

Roasted Chicken

by Johanne Killeen and George Germon

SERVES 6–8

2 whole chickens (about 3 pounds each), washed and dried

1–2 teaspoons kosher salt

1 head garlic

2 large onions (1 pound), peeled, cut in half lengthwise and sliced thinly

2 cups ripe cherry tomatoes

1/4 cup virgin olive oil

1 cup dry white wine

2 heads fresh watercress, washed and trimmed

1. Preheat the oven to 450°.

2. Liberally salt the inside and outside of the chickens. Lay them breast side up in a casserole with a tight-fitting lid. Break up the head of garlic, leaving the skin on, and scatter the garlic cloves around the chicken, along with the onion slices. Add the cherry tomatoes and pour over the olive oil and wine.

3. Cover the casserole and roast the chickens for 1/2 hour. Turn the chickens breast side down and roast another 1/2 hour. Uncover the casserole and roast about 15 minutes until the skin has browned; turn the chickens breast side up and roast an additional 15 minutes to brown. Set the chickens aside in a warm place to rest for 10 minutes.

4. Lay the watercress out on a large, warm serving platter, top with the chickens and some of the juice so the watercress wilts, and serve at once with the remaining sauce passed in a separate dish.

Joyce Goldstein

Joyce Goldstein agreed to answer our question on one condition: "It's got to be a Mediterranean island!"

INGREDIENTS:

1. **Wheat.** I'd want to make pasta, bread, pizza.

2. **Potatoes.**

3. **A tree that grows both lemons and oranges.** Citrus is one of the great balancers in my food—it adds sparkle.

4. **A cow or a goat.** For milk, cheese, yogurt.

5. **Grapes.** Wine enriches your life.

6. **Spinach.** One of the most satisfying vegetables I know. (See Joyce Goldstein's spinach salad recipe on page 340.)

7. **Chicken.** For eggs, soup.

8. **Olives.** For olive oil—plus I like them by themselves.

9. **Mushrooms.** They're like meat. And they're very versatile.

10. **Vegetables.** Asparagus, peas, eggplant!

TECHNIQUES:

1. **Sautéeing.** I'm a line cook—I love the energy of keeping all the burners going!

2. **Braising.** There's nothing like the smell when something's braising.

3. **Grilling.** I love the smell and the crunch of the texture and the char. The power of the grill is primitive.

Mushroom, Walnut, and Spinach Salad with Mustard Vinaigrette

by Joyce Goldstein

It's interesting that many Mediterranean countries pair mushrooms and nuts. In Italy, hazelnuts are the complement for assorted mushrooms. In Spain, almonds are often part of the duet. In this Greek-inspired salad, walnuts are combined with spinach in a spicy mustard vinaigrette. This is very nice served with *tiropetes*, the classic cheese-filled phyllo pastry.

SERVES 6

Mustard Vinaigrette

1 teaspoon dry mustard

2 tablespoon red wine vinegar

1 tablespoon prepared Dijon mustard

3 tablespoon lemon juice

3/4 cup olive oil

salt and pepper

optional: 3 tablespoons chopped dill

Salad

1 1/2 cups thinly sliced mushrooms

1 cups toasted walnuts, very coarsely chopped

6 cups small spinach leaves, well washed and dried

1. Make a paste of the dry mustard and vinegar. Add the rest of the vinaigrette ingredients and whisk together. Season to taste. Add optional dill.

2. Toss the mushrooms with 1/4 of the vinaigrette and marinate for 10 minutes. Toss the walnuts with some of the vinaigrette and marinate for 10 minutes. At serving time, toss spinach with remaining vinaigrette, and fold in the mushrooms and walnuts.

Hubert Keller

FLEUR DE LYS
San Francisco, California

INGREDIENTS:

1. **Vanilla ice cream.** This is a flavor I love from childhood. My father used to make it in his pastry shop when I was growing up, and I'd always be nearby with a spoon and a bowl. You have to eat vanilla ice cream right from the machine, three minutes before it's done, so it's just a little under. Vanilla is a flavor that's great for *crème anglaise,* sorbets, or anything! It's absolutely the best, despite all the complicated flavors out there.

2. **Caviar.** Not because it's expensive— I just love to eat it with a spoon, as long as it's fresh and not oversalted. Its creaminess and texture are unique. (See Hubert Keller's recipe for Cauliflower Purée with Caviar on pages 342–343.)

3. **Rose hip jam.** My father still sends it to me! It's an elegant confiture. My grandmother used to make a syrup of rose hip, and we would add water and make it into a drink like lemonade when we were children.

4. **Caprina** [the Brazilian national drink]. My wife and I serve it at home at the start of parties. It gets a party going in a hour!

5. **Limes.** Lime goes with the Caprina!

6. **Champagne.** It's festive, and great for special occasions. In a recent article about what chefs have in their refrigerators, all of us had champagne! Mine also had rose hip jam—and chocolate, for my wife.

7. **Rack of lamb.** It's the meat I eat the most. Lamb is very simple; simply roast it and add some roast garlic and a simple, uncomplicated sauce.

8. **Wild strawberries** *[fraises des bois].* It's a fancy thing. As a kid, my parents had a house in the mountains, and we would pick them in the woods. Their flavor cannot be beaten. They're like the ultimate jewels, or diamonds—so full of flavor! And I could put them on my ice cream.

9. **Oysters (Belon triple-zero).** They're big, but not overpowering—so delicate, you could eat one or twelve.

10. **Truffles.** It's an ingredient that is a miracle. With all the money, scientists, and technology, these are only a product of nature. And with scrambled eggs, they're the ultimate!

TECHNIQUES:

1. **Roasting (with a convection oven).** We roast 80 percent of our fish this way. It seals in the juices and flavors. We do everything this way—small cuts of fish and meat, even scallops—and let it rest for three minutes, just like meat. And all our cooks have small spray bottles of oil, to spray the meat.

2. **Braising.** Living in a fast-paced world, there is no time to cook anymore. This takes longer, but you get to use cheaper cuts of meat that have a lot of flavor. We'll do braised lamb next to lamb loin or chop, for contrast on the plate. It's a forgotten technique that has great delicacy.

3. **Pan-frying.** It's a technique you'd use for veal medallions or thin cuts of meat. Or for vegetables or potatoes, to give them crispness.

Cauliflower Purée Topped with Caviar and Blue Potato Chips

by Hubert Keller

For New Year's Eve every year, we prepare dishes that our customers have never seen before. Caviar and cauliflower is a combination that has existed before—it's just not that common. So we brought it back and made it festive with the blue chips. It makes for a visually stunning plate. Plus, the caviar and the crisp chips are a nice contrast to the puréed cauliflower.

SERVES 4

2/3 cup white wine vinegar

1 1/2 tablespoons salt (for blue potatoes)

2 medium blue potatoes

3 teaspoons olive oil

1 large cauliflower

4 tablespoons cream

1 small bunch watercress

1 tablespoon shallots, finely chopped

2 tablespoons dry white wine

3 tablespoons caviar (golden, salmon, or sturgeon)

1 tablespoon chives, finely chopped

1 hard-boiled and chopped egg yolk

salt and freshly ground pepper

Blue Potato Chips

1. Preheat oven to 350°. In a saucepan, combine 1 quart of water with 2/3 cup of white wine vinegar and 1 1/2 tablespoons salt. Bring to a boil. Remove from the heat and cover.

2. Meanwhile, slice the unpeeled blue potatoes paper thin with a mandoline. Drop the potato slices into the hot water one by one and cover. Let sit for 1/2 hour.

3. Cover a baking sheet with parchment paper. Brush the paper lightly with olive oil. Drain the potatoes in a strainer. Lay the potato slices side by side on the paper. (Keep a little space between the potatoes so that they do not touch each other—otherwise, they will stick together.)

4. Brush a second sheet of parchment paper with olive oil and place on top of the potato slices. Bake them in the oven for 15 to 18 minutes. The potato chips will turn into a beautiful dark-blue color and be almost translucent. Remove from the heat and set aside in a dry spot.

Cauliflower Purée

Take off the outside leaves of the cauliflower, separate it into florets, and wash it. Cook the cauliflower in a pot of lightly salted boiling water. When it is absolutely soft, drain it. Place the cauliflower in a medium-size saucepot. Add 3 tablespoons of cream and, using a whisk, mash it into a purée over medium heat. Go on stirring for 4 to 5 minutes to eliminate any excess of moisture—otherwise when blended, the purée will be too runny. Transfer the mixture to a blender and purée until you obtain a very smooth texture. Season to taste. Transfer the purée to a small pot and keep hot.

Watercress Sauce

1. Wash the watercress and trim off the leaves. Discard the stems. Cook the leaves in a pot of boiling salted water just until tender, about 3 to 4 minutes. Drain in a strainer. Save 1/2 cup of cooking liquid. Refresh the leaves under cold running water. In a small saucepot, heat one teaspoon olive oil.
2. Add the chopped shallots and cook to a light golden color. Deglaze with white wine and reduce to almost dry. Add 1/2 cup of the cooking liquid and one tablespoon cream; season with salt and pepper. Bring to a boil and lower the heat to a simmer for 2 minutes, then add the cooked watercress leaves. Transfer to a blender, blend the mixture for one minute, and you will obtain a light and very tasty watercress sauce. Check the seasoning.

Finishing and Presentation

Carefully divide the cauliflower purée in the center of four plates. Top the purée with the caviar. Spoon the watercress sauce all around the cauliflower. Decorate with the potato chips by sticking them around the cauliflower purée. Sprinkle with chives and chopped egg yolk.

Note: The blue potato chips definitely add a dramatic look to this delicious dish. As an option, but a less dramatic one, red potatoes can be used for chips; so can blanched asparagus tips. About blue potatoes or purple potatoes: they have a deep blue skin. The flesh is bright blue and the flavor and texture are similiar to russets. They originate and are very popular in the South American Andes.

Gray Kunz

LESPINASSE
New York, New York

INGREDIENTS:

1–4. **Potatoes, carrots, leeks, onions.** I'd want to bring some nourishment, first.

5. **Coriander.**

6. **Bay leaves.**

7. **Coconut.**

8. **Sugar cane.**

9. **Salt.**

10. **Water.**

Kunz rattled off his list with the assurance of someone who had just finished thinking about exactly this question. No meat? Kunz claims, "I wouldn't miss it so much." And he says he'd look for fish and other local ingredients to cook with.

TECHNIQUES:

1. **Braising.**

2. **Simmering.**

3. **Steaming.**

Kunz explains that all of these techniques concentrate the flavor of the ingredients being cooked into the liquid.

Mary Sue Milliken

BORDER GRILL
Santa Monica, California

INGREDIENTS:

1. **Black pepper.** I love it.

2. **Olive oil.** It's too hard to make from scratch.

3. **Vinegar.** I need it to flavor everything.

4. **Basmati rice.** I adore it. It has such a fabulous aroma—I could eat it every day.

5. **Salt.** I don't want to get it out of the ocean.

6. **Tomatoes.** Ripe and beautiful ones.

7. **Raspberries.** Perfectly ripe, they're my favorite fruit.

8. **Cheese.** Vacherin. It's only available around my birthday (which is in February).

9. **Arugula.** A good source of calcium.

10. **Red wine.** A really incredible one, to go with the cheese.

Milliken took some coaxing to answer the question. "I want to have anything I want whenever I want it," she complained. But then her ingenuity jumped into action. "Can you fish there?" she asked hopefully.

TECHNIQUES:

1. **Pan-searing.** If you pan-sear, you get juices in the pan and can make a sauce. I like the caramelization.

2. **Braising.** I love braisable cuts of meat—they have more flavor, more character.

3. **Baking.** I could make pastries. I worked seven years in a bakery.

Wayne Nish

MARCH
New York, New York

Ingredients:

1. **Olive oil** (Mosto).

2. **Sea salt.** When I went to Barbados two months ago, I took a bottle of olive oil and a bag of sea salt. So those are far and away my priorities.

3. **Vermouth.** It's a liquid element that can be used effectively in building up layers of flavor without calling attention to its specific existence within the dish. You simply make a dish more complex without adding something that's immediately identifiable.

4. **Chives.** Chives are one of the most successful herbs to me because they do have a distinct flavor, yet they work with a lot of different things.

5. **Coriander seeds.** They have a perfume that's very alluring, and a sweetness and flavor that works with a lot of different things.

6. **Roasted tomatoes.** When good tomatoes are simply impossible to get during the winter months, it's a way to extract the most flavor from not-so-great tomatoes in the winter. The liquid evaporates, and the flavor becomes intensified.

7. **Confit of garlic.** It's one of those great items because it's so versatile and usable.

8. **Chicken stock.** The key here is versatility. Good chicken stock is neutral, and will allow the acceptance of other items and work with things as disparate as meat and fish.

9. **Herb mix.** All the soft herbs—basil, tarragon, chervil, parsley—in more or less equal quantities.

10. **The Holy Trinity of luxury restaurants: caviar, truffles, and *foie gras*.**

Techniques:

1. **Sautéeing.** It's often the quickest way to get something cooked.

2. **Grilling.** The grill is often the second quickest way to get something cooked.

3. **Poaching and/or braising.** I'll often increase the liquid when braising so that it effectively becomes poaching.

Patrick O'Connell

THE INN AT LITTLE WASHINGTON
Washington, Virginia

I don't think I'd bother with anything but water. I'd regard it as a great cleansing, to rise above food. Why would I want food on a desert island? To survive? Why would I want to survive on a desert island? I just find being thirsty rather unpleasant. I think I would fast and die. And transcend. Certainly one wouldn't want to cook, for God's sake! For myself?! I can't relate to that.

I think I'd be perfectly content eating raw food, and foraging, or whatever. I think there's going to be much learned in the next hundred years about why we do what we do to food even though very often it's unnecessary. Why we cook food, why we replicate tastes from childhood, why we go through the whole process when raw food would be fine. Obviously, it's doing it for others. It's doing it to express love and coddling and all of this. But it isn't something that I would ever feel I needed to do for myself. I'm looking to get beyond it.

I recognize that food is a focus—it's a way of manipulating and controlling people into a sort of heightened state and it's a vehicle that provides them with a connection. And it is powerful. But there's a dimension and a level beyond it. There's sort of a high without it. And even fasting is a fabulous high. But food is a fabulous anchor, too—food, and working with food. And that's what it's done for me, as a person—it's kept me from flying off. Or being shot down.

What on earth do people say they'd bring to a desert island? Butter? Olive oil?

I would welcome the experience of starting fresh—of going to a desert island not having any idea of what was there, and looking upon it as dropping all the old baggage and developing an entirely new palate and new mode of survival.

Bradley Ogden

LARK CREEK INN
ONE MARKET RESTAURANT
San Francisco, California

INGREDIENTS:

1. **Corn.** There's nothing better than fresh corn, right off the stalk. I still remember sitting in a corn patch on my grandmother's farm, eating it right off the stalk.

2. **Tomatoes.** There's nothing better than vine-ripened tomatoes, with a sprinkle of salt. When I was growing up, we used to eat them in movie theatres. (See Bradley Ogden's recipe for Chilled Fresh Tomato Soup on page 349.)

3. **Beluga caviar.** I love it with warm blinis.

4. *Fraises des bois* **(wild strawberries).** Right off the vine, they have the most intense flavor.

5. **Lobster.** Maine lobster, right out of the water.

6. **Free-range chicken.**

7. **Basil.** If I had to go to sleep with an herb, this is the one. It's my favorite to cook with.

8. **Chiles.** They enhance and add spice and life to ingredients.

9. **Artichokes.** They're one of my favorite vegetables; I use them with almost anything.

10. **Balsamic vinegar.** It's my all-time favorite vinegar. I've been accused of carrying around a bottle in my back pocket.

Ogden balks at not being able to also take along apples, blueberries, cherries, musk melons, and morels: "When they're in season, there's nothing better!"

TECHNIQUES:

1. **Spit-roasting.** It's a clean way of cooking.

2. **Grilling.** You don't have to use a lot of fat, and you can get things crisp on the outside.

3. **Steaming.** It allows you to retain all the nutrients and depth of color.

Chilled Fresh Tomato Soup with Pepper Relish

by Bradley Ogden

SERVES 4 – 6

2 pounds firm, ripe tomatoes

1/4 cup minced red onion

1/4 cup minced yellow bell pepper

1 tablespoon chopped fresh basil

2 teaspoons balsamic vinegar

2 tablespoons extra virgin olive oil

1 teaspoon kosher salt

1/4 teaspoon fresh cracked black pepper

1. Cut the tomatoes into 1-inch chunks. Purée them through the fine blade of a food mill to extract the juice and pulp and leave the skins and seeds behind. (A food processor or blender should not be used for this step as too much air is incorporated into the purée.) Cover the purée tightly and refrigerate for 2 hours.

2. Just before serving, mince the red onion and yellow bell pepper and chop the fresh basil. Toss together in a small bowl. Stir the balsamic vinegar, olive oil, salt, and pepper into the chilled tomato purée. Adjust the seasoning with more vinegar, olive oil, salt, and pepper if necessary.

3. Serve the soup in chilled soup bowls and place a heaping tablespoon of the relish in the center of each bowl.

Jean-Louis Palladin

INGREDIENTS:

1. **Poultry.** I'd bring duck.

2. *Foie gras.* I'm addicted to *foie gras.* (See Jean-Louis Palladin's *foie gras* recipe on pages 351–352.)

3. **Bananas.** They give you strength.

4. **Salt.** I'm nuts about salt.

5. **Spices and herbs.** I like *verveine* (verbena) so much that I named my daughter after it.

6. **Olives.** Likewise, I named my son Oliver.

7. **Wine.** When I smell it, it's so fantastic...

8. **Grappa or Armagnac.**

9. **Dried cod.**

10. **Water.** I'm addicted to water—I drink four or five liters of Evian a day!

TECHNIQUES:

1. **Grilling in a fireplace.** I've done it all my life.

2. **Braising in the oven.** In the winter...

3. **Sautéeing.** It gives food a nice color—and I like having a crispy top and a moist bottom.

Palladin also admits to loving *pot au feu*—"things that are cooked a l-o-n-g time." He'd also want to bring a Cuisinart and a blender. "I love making concoctions of herbs, when the raw juice tastes just of the herb. You can use herb juices for so many things." A cooking technique he could do without? "Poaching—I hate it when the food disintegrates into the liquid."

Braised *Foie Gras* with Rhubarb

by Jean-Louis Palladin

SERVES 4

Sauce

1/2 cup sugar

twelve 1/2 ounces trimmed rhubarb stalks (seven 5 1/2-inch stalks)

1 cup meat or vegetable consommé (preferred) or meat or vegetable stock (liquid and clear broth)

1/4 cup unpeeled chopped carrots

2 tablespoons chopped celery

2 tablespoons of chopped leeks (mostly white part)

1 tablespoon chopped onion

2 tablespoons unpeeled chopped turnips

1 tablespoon chopped shallots

1 cup of *fond de veau* (veal stock—thick in consistency)*

About 4 to 6 tablespoons braising liquid
(reserved from braising *foie gras*)

1 whole fresh uncooked duck or goose *foie gras* (Grade A; about 1 pound)

fine sea salt and freshly ground black pepper

Braised bed

1 cup unpeeled chopped carrots

1/2 cup chopped celery

1/2 cup chopped leeks (mostly white part)

1/2 cup chopped onions

1/2 cup chopped unpeeled chopped turnips

1/4 cup chopped shallots

10 very leafy thyme sprigs

3 medium-size bay leaves

1 teaspoon fine sea salt

1 teaspoon whole black peppercorns

2 tablespoons vegetable oil

1/2 cup meat or vegetable consommé (preferrred)
or meat or vegetable stock

1 cup of port wine

(continued on next page)

---

* *Fond de veau* is made from a reduction of the feet of veal, tomato paste, vegetables, and water. It is thick in consistency, compared with the consommé. The *fond de veau* is used to finish the sauce.

(continued from preceding page)   *Start the sauce*

Place the sugar in a heavy 4-quart saucepan and cook over high heat until a rich caramel color, 3 to 4 min-utes, stirring almost constantly with a wooden spoon; be careful not to let it burn. Add the rhubarb, stir-ring until pieces are well coated, then promptly add the consommé (not *fond de veau*), carrots, celery, leeks, onions, turnips, and shallots; cook until mixture reduces to about 1 cup, about 20 minutes, stirring occa-sionally. Remove from heat and strain through chinois, using the bottom of a sturdy ladle to force as much through as possible. Return to saucepan and cook over medium heat until reduced to 1/2 cup, about 15 min-utes, and set aside. (This may be done up to two days ahead; keep refrigerated.)

To finish the dish

Heat oven to 350°. With a sharp thin-bladed knife, carefully trim away any green spots on the *foie gras* caused by contact with the gall bladder. Season both sides of the *foie gras* very generously with salt and pep-per; set aside.

In a medium sized bowl, combine all the ingredients for this braising bed. Place the oil in a heavy 13 x 9-inch roasting pan and heat over high heat on top of the stove about 1 minute. Add the braising-bed mixture and sauté until it starts to brown, about 10 minutes, stirring frequently. Add the consommé and continue cooking and stirring about 3 minutes more, then mound the vegetables in the center of the pan and place the *foie gras* on top. Remove from heat and seal pan with aluminum foil, pierce foil 2 or 3 times with the tip of a pointed knife so steam can escape during cooking. Bake in the preheated oven for 8 minutes; then momentarily remove pan from the oven, uncover, and turn *foie gras* over with two sturdy rubber spatulas to prevent marring the *foie gras*'s smooth surface, being very careful to keep it intact. Cover the pan and continue baking until done, about 10 minutes more; **do not overcook,** or the *foie gras* will lose its unique buttery texture. (To test doneness, pierce *foie gras* with a thin wood or metal skewer; then press very gently around skewer hole. If juices run slightly pink, not clear and not bloody, it's done.) Transfer *foie gras* to a plate and cover loosely with foil to keep warm while finishing the sauce.

To finish the sauce, place the roasting pan with the braising liquid and vegetables in it over high heat on top of the stove and bring to a boil. Add the port and return to a boil; then continue boiling until liquid reduced to about 2/3 cup, about 8 minutes more, stirring occasionally. Strain braising liquid through the chinois into a bowl, using the bottom of a sturdy ladle to force as much through as possible. Skim all fat from surface and add remaining liquid to the reserved rhubarb sauce. Reheat sauce and, if needed, let it reduce to a thin sauce consistency. Season to taste with salt and pepper and serve immediately

To serve

Cut the *foie gras* crosswise into 1-inch-thick slices on the diagonal. Spoon 2 to 3 tablespoons sauce on each heated serving plate and arrange a slice of *foie gras* on top of sauce.

Charlie Palmer

AUREOLE
New York, New York

INGREDENTS:

1. **Fish, specifically tuna.** It's very universal. You can do a lot of different stuff with tuna.

2. **Guinea fowl.** Again, it's universal—and I'd get tired of eating chicken.

3. **Potatoes.** I could live without rice or pasta, but not without potatoes.

4. **Artichokes.** There's a lot you can do with them—serve them with a vinaigrette, or braised in broth with beans, or roasted, or marinated. And their flavor's great—they're almost sweet.

5. **Butter.** From Egg Farm Dairy [the dairy in which Palmer is a partner], of course.

6. **Spinach.** It's versatile—I like it raw and cooked.

7. **Chives.** I'm crazy about chives.

8. **Eggs.** It would be hard to live without eggs.

9. **Apples.** I could do without them, but I'd have to have apples for my two sons, who love them.

10. *Foie gras.* Every time Alicia [Palmer's wife] has *foie gras*, it puts her in a good mood.

Charlie Palmer comments, "I could make salt from the ocean, so I wouldn't have to bring it. The island would probably have coconuts, so I could get milk from them. And there'd probably be some source of sugar."

François Payard

RESTAURANT DANIEL
New York, New York

MAKING DESSERTS ON A DESERT ISLAND

INGREDIENTS:

1. **Meyer lemons.** They're amazing to eat whole, skin and everything!

2. **Dark chocolate.** Chocolate that's about 60–70 percent cocoa—not extra-bitter [over 70 percent]. (See François Payard's Warm Chocolate Soufflé recipe on page 355.)

3. **Coffee.** I drink about ten to twelve cups a day.

4. **Nuts.** I love pistachio nuts and macadamia nuts, which we don't use in France.

5. **Red wine.** A Burgundy or Bordeaux—I've only started to love white wine.

6. **Armagnac.** My grandfather used to eat prunes soaked in Armagnac.

7. **Cognac.**

8. **Black figs.** I prefer them to green figs.

9. **Strawberries.**

10. **Raspberries.** I love berries!

Warm Chocolate Soufflé

by François Payard

10 INDIVIDUAL SOUFFLÉS

10 ounces sweet butter

7 egg yolks

6 ounces granulated sugar

12 ounces extra bitter chocolate, cut in small pieces

7 egg whites

juice of 1/2 lemon

1 ounce granulated sugar

ten individual soufflé cups, prebuttered and dusted with sugar

1. In a small pot over medium heat, melt butter and keep warm on the side. In a bowl, whip firmly the egg yolks and the 6 ounces of sugar until it becomes whiter and foamier (about 6 minutes). Pour hot butter over the chocolate, mix well with a whip until chocolate is melted and then blend with the yolks and sugar mix.

2. Whip 7 egg whites with the lemon juice. When they become stiff, add 1 ounce of sugar. Whip for a few more minutes and then incorporate the chocolate and yolk mixture into the whipped egg whites. Gently fold the two together with a spatula to keep the preparation light and foamy. Transfer the mix into the cups.

3. Preheat the oven to 350°. Place the cups in a pan of water and cook for 5 to 6 minutes. Remove and unmold onto the serving plate. The soufflés can be served with whipped cream or ice cream on the side.

Mark Peel

CAMPANILE
Los Angeles, California

INGREDIENTS:

1. **Salt.**

2. **Bread.** [After first saying, "Definitely salt and pepper—you need some seasoning," Mark later gave up pepper in order to bring bread.]

3. **Greens.** Everything from spinach to arugula to collard greens—I love their flavor, their bitterness, the sharpness you get from their acid. In a diet, you need their vitamins and fiber.

4. **Olive oil.**

5. **Potatoes.**

6. **Lemons.** I'd take lemons over balsamic vinegar. Lemon is such a basic flavor, and is so versatile; you can use it on a salad, on a piece of chicken, on fish.

7. **Chicken.** I love its versatility. And it's great roasted with a crispy skin! (See Mark Peel's recipe for Herbed Baby Chicken on pages 357–358.)

8. **Thyme.** I love thyme. It's not an esoteric herb. It's universal. It seems to enhance the flavor of just about everything—any dish, except for dessert: fish, chicken, meat, pastas, polentas.

9. **Onions.** [Again, Mark eliminated his original choice of chocolate in order to bring onions.] You have to have onions!

10. **Red wine.**

"Remember, you're on a desert island, so you're going to have salt available because it's in the sea," Mark comments. "And presumably you can get fish."

TECHNIQUES:

1. **Grilling.**

2. **Roasting.** I like the flavor of grilling and roasting. There are some things that lend themselves to grilling, like grilled whole fish, and others that lend themselves to roasting, like roasted chicken.

3. **Steaming.** It's a gentler method of cooking that's perfect for fish, vegetables, potatoes.

Herbed Baby Chicken *(Poussin)* with Lemon-Thyme Butter

by Mark Peel

SERVES 4

This recipe came about backwards. I had a wonderful, crisp, buttery potato galette and wanted a tender and flavorful chicken dish to complement it. A *poussin* (a six-week-old chicken) has the tender texture that I want for this dish, but it isn't all that full-flavored, so a quick splash of lemon thyme butter is tossed on to add an intense accent. To butterfly the chickens, the backbone must removed, but with a little practice, it isn't a difficult procedure.

Herbed Baby Chicken

4 baby chickens, about 1 pound each

1/4 cup extra virgin olive oil

3 tablespoons chopped fresh herbs (parsley and thyme)

kosher salt

freshly ground black pepper

Lemon Thyme Butter

6 tablespoons (3 ounces) butter

2 large garlic cloves, peeled and chopped (2 tablespoons)

zest of 1 medium lemon, finely chopped

2 tablespoon fresh lemon thyme leaves

kosher salt

freshly ground black pepper

2 tablespoons fresh lemon juice

(continued on next page)

(continued from previous page)

1. Using a large, very sharp knife, remove the backbones and ribs from the chickens. Place each chicken breast side up on a cutting board; insert the tip of the knife into the cavity as far as it will go. Line the knife blade up parallel to the backbone and cut through the ribs on both sides of the backbone. Remove and discard the backbones of all the chickens. Spread each chicken out on the cutting board, and press down on each in turn with the heel of your hand, until the breastbone cracks, and the chicken will lie flat. Turn each chicken over and, using your fingers, pull out and discard the ribs.

2. In a large mixing bowl, marinate the chickens, refrigerated, with the olive oil and the chopped herbs for 2 to 3 hours. Remove the chickens from the refrigerator about 15 minutes before cooking. Just prior to cooking, season the chickens lightly with kosher salt and black pepper.

3. Start a fire in the grill and allow it to burn to medium-high temperature.

4. Grill the chickens skin-side down until the skin is browned and crispy, almost charred, about 6 to 8 minutes. Turn the chickens and place them on a part of the grill that gives off only a moderate amount of heat, so as not to burn them. Continue to grill the chickens until they are firm to the touch all the way through, about 15 to 20 minutes longer. When the thigh is pierced and the juices run clear, the chicken is done.

5. In a cast-iron skillet melt the butter over medium heat. When the butter begins to sizzle and foam, just before it browns, stir in the garlic and lemon zest, remove the pan from the heat, add the lemon thyme, and swirl briefly. Correct the seasoning to taste with kosher salt, black pepper, and up to 2 tablespoons of fresh lemon juice.

6. To serve, put one chicken, skin side up, on each plate and splash a little lemon thyme butter over the chicken, and serve immediately with potato galettes.

Michael Romano

UNION SQUARE CAFE
New York, New York

INGREDIENTS:

1. **Olive oil.** It's what greases good cooking. You can take a can of mediocre soup, drizzle it with olive oil, and it becomes a wonderful thing.

2. **Bread.** I have a hard time eating without bread near me—it's so basic.

3. **Tomatoes.** Only in the summer months.

4. **Eggplant.** It's close to home for me, and it's like meat in terms of what you can do with it.

5. **Bitter greens—chard, dandelion, kale, mustard.** I eat them daily. They're like a tonic—they make me feel so good.

6. **Wine.** Both my grandfathers made their own wine, so we grew up with it as a part of our life. It's a miraculous thing—it's incredible what can be made from grapes!

7. **Lentils.** There are so many different ones.

8. **Salt—kosher or sea salt.** Table salt has a sharp, stinging, acrid taste.

9. **Pepper.** I love what it does for food, the warmth it brings.

10. **Arborio rice.** (Romano first chose basmati rice, then switched when he realized he couldn't make a menu with the other ingredients.) Basic to any cuisine is some sort of starch and protein. And I'd choose rice over potatoes. (See Michael Romano's recipe for Risotto d'Oro on pages 360–361.)

Romano said, "I would give up all manner of meats and fish before I'd give up vegetables." And he appeared heart-broken when he realized he'd omitted garlic from his list. He also wished aloud to have taken herbs like basil, chervil, parsley, and tarragon, and spices like black cumin, cardamom, and nutmeg.

TECHNIQUES:

1. **Sautéeing.** It's the quickest way to combine ingredients, heat them through, and get them on a plate quickly without altering them too much.

2. **Deep-fat frying.** It has a homey kind of feeling, yet done correctly, it can be exquisite for things like calamari, potatoes, fritters.

3. **Braising.** It's homey. It harkens back to a time when people cooked with less expensive types of meat.

Risotto d'Oro

by Michael Romano

SERVES 4–6

This golden-colored risotto looks convincingly like *risotto alla Milanese*, the saffron-infused Lombardy classic. But appearance is where the similarity ends. Substituting fresh carrot and celery juices for the standard chicken stock adds a gentle sweetness to this summery, all-vegetable risotto. A vegetable juicer makes this recipe convenient to prepare, but fresh vegetable juices are widely available in health food stores. Choose a white wine with lots of fruit to stand up to the sweetness of the carrot and celery juices. Ripe Chardonnays from Australia and California will do the trick.

3 cups carrot juice

3 cups celery juice

1/4 cup olive oil

1 3/4 cups arborio rice

1/2 teaspoon minced garlic

1/2 cup white wine

1/2 cup peeled, split lengthwise, and sliced carrots

1/2 cup 1-inch pieces green beans

1/2 cup split lengthwise and sliced zucchini

1/2 cup 1/2-inch pieces of asparagus, tough ends discarded

1/2 cup sliced red bell pepper

1/2 cup fresh shelled peas

1/3 cup sliced scallions

4 tablespoons butter

3/4 cup finely grated Parmigiano-Reggiano

1 teaspoon kosher salt

1/8 teaspoon freshly ground black pepper

1 tablespoon chopped parsley

1. In a saucepan, combine the carrot and celery juices and bring to a simmer.

2. In a 3-quart skillet heat the olive oil over medium heat. Add the rice and garlic and stir together until the rice is coated with the oil. Add the white wine and bring to a boil, stirring constantly until the wine is absorbed by the rice. Add the carrots and the green beans to rice.

3. Ladle 1/2 cup of the hot juice mixture into the saucepan and stir until it is absorbed. Continue with the rest of the juice, adding more liquid. The constant stirring allows the rice to release its starch into the cooking liquid, resulting in the characteristic risotto creaminess. When 3/4 of the juice has been used, about 15 to 20 minutes, stir in the remaining vegetables. Continue ladling and stirring in the remaining juice, about 10 additional minutes. The grains of rice should be *al dente*.

4. Swirl in the butter, 3/4 of the Parmigiano, and season with the salt and pepper. Serve the risotto sprinkled with parsley and the remaining Parmigiano.

Anne Rosenzweig

ARCADIA and THE LOBSTER CLUB
New York, New York

INGREDIENTS:

1. **Chocolate-covered pretzels.** It's the perfect food—yin and yang, sweet and salty, crunchy and creamy—all at once.

2. **Milk.** It's the perfect drink with the perfect food.

3. **Butter.** Why? I'm the butter queen of New York. It's an essential thing for good cooking.

4. **Kasha.** From my roots—it's a homey, ethnic thing.

5. **Onions.** Like butter, it's a basic, essential ingredient—and there are lots of ways to eat them. You can use them for flavor, or as a vegetable.

6. **Lobster.** It's my favorite protein right now.

7. **Corn.** I just had some roasted corn at a street fair, and it was great!

8. **Pasta.** Eventually you'll get tired of everything else, and you can have it with just butter.

9. **Tomatoes.** I'll need some vegetables, and these are healthy and good.

10. **Steak.** It's my second-favorite protein.

Rosenzweig said she's sneak along some salt and pepper, too—"hidden in my onions!"

TECHNIQUES:

1. **Sautéeing.** It's the most fun, and you can use a lot of finesse. It's very immediate.

2. **Roasting.** It's a technique that brings out flavors.

3. **Grilling.** It's easy, and it's fun.

Chris Schlesinger

THE EAST COAST GRILL
Cambridge, Massachusetts

INGREDIENTS:

1. **Salt.** You can't make food taste good without salt.

2. **Pepper.** I love pepper—salt, pepper, and ginger make things taste good.

3. **Lime juice.**

4. **Hot sauce.** I like it to spice up food—I'm not really impressed with subtlety in food. I'd take El Yucateco [hot sauce].

5. **Bacon.** I could make a salad with the bacon fat and lime juice—and some tomatoes.

6. **Greens.** I like leafy greens, like baby collards and kale. I use it as lettuce as well as in cooking.

7. **Ginger.** It's a nice, fresh spice.

8. **Oysters.** It's my favorite type of seafood. I like the East Coast variety, which are salty and briny, as opposed to West Coast oysters, which are more subtle.

9. **Tomatoes.** I like really nice, fresh tomatoes. I'd make a salad to go with the oysters.

10. **Sweet potatoes.** They're versatile and tasty, and you need a starch to balance dinner.

Schlesinger also commented that if he caught, for example, a beautiful striped bass out of the ocean, "It's good to just cook that with salt and pepper and put a little bit of lime on it. A lot of food is good just as food; we're not obligated to do a lot to it. And if I had fish, I'd wish I had some mangoes, which are my favorite fruit, to go with it."

TECHNIQUES:

1. **Grilling/spit-roasting.** I love it. To me, grilling means cooking. I love the connection to live fire. Escoffier defines grilling as "the remote starting point of our art."

2. **Deep-fat frying.** I love fried food—especially the crispy crunchiness of it.

3. Chris pleaded for an eleventh ingredient when he realized he hadn't brought **beer,** and offered to trade in his third technique: "Any kind of cold beer—but preferably Samuel Adams."

(See Chris Schlesinger's recipes on pages 364–365.)

Stranded on a Desert Island Menu

by Chris Schlesinger

Buttermilk-Fried Oysters with Chili-Ginger Sauce
Wilted Greens with Smoked Tomato, Bacon Bits, and Lime Dressing
Ash-Roasted Sweet Potatoes
Beers

Buttermilk-Fried Oysters

SERVES 4 GENEROUSLY

(Do you really think that you want less than half a dozen of these babies? I don't think so!!!)

2 cups yellow cornmeal

1 tablespoon cayenne

salt and pepper

2 dozen oysters, shucked

buttermilk, to cover

1. Have deep-fat fryer ready to go at 350°.

2. Mix cornmeal with cayenne and liberal amounts of salt and pepper to taste.

3. Soak oysters in buttermilk for 1 minute.

4. Dredge in cornmeal mixture.

5. Put in basket and fry for about 3 minutes or until the oysters turn a toasty color.

6. Eat immediately.

Chili-Ginger Sauce

YIELD: 1 CUP

1/2 cup red wine vinegar

juice of 3 limes

1 tablespoon fresh hot pepper (your choice), finely chopped

1 tablespoon fresh ginger, minced

2 tomatoes, finely chopped

Cook all ingredients over low flame for 5 minutes. Let cool.

Wilted Greens with Smoked Tomato, Bacon Bits, and Lime Dressing

1/2 cup bacon bits (fry 'em up)

juice of 2 limes mixed with a little leftover bacon fat

salt and pepper to taste

1 head washed chicory

1 head washed kale

6 plum tomatoes, smoked over low fire on grill and cooled

Heat bacon fat with lime juice, salt, and pepper. Toss hot dressing over washed greens and toss greens until slightly wilted. Serve with smoked tomatoes and bacon bits.

Ash-Roasted Sweet Potatoes

4 sweet potatoes, washed and wrapped in foil

Place potatoes in coals and cook until they are soft. Cut up large or mash to eat.

Jimmy Schmidt

THE RATTLESNAKE CLUB
Detroit, Michigan

INGREDIENTS:

1. **Chile seeds.** Chiles are really adaptive; you can use them for coloration, heat, spiciness. You can consume them fresh or dried. With the peppers, you wouldn't need as much salt in the food—and I hate bland food.

2. **Grape seeds.** You've got to have wine. While you'd have to find a variety that would do well in that climate, I love pinot noir. You can make white or red from pinot noir pretty effectively. And at the second dosage, you could ferment it and have Champagne!

3. **Wheat.** Obviously, you'd need wheat for breadmaking, and pasta. I think that's a very important staple.

4. **Corn.** I love corn—you have to love corn if you grow up in Illinois. Corn's a good storage food; it grows really quickly, and it's very high yield. And you can roast it, boil it, bake it—you can do a hundred different things to it.

5. **Tomatoes.** They're very adaptable—you can make a sauce out of them, you can eat them raw, you can dry them and put them into salads and sauces. They've got good, high acid.

6. **Potatoes.** They're a great staple. You can mash them, you can use potato starch for thickening, you can make gratins, or fry them—you can do tons of different things to them.

7. **Citrus—limes.** For vitamin C. I like them all, but I'd probably take limes. I think they're the most adaptive for being blended with other things. I like limes better than lemons, and I think they go better with the chiles. They add a characteristic that is beyond citrus itself. Oranges are not that concentrated, which is why I passed over them.

8. **Spinach.** You could use it as a salad or as a vegetable, or for fillings in ravioli, or for soups. And I love spinach. It's got lots of iron. And it grows very quickly.

9. **Garlic.** I've got to have garlic. Besides that, it's good for you. It's a great flavor enhancer on anything that you use. It's also very stable. And it protects you from vampires!

10. **Basil.** It's a good overall herb. I wouldn't say that it's my favorite—I like cilantro, I like thyme and rosemary, I love savory—I love them all. But you can turn basil into a sauce, whereas you can't really with the other herbs.

"What's on the island?" Schmidt asked. "You could get salt from the water, so that takes care of salt. And you could get fish from the ocean. Since I grew up on a farm, I'm covering all my bases first. I use more spices than I do herbs. And I love coriander, even though I don't have it on my list."

TECHNIQUES:

1. **Grilling.** It's good for flavor development. You get a lot of flavor off the wood on what you're grilling. It's adaptable to meat, fish, and vegetables.

2. **Baking** (so I can sneak **roasting** in). For breads. And high-temperature roasting of meats and larger fish.

3. **Cooking in a pan (sautéeing/boiling).** I do like the high-temperature effects of searing things, being able to affix spices and such to the flesh of a fish.

Dieter Schorner

MAKING DESSERTS ON A DESERT ISLAND

INGREDIENTS:

1. **Seltzer water.**

2. **Eggs.**

3. **A good Cognac.**

4. **Flour.**

5. **Sugar.**

6. **Flavorings.** I'd bring lemons and vanilla beans—and marjoram! I especially love marjoram on potatoes.

7. **Apples.** I could survive on apples alone. I love apples! There's nothing more universal.

8. **Cinnamon.**

9. **Hazelnuts.** I like them more than almonds—they have a stronger flavor, especially when they're roasted, when their smell and taste become so robust!

10. **Chocolate.** Semi-sweet.

"I wouldn't need butter—I'd get coconut oil from the coconuts," Schorner says.

Lindsey Shere

CHEZ PANISSE
Berkeley, California

INGREDIENTS:

1. **Sheep.** For cheese and meat.

2. **Wheat.** It's a staple of one's diet—I could never live without bread or cereal.

3. **Corn.** I'm an Italian, and I like my polenta.

4. & 5. **Apple tree and pear tree.** I love them both. And they're constantly usable; I could eat the fruit fresh, or cooked, or even make liqueur from them.

6. **Grapes.** To have wine.

7. **A pig.** I love pork.

8. **Salad greens.** A variety, or any kind.

9. **Chickens.** I love eggs.

10. **An orange or tangerine tree.** It's a flavor I really love a lot.

When reminded that she could bring along seasonings, Shere responded, "I don't need seasonings. If you have something that's wonderful, you don't need to do a lot to it."

TECHNIQUES:

1. **Baking.** How could you have bread if you couldn't bake, not to mention the occasional apple tart, fruit crisp, and cake?

2. **Stovetop pot-cooking.** I'd want to be able to make custards and soups and stocks.

3. **Cooking over fire coals.** For variety and flavor—and there are times that it's just too hot to cook inside!

Lydia Shire

BIBA and PIGNOLI
Boston, Massachusetts

INGREDIENTS:

1. **Garlic.** I love garlic. It's my favorite thing in the world. (See Lydia Shire's recipe for Crab Fideos with Broken Garlic Oil on pages 371–372, which she characterizes as "major garlic!")

2. **Olive oil.** Garlic and olive oil go hand in hand.

3. **Salt.** I cannot eat food without salt—it has zero flavor. Salt might actually be my number one choice.

4. **Bacon.** I love good bacon. I love fat.

5. **Pasta.** Spaghetti goes great with olive oil and garlic—it's my comfort food.

6. **Mayonnaise.** I'm a closet mayonnaise eater. I can eat mayonnaise sandwiches.

7. **Spinach.** I crave spinach.

8. **Broccoli rabe.** I crave greens—I love their bitterness.

9. **Lemons.** I use lemons like salt—as a flavor enhancer.

10. **Beef.** To have a great steak, with fat—nothing else quite does it for me.

If given a bonus ingredient, Shire says she'd bring caramel sauce.

TECHNIQUES:

1. **Sautéeing.** It's a great, quick method of cooking that intensifies the flavor on the seared side.

2. **Frying.** What's better than a perfect fried clam in the summer?

3. **Roasting.** The smell of a chicken roasting in your house is one of the top smells in the world.

While Shire says she also loves the charcoal flavor imparted by grilling, she admits, "I'm not much of a steaming person."

Crab Fideos with Broken Garlic Oil

by Lydia Shire

1 cup olive oil, pure

3 live rock crabs, quartered with cleaver. Save all liquid. Discard head sac.

2 heads garlic, crushed with most skins removed

1/2 bottle white wine

6 ripe roma tomatoes or 1 pint cherry tomatoes, chopped

1 bunch scallions, chopped

1 cup celery leaves

parsley stalks, fennel fronds

rind of 1 orange

pinch of saffron

sprigs of fresh thyme and 1 bay leaf

2 tablespoons canned crushed tomato

salt, pepper, cayenne

lemon juice

1 pound Goya fideos (vermicelli-type noodles)

1 pound fresh crab meat

1. In a large stock pot pour in 1/2 cup olive oil. Heat to smoking and drop in 1/2 of the crab bodies. Do not shake pan. When browned, remove and brown the second half. Add 1/4 cup more oil to pan and sauté the crushed garlic heads until lightly golden. Return crab bodies to pan, deglaze with white wine. Add enough water (1 quart) to cover crabs and add remaining ingredients except for salt, pepper, and lemon juice.

2. Simmer slowly for 1 hour skimming any froth off surface. Add 2 tablespoons crushed tomatoes. Shake the crabs to get the tomalley (liver) into the stock. Strain through a China cap pressing down on vegetables. Season with salt, pepper, cayenne, and lemon juice.

(continued on next page)

(continued from previous page)

3. Break 1 pound Goya fideos into approximately 1- to 2-inch pieces. Toss in 1/4 cup olive oil and bake in 350° oven until lightly golden. This should take 5 to 8 minutes. Be careful not to let the noodles get too brown.

4. Boil fideos in crab stock until *al dente*. Drain in colander. Set over bowl. Reduce 4 cups of liquid to 1 cup. Reserve.

5. Rub a shallow casserole dish with a cut clove of garlic and butter lightly. Arrange the cooked noodles tossed with the picked-over crab meat to a depth of 1 inch. You may need two casseroles. It is important that the noodles only be 1 inch high.

6. Drizzle the noodles with the reserved cup of stock and bake in a 400° oven until the top is crispy and the stock absorbed.

7. The beauty of this dish is the contrast of the crisp noodles on top, and the soft and somewhat dry underneath.

8. Pass the broken garlic oil separately, as your guests will want different amounts.

Broken Garlic Oil

1 ancho chile

8 cloves garlic, peeled

1 cup good Spanish extra virgin olive oil

1 teaspoon salt

2 teaspoons cracked black pepper

In 3 tablespoons of water, steam the ancho chile in a covered sauté pan for 5 minutes till tender. Remove excess water, add oil and 1/2 of the garlic. Cover pan and roast slowly for 45 minutes. Remove garlic and chile. Place in food processor and chop till coarsely puréed. Slowly drizzle oil into the machine till well mixed. Remove into bowl. Take remaining garlic and begin chopping with a knife. Add salt and mash it with your knife into the garlic. Go back and forth over the garlic in a circular motion. Add salt, garlic and cracked black pepper.

Nancy Silverton

CAMPANILE
Loss Angeles, California

INGREDIENTS:

1. **Salt.**

2. **Pepper.** I really think that, to make something good, you don't need anything more than a good ingredient and salt and pepper.

3. **Arugula.**

4. **Potatoes.**

5. **Olive oil.**

6. **Bread.** [Silverton gave up her original choice of balsamic vinegar in order to bring bread.]

7. **Parmesan cheese.** Everything about a baked potato, olive oil, Parmesan, and arugula with salt and pepper is so satisfying that I always say I could eat this every day for the rest of my life.

8. **Dried pasta.** I love dried pasta. I love the texture, the toothiness. I love fresh ravioli, but too many times fresh pasta is gummy. It's not always a benefit to make it fresh.

9. **Coffee.** I have to have coffee. (See Nancy Silverton's recipe for Coffee Ice Cream on page 374.)

10. **Red wine.** I need red wine.

Silverton asked, "Is it a Hawaiian island? Do I have to bring sugar, or is there sugar cane there?"

TECHNIQUES:

1. **Sautéeing.** It's very quick and it's very simple—and the results can be delicious.

2. **Boiling.** I love pasta—and coffee.

3. **Braising.** I love the cuts of meat that lend themselves to being braised, and the results.

"I can easily live without deep frying. Grilling is nice, but I don't have to have it. And I could easily live without sweets. For obvious reasons, I love baking because of what I do—but not necessarily because of what I eat."

Coffee Ice Cream

by Nancy Silverton

YIELDS 1 QUART

A coffee flavor at the end of a meal can be doubly pleasing; it can satisfy the desire for both coffee and dessert. Our coffee ice cream has an intense coffee flavor, much more so than traditional coffee ice cream because we use no eggs and less cream. It may not be quite as smooth, but I find it more refreshing.

Crush the coffee beans with a rolling pin or with the back of a pan. Do not use a grinder or food processor because the resulting grind is too small and it causes the ice cream to take on an unpleasant gray color. I find that decaffeinated beans produce a smoother ice cream than regular coffee beans.

4 1/2 cups whole (4%) milk

1 1/2 cups heavy cream

1/2 cup plus 1 tablespoon granulated sugar

1 1/2 tablespoons corn syrup

1/2 cup decaffeinated coffee beans, espresso roast, crushed

1 1/2 teaspoons coffee extract or instant espresso

1. In a medium saucepan over medium heat, bring the milk, cream, granulated sugar, corn syrup, and coffee beans to a boil. Boil gently, stirring continuously using a rubber spatula, reducing until the mixture has thickened very slightly, about 20 to 25 minutes with sufficient body to provide an enveloping richness, as opposed to a watery milkiness, in your mouth.

2. Remove the saucepan from the heat, add the coffee extract or instant espresso, and mix just to combine. Using a fine mesh stainless steel strainer, strain the mixture into a large mixing bowl and allow to cool at least 15 minutes, then refrigerate for at least 30 minutes. Discard the coffee beans.

3. Remove the mixture from the refrigerator. If a skin has formed on the cream, simply stir it back into the mixture. Pour the cooled cream mixture into the container of an ice cream freezer. Freeze according to the manufacturer's instructions. Reserve the ice cream in the ice cream machine container until needed.

4. Serve the ice cream within 1 or 2 hours of freezing, as personally made ice cream does not keep well in the freezer—it becomes too hard and grainy.

Joachim Splichal

PATINA
Los Angeles, California

INGREDIENTS:

1. **Potatoes.** You can do so many different things with potatoes: stuff them, fill them, make them into canneloni, layer cake, even ice cream. They work well in salads, roasted, mashed, or whole with caviar. (See Joachim Splichal's recipe for Potato Lasagna on pages 376–377.)

2. **Olive oil.** I like to cook with olive oil.

3. **Skate.** I only eat it once in a while, when I'm craving it. I like its texture and flavor, especially with brown butter and capers.

4. **Peppercorns.**

5. **Chicken.** You have to eat something.

6. **Chocolate.** To make a great chocolate sauce.

7. **Sweetbreads.** Even though they're not good for me. I like to eat them just seared, with salt and pepper and flour.

8. **Basil.** I use it steadily on my menu.

9. **Red bell peppers.** I like their flavor, especially when making a coulis. It's a nice taste.

10. **Tomatoes.** I like tomato salad—sliced tomatoes with salt, pepper, olive oil, balsamic vinegar and onion.

TECHNIQUES:

1. **Steaming.** Most of the fish dishes I do are steamed. It keeps their natural flavor.

2. **Braising.** Many cooks don't know how to braise, or what it's all about.

3. **Rotisserie-cooking.** I like it from an aesthetic standpoint—doing a big piece of meat or a suckling pig this way.

Potato and Forest Mushroom Lasagna with Nage Butter Sauce

by Joachim Splichal

I think this dish can challenge any lasagna made from conventional pasta, and the technique of making tender potato sheets is really quite easily mastered once you have done it two or three times. The recipe calls for four different types of mushrooms, but in a pinch you could use 3/4 pound of one kind of mushroom, although, of course the flavor will not be as rich. You could cook the potato layer earlier in the day and leave them, covered with the parchment paper, until just before assembling the dish.

SERVES 4

Potatoes

1/4 cup unsalted butter, melted

salt and freshly ground white pepper

2 large Idaho potatoes, peeled and trimmed into approximately 3-inch by 2-inch blocks
(reserve the trimmings in a bowl of cold water to make mashed potatoes, if desired)

Preheat the oven to 350°. Line 2 baking sheets with parchment paper and brush them with some of the melted butter. Sprinkle a little salt and pepper onto the paper. With a mandoline or a sharp knife, cut the potato blocks carefully crosswise into 1/8-inch-thick rectangles (each potato should yield 9 to 10 slices) and arrange them in a single layer on the baking sheets. Brush the slices well with the butter and sprinkle with a little more salt and pepper. Cover with another sheet of parchment paper and bake for 12 to 15 minutes or until fork-tender. Set aside, on the baking sheets.

Mushrooms

1/4 cup unsalted butter

1 1/4 cups (3 ounces) thinly sliced white mushrooms, stems removed

1 1/4 cups (3 ounces) thinly sliced shiitake mushrooms, stems removed

1 1/4 cups (3 ounces) thinly sliced oyster mushrooms, stems removed

1 1/4 cups (3 ounces) thinly sliced chanterelle or porcini mushrooms, if available

1 large shallot, finely chopped

1 tablespoon finely chopped chives

salt and freshly ground white pepper

1. In a large sauté pan, melt the butter over medium-high heat. When the foam has subsided and the butter is just beginning to turn brown, add the white mushrooms and sauté, stirring, for 1 minute; then add the shiitakes and stir for another minute; finally, add the oysters and chanterelles, if using. Cook the mushrooms until all their liquid has evaporated, about 5 to 6 minutes more. Add the shallot and the chives, stir to mix well, season to taste with salt and white pepper, and remove from the heat.

2. On a baking sheet, make 4 individual lasagnas by layering first a single sheet of potato, then a nice thick layer of the mushroom mixture, then another sheet of potato, and so on. Use 3 layers of mushroom mixture and end with a potato layer. Place the other baking sheet on top of the lasagnas with a weight on it and allow the lasagnas to compress for 1 hour; otherwise, they will tend to fall apart.

Nage Butter Sauce and Assembly

2/3 cup vegetable *nage* (stock)

3/4 cup unsalted butter, at room temperature, cut into 6 equal pieces

salt and white pepper

1 tablespoon finely chopped chives

1 medium plum tomato, peeled, seeded and diced

1. Half an hour before serving, preheat the oven to 350°. When you are ready to finish the dish, bring the vegetable *nage* to a boil in a medium saucepan over medium heat, then reduce the heat to low. Add 2 pieces of butter and stir until melted, then pour the *nage* into a blender. Blend at high speed, removing the lid to add the remaining butter a piece at a time, and blend just until emulsified. Season to taste with salt and white pepper, pour into a glass measuring cup, and skim off any foam that rises to the surface. (Use within half an hour; to reheat, if cold, bring the sauce back to a simmer and blend again for 10 to 15 seconds to reemulsify.) Stir in the chives and diced tomato.

2. Place the lasagna in the oven and reheat until it is warmed through, about 4 to 6 minutes. Using a flat-ended metal spatula, transfer the lasagna to individual heated appetizer plates. Spoon a little of the sauce over and around each one.

Jeremiah Tower

STARS and J.T.'s
San Francisco, California

INGREDIENTS:

1. **Potatoes.** They're so flexible—sugared, with milk, I could even make a dessert of them. And I could make vodka.

2. **Turbot.** It's my favorite fish, and makes a fabulous stock. It's very, very delicate with a very pure taste.

3. **A cow, pregnant with a male calf.** For milk and beef.

4. **Sugar.** I could use it to cure pork and to make rum.

5. **Olives.** I could make olive oil from them and use them for flavoring. I love them—and they're very nutritious.

6. **Seed packet: a Burpee "Grand Slam" cornucopia of seeds.** With seeds for thyme, beans, citrus, tarragon, parsley, lettuces, chile peppers, and some kind of grain (like buckwheat).

7. **Lamb.** It's the meat I can eat the most and not get tired of. Plus I'd have wool and lanolin.

8. **Mangoes.**

9. **Grapes.** I could make wine, and dry them to make raisins. And I could make vinegar.

10. **Pork.** I couldn't live without a pig. I adore ham and bacon and things. (See Jeremiah Tower's recipe for Roast Pork Loin on pages 379–380.)

Tower commented that he could make his own salt.

TECHNIQUES:

1. **Grilling.** Over live fuel—then I could also cook by spit-roasting.

2. **Boiling/poaching.**

3. **Braising.** In a pot in a fire.

Roast Pork Loin Stuffed with Ham and Rosemary

by Jeremiah Tower

I learned from Jane Grigson's excellent book on charcuterie that if you brine pork for a day before cooking it you have a sure way to guarantee moist and very flavorful pork, as long as you do not overcook it. Remember that pork can be very slightly beige-pink and still be safe in terms of trichinosis, the trichinae being killed at a meat internal temperature of 137 degrees. This dish could be served with a warm vegetable stew, roasted peppers, black-eyed peas, or red cabbage salad.

SERVES 5

3 pounds center-cut pork loin

1/4 cup salt

1/4 cup sugar

2 quarts water

2 bay leaves

1 tablespoon allspice berries

1 tablespoon dried thyme

2 cloves garlic, left whole

2 large shallots, finely chopped

3 tablespoons olive oil

1/2 pound country ham or prosciutto, finely chopped

2 tablespoons fresh rosemary leaves, finely chopped

salt and freshly ground pepper

1 cup chicken stock

2 tablespoons Dijon-style mustard

4 tablespoons butter

1. Trim the loin so that there is only 1/4-inch fat on top. Mix the salt, sugar, water, bay leaves, allspice, and thyme in a pan and heat until the salt and sugar are dissolved; let cool. Put the loin in a pan just large enough to hold it and the liquid and pour the brine over the pork. Let marinate overnight or at least 6 hours in the refrigerator.

(continued on next page)

(continued from previous page)

2. When the pork is fully brined, remove it and wipe it dry. With the handle of a wooden spoon or with a round knife-sharpening steel, poke a hole carefully through the very center of the loin.

3. Put the garlic, shallots, 1 tablespoon of the oil, and 1 tablespoon water in a small sauté pan. Cover and sweat over low heat for 10 minutes; do not let the mixture brown. Stir in the ham and half the rosemary. Set aside to cool. When it is cool, push the mixture into the center of the loin so that it is evenly distributed. Mix the remaining oil and rosemary and rub all over the loin. Season and let marinate at room temperature for 2 hours.

4. Heat the oven to 325°.

5. Heat a sauté pan over high heat and sear the loin and brown on all sides, about 5 minutes. Put the loin in a roasting pan just large enough to hold it and cook for 30 minutes. Remove the loin and let it sit for 20 minutes in a warm place, covered with a piece of foil.

6. Pour any fat out of the pan and wipe it gently to remove all the fat. Pour in the stock and reduce it to 1/2 cup, scraping the pan to dissolve any of the browned meat juices. Strain the stock into a saucepan. Whisk in the mustard and the butter until incorporated. Keep the sauce warm.

7. Cut the pork into 1/8-inch slices. Put the slices on hot plates and pour the sauce over them.

Norman Van Aken

NORMAN'S
Coral Gables, Florida

INGREDIENTS:

1. **Plantains.** Plantains were the first fruit I had in Key West that caused me to marvel at this cuisine and to feel trust that there were all-new avenues for me to experience.

2. **Mangoes.** When they're the right kind, and at their juiciest, they're the most perfect fruit I've ever experienced in their lusciousness.

3. **Black beans.**

4. **Coconut.** All of the ingredients I'm mentioning are part of such a welcomeness I felt when I first got here. It made my cooking accelerate and become distinguished from cooking from anywhere else in America.

5. **Salt cod, or *bacalao*.** It's such a part of the Caribbean tradition, probably because it's the absolute opposite of the fresh fish it would be so impossible to choose among.

6. **Ginger.**

7. **Chiles.** I'd want the pungency and bite that ginger and chiles would provide. And there's such a broad range of flavors in chiles. One of the most common chiles that we would use here [at Norman's] would be Scotch bonnets or habeñeros, which are definitely distinct from jalapeños or serranos, in that the florality and incredible aroma they have is so much different from the other chiles. Ginger and chiles work together as well as resonate with each other in a very clear way. The flavors bounce quickly back and forth between each other. They're sort of standing on the side like a little chorus that provides a synergistic opportunity to "rock the boat" or the dish.

8. **Citrus—limes.** One of the key things that creates the opportunity for a sauce or a dish to work is the ability of acidity to provide relief from the meaty richness of the dominant protein or the softening foundation of the starch. The benefit of citrus on the island is that I could also drink it. I'd have a hard time drinking balsamic vinegar.

9. **Conch.** Those born in Key West, like my son was, are called conches. When I first got here, I asked, "What is this stuff?" But because of its abundance, it got used in everything. To this day, one of the most popular dishes on my menu is a conch chowder. It's become emblematic of my cooking. (See Norman Van Aken's recipe for Conch Chowder on pages 383–385.)

10. **Pig.** James Beard said that pork was his favorite animal of all. I guess that's because you can use so many different parts of it. My favorite part is somewhere between bacon and ribs and pork tenderloin.

"When I reached ten ingredients, how could I not continue to think, Well, I'd really like an herb in there, and I can't believe I didn't say anything about black pepper, and lemongrass is very important to me, and I can't not have soy sauce. It would be very, very difficult to have less than a whole lot of ingredients," Van Aken told us. Apparently so difficult that it prompted a follow-up fax the next day: "I thought about my list of ingredients and going to the deserted island and then I began to wonder...hey, what's on this island?! If there would be mangoes and citrus growing there, allowing me to subtract those ingredients, then I'd add olive oil and bread to the list. And I'd be likely to catch some fresh fish. Things are looking up! Wait! Is that a Chinese junk pulling up to my beach?!?"

TECHNIQUES:

1. **Grilling/smoking.** As much as we intellectually can talk about chefs as artists, we're basically beasts cooking over fire. Or at least we want to be, because that is really what connects us so much to the primordial past that I think is still very important to our being complete humans. Watching and smelling nature go through that transformation—that is good yoga!

2. **Stir-frying.** I love the suddenness of it. I like the absolute balls-to-the-walls, full-steam-ahead, everything-gets-to-be-done-rapidly-and-maintain-its-integrity in stir-frying.

3. **Roasting (sneaking a little braising into it).** It's slow, ancient, homey, healthy.

"There's a triumvirate of opportunity among those three techniques—whether it's vegetables or fish or meat, there's a way of finding such great flavors in there that, for me, poaching does not begin to compare."

Cracked-Hacked Conch Chowder with Saffron, Coconut, and Oranges

by Norman Van Aken

YIELDS 10 8-OUNCE PORTIONS

For the shellfish broth/cream and garnish

1/4 cup olive oil

1 Scotch bonnet, stem and seeds discarded, minced

6 shallots, peeled and sliced thinly

4 cloves of garlic, peeled and sliced thinly

12 small clams, scrubbed

12 mussels, scrubbed and de-bearded

1 star anise

1 tablespoon roughly cracked black pepper

3 cups freshly squeezed orange juice

1 scant tablespoon saffron

1 quart heavy cream

1 cup coconut milk

1. Heat the olive oil in a large, heavy-bottomed saucepan over medium-high heat. Add the Scotch bonnet, shallots, and garlic. Stir. Let vegetables flavor the oil (about 1 minute). Then add the clams, mussels, star anise, and black pepper. Stir. Then add the orange juice and cover the pot. Remove the clams and mussels as they open to a colander set over a bowl to catch the liquid. (They start opening after about 3 minutes; just take them out as they open and cover the pot again and keep checking for more open ones.)

2. Allow the orange and shellfish juices to reduce, uncovered, until about 1 cup of liquid remains, about 10 minutes. Now add the saffron, heavy cream, and coconut milk. Allow to boil, stirring occasionally. (Be careful; cream can boil over in a split second.) Reduce the cream until it will just barely coat the back of a spoon (about 15 to 20 minutes).Turn off and strain. Discard the solids and reserve the flavored cream. Meanwhile, take the cooled mussels and clams out of their shells, reserve the meat, and toss the shells.

(continued on next page)

(continued from preceding page)

For the vegetable garnish

6 new potatoes, scrubbed and diced medium

1/2 cup of pure olive oil

2 ounces smoked slab bacon, rind removed, about 1/2 cup

4 cloves garlic, sliced thinly

1 poblano chile, stem and seeds discarded, minced

1/2 red onion, peeled and diced medium

2 large carrots, peeled and diced medium

1/2 bulb fennel, cored and diced medium

2 celery stalks, cleaned and diced medium

1 red bell pepper, stem and seeds discarded, diced medium

1 ear corn, kernels cut off the cob

1/4 cup roughly chopped cilantro leaves

2 bay leaves, broken

salt and pepper to taste

1. Put potatoes in a small saucepot of lightly salted water. Bring to a boil and turn down heat; simmer till just underdone (this only takes a few minutes, since the potatoes are so small).

2. In a large heavy soup pot, cook the bacon with the olive oil over medium-high heat until bacon is half-way cooked. Add the garlic and chile and stir briefly. Add the rest of the vegetables except the potatoes; stir to coat, add salt and pepper; cilantro, and bay leaf. Cook until firm, stirring occasionally (about 8 minutes). Add potatoes, saffron cream, clams, and mussels.

For the conch

3/4 pound cleaned, pounded conch

salt and pepper, to taste

1/4 cup flour

2 eggs beaten with 4 teaspoons of half-and-half

1 1/2 cups panko crumbs

peanut oil to sauté the conch

1. Season the conch with salt and pepper. Now dredge the conch pieces in the flour, then the eggs, and then in the panko. Place them on a large plate. You can layer them if you separate the breaded pieces with wax paper or plastic wrap.

To finish the dish

1. Heat the soup until quite warm. Now heat a large skillet and sauté the conch until nicely colored on both sides. Remove to paper towel until all the conch is cooked. Now quickly chop the cooked conch into pieces. Ladle the soup into warm bowls and scatter the cooked conch over the soup.

Note: Any uncooked, breaded conch risks turning color overnight. It is best to cook any conch that may be deemed extra and add it to the cooked soup or save for leftovers. Also, for a less chock-full-of-stuff soup, you can add a cup or so of half-and-half and season again to taste.

Garnish Notes: I like to garnish this soup with orange sections, toasted coconut, and, sometimes, saffron pistils.

Jean-Georges Vongerichten

JOJO, VONG, and THE LIPSTICK CAFÉ
New York, New York

INGREDIENTS:

1. **Lemongrass.** It's my favorite herb. I love its fragrance. It's addictive. I could cook it with my eyes closed. It's like a friend, I'm so comfortable with it.

2. **Sweetbreads.** I need to eat them once a week. I love the flavor and the texture—which go with everything.

3. **Salad greens.** I like Asian greens, watercress. I put them everywhere.

4. **"Liquid salt"** (*nam pla* and/or soy sauce). I use it in marinades, in seasoning—it's different.

5. **Parsley.** It's the first herb I knew—I grew up with it. I chop it as needed, because within two minutes, it starts losing its flavor.

6. **Mustard.** I love it as a condiment.

7. **Truffles.** Both black and white—they're gems of the earth.

8. **Curry paste (red, green and yellow).** I like mixing all three for lobster with herbs.

9. **Fish.** I'm a fish freak.

10. **Licorice.** I grew up with it—as a kid, I always chewed it. I like it in desserts, on pears, ice cream, sweetbreads.

TECHNIQUES:

1. **Rôtisserie.** For birds, fish, sweetbreads.

2. **Steaming.** It's the most technical and the most difficult technique. It can bring flavor if you infuse the water with something like lemongrass or tea. And I like dry steaming, insulating the food in plastic wrap or a banana leaf.

3. **Slow-roasting.** It involves a long-term, compassionate relationship between the cook and the oven. I don't like the harshness of flavor that results from high-temperature roasting.

Alice Waters

CHEZ PANISSE
Berkeley, California

INGREDIENTS:

1. **Bread.**

2. **Olive oil.**

3. **Garlic.**

4. **Tomatoes.** (See Alice Waters' recipe for Pasta with Tomato Confit below.)

5. **Herbs**—Basil or rosemary, perhaps.

6. **Salad greens**—Wild rocket or chicories.

7. **Noodles**—Any kind. I had great soba noodles recently, and I love Italian pasta.

8. **Citrus.** I like citrus a lot—everything from limes to blood oranges.

9. **Figs.** I like them fresh. I like baking fish in fig leaves, which gives it a coconut-like flavor and is very aromatic. And I like cooking over fig wood.

10. **Nuts.** It's hard to choose—probably almonds or walnuts.

TECHNIQUES:

1. **Cooking over fire/grilling.** I'd cook over a fire all the time. It feels somehow fundamental.

2. **Wood-burning oven.** I love the flavors it imparts.

3. **Sautéeing.** Ingredients can come together very quickly; you can marry things in a hurry.

Pasta with Tomato Confit

by Alice Waters

Allow about two tomatoes per serving. Make a bed of basil leaves in the bottom of an ovenproof dish that will hold the tomatoes snugly in one layer. Peel and core the tomatoes and place them core-side down on the basil. Lightly salt and pepper. Pour in enough extra virgin olive oil to come halfway up the sides of the tomatoes. Bake for 1 1/2 hours in a preheated 350° oven, until the tomatoes are soft and lightly caramelized and have infused the oil with their perfume. Season to taste and serve spooned over cooked and drained fresh noodles.

Jasper White

Boston, Massachusetts

INGREDIENTS:

1. **Oysters.** I absolutely adore them. I always have, and always will. They're one of my favorite things in the world. I never tire of them.

2. **Shellfish—lobster.** It might be sentimental; I've just spent a whole year in an intimate relationship with this creature [White's next book is *Lobster at Home*]. It's very versatile.

3. **Spinach.** [While White initially planned to take butter to cook with, when he later realized he could cook with rendered pork fat, he opted to take spinach instead.] I love spinach. I could eat it as a salad or cook it as a vegetable.

4. **Pork.** I adore it. It's so versatile—I'd be able to use it as my only meat.

5. **Starch—potatoes.** Because I'm Irish! Seriously, they're a real staple for me. Given the grains of the world, I'm definitely a potato guy.

6. **Citrus fruit—oranges.** I'd need a citrus fruit, since I have all that seafood. I'd really want to have limes and oranges and grapefruits and lemons. I feel like my body needs citrus—it's beyond the flavor, which I really enjoy.

7. **Onions.** They're the king of vegetables. Pick up any cookbook off your shelf and see what the most used vegetable is in every recipe. It's onions.

8. **Spices—chiles or black pepper.** Personally, I like pretty spicy food, so I'd need a "heat" ingredient. It would add a little zest.

9. **Herbs—mint or basil or thyme.** It would make my food have some extra dimension.

10. **Corn.** I love corn. I grew up eating corn; it's a very satisfying vegetable for me. It's kind of a starch/vegetable.

"I can make my own salt; I could boil ocean water in a pan. My mind is racing now—I'm thinking about ginger and garlic. I guess Peking duck doesn't fit. And you can tell I'm not a dessert person," says White.

TECHNIQUES:

1. **Grilling.** I love the flavor of the grill—that wood flavor. I like what the intense heat can do, the way it caramelizes the fat on the outside of meats and kind of chars the shells of shellfish. It's not just the flavor that the grill adds to the food, but it's the way it brings out the flavor in the food, too, and kind of seals it in.

2. **Pan-frying.** It's a good way to seal in flavors. The other good thing is it's a technique I can use to introduce fat into the food.

3. **Boiling.** You need a versatile way to cook foods. You can make soups and broths.

Communion: communication (a sharing of thoughts or feelings);

community (spiritual fellowship);

also, the sacred consumption of bread and wine.

Food—whether flavors, dishes, menus, or entire cuisines—is a medium through which chefs can express their point of view. However, the potential for communication is not limited to the plate. Just as in the art world, where the lines of distinction have blurred between works of art and performance art, every aspect of a dining experience provides an opportunity for artistry.

"I never limited my interest in food to one dimension on a plate," says Patrick O'Connell. "I've never seen it that way. It seems as though theater [his college major] just swept into food and they became one.

I think of food as an experience, not as an entity or a product, and it's given me a tremendous edge. I think of it as performance art, and of every detail as being equally important. The whole experience has to be conscious. So the chef needs to emerge as the controlling influence from the kitchen and direct the entire production, keeping it all on the same level."

O'Connell observes that more people are regarding the restaurant experience as theater. "And it's either a good play or a bad play. It's fresh or it's tired. And it's genuine or it's fake. More and more, it seems to boil down to that for me," he says. "It's either right or it's wrong. And you're continually aiming for that right-on feeling."

Certain chefs believe that some of food's expressiveness has been lost due to its abstraction from its meaning in life and its meaning in society. "What we've done is demeaned it by creating celebrity chefs and hot restaurants," says Mark Miller. "We've stripped it of some of its possibilities, and some of its humanness, and some of its sensuality—its simplest level of an experience. Too many young chefs are accepting what the media has promoted food and the restaurant industry as being about."

Culinary artists, on the other hand, understand the multifaceted potential within the dining experience. "Al Forno is a combination of things—I don't think you can pinpoint any particular aspect of the experience. We started with the front door, and gave thought to the entrance and working your way through the restaurant—the visuals, the smells, activating all the senses," says George Germon. "I think we have everything working in the same direction, so that we try to make the picture complete."

Johanne Killeen points out, "George designed everything in the restaurant, including the equipment. There's a unity to the look of the restaurant and the look of the food. We've had total control." Germon adds, "And because we are so self-contained, in that we do about 99 percent of everything ourselves, it really is a pure vision."

Susan Feniger says that at Border Grill with partner Mary Sue Milliken, "We've always been huge believers that everything matters—everything from the valet to the bathroom to the busboys to the table settings. It's not that things have to be fancy, but there is a cutting edge to them. In the beginning, we were really extreme about everything that was part of the actual eating experience."

Several examples of extraordinary Japanese restaurant experiences were cited by chefs as inspirational in this regard, and worth emulation. Milliken raves about the attention to detail at Ginza Sushi-Ko in Los Angeles, a sushi bar she says seats only seven people. "It was absolute perfection," she enthuses. "You're eating things just minutes after preparation—it's so immediate. That part of it's really impressive. But it's not just the food—it's everything. This guy has collected dishes from all over the world, and has made a lot of his own pottery for you to eat from."

Mark Miller recalls as one of the greatest food experiences of his life a *kaiseki* meal he had in Japan in 1990. "I've had lots of great meals, but I had never had a meal where I felt like it was a single performance, being done for me, that came from hundreds of years of tradition being brought forward," says Miller. "Obviously, it was exotic and strange. But it was their consciousness about food—it was about pure aesthetics. It was a sensibility about the food, the environment, the people, the time, the culture, the room.

"There was not one element that was not part of the food experience. And yet, food was only a part of something so holistic. Everything had been arranged—it had been thought out consciously. And, as a diner, what you did and how you acted was just as important a part of the experience," says Miller. "By comparison, a French three-star restaurant has a lot to learn about creating a sense of care and concern for customers."

How can a restaurant ensure that it is communicating effectively with its customers? "I think it is more often than not a matter of having [restaurant employees] ask themselves, 'What feeling am I imparting to a customer, or to a guest?'" says Patrick O'Connell. "This is often where the breakdown is.

"In cities like New York, I believe they hire on what they consider 'talent,' and attitude is tertiary. You get a lot of misguided, independent thinkers who aren't reflecting the point of view which is the restaurant. It isn't just in the food—it's who they are, and what makes them unique. I used to go in and ask who owned the place—and three out of four times, the server didn't know. I always thought, How sad. They don't know who they work for. And not only that, they don't know what the owner is trying to accomplish with the restaurant, what its function is—they're not plugged in. It's never their fault. It is a fail-

The good, the excellent, the grand cuisine, is a great deal—but it is not everything. One must still know how to orchestrate it, that is to say, to present it, to enhance it, to bring out its full glory by carefully attending to all the details that go along with it—from the temperature of the room to the temperature of the wines, the thickness of the crust of the pâté, the thinness of the glassware, the lustre of the china, the quality of the linen, and the beauty of the fruit, not to mention the appearance and manners of the staff."
—composer Reynaldo Hahn, in Fernand Point's *La Pyramide Golden Book*

ure on the part of the owners or managers to communicate what they're there for, and what they're trying to do."

What's the bottom line in a dining experience? "For me, it's always the feeling I get," says O'Connell. "And as critical as I can be about food, I'm willing to overlook lack of talent, lack of imagination, lack of cooking techniques more often than rudeness, bad attitude, or feeling abused or mistreated in a restaurant."

In order to maximize the effect of a dining experience, "We should try to create a continuum of experiences that are more meaningful and more connected," says Mark Miller. "Someone who wants to be a great chef has to be involved in all of these decisions regarding the subtleties of these experiences."

Discontinuity in the messages communicated by a restaurant experience can be jarring. "We have these experiences where we go in and find the decor wonderful, and the service to be terrible, and the

I like having a wood-burning oven right in front and having an open kitchen—it adds to the restaurant's warmth and energy, and lets the customers feel that energy. It's great to have cooks see the customers they're cooking for—it adds a lot to a cook's mentality and sense of well-being.
—Bradley Ogden

Patrick O'Connell on "A Life's Work"

I was speaking with a musician once who told me, "No, I don't enjoy music—I just hear the echo chambers and the number of violins and who was off and where it should have speeded up and didn't. But that's an enjoyment in itself."

I once read, ages ago when French cuisine was considered the ultimate, something that said, "What a pity that French chefs can't ever enjoy their cuisine." And I wondered, Why not? I've come to understand that you give that up. It may be my ancient Catholicism coming through, but it's as though you have a calling, and you're a vehicle for providing this. As with food, I felt like I could never get it right, so why run around trying to get it right—just try to do it, for other people. You understand so much when you are obsessed with the flaws. Negative lessons are what you learn when you have a bad experience, and they're very valuable. You learn what rankled you, what didn't work, how it should have been. And they reinforce your own direction in doing it well.

What's hard about it is that degree of sacrifice. It's not so hard. Anybody could do it for one or two nights, for a week. It's mustering that energy and dealing with the other areas of your life that you have put on hold that you wish you could develop—like seeing a movie this year, maybe? It's the constancy—it's almost hysterical.

food to be good, but you go in the bathroom and it's filthy," says Miller. "There's this continuum, even within the restaurant, that you need to have at some level—of smells and flowers and china and texture and visuals. Mirrors are important, because they bring the sociability back—people looking at other people, into each other."

The art of the table goes beyond merely putting recipes into practice; it embraces good manners, the balance of the menu, the skills of being a host, and of best organizing that privileged moment when a meal is shared with guests or family.
—Curnonsky

At its best, a restaurant tries to communicate something about who and what it is—and that it cares about the people who are dining there. "Everyone goes about it in a different way, but it's ultimately a question of how you can manipulate [a diner] into a state of euphoria, using a broad spectrum, the complete palette," says Patrick O'Connell. "I think young chefs in particular feel limited to the confines of the plate. I have been astonished at the impact that minuscule things will have on the press and on clients—just being a little playful in the wording of the menu, letting them know that we're not stuffy. They want to feel that the people behind the restaurant are having fun, too. Once again, they're seeing a personality. That's basically what the public is seeing on a plate, but they may not be adept enough to see it in its broadest dimensions. If a chef or owner is passionate about something, anything, they should weave that into the experience somehow—that's a dimension that the public craves.

Every time we plan a trip, the day after we pay a nonrefundable deposit on it, there's a call from someone for whom you simply cannot be away for their arrival—an important chef, an important journalist. And you don't dare ever say anything. I have five brothers—they all got married on a Saturday. I couldn't go to any of their weddings. We believe that almost 10 percent of our clientele is either in the business or writing a critical piece. If you consider all the guides—the Mobil guide has four anonymous visits a year, the AAA guide has four unannounced visits a year. Almost every night there's a single person in the room taking notes. It's stressful. It's not easy to spray the pixie dust and have them succumb! Even though our staff is large and capable, you'll find that things will go better if you're present. And even if someone gets a perfect meal, they expect some interaction also, with a key person.

When you do reach somebody, often it's very powerful, the energy transfer. And you have a great satisfaction in making that connection. It reaffirms that what you're doing is important. We open the mail every day, and there are about twenty letters—and some of them just make you bawl! And they usually say, "I have never written to a restaurant in my entire life for any reason, but I feel compelled to write you about the experience." It's often just tiny, little acts of human kindness, for the most part, that were so touching to them—how they were treated by the staff, or how the staff went out of their way without being showy about it to accommodate them.

So it's important to remember that this is not a business. It's a life's work.

"As a bizarre example, our dog Rose [a dalmation] is in the restaurant, at the front door. Sometimes it's almost comical—you think, Haven't these people ever seen a dog before, for God's sake? Of course she's pretty and we love her to pieces and all this. But they get up from their dinner and they roll on the floor with her in their little Chanel suits, and the next thing you know she's got a string of pearls on. It's entertainment! It's novel.

"Chefs and restaurateurs could ask themselves whether there are one or two novel ideas about how they could communicate a broader dimension of themselves to their clients—whatever it might be. They would probably be astonished by the impact that might create," says O'Connell. "It's all inside you—if you will just take the sandbags off."

An Opportunity for Community

In her fascinating book *A Natural History of the Senses*, Diane Ackerman points out that, "The other senses may be enjoyed in all their beauty when one is alone, but taste is largely social. Humans rarely choose to dine in solitude, and food has a powerful social component."

Leading chefs agree. "Food should always be eaten in company," says Dieter Schorner. "To eat it alone brings only half the pleasure. Being with other people is what makes food so beautiful." Lindsey Shere concurs, "Food should be enjoyable, and bring people together somehow. If people ate together every day, things would be different. And if people ate *and cooked* together, things would be *very* different!"

Mark Miller has praise for restaurants that recognize the importance of a holistic approach to the dining experience. "I think that Patrick [O'Connell] and Reinhardt [Lynch] have been there for almost twenty years out in the middle of the wilderness [at The Inn at Little Washington in Virginia] creating some of the best of American hospitality and the best of style on their own. There aren't enough people like them who are pioneers, who are striving to create their own message. It's given American food and restaurants and inns and hotels a complexity that wouldn't be there without them."

But even O'Connell himself acknowledges, "This is a hard time to be a chef. It reminds me of the era in which French cuisine was born. That's the period when the great chefs had to please the kings, and the court, and they were the most jaded people in the world—because they could have anything, they'd tried it all, they'd done it all. This is very much like the American public today. The fresh wonderment and excitement of trying something they've never had before is virtually lost. It's a little difficult to get the public at large excited about a plate of food right now.

To entertain a guest is to make yourself responsible for his happiness so long as he is beneath your roof.
—Jean-Anthèlme Brillat-Savarin

"That's why we have to move on to the next dimension. The plate of food is only one component. Chefs have to busy themselves with creating an entire experience, a sort of mystical experience which, ironically, America is starving for," he says. "There is no spirituality left. There is no sacredness left. Food is the last connection to sacred reality. Everything else has been defiled. There's no belief structure, there's no real faith, there's not much hope—but there *is* sort of a desperate yearning. And food can still be a large part of dealing with that.

"A great restaurant has the ultimate potential of providing a transcendental experience. You go beyond fantasy into a state of having all of your needs better cared for than you could do for yourself, and you are allowed to sort of become psychically weightless and communicate more successfully and in a more pure way than you can in perhaps any other environment. And this is a big measure of why America is so bankrupt spiritually—there has been a tremendous communication break*down* with the communication break*through* of all of the mechanized tools and machinery put in place to further communications. Real communication, which is much more intangible, is taking place with much less frequency.

The great trumpet player Louis Armstrong once said of musicians, "What we play is life."

"I think the pendulum swing, with sexuality becoming fraught with tremendous anxiety and even a return to puritanism in some respects, has shut down another avenue for people. So, people are looking for something real to take place, and something meaningful," says O'Connell. "And food is a good vehicle to begin with."

Culinary art, like other great works of art, has the power to inspire and rejuvenate through offering a unique opportunity for communion. "Through a dining experience, people will connect and share and exchange and support and heal and do all the things that people crave," says O'Connell. "They reaffirm that life is worth living. And they live."

The purpose of art is not a rarified, intellectual distillate. It is life—intensified, brilliant life.
—Alain Arias-Misson

And, as M.F.K. Fisher asked in *Serve It Forth,* "When shall we live if not now?"

Ali-Bab. *Encyclopedia of Practical Gastronomy.* New York: McGraw-Hill, 1974.

Apicius. *Cookery and Dining in Imperial Rome.* New York: Dover Publications, 1977.

Bayless, Rick and Deann. *Authentic Mexican.* New York: William Morrow, 1987.

Beard, James. *James Beard's American Cookery.* New York: Little, Brown, 1972.

Beard, James. *Delights and Prejudices.* New York: Macmillan, 1990.

Beard, James. *Simple Foods.* New York: Macmillan, 1993.

Behr, Edward. *The Artful Eater.* New York: Grove Atlantic, 1993.

Bertolli, Paul, with Alice Waters. *Chez Panisse Cooking.* New York: Random House, 1988.

Blanc, Georges. *The Natural Cuisine of Georges Blanc.* New York: Stewart, Tabori & Chang, 1987.

Bocuse, Paul. *Bocuse's Regional French Cooking.* Paris: Flammarion, 1991.

———*Paul Bocuse's French Cooking.* New York: Random House, 1977.

Boulud, Daniel. *Cooking with Daniel Boulud.* New York: Random House, 1993.

Child, Julia. *Mastering the Art of French Cooking.* New York: Alfred A. Knopf, 1961.

Claiborne, Craig. *The New York Times Cookbook.* New York: HarperCollins, 1990.

Curnonsky. *Traditional French Cooking.* New York: Doubleday, 1987.

David, Elizabeth. *An Omelette and a Glass of Wine.* New York: Penguin, 1984.

————— *English Bread and Yeast Cookery*. New York: Penguin, 1977.

—————*French Country Cooking*. New York: Penguin, 1966.

—————*French Provincial Cooking*. New York: Penguin, 1970.

—————*Italian Food*. New York: Penguin, 1987.

—————*Spices, Salt and Aromatics in the English Kitchen*. New York: Penguin, 1970.

—————*Summer Cooking*. New York: Penguin, 1987.

Dornenburg, Andrew, and Karen Page. *Becoming a Chef: With Recipes and Reflections from America's Leading Chefs*. New York: Van Nostrand Reinhold, 1995.

Escoffier, A. *The Escoffier Cook Book*. New York: Crown, 1969.

Feniger, Susan, and Mary Sue Milliken. *City Cuisine*. New York: Morrow, 1989.

Fisher, M.F.K. *The Art of Eating*. New York: Macmillan, 1990.

Foo, Susanna. *Susanna Foo Chinese Cuisine*. San Francisco: Chapters, 1995.

Gardner, Howard. *Creating Minds*. New York: Basic Books, 1993.

Goldstein, Joyce. *Back to Square One*. New York: Morrow, 1992.

Grigson, Jane. *English Food*. New York: Penguin Books, 1974.

—————*Good Things*. New York: Penguin Books, 1971.

—————*Jane Grigson's Fruit Book*. New York: Penguin, 1983.

—————*Jane Grigson's Vegetable Book*. New York: Atheneum, 1978.

—————*The Mushroom Feast*. New York: New York: Alfred A. Knopf, 1991.

Grigson, Sophie. *Gourmet Ingredients*. New York: Van Nostrand Reinhold, 1991.

Guérard, Michel. *Michel Guérard's Cuisine Gourmande*. New York: Morrow, 1979.

Kamman, Madeleine. *In Madeleine's Kitchen*. New York: Macmillan, 1992.

—————*The Making of a Cook*. New York: Macmillan, 1980.

—————*Savoie*. New York: Macmillan, 1989.

—————*When French Women Cook*. New York: Macmillan, 1976.

Killeen, Johanne, and George Germon. *Cucina Simpatica*. New York: HarperCollins, 1991.

Lang, Jenifer Harvey. *Larousse Gastronomique*. New York: Crown, 1988.

MacLauchlan, Andrew. *New Classic Desserts*. New York: Van Nostrand Reinhold, 1995.

Meyer, Danny, and Michael Romano. *The Union Square Cafe Cookbook*. New York: HarperCollins, 1994.

Miller, Mark. *Coyote Cafe*. San Francisco: Ten Speed Press, 1989.

Ogden, Bradley. *Bradley Ogden's Breakfast, Lunch & Dinner*. New York: Random House, 1991.

Olney, Richard. *Simple French Food*. New York: Simon & Schuster, 1970.

—————*The French Menu Cookbook*. Boston: David Godine, 1970.

O'Neill, Molly. *A Well-Seasoned Appetite*. New York: Viking, 1995.

Palladin, Jean-Louis. *Jean-Louis: Cooking with the Seasons*. Charlottesville, Virginia: Thomasson-Grant, 1989.

Peel, Mark, and Nancy Silverton. *Mark Peel & Nancy Silverton at Home: Two*

Chefs Cook for Family & Friends. New York: Warner, 1994.

Peterson, James. *Sauces: Classical and Contemporary Sauce Making.* New York: Van Nostrand Reinhold, 1991.

Point, Fernand. *Ma Gastronomie.* Paris: Flammarion, 1969.

Robuchon, Joel. *Cooking Through the Seasons.* New York: Rizzoli, 1993.

Rombauer, Irma S., and Marion Rombauer Becker. *Joy of Cooking.* New York: Macmillan, 1975.

Root, Waverly. *The Food of Italy.* New York: Vintage, 1992.

Rosenzweig, Anne. *The Arcadia Seasonal Mural and Cookbook.* New York: Abrams, 1986.

Roux, Albert and Michel. *New Classic Cuisine.* New York: Barron's, 1984.

Schlesinger, Chris, and John Willoughby. *Big Flavors of the Hot Sun.* New York: Morrow, 1994.

————*Salsas, Sambals, Chutneys & Chow Chows.* New York: Morrow, 1993.

————*The Thrill of the Grill.* New York: Morrow, 1990.

Schmidt, Jimmy. *Cooking for All Seasons.* New York: Macmillan, 1991.

Shere, Lindsey Remolif. *Chez Panisse Desserts.* New York: Random House, 1985.

Silverton, Nancy. *Breads from the La Brea Bakery.* New York: Villard, 1996.

Splichal, Joachim. *Joachim Splichal's Patina Cookbook.* San Francisco: Collins Publishers, 1995.

Tower, Jeremiah. *New American Classics.* New York: Harper & Row, 1986.

Troisgros, Jean and Pierre. *The Nouvelle Cuisine of Jean & Pierre Troisgros.* New York: Morrow, 1978.

Tropp, Barbara. *China Moon Cookbook.* New York: Workman, 1992.

————*The Modern Art of Chinese Cooking.* New York: Morrow, 1982.

Van Aken, Norman. *Feast of Sunlight.* New York: Ballantine, 1988.

Vongerichten, Jean-Georges. *Simple Cuisine: The Easy, New Approach to Four-Star Cooking.* Englewod Cliffs, N.J.: Prentice Hall, 1990.

Waters, Alice. *Chez Panisse Menu Cookbook.* New York: Random House, 1982.

Wells, Patricia, and Joel Robuchon. *Simply French.* New York: Morrow, 1991.

White, Jasper. *Jasper White's Cooking from New England.* New York: Harper & Row, 1989.

Wolfert, Paula. *World of Food.* New York: Harper & Row, 1988.

If you're having a hard time finding a particular culinary resource at your local bookstore, you might want to try one of the following:

Kitchen Arts & Letters
1435 Lexington Avenue
New York, New York 10128
(212) 876-5550
Owner: Nahum Waxman

Books for Cooks catalog
(800) 355-CHEF
Owner: Lydia Cheng

Books for Cooks
301 South Light Street
Baltimore, Maryland 21202
(410) 547-9066
Owner: Arlene Gillis

The Cookbook Store
850 Young Street
Toronto, Ontario M4W 2HI Canada
(416) 920-2665
Owner: Alison Fryer

The Cook's Book Shop
3854 Fifth Avenue
San Diego, California 92103
(619) 296-3636
Owner: Kira Kane

The Cook's Library
8373 West Third Street
Los Angeles, California 90048
(213) 655-3141
Owner: Ellen Rose

Hoppin' John's
30 Pinckney Street
Charleston, South Carolina 29401
(803) 577-6404
Owner: John Martin Taylor

Jessica's Biscuit catalog
(800) 878-4264
Owner: David Strymish

Powell's Books for Cooks
3739 Southeast Hawthorne Boulevard
Portland, Oregon 97214
(800) 354-5957

The Wine and Food Library
1207 West Madison
Ann Arbor, Michigan 48103
(313) 663-4894
Owner: Jan Longone
Specializes in out-of-print cookbooks.

Rick Bayless is the chef-owner of Frontera Grill and Topolobampo and owner of Zinfandel, all in Chicago. Bayless was named one of America's Best New Chefs of 1988 by *Food & Wine* magazine. In 1991, he was named Best Chef of the Midwest and in 1995 he received the Outstanding Chef Award from The James Beard Foundation. He is also the author, with his wife Deann, of *Authentic Mexican,* and a member of the Who's Who of Food and Beverage in America.

Daniel Boulud is the chef-owner of Restaurant Daniel at the Surrey Hotel in New York City, which was awarded four stars from *The New York Times*. He was formerly the chef of Le Cirque. In 1992, he was named the Best Chef of New York and in 1994 he received the Outstanding Chef Award from The James Beard Foundation. A member of the Who's Who of Food and Beverage in America, he is the author of *Cooking with Daniel Boulud*.

Terrance Brennan is the chef-owner of Picholine in New York City. An alumnus of Le Cirque, The Polo Lounge, and Prix Fixe, in 1995 he was named one of the Best New Chefs in America by *Food & Wine* magazine, and *Condé Nast Traveler* magazine's Readers Poll voted Picholine the Best Restaurant in New York City. Picholine was awarded three stars from *The New York Times* in 1996.

Gary Danko was the executive chef of The Dining Room at The Ritz-Carlton Hotel in San Francisco, for which he earned five stars from the Mobil Travel Guide. He was named one of America's Best New Chefs by *Food & Wine* magazine, and in 1995 he was named the Best Chef of California by The James Beard Foundation.

Susan Feniger and Mary Sue Milliken are the chefs and co-owners of Border Grill in Santa Monica, California. They are members of the Who's Who of Food and Beverage in America, as well as the co-authors of *Cantina, City Cuisine,* and *Mesa Mexican*. They also co-host their own radio show as well as the series "Too Hot Tamales" on the Television Food Network.

Biographies of Chefs

Daniel Boulud

Susanna Foo is the chef-owner of Susanna Foo in Philadelphia. A former librarian from the University of Pittsburgh, she attended the Culinary Institute of America's continuing education division. She was named one of America's Best New Chefs by *Food & Wine* magazine. In 1996, her book *Susanna Foo Chinese Cuisine* won a James Beard Foundation Book Award.

George Germon and **Johanne Killeen** are the chefs and co-owners of Al Forno in Providence, Rhode Island. Al Forno was named one of the Distinguished Restaurants of North America in *Food & Wine* magazine. In 1993, they were named the Best Chefs of the Northeast by The James Beard Foundation. They are the co-authors of *Cucina Simpatica*.

Joyce Goldstein was the chef-owner of San Francisco's Square One Restaurant, which has won numerous awards for food, wine, and service since its founding in 1984. The restaurant closed in 1996. Goldstein is the author of many cookbooks, including *Back to Square One: Old World Food in a New World Kitchen* and *The Mediterranean Kitchen*. She was named the Best Chef in California in 1993 by The James Beard Foundation.

Hubert Keller is the chef-owner of Fleur de Lys in San Francisco. The restaurant holds one of the three highest food ratings in San Francisco according the the 1996 Zagat Survey. Keller has been nominated several times for the title of Best Chef of California by The James Beard Foundation.

Gray Kunz is the executive chef of Lespinasse at Manhattan's St. Regis Hotel, and earned a four-star rating from *The New York Times*. Kunz spent five years working with Fredy Girardet in Switzerland, and was later executive chef of both the Hong Kong Regent's restaurant Plume and of the Peninsula Hotel in New York City. In 1995, he was named the Best Chef of New York by The James Beard Foundation.

Mark Miller is the chef-owner of Red Sage in Washington, D.C., and of the Coyote Cafe in Santa Fe, New Mexico. He is an alumnus of Chez Panisse. In 1984, he was inducted into the Who's Who of Food and Beverage in America; he has also been named Best Chef in the Southwest by the James Beard Foundation. He is the author of several books including *Coyote Cafe*, and also produced the *Great Chile Poster*.

Patrick O'Connell is the chef-owner of The Inn at Little Washington in Virginia. A member of the Paris-based Relais & Chateaux Association, The Inn in 1989 became the first and only establishment in America to achieve five stars from the Mobil Travel Guide, five diamonds from the AAA, and the top national rating in the Zagat Hotel Survey with the first "perfect" score for its cuisine in the history of the Zagat rating system. O'Connell was named Best Chef of the Mid-Atlantic by The James Beard Foundation in 1992.

Bradley Ogden is the chef-owner of several restaurants in the San Francisco Bay Area, including The Lark Creek Inn in Larkspur, California, and One Market Restaurant in San Francisco. He is a graduate of the Culinary Institute of America. In 1984, he was inducted into the Who's Who of Food and Beverage in America and in 1993, he was named the Best Chef of California by The James Beard Foundation.

Jean-Louis Palladin is the chef-owner of Jean-Louis at the Watergate Hotel and Palladin in Washington, D.C. At the age of twenty-eight, Palladin was awarded two Michelin stars—at that time, the youngest chef in France ever to be so honored. In 1991, he was named the Best Chef of the Mid-Atlantic, and in 1993 he received the Outstanding Chef Award from The James Beard Foundation. He is the author of *Jean-Louis: Cooking with the Seasons*.

Charlie Palmer is the chef-owner of Aureole and an owner of The Lenox Room in New York City and the Egg Farm Dairy in Peekskill, NY. Aureole holds the second-highest food rating in the New York City *Zagat Survey* and was named one of the top 25 restaurants in America by *Food & Wine*. Palmer, a graduate of The Culinary Institute of America, is the author of *Great American Food*.

François Payard is the pastry chef at Restaurant Daniel in New York City, which was awarded four stars from *The New York Times*. In 1995, he received the Outstanding Pastry Chef Award from The James Beard Foundation. He was previously the pastry chef of Le Bernardin in Manhattan.

Mark Peel is the chef and co-owner (with his wife Nancy Silverton) of Campanile in Los Angeles. An alumnus of Chez Panisse and the opening chef of Spago, Peel is the co-author of *Mark Peel & Nancy Silverton at Home: Two Chefs Cook for Family & Friends*. He has been nominated several times as Best Chef of California by The James Beard Foundation.

Michael Romano is the chef at Union Square Cafe in New York City, which was named the most popular restaurant in the city by readers of the *Zagat Survey*. He is an alumnus of several Michelin-starred restaurants in France and Switzerland, and has been nominated as the Best Chef in New York by The James Beard Foundation. Romano is the co-author with Danny Meyer of the award-winning *Union Square Cafe Cookbook*.

Anne Rosenzweig is the chef-owner of Arcadia and The Lobster Club in New York City. Arcadia was named one of the Distinguished Restaurants of North America in *Food & Wine*. Rosenzweig was inducted into the Who's Who of Food & Beverage in 1987, and has been nominated as Best Chef of New York by The James Beard Foundation. She is the author of *The Arcadia Seasonal Mural and Cookbook*.

Chris Schlesinger is the chef-owner of the East Coast Grill in Cambridge, Massachusetts. In 1996, he was named the Best Chef of the Northeast by The James Beard Foundation. He is the co-author of several books with John Willoughby, including *Big Flavors of the Hot Sun; Lettuce in Your Kitchen; Salsas, Sambals, Chutneys and Chow Chows;* and *The Thrill of the Grill*, which won a James Beard Foundation Book Award in 1991.

Jimmy Schmidt is the chef-owner of several restaurants in the Detroit area—including The Rattlesnake Club, Stelline, and Tres Vite—and others under the corporate umbrella of META Restaurants. He studied with Madeleine Kamman in Boston and France. A 1984 inductee into the Who's Who of Food and Beverage in America, Schmidt was named the Best Chef of the Midwest by The James Beard Foundation in 1993.

Dieter Schorner has been the chef-owner of Patisserie Café Didier in Washington, D.C.'s Georgetown. Having worked as the pastry chef at leading restaurants on both sides of the Atlantic, ranging from Le Cirque in New York to the Savoy Hotel in London, he has been called one of the country's two leading pastry chefs by *Time* magazine, and "possibly, next to Lenôtre, the most famous pastry chef in the world."

Lindsey Shere has been the pastry chef at Chez Panisse in Berkeley, California, since its opening in 1971. In 1987, she and her partners opened the Downtown Bakery and Creamery in Healdburg, California. Shere received the Outstanding Pastry Chef Award from The James Beard Foundation in 1993. She is a member of the Who's Who of Food and Beverage in America, and the author of *Chez Panisse Desserts*.

Lydia Shire is the chef-owner of Biba, Pignoli, and the LMNOP Bakery in Boston. She is a graduate of Le Cordon Bleu in London. An alumna of Harvest, Maison Robert, and Seasons in Boston, Shire was one of the first women ever named to head an American hotel kitchen. In 1984, she was inducted into the Who's Who of Food and Beverage in America and, in 1992, she was named the Best Chef of the Northeast by The James Beard Foundation.

Nancy Silverton is the pastry chef and co-owner (with husband Mark Peel) of Campanile and the La Brea Bakery in Los Angeles. She was the first recipient of the Pastry Chef of the Year Award from The James Beard Foundation in 1991. Silverton is the co-author of *Mark Peel & Nancy Silverton At Home: Two Chefs Cook for Family & Friends*, and the author of *Nancy Silverton's Breads from the La Brea Bakery*.

Joachim Splichal is the chef-owner of Patina restaurant, which he opened in Los Angeles in 1989, and later Pinot Bistro, Patinette at MOCA, Cafe Pinot, Pinot Hollywood, Pinot Blanc, and Patina Catering Corporation. Splichal was named Best Chef of California by The James Beard Foundation in 1991, and to the Who's Who of Food & Beverage in America in 1995. He is the author of *Patina Cookbook*.

Jeremiah Tower is the chef-owner of a number of restaurants in the San Francisco Bay Area including Stars, which opened in 1984, and J.T.'s, which opened in 1995. An alumnus of Chez Panisse, Tower was named Best Chef in California in 1993, and received the Outstanding Chef Award from the James Beard Foundation in 1996. A member of the Who's Who of Food and Beverage in America, he is the author of *Jeremiah Tower's New American Classics*.

Norman Van Aken is the chef-owner of the Miami restaurant Norman's, which opened in Coral Gables in 1995 and was named one of the best new restaurants in the country by *Bon Appétit*. Ten Speed Press/Celestial Arts has published *Norman Van Aken's Exotic Fruits Posters*, *The Great Exotic Fruit Book*, and *The Great Exotic Fruit Postcards Book*; Van Aken is also the author of *Feast of Sunlight*.

Jean-Georges Vongerichten is the chef-owner of Jojo, Vong, and The Lipstick Cafe in New York City, and of Vong in London, which he opened in 1995. He earned four stars from *The New York Times* while the chef of Restaurant Lafayette. He received the 1995 Robert Mondavi Culinary Award of Excellence for his contributions to the world of gastronomy and was named the Best Chef of New York in 1996 by The James Beard Foundation. Vongerichten is the author of *Simple Cuisine*.

Alice Waters is the chef-owner of Chez Panisse in Berkeley, California, which has revolutionized American cuisine since its founding in 1971. Her publications include: *The Chez Panisse Menu Cookbook*; *Chez Panisse Pasta, Pizza and Calzone*; *Chez Panisse Cooking*; and *Fanny at Chez Panisse*. She received the Outstanding Chef Award and Chez Panisse received the Outstanding Restaurant Award from The James Beard Foundation in 1992.

Alice Waters

Jasper White is a 1973 graduate of the Culinary Institute of America, and opened Jasper's in Boston as its chef-owner ten years later. The restaurant, which closed in 1995, emphasized fresh, local seafood, and was consistently ranked among the city's top eateries; White is now a restaurant consultant. In 1991, he was named the Best Chef in the Northeast by the James Beard Foundation. White is the author of *Jasper White's Cooking from New England*.

Index

Butternut squash, 178
Butter sauce, nage, 377

C

Cabbage, 99
Cajun flavors, 209
California cuisine, 292, 293, 318
California food movement, 79. *See also*
    Nouvelle cuisine
California Regional dinner menu, 258
Calves' brains, 99
Calves' head, 100
Calves' liver, 100
Canadian flavors, 210
Cantonese flavors, 210
Capers, 197
Capon, 100
   accompaniments to, 261
Caramelizing, 42
Caraway, 197
Cardamom, 197
Cardoons, 102
Carib-Asian desserts, 286
Caribbean flavors, 210
Carnaroli rice, 46
Carrots, 102
Carrot soup, 280
Cassia, 197
Catfish, 102
   accompaniments to, 261
Cauliflower, 103
Cauliflower purée with caviar, 342-43
Caviar, 103
   accompaniments to, 261
Cayenne, 197
"Celebrity chefs," 392. *See also* Chefs
Celery, 103
Celery root, 104
Celery seeds, 198
Cèpes, 104
Chanterelles, 104-5, 248
Chapel, Alain, 305
Chard, 105, 182
Cheese, 248-49
   ricotta, 166
Cheesecake, variation on, 67
Chef-couples, 70
Chefs
   as artists, 1-21

categories of, 7
evolution of the cuisines of, 307-22
favorite menus of, 276-87
individual preferences of, 16
as owners, 298-300
perceptive abilities of, 2
point of view of, 304-6
professional cooking and, 6-8
Chefs' styles. *See also* Composition
   distinguishing, 290-92
   influences on, 292-95
   personification of, 305
Cherries, 105
Chervil, 198
Chestnuts, 105
Chez Panisse restaurant, 76-77, 224,
    225-26, 232, 250, 296
   menus from, 244, 258, 320-21
   recipes from, 154, 387
   regional menu from, 258
Chicken, 107-8. *See also* Poultry;
    Poussin
   accompaniments to, 262
   herbed, with lemon-thyme butter,
    357-58
   roasted, 338
Chicken livers, 109
Chick peas, 107
Chicory, 109
Child, Julia, 12
Chilean flavors, 210
Chiles, 198
   varying flavors of, 44-45
Chili-ginger sauce, 365
Chinese cuisine, 32-33
   Americanizing, 211
   classical, 66
Chinese desserts, 251
Chinese five-spice powder, 54
Chinese flavors, 210
Chives, 198
Chocolate, 109-10
   bitter, 198
Chocolate desserts, 249, 250
Chocolate soufflé, 355
Christ Cella restaurant, 234
Ciacci, 246
Cilantro, 198
Cinnamon, 199
Cinnamon basil, 199

K

Kaiseki meals, 228-29, 393
Kale, 131
Kasha, 98
Keller, Hubert, 106, 120, 121, 124, 139, 141, 169, 187
  biography of, 404
  cauliflower purée with caviar recipe, 342-43
  "Desert Island" ingredient list by, 341
Kidneys, 132
  accompaniments to, 264
  veal, 190, 275
Killeen, Johanne, 90, 105, 108, 109, 110, 139, 145, 161, 162, 171, 183, 238
  Al Forno menu by, 308-9
  biography of, 404
  "Desert Island" ingredient list by, 337
  roasted chicken recipe, 338
Kitchen Conversations (Goldstein), 58-59
Kitchen tools, using, 43-44
Kiwi fruit, 132
Kohlrabi, 132
Korean flavors, 215
Kump, Peter, 5
Kumquats, 132
Kunz, Gray, 3, 89, 110, 116, 122, 126, 134, 154, 163, 167, 189
  biography of, 404
  "Desert Island" ingredient list by, 344
  Lespinasse menus by, 278-81
  sautéed *foie gras* with quince confits recipe, 122

L

Lagasse, Emeril, 13
Lageder, Alois, 238, 239
Lamb, 133-34. *See also* Mutton
  accompaniments to, 264-65
  boneless rack, in pecan crust, 135-37
  cooking, 77
Lamb chops, 134
  accompaniments to, 265
Lamb crown roast, accompaniments to, 265
Lamb's lettuce, 141
Lamb's liver, 138

Lamb shanks, 138
  accompaniments to, 265
Lamb's tongue, 138
La Pyramide Golden Book, 393
La Ratte potatoes, 304
Lark Creek Inn, 272
Lasagna
  potato and mushroom, 376-77
  thin, 70
Latin American flavors, 215
Lavender, 202
Lebanese flavors, 215
Leeks, 138
Lemon, 138-39, 202
Lemongrass, 202
Lemongrass soup, 278
Lemon thyme, 202
Lemon thyme butter, 357
Lemon verbena, 202
Lentils, 139
Lespinasse restaurant
  menus from, 278-81
  recipe from, 122-23
Lettuces, 139
Levain bread, 245
Lima beans, 94
Lime, 140
Litchi nuts, 140
Liver
  accompaniments to, 265
  calf's, 100
  lamb's, 138
Lobster, 140-41
  accompaniments to, 265
  with quinoa risotto, 142
Lobster Club restaurant, 74, 257
Lobster salad, 278
London Chop House, menus from, 316-17
Lovage, 202

M

Mâche, 141
Mackerel, 141
  accompaniments to, 266
Ma Cuisine (Escoffier), 8-9
Mahimahi, 144
"Maillard effect," 40
Main courses, reduced-calorie, 230
Malaysian flavors, 215

Peaches, 152-53
Peanuts, 204
Pea pods, 152
Pears, 153-54
  poached in Beaumes-de-Venise and
    honey, 154
Peas, 155
Pecans, 155
Peel, Mark, 91, 96, 100, 108, 117, 134,
    147, 150, 163, 167, 190, 208
  biography of, 405
  "Desert Island" ingredient list by,
    356
  herbed chicken recipe, 357-58
Pepper, black, 205
Peppers, bell, 155
Persimmons, 155-56
Peruvian flavors, 216
Peterson, James, 55
Petit fours, 251
Pheasant, 156
  accompaniments to, 266
  menu using, 267
Philippine flavors, 217
Pic, Jacques, 305
Picada, 54
Picholine restaurant, 257
  menu from, 129
Pig, suckling, 181, 271
Pig's ears, 156
Pig's feet, 157
Pignoli restaurant, 299
  menu from, 284-85
Pike, 157
Pineapple, 157
Pineapple gratin, 280-81
Pinto beans, 94
Pistachios, 205
Pizza, grilled, 74, 259
Place, as a menu theme, 232-33
Plantains, 63, 157-58
Plums, 158
Point, Fernand, 16, 38, 85, 247, 305,
    393
Point of view, communicating, 304-6
Polenta, 158
Polish flavors, 217
Pomegranates, 159
Pomegranate syrup, 205
Pompano, 159
Poori bread, 254

Poppy seeds, 205
Porcinis, 159
Pork, 159-160
  accompaniments to, 268
Pork belly, braised spiced, 328-29
Pork chops, 160
  accompaniments to, 268
Pork loin, roast, with ham and rose-
    mary, 379-80
Portion size, 234-35
Portuguese flavors, 217
Potato and mushroom lasagna, 376-77
Potato chips, blue, 342-43
Potatoes, 160-61
  sweet, 181
Potato soup, 79
Pot au feu, 350
Pot roast, accompaniments to, 268
Poultry, accompaniments to, 268
Poussin, 357
Presentation, 81-84
  dramatic, 82-83
  pleasing, 16
Produce
  differences in, 297
  seasonal changes in, 255
Products, high-quality, 304-6
Professional cooking, 6-8. See also
    Cooking; Chefs
"Progressive cooking," 312
Prosciutto, 161
Prunes, 161
Puerto Rican flavors, 217
Pumpkin, 162

Q

Quail, 162-63
  accompaniments to, 268-69
Quatre-epices, 54
Quince confits, 122-23
Quinces, 163
Quinoa risotto, 142-43

R

Rabbit, 163-64. See also Hare
  accompaniments to, 269
Radicchio, 164
Radishes, 164
Raisin-caper purée, 70
Raspberries, 164-65

J.T.'s menu by, 319
pheasant menu by, 267
roast pork loin recipe, 379-80
Stars menu by, 318
Travel, importance of, 291
Tripe, 184
Troisgros, Pierre, 6
Troisgros Brothers, 65, 305
Trotter, Charlie, 13
Trout, 184-85
salmon, 169
Truffle dishes, 278
Truffle menu, 186
Truffles, 185
Tuna, 187
accompaniments to, 273
Tunisian five-spice mix, 54
Tunisian flavors, 220
Turbot, 188
Turkey, 188
accompaniments to, 273
Turkish flavors, 220
Turmeric, 207
Turnips, 188
"TV dinner" approach, 75

U

Ukrainian flavors, 220
Umami, 39
Union Square Cafe, menu from, 101

V

Valentine's Day dinners, 34-35
Van Aken, Norman, 4, 56-57, 89, 91,
92, 100, 111, 113, 119, 165, 171,
183, 189, 201
biography of, 407
conch chowder recipe, 383-85
"Desert Island" ingredient list by,
381-82
on inspiration, 69
menu from Norman's by, 286-87
on New World cuisine, 302-3
Vanilla, 208
Veal, 189
accompaniments to, 273
Veal chops, 190
accompaniments to, 273
Veal kidneys, 190
accompaniments to, 275

Veal shanks, 190
Veal sweetbreads, 191
Vegetables, preparation methods for, 42.
See also Produce
Vegetarian menus, 280
Vegetarian tasting menu, 281
Veneto Dinner, 276-77
Venezuelan flavors, 220
Venison, 191
accompaniments to, 275
mignons of Cervena, 192-93
Veracruz-style greens and beans, 325-26
Vergé, Roger, 293, 294, 305
Verjus, 59
Vertical food, 84
Vietnamese flavors, 220
Vinegar, balsamic, 208
Vinegar pie, 80
Visual presentation, 81-84
Vongerichten, Jean-Georges, 52, 89,
105, 108, 113, 115, 117, 125, 132,
134, 146, 164, 172, 174, 180, 182,
219
biography of, 407
"Desert Island" ingredient list by, 386

W

Walnuts, 191
Wasabi, 208
Watercress, 194
Watercress sauce, 343
Waters, Alice, 90, 91, 102, 104, 111,
113, 117, 119, 124, 126, 139, 145,
147, 150, 161, 163, 164, 167, 172,
183, 185, 187
biography of, 407
on cheese/fruit combinations, 249
on Chez Panisse menu, 244
Chez Panisse menus by, 320-21
"Desert Island" ingredient list by, 387
pasta with tomato confit recipe, 387
on regional menus, 258
Weather, influence on food, 70-71
White, Jasper, 118, 121, 127, 140, 141,
147, 151, 156, 160, 164, 170, 171,
172, 173, 174, 179, 183
biography of, 408
"Desert Island" ingredient list by,
388-89
White, Jonathan, 304

Andrew Dornenburg and Karen Page are the co-authors of the best-selling book *Becoming a Chef: With Recipes and Reflections from America's Leading Chefs* (Van Nostrand Reinhold, 1995), which won the 1996 James Beard Book Award for Best Writing on Food. The authors and *Becoming a Chef* have been featured on The Today Show, America Online, America's Talking, CompuServe, NPR radio stations, Television Food Network, and Voice of America as well as other TV and radio shows across the country, and highlighted in leading publications including *The New York Times*, *The Chicago Tribune*, *The Boston Globe*, *The Detroit News*, *Gourmet*, *Restaurant Hospitality*, and *The Village Voice*. They have also cohosted a show featuring America's leading chefs, as well as Julia Child's first online chat, on America Online, which has received mention in publications ranging from *The Los Angeles Times* to *New York* magazine to *USA Today*. The couple is contributing 15 percent of their royalties from *Becoming a Chef* to The *Becoming a Chef* Scholarship Fund, which assists aspiring chefs seeking formal culinary education.

Andrew Dornenburg has spent the last eight years cooking in some of the top restaurants in New York City and Boston, including Arcadia, Biba, the East Coast Grill, March, 9 Jones Street, and Rosemarie's. He and Karen Page were married in 1990 at Biba, where he cooked at the time. He was one of thirty-two chefs selected to attend The School for American Chefs in 1992, where he studied with the legendary Madeleine Kamman. With his wife, he cofounded the nonprofit organization FEED*BOSTON, which provided memorable holiday meals to the city's homeless prepared by chefs from top Boston restaurants. In prior lives, he fought fires for the California forestry, and processed salmon and salmon roe in Alaska. Dornenburg currently runs his own catering company and plans to open a restaurant in New York.

Karen Page has consulted with *Fortune* 500 food companies on management and marketing strategy, culinary trends, and new product development. She is a graduate of the Harvard Business School, where she was a General Mills/AAUW

About the Authors

Foundation Fellow, and Northwestern University, where she was a Scripps-Howard Foundation Journalism Scholar. She chairs the Harvard Business School Network of Women Alumnae, and was named by the President of Northwestern University to The Council of 100, an organization of Northwestern's 100 leading alumnae. She also served a one-year term as one of the first non-chef/restaurateurs named to the Board of Directors of the San Francisco-based International Association of Women Chefs and Restaurateurs.

Andrew Dornenburg and Karen Page
527 Third Avenue Suite 130
New York, New York 10016
BACsters@aol.com http://home.aol.com/BACsters

VAN NOSTRAND REINHOLD

Your Name_____ Address_____
Title_____ City/State/Zip_____
Function_____ Phone_____
Company_____ Fax_____
Date of book purchase_____ E-Mail_____

Thank you for your interest in Van Nostrand Reinhold publications. To enable us to keep you abreast of the latest developments in your field, please complete the following information.

1. With respect to the topic of this book, are you a:
a. student in this field
   name of your institution: _____
b. working professional in this field
c. hobbyist in this field

2. For how many years have you worked/studied in this field? _____

3. Of which professional associations are you a member?
_____
_____
_____

4. To which industry or general food-related publications/resources do you subscribe for important information?
_____
_____
_____

5. Describe your professional title:
a. chef   h. sommelie
b. caterer   i. consulting services
c. restaurant owner/manager   j. government
d. food and beverages manager   k. librarian
e. student   l. education/research
f. professor/teacher   m. other (please specify)
g. pastry chef
_____

6. How/where was this book purchased? (circle one)
a. bookstore
b. publisher's outlet
c. through offer in mail
d. through book club
e. other _____

7. How/where do you usually purchase professional books? (please circle all that apply)
a. bookstore
b. publisher's outlet
c. through offer in mail
d. through book club
e. other_____

8. Do you own or have access to a computer with a modem?
a. yes b. no

9. To which electronic on-line services do you have access? (please circle all that apply)
a. America On-Line   e. World Wide Web
b. Prodigy   f. other (please specify)
c. Compuserve   _____
d. Internet   g. none

10. Do you own or have access to a computer with a CD-ROM reader?   a. yes b. no

11. Would you purchase updates, supplements and/or additional chapters to this book in an electronic format?
a. yes b. no

12. Which format would you prefer?
a. disk (circle one) Mac Dos Windows
b. CD-ROM
c. online
d. other_____

13. What was the primary reason for purchasing this book?
a. professional enrichment
b. academic coursework
c. personal interest/hobby
d. other_____

14. Would you be interested in or subscribe to a Professional Chef's Newsletter? a. yes b. no
If yes, which do you prefer?
a. online b. print

15. In which of the following areas would you be interested in new books?
a. International cuisine   e. buffets
b. catering   f. wines
c. baking and pastry   g. other (please specify)
d. beverage management   _____

16. Please indicate author/title and ISBN# of book purchased:
_____
_____

VNR is constantly evaluating its services to better meet your needs.

If you need further information please contact us by fax at
212-475-2548.

BE SURE TO VISIT US AT OUR WEB SITE
http://www.vnr.com

Please check the book you are responding to:

☐ Becoming a Chef, Dornenburg/Page 0-442-01513-5
☐ Culinary Artistry, Dornenburg/Page 0-442-02333-2
☐ The Becoming a Chef Journal, Dornenburg/Page 0-442-02332-4

an International Thomson Publishing company I(T)P®

BUSINESS REPLY MAIL

FIRST CLASS MAIL   PERMIT NO. 704   NEW YORK NY

POSTAGE WILL BE PAID BY ADDRESSEE

VAN NOSTRAND REINHOLD
Culinary and Hospitality
115 FIFTH AVENUE
4th Floor
NEW YORK, NY 10211-0025